THE FUTURE OF THEOLOGY

The Future of Theology

Essays in Honor of Jürgen Moltmann

Edited by

Miroslav Volf
Carmen Krieg
Thomas Kucharz

WILLIAM B. EERDMANS PUBLISHING COMPANY
GRAND RAPIDS, MICHIGAN / CAMBRIDGE, U.K.

© 1996 Wm. B. Eerdmans Publishing Co.
255 Jefferson Ave. S.E., Grand Rapids, Michigan 49503 /
P.O. Box 163, Cambridge CB3 9PU U.K.
All rights reserved

Printed in the United States of America

01 00 99 98 97 96   7 6 5 4 3 2 1

Library of Congress Cataloging-in-Publication Data

The future of theology: essays in honor of Jürgen Moltmann /
edited by Miroslav Volf, Carmen Krieg, and Thomas Kucharz
p.   cm.
Includes bibliographical references.
ISBN 0-8028-4953-9(pbk. : alk. paper)
1. Theology. 2. Moltmann, Jürgen.
I. Moltmann, Jürgen. II. Volf, Miroslav.
III. Krieg, Carmen. IV. Kucharz, Thomas.
BR50.F84   1996
230'.09'049 — dc20   96-919
                                                  CIP

The essays by Jon Sobrino, Gustavo Gutiérrez, Elsa Tamez, and Paul
Ricoeur were translated by Robert R. Barr.

The essays by Dorothée Sölle, Johann Baptist Metz, Dietrich Ritschl,
Michael Welker, Ingolf U. Dalferth, Wolfhart Pannenberg, Elisabeth
Moltmann-Wendel, and Hans Küng were translated by Douglas Stott.

Contents

CONTENTS

PART II: PERSPECTIVES

PART III: THEMES

Contents

INTRODUCTION
A Queen and a Beggar:
Challenges and Prospects of Theology

Miroslav Volf

Perhaps no single other theologian of the second half of our century has shaped theology so profoundly as has Jürgen Moltmann. He appeared on the world theological scene with his *Theology of Hope* (1964) and took most of its capitals by storm. Not only were his subsequent performances "sold out," but the power of his vision and the originality of his method helped inspire a host of new directors — above all, the originators of various theologies of liberation — who modified his approach and put it to creative uses. Coming from what were considered theological peripheries, some of the new directors transformed these margins into center stages with a worldwide impact. In terms of fecundity, Moltmann's opus remains unmatched among his generation of theologians. Over 130 dissertations written so far on his thought — most of them in the past decade — testify eloquently to its continued attractiveness.

For his 70th birthday, an international circle of "shapers of theological thought" — his friends, colleagues, interlocutors, and former students — wishes to honor Jürgen Moltmann with this *Festschrift* on the future of theology.[1] Moltmann himself always sought to be both contemporary and future-oriented. From the *Theology of Hope* (1964) to *The Coming of God* (1995) — the latest in the series of his "Contributions to Systematic Theology" — his theology was an exercise in thinking not only *from* the perspective of God's future but also *toward* a new human future. A book on the future of theology takes up an aspect of "his" theme and "his" concerns. Moreover, as the next big

---

1. For a previous *Festschrift* in honor of Jürgen Moltmann see *Gottes Zukunft — Zukunft der Welt: Festschrift für Jürgen Moltmann zum 60. Geburtstag,* ed. H. Deuser et al. (München: Chr. Kaiser Verlag, 1986). See also *Love: The Foundation of Hope: The Theology of Jürgen Moltmann and Elisabeth Moltmann-Wendel,* ed. Frederic B. Burnham et al. (New York: Harper & Row, 1988).

project after *The Coming of God,* Moltmann has announced a theological methodology. It seems appropriate to offer him a volume that in its multiple harmonies and dissonances may serve as a polyphonic companion to his own composition on the past and future of theology — that intellectual discipline which of all disciplines has a singular responsibility to attend to the "coming of God" as the future of God's wounded world.

But beyond the reasons related to the honoree's theological biography, what justifies a volume on the future of theology? The answer is simple: it is the present crisis of theology, which generates both fears and hopes for its future. On the threshold of the third millennium, the presumed queen of sciences has grown old and feeble, unable to see that what she thinks is her throne is just an ordinary chair, uncertain about what her territories are, and confused about how to rule in the realms she thinks are hers, seeking advice from a quarrelsome chorus of counselors each of whom thinks himself the king, and ending up with a divided, even schizophrenic, mind. This is not the place to rehearse, let alone adequately analyze, all the varied and serious challenges of theology that the metaphor of an old queen suggests. Here are only a few.

Consider, first, the fact that today we inhabit a plurality of often contradictory social worlds and are surrounded by a plurality of cultures that are moving ever closer together as the process of globalization advances. The plurality of social worlds is reflected in an increasing plurality of theologies. Some fear that theology may soon sink into a quagmire of "anything goes" in which the only "kings" are the conflicting and ever changing tastes of theological consumers, hungry for new and exotic fruits. Is not all this talk about plurality just one more seduction of theology, luring it to forget that behind all the difference of social worlds and all the de-centered plurality within them lies an even more fundamental sameness — some form of Nietzschean "*no* herdsman and *one* herd," they may ask?[2] Others rejoice over new, perhaps even adventurous paths, opened to theology, over new themes, new methods, new dialogue partners. But whether one feels burdened or excited by the multiplication of theologies, one has to reflect seriously on the questions how should individual theologies relate to the pluralization of the discipline and in what sense can we still speak of theology as a single discipline?

Consider, second, the progressive marginalization of theology in the public discourse. The erstwhile queen of sciences who believed herself to have enough wisdom and authority to rule both over the submissive and the rebellious must now descend from her throne on which she enjoyed hushed attentiveness and enter the marketplace in which many clamoring voices vie for attention. Hers is one among many voices, a voice often trembling with uncertainty about what to say and how to command attention. For some this dethroning offers theology an opportunity to free itself from its "Constantinian

---

2. Friedrich Nietzsche, *Thus Spoke Zarathustra: A Book for Everyone and No One,* trans. R. J. Hollingdale (London: Penguin Books, 1969), p. 46; italics added.

captivity" and rediscover its own proper and independent voice. Others fear that the uncertainty of today may give way to perplexity or even total silence tomorrow, and they scheme about how to put theology back on the throne. Both the nostalgic theological royalists and the impatient anarchists are faced, however, with the question how theological reason relates to nontheological reason(s) and, more significantly, what to do about the lack of sync between the attempts of theology to gain a hearing and the kinds of receptivity it finds among the constituencies it addresses.

Academic theology in particular faces a third challenge. Caught in the movement of increased specialization, theology today often avails itself of specialized areas of research and moves on a relatively high level of abstraction. This seems a necessary condition of fundamental research. And yet in the process of specialization the overarching subject of theology often gets lost, if not on teachers certainly on students of theology. After their first experiences in the church, many young pastors are no longer certain that the long years of theological study were useful. The theological interests of their former professors do not intersect with the life realities of their parishioners. With much toil these pastors have learned to use theological tools that seem singularly unsuitable for the work that needs to be done in the parish. Have the students been taught the wrong things, or have they learned the right things too superficially? Were they given the wrong tools, or were they not taught well enough how to use the right tools? A fresh reflection on the relation between theology as a scholarly endeavor and theology as a helpmate of the church, between academic exercise and spirituality, is urgently needed.

Add to these more formal challenges a whole line of significant issues theology is uncertain how to address — issues that concern happiness and misery, the life and death of millions, and, in the mind of some theologians, issues that require a reorientation of the whole theological enterprise to address them adequately. On the global plane there is an ecological crisis of such magnitude that it endangers not simply human well-being but the very survival of our planet. There is the scandal of worldwide poverty, exacerbated by the scarcely controllable population explosion, coupled with the depletion of natural resources; the gap between the overfed rich and the overworked, underpaid, and malnourished poor — "the crucified people" — is enlarging. There are also deep rifts between people of different genders, cultures, races, and religions; multiple forms of intersecting and overlapping oppressions sometimes lead to brutal domestic, national, and international conflicts that leave behind rivers of blood and mountains of corpses. On which of these problems ought theology to focus its attention? Gender? Race? Poverty? Ecological survival? All four together? Do these problems singly or together require a radical rethinking of classical Christian perspectives on God, humanity, and the world, or would attempts at minor adjustments or even the simple retrieval of genuine Christian tradition be more appropriate? Ought theology to be primarily "issue oriented" at all, or does it not thereby lose one of its most important functions, namely, its overarching perspective on the one world in the name of the God of all peoples? Is a singular concentration on issues a diversion from theology's most proper theme — God — or a necessary consequence of the most basic theological insight that the love of God and of neighbor are inseparable and that the love of God is only real in the love of the neighbor?

But how do theologians address the great public issues of the day if, as in many Western countries, they live in genuinely post-Christian societies in which, when all is said and done, their voice is heard as an echo from a bygone age? How do theologians speak to the wider public if, as in many non-Western societies, their faith has not taken root in their cultures and their speech therefore appears as a message from some foreign land in the name of some unknown god? Do the problems of progressive de-Christianization and unsuccessful enculturation make theology's public responsibility an impossible task? Or could it be that theologians, for lack of commitment and imagination, have lost nerve and become either silent spectators or compulsive parrots whose skill in repeating with a strange accent what others say in Oxford English is admired precisely because they are judged incapable of proper speech, let alone of having a mind of their own? Could it be that the problem is not so much that theological language is foreign but that theologians themselves are deracinated — they have severed their ties with concrete communities of faith, the sole crucibles in which the virtues and practices of which they speak can be forged in culturally specific ways, and become free-floating intellectuals, proudly suspended by their superior knowledge above the hustle and bustle of ecclesial life, speaking from nowhere and to nobody in particular? Of course, it could be that the most appropriate theological language and most responsible theologians' lives would make plain only that some hearers do not have ears to hear because their spirits are either "imprisoned in their good conscience,"[3] as Nietzsche said of Jesus' contemporaries, or ensnared in the self-perpetuating cycle of evil practices.

The future of theology! Most theologians (along with many of their colleagues in other disciplines) believe that theology has had a glorious past. Augustine and Maximus the Confessor! Aquinas and Palamas! Luther and Calvin! Schleiermacher and Barth! Veritable intellectual giants by any standards! But will theology have a matching future? Will it have a future at all, except as an article in a museum, studied by historians and occasionally surveyed by a few intellectual tourists when bad weather prevents them from doing better things? To return to the metaphor of the queen, can the old queen be saved? Will her head be put under the guillotine of unfulfilled promises, missed opportunities, misplaced interests, disorientation and confusion, or sheer incompetence and pathetic impotence? If she is granted a reprieve, what new responsibilities will her deposed majesty be able to master? Will she ever climb up the throne again? Would she be wise to *want* a throne?

3. Nietzsche, *Thus Spoke Zarathustra*, p. 229.

These are some of the challenges facing theology that the contributors to the present volume seek to address. Though none advocates reinstatement of theology to royal glory, neither is any of them ready to take theology out of circulation and freeze it up for safekeeping. All believe in the future of theology as a vibrant discipline, its present crisis notwithstanding. Each contribution is an attempt to revitalize theology, an attempt that may go at cross-purposes with other attempts even in this volume but that precisely through such contestation testifies to the vigor of the discipline as a whole.

The present volume is loosely structured in three parts: challenges, perspectives, themes. "Challenges" deals with the external or internal problems theology is facing. "Perspectives" offers proposals as to how to meet the challenges. "Themes" concentrates on various issues that need special attention today. In a sense, this division is arbitrary. All contributions point to the challenges and offer perspectives, and many suggest themes that must not be neglected. Yet the *focus* of the contributions justifies the division. With some, challenges function as a background for offering new perspectives. With others, perspectives surface only on the horizon, most of the attention being focused on the immediate surrounding of challenges. With still others, themes dominate the discussion and refract both how challenges are perceived and what perspectives are offered.

The First Part ("Challenges") is framed by two contributions that give two rather different accentuations to the challenge of the future. Observing the global trends, *Konrad Raiser* claims that the present course of human development is unsustainable and suggests new forms of human peaceful living in interaction with the natural environment. *John H. Yoder* warns against too much fascination with reading and manipulating the future, lest we fall into the trap of theologically underwriting some new surrogate for Constantine. Instead, theology should attend to what "will not be different, except superficially, about the twenty-first century."

Dietrich Ritschl pursues the question whether in theology itself what is new is different in any other than a superficial way. He argues for the possibility of genuine novelty in theology as a result of the "interplay between a present experience of the new in God, on the one hand, and the search for the implicitly new in the old writings of the Bible and in the postbiblical witnesses on the other." Both those who see the only source of salvation in aggressively imposing on everyone what "the old writings" teach (fundamentalists) and those who give themselves with abandon to any and every "present experience of the new" (radical liberals) advocate in *Douglas John Hall's* opinion unacceptable forms of adolescent Christianity. He is calling theologians to turn away from their narrow professional interests and, in dialogue with the tradition, contribute to a mature Christianity that seeks to preserve not so much the churches but "the life of God's beloved creation."

Dorothée Sölle and *Stanley Hauerwas* concentrate on the challenge of modernity, though each construes the interplay between theology and modernity rather differently. Accepting the modern critique of religion by masters of suspicion (Marx, Nietzsche, and Freud), Sölle argues that both premodern and postmodern forms of religion ought to be discarded and a new critical form of Christianity developed. Its program should be the preferential option for life, its enemy the new religion of science which is a religion of death. Hauerwas, on the other hand, prefers to exercise a good deal of suspicion of his own against self-portrayals of modernity and postmodernity and insists on reading social realities and their nontheological interpretations from a theological perspective. His account of modernity and postmodernity leads him to advocate what may be described as a bellicose version of pacifist Christianity: he is issuing a declaration of war with no sword but truth against people corrupted by tolerance.

Johann Baptist Metz and *Nicholas Wolterstorff* both deal with the issue of the universality and particularity of theology within the public university. In a time when plurality and difference reign, maintains Metz, God must be upheld as a universal theme. For the sake of the one God and of the memory of suffering, theologians must be universalists — even if they may be the last ones around. Wolterstorff seeks to show how Christian theologians, whose perspective is quite particular, can discover a new kind of universality and remain legitimate members of the university. Some recent developments in philosophy of science — such as the death of the notions of generically human learning and of a single logic of *Wissenschaften* — give, in his view, grounds for hope that Christian theology may once again thrive as it has not in the public universities of late modernity.

In the Second Part ("Perspectives") *Michael Welker* takes some major theological loci to indicate how their reconceptualization may overcome the present crisis of theology. He argues that we need a "(1) Trinitarian-theological concentration on God's vitality, (2) a preeminent orientation toward the witnesses of the biblical tradition, (3) freedom under the word of God in both the congregational and ecumenical church, and (4) the ever new reflection back to the revelation of the lost condition of the world beneath the cross."

Any adequate reconceptualization of Christian faith must seek "ressourcement by way of retrospection," suggests *Geoffrey Wainwright*. Examining the cases of liturgy, ecumenism, dogmatics, and hermeneutics, he argues that the churches must continue to look "towards the past in order to gain their bearings in the present and get guidance for the ongoing journey" on the grounds that when we look back we "see our contemporaries" with whom God has made an eternal covenant. My own contribution is an attempt to formulate a more formal vision of "a public theology for a public gospel" under the conditions of late modernity: "Looking through the spectacles of its own culture, [theology] sees a city whose builder and architect is God; situated in multiple relations of power, it advocates the weakness of the Crucified as a new form of power; dwelling on the margins, it seeks to bring the reign of the triune God to bear

xiv

on all domains of life." The driving force behind such a theology, I suggest, following Moltmann's own recent reflection on the nature of theology, should be the pain and delight of God, the passionate lover of life.

Both *Ellen T. Charry* and *Ingolf U. Dalferth* seek to rediscover God as the one, single theme of theology. Instead of wandering through its own peripheries (such as reflection on various single issues or on the function of the language of God), Dalferth calls theology to find its way back to the center of its interest, which is God and the truth about God. "The more it [theology] concentrates unmistakably on *God*, the more it will have to say, and the less it will need to worry about its own future," he claims. Whereas Dalferth focuses on the critical knowledge of God's love that is at work here and now, Charry is interested in the shaping of the human self through knowing and loving God. As an alternative to two equally unacceptable models of theology — academic and activist — behind which there lurks the mythical autonomous self, she proposes a pastoral theology whose primary task, to be undertaken with "intellectual rigor and social sensitivity," would be persuading people "that the life grounded in knowing, loving, and giving glory to God is the highest human calling."

Seeking refuge from crises in theology caused by false polarities, both *Catherine Keller* and *D. Lyle Dabney* turn to the reconciling power of divine Spirit. In dialogue with Moltmann's *The Spirit of Life*, Keller seeks to heal the rift between messianism and mysticism, immanence and transcendence, femininity and masculinity. Helped by a dose of healthy pneumatology, theology can proceed, she suggests, "with the lively bounce of a messianically and mystically charged present." In dialogue with Friedrich Schleiermacher and Karl Barth, Dabney seeks to reconcile a theology of ascent and a theology of descent. As an alternative to both, he proposes a theology of relationship that is a theology of the Spirit of God, because human beings are from the very first "Otherwise engaged in the Spirit."

In their contributions, *Gustavo Gutiérrez* and *Jon Sobrino* center on the "crucified people" because they are the privileged place of God's presence. Sobrino insists that the theology of future should be a theology of liberation because "the ever more dense element of reality continues to be the oppression that generates victims." Gutiérrez, who has interpreted his original *A Theology of Liberation* as a love letter both to God and to the poor, is willing to write slightly different letters so that the same love, but deepened now through experience, may be expressed. Rediscovery of contemplation, of the gratuity of God's grace, and of martyrdom, in addition to the historical commitment to liberation, all serve to enrich the love for the "crucified people" and their "crucified Lord."

John B. Cobb, Jr., argues that the multiple spheres in which the Christian life is lived call for a multifaceted theology. He suggests that we think of theology as a four-pronged exercise: academic theology which offers overarching perspectives, church theology which brings Christian faith to bear upon the actual life of the believers, lay theology which lets lay people reclaim their role as theologians, and liberation theology which is bound to diverse groups and can speak for them to the church as a whole. *James H. Cone* shows what one such liberation theology (black theology) needs to look like if it is to speak authentically for its own community and issue a prophetic call to the church as a whole. Combining the "politics of equal dignity" and the "politics of identity" (to use the categories analyzed so skillfully by Charles Taylor), Cone argues that an adequate black theology must weave together racial justice and black identity, that Martin and Malcolm must march hand in hand.

In Part Three ("Themes") *Elsa Tamez* and *M. Douglas Meeks* reflect on the shape of Christian thought in the context of market society. Tamez offers theological-sociological reflections on the utopian reason of the seemingly most thoroughly nonutopian book in the Bible. Qoheleth's alternative to the kinds of false hopes similar to those produced by a capitalist system is "the affirmation of concrete life in the gladness of eating bread and drinking wine and enjoying one's beloved. There is neither irresponsibility nor irrelevance here," she continues. "There is only wager on life, for we rest in the grace of God in the midst of enslaving toil and against its antihuman logic." Meeks argues that the viability of theology in the 21st century depends on the ability of church to provide an alternative to the market society. He seeks to revive the church as "the household of Jesus Christ in which God's love as gift is embodied in relation to the stranger" and thereby create space and time for theology.

From a feminist angle, *Elisabeth Moltmann-Wendel* and *Rosemary Radford Ruether* address two interrelated false dualities they detect in nonfeminist anthropologies. Moltmann-Wendel strives to overcome the duality of body and spirit, an effort guided by a vision of "a totality in which heaven and earth, immanence and transcendence, soul and body, nature and technology come together once again." In her rethinking of Christian anthropology, Ruether wishes to transcend both androcentric monism and the romantic binary split of masculine men and feminine women and to contribute to a "transformed synthesis in which rationality and intuition, autonomy and relationality, are mutually transformed."

Each in his own way, *Wolfhart Pannenberg* and *Hans Küng* are concerned with global unity. Pannenberg has directed attention to the problem of establishing and maintaining the unity of the larger church, especially in the Protestant tradition, which has lost concern with the *consensus de doctrina*. He argues for a new kind of Petrine service that would be responsible both to mediate "between the various constituent churches of Christendom" and to preserve "unity in the apostolic faith." Unlike Pannenberg, who focuses on the doctrinal disintegration of the church, Küng thematizes the moral disorientation of the world. A shared "global ethic" of different world religions takes the place of the single office of unity. By promoting a general consensus regarding binding values, religions can educate the young people of the world for peace — those malleable creatures lost in the "orientation jungle" that seduces them to violence.

Finally, *Paul Ricoeur* advises not to fall into the temptation of seeking a way out of the "orientation jungle" by operating with the exclusive alternative "autonomy" vs. "theonomy." On the twofold premise that God is love and that it is this Lover's love that obliges to loving obedience, he argues that theonomy is by no means incompatible with autonomy. Instead, just as love perfects justice, so theonomy — loving obedience — perfects autonomy — for instance, by creating the kinds of persons willing to solve their problems through uncoerced dialogue rather than through violence. Applied to theology as a discipline, Riceour's argument would imply that theology would be ill-advised to seek its orientation in modernity's fascination with autonomy at the expense of the singular commitment to the God of love. For, paradoxically, it would then become ensnared in the kind of heteronomy that would rob it of its proper dignity. Which brings me to the one point I want to make in conclusion.

If we are to judge by the contributions to this volume, theology need not fear for its life. No discipline whose practitioners show such ability, passion, imagination, and diligence can be on its deathbed! Yet the question is not simply whether theology will survive, but what kind of life it will lead. With respect to this question, too, the present volume, I believe, makes plain that even though theology may never ascend a throne (again?) and reign as a queen, it need not become a beggar — unless it recoils from being a beggar in that profound sense in which the gesture of holding our empty hands open before God symbolizes the very structure of our humanity.

Commenting on the task of theology, the honoree of this volume said recently, "It is simple, but true, to say that theology has only one, single problem: *God*. We are theologians for the sake of God. God is our dignity. God is our agony. God is our hope."[4] The answer to the question about the future of theology is simple: *God* is the future of theology. Whatever else theology does — whichever methods it uses, sources it chooses, or issues it addresses, whichever dialogue partners it entertains, cultural contexts it inhabits, or social settings it prefers, whichever theological loci it privileges, or spiritualities it wishes to presuppose — whatever else theology does, theology must not lose sight of God. Though God by no means lives and dies with theology, theology lives and dies with God. If the old queen gets saved, she will be saved by becoming a subject in God's realm, or not at all. But if the desperate queen starts looking for salvation elsewhere, she will turn into a beggar, maybe a gifted, passionate, imaginative, and diligent beggar, yet in the end nothing but a pitiful little beggar — hand outstretched for an undeserved coin or two and eye always searching for something to recycle and peddle as her own. The one thing more pitiful

4. Jürgen Moltmann, *Theology and the Future of the Modern World* (Pittsburgh: ATS, 1995), p. 1.

than such a theologian is such a theologian's god, tottering behind its mistress's cart and polishing its scrap contents to give them a bit of sacral shine.

Using Nietzsche's formulation from *Thus Spoke Zarathustra,* which builds on a different metaphor to express a similar thought, we can envision two alternative futures for theology: if theologians with all seriousness opt for that burlesque god who "limps hither to bless what he has not joined,"[5] theology will have a secure future — in the museum of human follies; if theologians opt for the God of Abraham and Sarah who "calls into existence the things that do not exist" (Rom. 4:17) and in an important sense keeps joined even the things God does not bless, theologians' works will follow them into that imperishable future that God has prepared for our world (1 Pet. 1:4). This, I think, is the most basic and the most important lesson about theology as a discipline that we, the contributors, and the wider theological public can learn from the honoree of this volume.

---

5. Nietzsche, *Thus Spoke Zarathustra,* p. 95.

PART I
CHALLENGES

The World in the Twenty-first Century: Challenges to the Churches

Konrad Raiser

Introduction

Less than five years separate us from the beginning of the twenty-first century. As the twentieth century draws to its close, more and more people begin to realize that we may be approaching a watershed in human history. The last hundred years have been a period of dramatically accelerated growth in virtually all areas of human life. The world population has more than doubled, from 2.5 to more than 5 billion people. Industrial production, world trade, and the total wealth of the world population have increased to levels that were beyond imagination a hundred years ago. Scientific discoveries and the revolutions in modern technology, particularly with their consequences for transportation and communication, have turned the earth into an interconnected global space.

But this century has also been the period when the most destructive wars in human history have been fought, causing more victims than all previous wars in recorded history. Furthermore, the pattern of growth is very unequally distributed. Eighty percent of the world's wealth is concentrated in the hands of less than twenty percent of the world's population, who also control scientific research, technological innovations, the large transnational business corporations, and the means of military power. Population growth, however, is concentrated in the poorer regions of the Southern hemisphere. Not only have poverty, hunger, and disease increased dramatically in spite of the efforts of four decades of development, but more and more population groups in the poor countries find themselves totally marginalized and excluded from participating in social, economic, and political life.

All studies looking into the future that lies ahead in the twenty-first century agree that the present course of human development is unsustainable. The main limiting factors are the availability of arable land to produce sufficient

3

food for a still rapidly growing population and the availability of energy resources to fuel an energy-based mode of industrial production. Predictions are uncertain, but there are indications that if all potentially arable land were used for food production, the earth could sustain a maximum of 12 billion people, a figure that may be reached by the end of the next century. The negative consequences of this enormous growth may, however, bring the critical point much closer. Among these, the most important is the accelerated climate change due to the emission of greenhouse gases as a consequence of the burning of fossil fuels and of intensive forms of agricultural production. Already within the life span of this present generation, global warming may critically affect the patterns of agricultural production and the conditions for human living.

There is little time left to develop ways to make human life more sustainable in interaction with the natural environment. The changes required go beyond scientific, technological, or structural innovations and reach into the spiritual and moral foundations of humanity. The challenge is addressed to the Christian churches together with the communities of all religious faiths. The 1993 World Parliament of Religions in Chicago accepted a declaration toward a "global ethos" that can serve as a pointer toward the new consciousness of human values that will be required. The following remarks do not pretend to be more than notes for an agenda that still is to be established.

1. From Anthropocentrism to Life-centeredness

Most of the unprecedented growth during the past century has been the fruit of the long-term consequences of the European Enlightenment, which resulted from the interpenetration of Greek philosophy and the Christian faith. The most important feature of this tradition has been the separation of the human person and the human community from its natural setting. Nature became a resource to be used and exploited for the benefit of the human community. This development has been supported and strengthened by a particular interpretation of the Christian understanding of creation placing the human person in the center of God's creation with the mandate to dominate and rule over the earth. While this understanding is being challenged with good reason as being a distorted interpretation of the biblical tradition, no doubt it has had a profound influence on the development of Western culture based on the influence of science and technology. The idea of progress in terms of the continuous improvement of the conditions for human life became a secular expression of biblical eschatology.

At the end of the twentieth century, which has seen the most dramatic effects of the notion of progress being put into practice, we have to acknowledge not only the limits to growth, but the dark and destructive side of the philosophy of progress. The anthropocentric foundations of our dominant culture have neglected or forgotten that human life is dependent on the regenerating power of the natural life-cycles. The most essential factors on which the sustainability of human life depends are water, arable land, climate, energy resources, and the adaptability of natural species to changing conditions. In all these respects, the dominant industrial mode of production and the growth-oriented pattern of the economy and of consumption have led to serious disturbances in the ecosphere, with the danger of catastrophic developments increasing rapidly.

Only twenty years ago, after the first United Nations conference on the environment and the first report of the Club of Rome, concern for ecological sustainability was widely believed to be a preoccupation of the highly industrialized countries of the North and likely to distract public attention from the need to establish structures of justice in economic and political relationships between North and South. The earth summit in Rio twenty years later has dramatically demonstrated the global nature of ecological threats, which do not respect national, political, or ideological boundaries. In fact, the consequences of ecological degradation already now are more acutely felt in the developing countries of the Southern hemisphere. A change of consciousness is slowly emerging, but the processes of decision making are totally inadequate to meet the growing challenge.

In the ecumenical movement, the concern for a sustainable relationship between the human community and its natural environment has been given increasing attention for more than quarter of a century. The most focused effort has been undertaken in relation to the concern about accelerated climate change. Studies and reflections have not been limited to finding scientific, social, and political remedies, but have led to a rethinking of the Christian understanding of the relationship of humans to nature in God's plan of creation. The essential insight emerging from these studies is that we must overcome the anthropocentrism of our view of the world and of history and recapture the life-centeredness that is at the heart of most religious traditions, including that of the Bible. Life-centeredness implies that humans have to exercise a caring relationship to all living beings and to all life-sustaining processes. Human needs will have to be brought into a new balance with the needs and capabilities for regenerating life through the natural life-cycles. Human history is to be reassessed as an important but limited part of the history of nature, thus challenging the fundamental assumptions of the Enlightenment traditions. The human habitat is not self-contained, and its security over against the disruptive forces of nature must be seen as interdependent with the security of nature over against the destructive interventions of human activity. The change from anthropocentrism to life-centeredness goes to the root of our understanding of God, world, and humanity, our spirituality and our ethical norms. The increasing intercultural and interreligious encounter that has taken place over these last few decades has made us aware of the decisive insights that indigenous and

5

traditional religions as well as the Eastern faith traditions can contribute to the search for a new life-centered spirituality and ethic.

II. From the Dream of Hegemony to the Acknowledgment of Plurality

Much of recorded human history has been shaped by struggles for cultural, religious, social, and political hegemony among human groups. The emergence of the state and the imperial form of political rule has extended and increased the struggles for hegemony. European colonialism, beginning with the conquest of Latin America five hundred years ago, has been one of the most dramatic forms for establishing cultural, religious, and political hegemony over large parts of the earth. The last five decades have been characterized by the hegemonic struggle between the two superpowers during the period of the so-called cold war. With the collapse of state socialism and the disappearance of the Soviet Union, this hegemonic struggle has suddenly come to an end. The crucial question arising after the end of the cold war is whether these historic events open the way to the establishment of one hegemonic rule over all of the earth with power concentrated in the alliance of the highly developed Western industrialized nations under the leadership of the United States, or whether the end of this last hegemonic struggle marks the definitive transition from the pattern of competitive hegemony to a new state of acknowledged plurality.

The awareness of the plurality of religions, cultures, ethnic and racial identities, languages, and histories has dramatically increased as the different parts of the earth have become interdependent. While the spread of Western civilization based on science and technology to all parts of the world has produced a certain homogenization of lifestyles and cultural forms, the effort to defend and reaffirm indigenous cultures, religious traditions, and ethnic and racial identities has increased simultaneously. Just as the attempt to create a universal language, "Esperanto," has not met with much success, the expectation that the differences of traditional cultures would slowly disappear and be merged into a global culture has been proven false or at least premature. To be sure, the worldwide network of electronic communication creates the artificial semblance of a unified culture and language, but this is more and more clearly separated from the everyday world of the vast majority of people. The collapse of the last colonial empire, the Soviet Union, with its very repressive forms of ideological and political hegemony has brought to light the need among peoples and communities to reaffirm more immediate collective identities based on culture, religion, and ethnic or racial bonds.

The reappearance of religion in the public sphere, often in the form of militant fundamentalism, can be interpreted as a form of collective resistance against hegemonic claims, but at the same time it raises the question whether plurality is itself sustainable. Obviously there is no way to return to the premodern form of homogeneous and self-contained forms of human community, sharing the same culture, religion, ethnic origin, etc. The fact of human interdependence and of the common dependency on nature can be removed just as little as the knowledge of other cultures and traditions and the interpenetration of different cultures due to increased mobility. Humanity is obliged to develop ways of acknowledging cultural and religious plurality as a permanent social fact and to move from antagonistic competitiveness to communicative cooperation. This again constitutes a challenge to very basic social and moral orientations that are based on the clear distinction between "us" and "the others." This "parochial" shape of human consciousness and moral conscience needs to be overcome and widened to accept the difference of "the other" not as a threat, but as a potential enrichment. Most of the roots of the exclusivism of the parochial consciousness are religious in nature. The acceptance of religious plurality as a permanent feature of human society in the twenty-first century constitutes a challenge in particular to Christianity with its long-standing exclusivist orientation. One of the basic tasks that the churches have to address is how to develop, in dialogue between people of different religious traditions, forms of communication and standards of moral orientation that will make the situation of social, cultural, and religious plurality sustainable rather than self-destructive.

III. From Globalization to Life within Limits

The most obvious expression of the spirit of this outgoing century is the emerging globalization of human life, in particular in the areas of economy, finance, and communication. Globalization, which is symbolically expressed in the unlimited network of high-speed electronic communication, is beginning to change all traditional forms of organizing society, of the exercise of power, and of the modes of production. The global economic and financial system does not recognize any limits of national boundaries, political sovereignty, or ecological sustainability. Driven by the logic of competitive growth, it treats the whole earth as a resource for the continued accumulation of power and wealth. The most immediate consequence of this emerging globalization is the fact that increasing numbers of people are being excluded and condemned to mere survival on the fringes of this integrated system.

Impressive as the achievements of globalization are, there are also increasing indications of its fragility. It symbolizes a form of human power that can no longer be controlled and thus becomes self-destructive. In spiritual terms, this attempt to construct global unity could be called a modern version of the tower of Babel. It assumes for humanity the position of handling the earth as an integrated whole, abolishing the distinction between Creator and creatures.

To regard the earth as an integrated whole is the perspective of God, which is expressed by humans in prayer and adoration. Humanity is part of God's creation; it is placed within the limits of human finitude — that is, ultimately the limits of death. The potentially self-destructive dynamics of the process of globalization can only be met if humans, individually and collectively, learn again to live within limits.

Globalization has begun to challenge all traditional forms of social and political organization, in particular the traditional form of the nation state and of the national economy. In an age of globalization, national sovereignty and international organizations based on agreements between sovereign nation states have become ineffective forms of exercising and controlling power. In particular, the traditional interpretation of national sovereignty in terms of the acceptability of settling international disputes by military means has become dysfunctional. Security in an age of growing interdependence among peoples and states can no longer be established by accumulating the means of defense against a potential enemy, but only as common or cooperative security that takes the legitimate security needs of the other as seriously as the needs of the security of one's own group. Competition as the means to allocate scarce resources in a market framework becomes destructive where it leads to the marginalization of large parts of humanity and to lasting damage to the total ecosystem.

The present trend toward globalization will have to be transformed by recovering a sense of sustainable limits for human existence and production. Most of the fundamental ethical codes of the great religions are based on the essential insight that human life in community and in relationship with nature is sustainable only on the basis of intentional self-limitation of power and greed. The acknowledgment of the minimum limits that have to be respected if the basic needs of human beings are to be met has to be accompanied by a recognition of the acceptable maximum that can be tolerated before excess of power and greed leads to ruin.

The acknowledgment of limits corresponds to an understanding of human existence as "being in relationship." Each human person is a center of relationships; and human identity is formed in shaping relationships with other human beings, with the human environment, and ultimately with God, who, according to the trinitarian faith, is to be understood as the ultimate center of relationships. Living in relationships means acknowledging the "other" as the limitation to one's own freedom, power, need, and security. Since the "other" is himself/herself a center of relationships, the common task is to shape these constitutive relationships into communicative and mutually supportive links. Individual autonomy as well as national sovereignty and all other forms of exclusive and competitive claims has to be seen in its relative significance as being dependent on a wider network of sustaining and limiting relationships.

If the present trend toward globalization is being approached from this perspective, the existing structures for organizing human life have to be reevaluated in terms of their capacity to generate and sustain the vital relationships on which human life and survival depend. Hierarchical structures of control as well as competitive systems of establishing and accumulating political and economic power constantly threaten the maintenance of the network of relationships. They must be replaced by participatory and decentralized forms of social, economic, and political organization that recognize the priority claims arising from the everyday life of people over against the systemic demands of superstructures.

In the present situation of increasing fragmentation as the reverse side of the trend toward globalization, the primary task of Christian churches is to further the process of reconstructing sustainable human communities. This is reflected in the growing interest in processes of strengthening civil society over against the formal structures on the political, social, and economic levels. For centuries, churches have shaped their structured life in correspondence to the prevailing structures of the state, or more recently the patterns of the business world. The challenge as we move into the twenty-first century will be to understand the churches as a vital part of civil society transcending the potentially exclusive claims of culture, racial origin, or ethnic loyalties.

IV. Toward a New Face of the Church

In the preceding sections, a number of challenges that the churches will have to face as we move into the twenty-first century have already been indicated. These challenges are sharpened if the condition of Christianity in worldwide perspective is taken seriously. During the twentieth century, Christianity has become truly ecumenical — that is to say, embracing all the "ends of the earth." The center of Christianity, both numerically and in terms of vitality, has moved from Europe and North America to the Southern hemisphere. Historic Christianity, which has been the origin of the ecumenical movement and has given shape to its structural expression, is more and more giving way to new expressions of Christian faith, life, and witness that have been shaped by interaction with other cultural and religious traditions. Pentecostalism is emerging as the dominant form of Protestantism in Latin America, and in Africa the growth of African-instituted churches is continuing. While historic Christianity, even in its free church expression, has been marked by the Constantinian alliance between church and state, the new and growing forms of Christianity in the Southern hemisphere are increasingly shaped by a post-Constantinian consciousness. Furthermore, while the numerical presence of Christianity in global perspective has increased together with the growth of world population, the percentage of Christians has not changed significantly. Particularly in Asia, Christians continue to form a very small minority with the exception of South

Korea and the Philippines, which have to be considered special cases. In the twenty-first century, Christianity will remain a minority among other religious minorities in spite of all campaigns for evangelism and church growth. In this situation, the churches everywhere will have to learn again what it means to live as the salt of the earth rather than concentrating on the defense of supposedly Christian cultures.

When the ecumenical movement emerged in the first half of the twentieth century, it was called "the great new fact of our time." Since then, ecumenism has become integrated into the normal life, at least of the historic churches, and a wide network of interchurch relationships has emerged. At the same time, ecumenism has become a dividing line within worldwide Christianity, provoking a counterreaction from conservative evangelical or even fundamentalist tendencies within and among the Christian churches. As historical barriers between the different Christian traditions are being overcome, the need to affirm denominational and doctrinal identities has increased as well. If the challenges that the churches will have to face as they move into the twenty-first century have been correctly identified, it will be decisive whether the churches will be able to manifest in their relationships the distinctive form of universality that is rooted in the Christian faith. This is different from all forms of globalization, but it also qualifies the mere acceptance of plurality. "Catholicity," which is the term in the Christian tradition that points to the universal scope of the church, is based on the recognition that the fullness of God's presence is to be experienced in each local community that gathers in the name of Christ and recognizes its constitutive relationship with all other local communities. The tension between the local and the universal church, which is at the heart of present ecumenical discussions about ecclesiology, must be transformed into a relational understanding of the worldwide church that starts from the local community in each place. The ecumenical character and commitment of each local community is to be measured by the extent to which it is prepared to recognize its indissoluble relationship with all other communities as members of the worldwide body of Christ. This relationship finds expression in forms of mutual support and solidarity as well as in the recognition of differences and in mutual accountability. The early church gave expression to this constitutive relationship in developing forms of conciliar life from the local to ever increasing wider levels. Conciliarity, while it was coopted for the purposes of the imperial *oikoumene,* at the same time represented the most effective form of resistance: affirming the nature of the church as a community or *koinonia* in relationship with the triune God. Christian ecumenism, as the practice of conciliar forms of life, remains today one of the most important forms of counteracting the destructive effects of the globalization of modern culture.

Under the conditions of plurality as a continuing feature of human societies in the twenty-first century, the understanding of Christian mission will have to be reassessed fundamentally. Much of Christian mission in the last five hundred years has followed the model of the Crusades in aiming to establish Christian hegemony over other cultures and religious traditions. This was motivated by the desire to establish the rule of Christ over the whole world and to hasten the coming of God's kingdom. A process of rethinking this church-centered or Christ-centered understanding of mission has begun over the last few decades. It has been sharpened by the emergence of dialogue with people of other faiths and by the acknowledgment that God's saving presence in creation is not limited to the visible manifestation of the Christian community. In particular, the recognition of God's "option for the poor" has brought to light that the poor may already be closer to the kingdom than those who try to evangelize them. Mission following the way of Christ — that is, in accordance with the metaphors of the salt of the earth or the grain of wheat that has to die in order to bear fruit — offers a clear alternative to the crusading mind of much of the traditional missionary enterprise. This must lead to a fundamental re-assessment of the place of the Christian community in the wider human community. Christian witness must liberate itself from all hegemonic and exclusivist claims and accept the challenge of genuine dialogue with people of other faiths.

Given the dominant forms of Christian culture that have emerged in particular over the last two hundred years, the challenge to move from anthropocentrism to a life-centered spirituality and ethic is the most difficult to meet. It requires a new understanding of the world as God's creation and a new interpretation of history and eschatology. The traditional separation between creation and redemption will have to be overcome and human salvation will have to be seen in the perspective of the hope for a new heaven and a new earth shaped by God's righteousness — that is, by right relationships between humanity, nature, and God.

It has been said that while the twentieth century has been distinguished by the explosive developments in the field of economy, the twenty-first century will be dominated by the concern to develop a new balance between the needs of human survival and sustenance and the integrity of creation. Christian communities are ill prepared for this task, and they will have to enter into a process of learning from other cultures and religious traditions if they are to make a contribution to meeting this vital challenge. The development of new forms of living has to begin in small communities that accept their dependency and interrelationship with their natural environment. However, they need structures of mutual support; and it is here that the ecumenical movement receives a new significance.

This has been only a preliminary indication of challenges to be faced by the churches as they move into the twenty-first century. As I said at the beginning of this chapter, this exposition cannot offer more than notations for an agenda that is still to be built in the years to come. It will be decisive, however, whether the challenges are accepted or whether the churches retreat into defensive self-isolation. This is why the ecumenical movement today is as important as it was when it began to emerge at the start of the twentieth century.

Turning Point: Will the Christian Religion Overcome Its Adolescence?

Douglas John Hall

Jürgen Moltmann ends his provocative essay "Christianity in the Third Millennium" with a stirring challenge from which I shall derive the primary metaphor for this piece:

> Christianity is a young religion on this earth. It is only 2000 years old. As a young religion, it has filled most of all the young peoples with its messianic spirit. It has made Europe into a continent of reformations and revolutions. It has called the experiment of modern world civilization into being. As no other religion, Christianity is bound to the fate of the modern world. For this reason, *Christians must also overcome their puberty and become mature and wise.* We are not meant to dominate the world but rather can only survive together with other religions and work to the service of humanity's survival. We can learn how to relate to the earth from humanity's more ancient religions. Christianity will also come to adulthood and find its way from faith in progress to the balances of life. Christianity will also recover its own spirituality of creation and find resonance in the religion of the earth in order to harmonize in God's great song of creation, which will save the world.[1]

The metaphor of adolescence that is evoked by this statement seems to me an appropriate one for the historical positioning of the Christian religion *as a religion* at this juncture in its sojourn.[2] Though it may baffle Americans and Canadians, whose less than 500-year history makes Christendom's 2,000 years appear venerable, from the perspective of the ancient faiths to which Moltmann

---

1. *Theology Today* 51 (April 1994): 89 (my italics).

2. If we are to use this metaphor, however, we shall have to draw heavily on the distinction between religion and faith. Maturity of *faith* must certainly be attributed to many whose chronology places them in the stage of Christianity's "childhood," before any of the promptings of "puberty," and, indeed, to many at every other stage in the maturation of the religion.

12

refers, not to mention the natural history of Earth itself, Christianity really is, chronologically, just emerging from "puberty."

It is also adolescent in a more important sense: its inner, spiritual-intellectual estate. This is far more conspicuous in the North American context than it is in the "old" European motherlands. European Christianity has been undergoing the painful transition to adulthood for at least two centuries — perhaps even since the breakdown of the medieval synthesis. In the United States and Canada, on the contrary, the adolescent phase has been prolonged, partly because that very "messianic spirit" (which, as Moltmann rightly notes, the "young" religion of Christianity has inspired among the "young peoples" of Earth) has been so effectively at work in our relatively brief history. Indeed, at the level of public life and rhetoric, what still fuels the psychic engines of U.S.-America in particular is precisely an uncritically triumphalistic form of Christianity that bears all the earmarks of sheer adolescence. One cannot have observed the vital role of the Christian Right in the recent (1994) congressional elections without realizing this. Nor (lest we erroneously conclude that the phenomenon applies to one political party only) could one have listened to President Clinton's 1995 State of the Union address, with its overt references to God and its explicit challenge to the clergy to bolster the government's "Covenant [*sic!*] with America," without knowing how dependent the United States of America still is upon the religion with which its history is intertwined.

Moreover, as America itself emerges reluctantly from its adolescent phase, experiencing, as it must, the loss of its legendary innocence and the deep anxieties of global responsibility, the sociopolitical demand for unconditional affirmation on the part of its historic cultus becomes increasingly insistent. What is wanted by the dominant culture is precisely *not* a Christianity that has "become mature and wise," for such mature wisdom must of necessity be too nuanced for the purpose. What is wanted is a Christianity that can devote itself unquestioningly to the task of restoring the American Dream: that is, the same Christianity that was wanted by the Emperor Constantine, by Henry VIII and the German princes at the time of the Reformation, and (in its most truncated form) by Adolf Hitler — namely, adolescent Christianity.

Under such circumstances one wonders, "Will Christianity be able to move beyond its adolescence? Is the adulthood that Moltmann both exhorts and predicts for the Christian movement so clearly the future that awaits us?"

Adolescence is a time of turbulence, but also of excitement, daring, adventure. In the human being, especially the male of the species, it is inseparable from the wondrous discovery of one's power — potency! It erupts in bursts of exuberance verging on dangerous wrecklessness: the squealing tires of cars with young males at the wheels! Unless circumstances curb and direct its energies, it can lead to violence and machismo of the most abhorrent type. The externally constrained adolescent is an explosive device waiting to be detonated. If this pent-up energy is not channeled into constructive ends, it will almost certainly become destructive — perhaps most regularly *self*-destructive. The discovery of power within oneself is always a heady thing.

Christianity in the fourth century C.E., like "America" in the eighteenth, began to be conscious of its immense power. It is a mistake, I believe, to attribute this to external factors alone. If the army officer Constantine intuited the potentiality of this new religion for buttressing his tottering empire, it was because the Christian movement, though very young and still a minority, already conveyed the surge of energy that dying civilizations can easily recognize — for they need it! This energy emanated from the Christian message itself, which, despite its sometimes gloomy assessments of the human condition and the prospects of the *civitas terrena,* was essentially a hopeful and positive message. Indeed, given the political background of aristocratic decadence and spent authority, and the spiritual background of gross superstition at the popular level and fatalism among the elites, Christianity must have shone in the ancient world as a bright star of possibility.

The enthronement of Christianity during the brief eighty-year period between Constantine and Theodosius the Great meant that this socially undefined and (from officialdom's perspective) potentially dangerous spiritual energy was effectively conducted into political ends that would not only stave off the oblivion that Mediterranean civilization was courting but also provide a new lust for life in that spiritually exhausted world. And Christianity furnished that "enthusiasm" *(en theos)* for European civilization for more than a thousand years. Even when the marriage of Christ and culture began to fail with the demise of the Middle Ages, the energies that were poured into both Christian and secular movements from the fifteenth until the nineteenth centuries were basically Christian energies. The European "reformations and revolutions" of which Moltmann speaks, as well as the impetus for knowledge and exploration that led Europeans to find new worlds and usher in the Age of Science, can be traced to Christian spiritual assumptions even when, on the surface of history, they appear or wish to appear anti-Christian. A faith that affirms the world as God's own creation and humankind as the apple of God's eye, whatever else may be said about it and whatever it may say about itself, produces an enormous ardor for human potentiality in a world whose history is meaningful and progressive.

In the two northern nations of the North American continent, we are still very conscious of the power of Christian religious fervor to effect such ends; for not only are we one of the specific consequences of this surge of spiritual zeal in European history but we have still in our midst strident voices that urge us to recover the now-waning power of our own adolescence. Our perspective on the "turning point" alluded to in the title of this essay is therefore somewhat different from that of our European contemporaries. Having preserved rather longer than they the truly exhilarating, if naive, intensity of adolescence, we are more conscious of its benefits, more fearful of the loss of it, and (most significantly) more skeptical concerning the "maturity" that may well replace it.

Jürgen Moltmann's concluding sentences in the above quotation are premised on the belief that the transition from "puberty" to maturity can be a highly positive one. As an individual moving out of adolescence may become a reasonable, cooperative, and responsible citizen of the community, so the Christian religion undergoing its introduction into the great world of many faiths and shared problems can cease being evangelically aggressive, discover its own best resources for addressing common threats to life, and enter harmoniously into the chorus of "God's great song of creation, which will save the world."

This is a wonderful scenario, worthy of the man who gave us the "theology of hope." I do not wish to discredit it, for I fervently hope that the Christian movement may meet its *krisis* in just such a mature way. But as one who shares with Professor Moltmann a common background in the tradition that Luther named *theologia crucis*, I should like to enter some ifs and buts from the perspective of a church and society existentially closer to the transition in question on account of their continuing proximity to the adolescent stage.

While many adolescents make the difficult transition to adulthood with relative grace and with favorable results, many others do not. Under auspicious circumstances, especially if they are surrounded by understanding and wise adults, adolescents often emerge into maturity of a commendable sort. But if such guidance is lacking, the latter state may be worse than the former. The people we call adults are all too often disillusioned or cynical adolescents, whose youthful vigor and idealism have been dashed by the realities of life in a finite and sinful world. And the more inhospitable the world becomes to maturing adolescents who are equipped and willing to serve it, the more common is the phenomenon of such disillusionment. The "message" given to the young by a society that, for example, may need only a fraction of its potential workforce to provide its needs[3] is that it would be better to remain in a state of adolescence.

Certain factors in the North American context that concern me as I reflect on our Christian "turning point" and make me less sanguine of its ending so happily as Professor Moltmann invites us to believe it will. I shall concentrate on two of these factors militating against the "maturity and wisdom" that Moltmann envisages as characterizing the Christianity of the future.

The first could be considered an ecclesiastical form of the nostalgia for adolescence just alluded to. A robust and enterprising branch of Christianity in our context indicates by everything that it says and does that it is wholly unprepared to let go of the militant, exclusivistic, world-conquering faith that fought back all competitors and believed so unabashedly in the finality of its

---

3. Jeremy Rifkin, president of the Washington-based Foundation on Economic Trends, argues in his book *The End of Work* that "within 30 years the global marketplace will not require more than 20 percent of the population to operate" (quoted by Brenda Dalglish in "Looking for Work," *Maclean's*, 23 January 1995, p. 32).

doctrine that it was able to achieve results that would certainly have been denied more reflective and dialectically balanced expressions of religious belief. This type of Christianity, which in many of its specific embodiments was until recently persuaded of its own holy separation from the wicked world, has in the past few decades rushed in to fill the vacuum left by the historic, once-mainline denominations — namely, to assume the role of religious establishment. For the vast majority of North Americans, whose chief medium of information is television, fundamentalist-biblicist expressions of Christianity are perceived by now as normative Christianity. Not only is this Christianity unwilling to share the "fields that are white for harvest" with any other faith, or to look to ancient religions for wisdom; but it regards pluralism and secularity as aspects of the malaise of the society, and entertains bold missionary endeavors intended to Christianize the world — often enough "by the year 2000."

Using the metaphor we have employed here, this Christianity, currently dubbed "the Christian Right," is refusing to leave the adolescent phase. It intends to continue its quest for power, skidding its tires at will, and quietly countenancing, along its edges, whatever spiritual (and occasionally even physcial) violence may be necessary to ensure its dominance.

The second disturbing factor in our context is located on the opposite side of the spectrum among those Christians whom we might group together as the radical, vociferous wing of mainline liberalism. The watchword of this segment is inclusivity.[4] In the line of nineteenth-century liberal universalism, it opens itself to all faiths, races, sexual identities and preferences, and points of view, excluding only those whom it perceives as exclusive — in particular, other Christians who insist upon an explicitly Christian confession of faith.

It is practically impossible for the majority of those who remain in the "old-line" denominations, being mainly middle-class, relatively well-educated people whose natural inclination is toward toleration of difference, to entertain a critique of radical liberal inclusiveness, however uncomfortable some of the expressions of the latter may make them. Not only culturally but religiously as well, the persons in this category are conditioned to distrust any system of meaning that can appear "elitist." Indeed, the whole thrust of mainline Christianity on this continent has been toward the creation of gentle, accepting, hospitable communities of belief — "friendly churches" — whose corporate life

---

4. The use of "inclusivity" in contemporary discourse relating to religious pluralism is in part traceable to Karl Rahner's employment of the term. I am not using it here in Rahner's sense; rather, I intend it as a designation of the attitude that finds itself embarrassed by Christian particularity. The context in which such a term is employed always colors its meaning: It is one thing to deploy the concept of inclusiveness strategically, as Rahner does, in an ecclesial milieu that assumes the blatant exclusivity designated by the phrase *extra ecclesiam nulla salus;* it is something quite different when such a concept is employed in a social context where any claim to the uniqueness of Christian revelation is denounced by both the secular and the religious avant-garde.

exemplifies the Christ in whom "there is no longer Jew or Greek, . . . slave or free, . . . male and female; for all . . . are one . . ." (Gal. 3:28, NRSV).

But hope in the eschatologically reconciling labor of the triune God is not synonymous with an ideology of inclusivity, in which reconciliation is no longer a gift of grace but a reality and therefore a "right" inhering in the very structure of being. The truth is, for the ideologue of liberal Christian inclusivity the confession abbreviated in the name "Jesus Christ" is an embarrassment that can be overcome only by collapsing the particularity of the historical person Jesus into a "Christ" who is in reality a construct composed of the chief tenets of the ideology.[5]

We see here the type of embarrassed *reaction* to adolescence that leaps into the state of presumed maturity so injudiciously as to leave behind not only its *naiveté* but also the source of its exuberance. Not unpredictably, it regularly becomes academic and jaded, and frequently more aggressive in its "correctness" than are the others who cling tenaciously to their adolescent creeds. If Christians follow this route as we move from the Constantinian to the post-Constantinian phase of the Christian movement, we shall end by forfeiting the very thing that has created us — namely, the faith that sees in Jesus of Nazareth a concretization of the Ultimate which, while pointing beyond itself and thus refusing to absolutize *itself*, continues to be the entree ("door") to an expansiveness of love that otherwise remains purely abstract or altogether hidden from view.[6]

To summarize, two agendas for the future assail us: from the Right, a christomonism (Dorothée Sölle called it "christo-fascism") that elevates not only the Christ but also specific christological and other dogma to the sphere of finality; from the Left, an ideological faith that subsumes Jesus Christ under its own a priori assumptions about God and the world. The *danger* that looms on the horizon, given this polarization of the Christian movement in its North American expression, is that Christianity will either devolve into simplistic reductions of itself along sectarian lines, or that it will be absorbed into the general "Spirituality" that now attracts so many allegedly post-Modern people. In metaphoric terms, the danger is that Christianity will not manage a wise transition from puberty to maturity but, like many individuals, will either carry a militant adolescence with it into chronological adulthood or take upon itself

---

5. What Reinhold Niebuhr said of Christian liberalism in his "intellectual autobiography" forty years ago is just as true, if not truer, of the present-day self-styled radicals who chafe at the "scandal of particularity": "The whole of modern theology in its various aspects is involved in the effort to reduce the absurdity of the idea of God involved in history and taking action in historic terms. This is done by reducing the message of the Bible to 'eternal principles' of ethics or of ontology. . . . In the desperate effort of the modern Christian to make his faith acceptable to the intellectual scruples of modern men, he reduces it to ontological absurdities or to ethical truisms" (*Reinhold Niebuhr: His Religious, Social and Political Thought,* ed. Charles W. Kegley and Robert W. Bretall [New York: Macmillan, 1956], p. 19).

6. See Paul Tillich, *Systematic Theology,* vol. 1 (Chicago: University of Chicago Press, 1951), pp. 150-53.

a bogus maturity that robs it of the very life force that engendered it. Whether this is only a North American danger, I shall not venture to suggest, though I suspect that it is to be noticed, *mutatis mutandis*, at least in most of the other, "newer" churches of the planet.

There is, it seems to me, only one way in which such an undesirable scenario as either the continuation of such polarization or the ascendancy of one position over the other can be effectively altered. That possibility involves in particular the future course that will be taken by two groupings within the present makeup of the churches: the aforementioned nonaligned majority of the old-line churches, who incline toward inclusivity yet are uncomfortable with ideological versions of the same; and the professional scholars of the Christian religion, who might be able, if they are willing, to provide the necessary guidance to that majority as it moves out of the stage of "puberty" — a stage in which, for both internal and external reasons, it certainly cannot remain.

What is most conspicuous about this amorphous majority among all of the once-mainline churches of our context is its theological confusion, amounting in many cases to doctrinal indifference and historical amnesia but among a significant minority manifesting itself as a genuine desire for clarity and direction. This segment of the churches can be tempted by either "conservative" exclusivity or "radical-liberal" inclusivity, yet it feels at home in neither camp. Its very ethos begs for a more nuanced, thoughtful, less doctrinaire expression of belief — one that neither demands of it a narrowness of outlook foreign to its character nor, on the other hand, beckons it clear away from any adherence to the particularity of the Judeo-Christian tradition.

Such a situation amounts to nothing less than the implicit demand for a *theological depth* that only those who have undergone to years of professional training in the various theological disciplines and cognate areas can supply. *But* (and this is perhaps the most explicit of the caveats that I wish to append to Moltmann's admirable vision for the Christian future) the sad fact is that professional Christian scholars, at least in North America, have practically abandoned the churches and, under the impact of professionalism in all of its contemporary expressions, conduct dialogues and monologues within their guilds. As John Cobb, Jr., has recently written, "Since so little of the scholarly and intellectual work of faculties of theology is geared to the service of the church, it is not surprising that the church takes little interest in this work. Scholars write for one another and for the students to whom they assign their books."[7]

Let me therefore indulge in a tautology: only a *thinking* faith can overcome adolescence and "become mature and wise." The onus, humanly speaking, is thus on the scholars and teachers of the church to turn from their narrowly

---

7. Cobb, Jr., "Faith Seeking Understanding: The Renewal of Christian Thinking," *The Christian Century,* 29 June–6 July 1994, pp. 642-43.

professional pursuits and serve the community that constitutes, after all, the only reason for their being, helping it to become a truly *confessional* community. While the grace and providence of God are not dependent upon human agency, and while therefore the future of the church, like all future, is in the hands of God and not Christian educators, Christian *obedience* in our historical moment has quite explicitly to do with theology. It is a pathetically mistaken reading of the "signs of the times" to think that the act has priority over the thought. That assumption, which motivates perhaps the best efforts in old-line Protestant denominations, ignores the fact that an incalculable but obvious causative dimension of the complex *problematique* of our age must be located immediately in thought-*less* activity. No one in his or her right mind could sanction activity-less thought, or thought functioning as a fence upon which to sit! But unless the churches are helped to think again, the most that anyone can expect of them is to be blown about by every *dernier cri,* every ism and slogan and "theology of."

As an intentional Protestant, I am convinced that such a theological re-vitalization of Christianity can be undertaken now only by a genuinely ecumenical Christian movement in which those Christian bodies that have sustained a lively dialogue with the *tradition* have a vital role. Only those who remember the past can help us to get into the future. That certainly does not mean that we are to carry the past, *any* past, into the future; but it does mean that the future will be a very mixed bag indeed, a repetition of the *worst* of the Christian past, if there is no remembrance of and wrestling with where and what we have been — no "traditioning." The liberal Protestant denominations of this continent, having been the most accommodating to Modernity, are most at sea in the so-called post-Modern era. There is therefore a special vocation awaiting all those Christian bodies — Roman Catholic, Orthodox, Lutheran, moderate Baptist, Mennonite, and others — that for one reason or another have not been permitted to embrace Modernity uncritically because they were obligated to struggle with doctrinal positions predating the Enlightenment.[8]

Such a vocation is not an easy one for these bodies, for (with notable exceptions) they have characteristically withdrawn from worldly discourse, except where they could still count on a hearing for reasons extraneous to the Evangel (in various establishments, ethnic ghettos, etc.). The rest of us do *not* need from these ecclesial groupings the kinds of testimonies to unchanging *doctrina* that in their too-typical expressions they have always been ready to

---

8. This is also the conclusion of the sociological study by Wade Clark Roof and William McKinney called *American Mainline Religion: Its Changing Shape and Future* (New Brunswick: Rutgers University Press, 1987): "If a revived public church is indeed on the horizon . . . [it] will require forms and qualities of leadership that have seldom been forthcoming from the Protestant middle; a revitalized ecumenicity and new, bold theological affirmations are critical as well, especially a theology that resonates with and gives meaning to the experience of middle Americans" (p. 241).

share with (or impose upon!) us. What we need from them is a model of historical *responsibility* that is directed not toward the preservation of the church and its doctrine but toward the preservation of *life* — namely, the life of God's beloved creation.[9] Such a model of *theologische Existenz* could help the remnants of mainstream Protestantism to recover the memory of their own most significant past, so that together the divided Christian churches might find a sufficient integrity (which they do not now possess) to engage in that creative interaction with the more ancient faiths of the planet that will "work to the service of humanity's [and earth's] survival."

<hr>

9. A promising recent example of what I mean is a new work by Roman Catholic feminists entitled *Freeing Theology: The Essentials of Theology in Feminist Perspective,* ed. Catherine Mowry LaCugna (San Francisco: Harper San Francisco, 1994), a work described by its editor as being distinctly Catholic because the essays "are marked by the Catholic concern to be in continuity with the Christian tradition as much as possible, indeed, to search to the fullest possible extent for liberating elements within the Christian tradition." See the review by Maureen Dallison Kemeza in *The Christian Century,* 23 November 1994, p. 1121.

Kneeling and Walking Upright

Dorothée Sölle

In recent centuries, religion has been criticized in the Western world in a thorough and relevant fashion. The three great "masters of suspicion," as Paul Ricoeur calls them — Marx, Freud, and Nietzsche — unmasked it as the opiate of the masses, as collective neurosis, and as Platonism for the people. For a quarter century now, feminism has carried on this project of unmasking Scripture and tradition: androcentric language and symbolism as well as patriarchal structures seem to be integral components of both the Jewish and Christian traditions. Theology — in its enlightened, Protestant form — has integrated this criticism sometimes more, sometimes less effectively. It has passed "through the fire brook [*Feuer-bach*]" and has in its own turn developed a hermeneutic of suspicion capable of criticism of both the self and institutions, and thus critically evaluates both the Bible and the church ever anew. In this process, living Christian faith has lost its naiveté and its missionary imperialism, and has learned how to apply prophetic criticism of cult and sacrificial offerings — the "noise of your songs," as Amos puts it (Amos 5:23) — to Christianity itself and to the church that is ever in need of reform. *Ecclesia semper reformanda!*

Today, this critical Christian consciousness often seems to me like an expiring ideal — between fundamentalism on the one hand, and postmodernism on the other. I fear that in this critical, enlightened form, a form engaged in dialogue with the scientific explanation of the world, Christianity has increasingly less air to breathe and room to grow. On the one hand, the crudest fundamentalism continues to flourish with its fears of anything that is "different"; "strong" faith seems to be a bulwark *against* the apocalyptic scenarios that threaten us. On the other hand, post- or anti-Christian forms of new spirituality are emerging that make the Christian faith directly responsible precisely *for* these apocalyptic scenarios. Christianity is then perceived only as a kind of scrap religion; its message shrivels to "subdue the earth," the disastrous consequences of which are visible to everyone. Between these two — the pre- and postmodern forms of religion — the "Protestant principle" is being deflated.

21

The minority of critical Christians increasingly encounter the very real forces and powers of destruction, forces that have long ceased to be religion and the church. Today, money and power need religious legitimation less and less, and function best in the name of progress and of technological rationality. In this situation, one must ask whether traditional criticism of religion has not in some respects run out of gas, since it disregards and in no way really critically inquires concerning genuine religion; that is, concerning that particular religion in which, in the industrialized countries, the overwhelming majority actually believes. This real religion is science. It has its larger temples, as anyone knows who has visited Harvard University with its white columns and impressive halls, its main and secondary chapels, its sanctuaries and treasuries. It has its own priests, high priests, and popes. It performs certain rituals, dispenses accolades and chastisement, all according to models fixed beforehand, and declares what is sinful and what sacred. The only thing it has not learned quite so well, relatively speaking, is criticism of its own religion. The question concerning just who is to benefit from certain research projects is generally rejected as unscientific; any evaluation of priorities and of the applicability of research in actual practice, especially regarding military considerations, is considered secondary.

If science is the primary religion of the industrialized world, then I must confess myself to be a nonbeliever. Rather than preventing war, it has improved our capacity for killing. Rather than feeding the hungry, it has turned its attention to space exploration. It has generated a megamachine that rapes all of nature and all of creation. It believes in its own, second creation, one that is to be better than the first. The visions of science have long turned into horror stories. For example, let me mention merely the familiar, scientific implementation of torture as an interrogation method. Is it enough in our age merely to think scientifically? Is not a different perspective on the world needed, and different values for enlisting the service of scientists? Indeed, is not theology itself — which in the words of Walter Benjamin is small and ugly today — is not theology itself needed now more than ever if we are to acquire a different vision of the good life in a fellowship free of the strictures of domination?

Within this framework, I will try to articulate what I believe, and what seems indispensable to me. In liberation theology we often speak about the *opción preferential por los pobres*, "God's partiality toward the poor." Perhaps all religions have such "options," that is, choices and decisions of an obligatory character. I understand the Christian faith as an *"opción preferential por la vida,"* a partiality or preference for life over against death. To be is better than not to be. Kissing is better than not kissing, and eating is not only preferential to hunger, but it is also ontologically superior. The Christian religion, too, tries to articulate this ontological surplus of being over nothingness.

I once tried to explain to a depressed friend this kind of faith in life; he waved me off wearily and said, "You just want to lure me back to creation with flowers and sunrises." And indeed, that was and still is my intention. The ontological superiority of being over nothingness expresses itself religiously as faith in the creator God and in the goodness and blessedness of creation. On the sixth day, God saw that "all was very good." God's option is directed toward life, and I, too, wish to see with these eyes of God, though without denying everything that yet — as I add in faith — mortally contradicts this vision. It was no accident that brought us to this small, blue planet; life itself beckons us to participate in life with a kind of living thankfulness that even in the darkness does not cease to perceive life as grace, as a gift. Praise of life is a kind of devotion of existence that I both need and try to pass on to others.

I believe in God, in the creative power that "calls into existence the things that do not exist" (Rom. 4:17), the power that is good and that wants us to be good human beings, and that means completely and in the full blossom of our capacity to reflect God. In German, the word *glauben* ("believe") derives from the word *geloben* ("pledge") and does not have primarily the rational sense of "accept, consider true," but exhibits rather the existential dimension "engage in, pledge oneself to someone." I believe in God's good creation, as it was intended, encompassing the equality of man and woman, the responsibility for caring for and preserving the garden, and our capacity to work and to love and thus to be an image of God.

The origin is simultaneously the goal. Since we come from God, we also enter into God; every day we take steps toward this reality of God. From the triviality of daily life and from the trivialization of our life goals and wishes, we retrieve our partiality for life itself. My own tradition refers to this retrieval as *t^ešûḇâ*, or "turning, return," and one of the most profound experiences and hopes of faith is the assumption — guaranteed by absolutely nothing in this world — that we are indeed capable of such turning and return. I am to believe this of myself; unbelief in the possibility of one's own turn or reversal is perhaps the worst thing depression inflicts upon my friend. I am both called upon and invited to believe my fellow is capable of this turn, even if he or she continues to steer stubbornly toward the iceberg; and I am even supposed to believe the enemies of life are themselves capable of the *t^ešûḇâ*, truly an absurd undertaking given the obsession with which the lords of this world pursue the project of death. And yet I do believe from tradition that turning is our true potential.

How am I to love God, praise and preserve creation, and contribute to the reign of God without despairing? The assistance that my tradition offers to me is called Christ. I find believing in him to be comparatively easy; one need not be a Christian in the fundamentalist sense of the word in order to be drawn onto his path, and one need not make dogmatic distortions of his truth into the main point. After all, he was himself never concerned with any exclusivity attaching to his own person, but rather with that which appeared before him: God's reign. We are, all of us, sons and daughters of God, and he is merely the "firstborn of many brothers and sisters" (Rom. 8:29) who disclosed to the non-Jews of the ancient world the God of Israel. His own bond with the ground of all life was strong enough, and is present in everything we know of him; his orientation toward the goal is unequivocal. In his brief public life he more and more became that very love of which he spoke. To believe in Christ does not mean to admire him as a hero, but rather to follow him. "Let the same mind be in you that was in Christ Jesus" (Phil. 2:5).

But did he not fail completely? Were not both he and his dream of God betrayed and denied, condemned and tortured to death? And has his project, namely the reign of God, not then been genuinely betrayed and denied, distorted and burned a thousand times in precisely what followed from this, namely, the church? And as if the ancient Christians suspected just what would become of this church, and the despair into which this apparatus would plunge the later followers of this poor man of Nazareth — they added to the ground of life and to the leader and perfecter of life yet another puzzling figure of faith, namely, the Spirit of God, or as we might better say today, following the Hebrew word: the Spiritess, the *rû(a)ḥ* that grants life.

I cannot imagine my own life without this faith in the *rû(a)ḥ*. Reason, if it is not behaving as simply a neutral spectator, runs aground on despair. If it is honest, it can only founder on the project of death that now as before governs the most important productive force, namely, science. (The bare majority of all scientists and engineers is still working on this project of death, in "military related industries" and research projects.) Whence can any hope come for the minorities of conscience who are resisting this undertow of death, for those who take a stand in favor of trees and butterflies and the water their grandchildren are to use, and who are arrested and sentenced in nonviolent protest? I do not think it is saying too much if we see the Spiritess of God in the resistance to everything that is seeking to reconcile us with this killing. According to tradition, the Holy Spirit gives us two things: truth and courage. Truth means that God's Spirit makes human beings capable of truth. It is not as if we cannot know anything, or as if the experts are the eternal lords and judges over a people that from a faithless perspective are considered dumb and unsuspecting. When at the beginning of the 1980s both scientists and physicians took a stand "for peace," I had to smile a bit. My own experience was that the housewives in the various church congregations had a better understanding of the fact . . . that one cannot keep starving children alive with bombs and poisonous gas. The Holy Spiritess had made them truthful, and in a world of systematic, state-organized misinformation (a new word for lying), that is no small feat. Inasmuch as God's Spirit gave human beings truth and liberated them from the profound fear of being incapable of truth, this Spiritess led them further into courage.

I often perceive the present to be a kind of blanket surrounded by the mild depression of intelligent men, a blanket in which human beings remain incapable of action because they remain without faith. The alleged objective constraints of the industrialized world on the one hand, and the corresponding experiences of helplessness of those who know that "nothing can be done" on the other, correspond to one another. Knowledge has increasingly degenerated into a knowledge of death. Enlightenment alone will not suffice. It is incapable of overcoming the predominating spiritlessness. To believe in God's Spirit means above all to summon it. "Holy Spirit, come . . ." also into our emptiness and into our dependence on the drugs with which we have surrounded ourselves. A different life is possible; the stone heart can become flesh again. To believe in this is indispensable for my own life. I pledge myself to the Spiritess, precisely and especially when in my own presence among my own class, people, or world-historical role I sense very little of her fire.

What do I believe in? We live when we praise God, do what is just, and call upon the Spiritess. By learning to walk upright, we also learn how to kneel. Thus do we who are constructing so much apartheid and such a culture of death — thus do we reconnect with life and with the lover of life, as God is called in the Bible. "I call heaven and earth to witness against you today that I have set before you life and death, blessings and curses. Choose life so that you and your descendants may live" (Deut. 30:19). God offers us life — blessed, good life in Shalom. And we can choose it in freedom.

No Enemy, No Christianity:
Theology and Preaching between "Worlds"

Stanley Hauerwas

I have always admired Jürgen Moltmann's theological courage and imagination. Some years ago in the *New Yorker,* John Updike wrote a rather surprising positive review of the work of Kurt Vonnegut. He observed that Vonnegut was the most imaginative contemporary novelist helping us see the absurdity of the normal. Moltmann, I believe, is the Vonnegut of recent theology: he has been willing to force us theologically to imagine our world eschatologically. In the hope of indicating the debt we owe him, I offer this chapter in which I inadequately try to follow his example by exploring what it means to preach and do theology in an allegedly postmodern world.

I first wrote this chapter as an address for the 1994 annual meeting of the American Academy of Homiletics at Duke University. I tried to be faithful to their theme — "Preaching in a Post-Modern Age" — while avoiding the endless discussion of what "postmodernity" entails. Taking my cue from Moltmann, I tried to narrate the motif of postmodernity in a more determinatively eschatological fashion.

The focus of preaching was obviously dictated by the occasion, but I think Moltmann would approve of such a focus. Moltmann, unlike many recent theologians, has written theology that is sermonic. For Moltmann, the practice of theology is not separable from the practices of the church, such as preaching. He offers us no strong distinction between theory and practice. We have no difficulty understanding how his theology should shape the church's preaching.

That is one of the reasons that Moltmann's theology has rightly been so important for so many. You never have to ask how his theology might be applied because his theological work is from beginning to end practical. Indeed, he has taught us that if you have to ask how a theology can be or should be "applied" to preaching you know such a theology is based on a mistake. "Applied theology" is almost as absurd a project as the recent creation and interest in "applied ethics." "Practical" and "applied" are adjectives that were legitimated by the modernist penchant for "theory" that then must be "applied." In that respect, Moltmann was "postmodern" before we even knew we were postmodern.

I am just postmodern enough not to trust postmodern as a description of our times. The very description, postmodern, cannot help but privilege the practices and intellectual formations of modernity. For example, calling this a postmodern age reproduces the modernist assumption that history must be policed by periods. Modernity creates the "middle ages" that we all know can be safely left behind. The very description "postmodern" is far too comforting since it gives the illusion that we know where we are in contradiction to the postmodernist's epistemological doubt that such knowledge is available.

Modernity was created by a deliberate rejection of the past, but ironically modernity is now our past. Accordingly, "postmodernity is still in the line of modernity, as rebellion against rebellion is still rebellion, as an attack on the constraints of grammar must still be written in grammatical sentences, as a skeptical argument against the structures of rationality must still be put rationally."[1] As Reinhard Hutter observes, "it belongs to the ironies of modernity that exactly those who are most modern increasingly claim post-modernity as modernity's most recent advance."[2]

I confess that as a theologian I take perverse delight in the controversies surrounding postmodernism. Modernity, or at least the intellectual formations of modernity, sought to secure knowledge in the very structure of human rationality. Accordingly, God was relegated to the "gaps" or denied all together. Postmodernists are, thus, the atheists that only modernity could produce. Modernity said that since God is a projection of the ideals and wants of what it means to be human, let us serve and worship the only God that matters — that is, the human. Postmodernists, in the quest to be thorough in their atheism, now deny that the human exists.

I do find it puzzling, however, to watch theologians, both conservative and liberal, come to the defense of the human, the rational, objectivity, the "text," "moral values," science, and all the other cherished conceits of the modern university in the name of "humanism." It is as if Christians have forgotten that we also have a stake in atheism. Christians do not believe in the "human"; we believe in God — a God who we believe, moreover, intends to kill us all in the end. So we Christians oppose nuclear weapons not because they threaten to destroy "mother earth," but because the God we serve would not have one life unjustly killed even if such a killing would insure the survival of the human species. Indeed, it is not even clear that we Christians know what the human

1. J. Bottom, "Christians and Postmoderns," *First Things* 40 (February 1994): 29.
2. Reinhard Hutter, "The Church as Public: Dogma, Practice, and Holy Spirit," *Pro Ecclesia*, 3 (Summer 1994): 334.

species is or what status it may have since we have surer knowledge that we are creatures than that we are human.

Christians, therefore, have little stake in the question of whether we live in a postmodern time. For us, any divide in history, the way we tell the story of how we have come to the place where we are, requires a reading of God's providential care of God's creation through the people of Israel and the church. Israel and the church are not characters in a larger story called "world," but rather "world" is a character in God's story as known through the story that is the church. Without the church there is no world to have a story. From my perspective, postmodernism only names an interesting set of developments in social orders that are based on the presumption that God does not matter.

The imperialistic character of these claims for the significance of the church does not mean that it is unimportant for Christians to understand that peculiar development called modernity. Rather, as I just suggested, we must narrate the modern/postmodern divide on our terms. That, I fear, is what we have not done well in modernity. Christians' attitudes toward modernity have primarily been characterized by a sense of inferiority. As John Milbank observes, "the pathos of modern theology is its false humility."[3] Our preaching and theology have been one ceaseless effort to conform to the canons of intelligibility produced by the economic and intellectual formations characteristic of modern and, in particular, liberal societies.

Christians in modernity thought their task was to make the gospel intelligible to the world rather than to help the world understand why it could not be intelligible without the gospel. Desiring to become part of the modernist project, preachers and theologians accepted the presumption that Christianity is a set of beliefs, a worldview, designed to give meaning to our lives. As a result, the politics of Christian discourse was relegated to the private in the name of being politically responsible in, to, and for liberal social orders. Believing that neither we nor our non-Christian or half-Christian neighbors could be expected to submit to the discipline of Christian speech, we accepted the politics of translation.

Ironically, the attempt to make Christianity intelligible often sought support from those philosophical and literary theories that tried to protect discourse from translation — the most prominent example being new criticism. Under the influence of new criticism, some thought that Christianity could be conceived as a beautiful poem that is its own justification. Such a poem, of course, could and should illumine the human condition, but just to the extent that the poem provided such illumination, all attempts to make the poem "do something" must be condemned as crass. In quite different ways, Paul Tillich and Reinhold Niebuhr gave theological warrant to the high humanism intrinsic

---

3. John Milbank, *Theology and Social Theory: Beyond Secular Reason* (Cambridge: Basil Blackwell, 1990), p. 1.

to the powerful set of suggestions associated with such formalist theories. What could be more comforting to the modern consciousness than to discover that "ultimate concern" and "sin" are essential and unavoidable characteristics of the human condition? You do not even need to go to church to learn that. Reading Shakespeare will do just as well if not better.

The humanistic presumptions of new criticism nicely fit the aestheticism of the middle class that dominates Christianity, particularly in America — at least the Christianity that produces intellectuals who teach in most seminaries. That is why I take it that contemporary theology and preaching are still dominated by formalist presumptions even if theologian and preacher, or the teacher of homiletical theory, think they have theoretically left such theories behind. New critical habits are hard habits to break because they fit so well the class interests that dominate the seminary cultures in which most of us are located. Even "neoorthodoxy" was not free of their temptations exactly to the extent that "God's word" was made autonomous and self-validating.

In particular, new critical assumptions hide from us how our theological presumptions are shaped by class interests. Frank Lentricchia, in his *Modernist Quartet,* makes the fascinating suggestion that the modernist writer defined himself against the standards of the mass market by becoming the champion of radical originality and the maker of a "one-of-a-kind-text." He observes, however, that "the modernist desire in Frost and Eliot — to preserve an independent selfhood against the coercions of the market, a self made secure by the creation of a unique style — is subverted by the market, not because they wrote according to popular formulas, but because they give us their poems as delicious experiences of voyeurism, illusions of direct access to the life and thought of the famous writer, with the poet inside the poem like a rare animal in a zoo. This was the only commodity Frost and Eliot were capable of producing: the modernist phenomenon as product, mass-culture's ultimate revenge on those who would scorn it."[4]

In like manner, the preaching and theology shaped by new critical presumptions to illumine the human condition hid from us that the human condition being illuminated was that of the bourgeois. That is why the sermon meant to illumine our condition, which is often eloquent and profound, is also so forgettable and even boring. Insights about the human condition are a dime a dozen. Most days most of us would rightly trade any insight for a good meal.

The high humanism of contemporary theology and preaching not only hid the class interest intrinsic to such preaching, but also reinforced the presumption that Christians could be Christians without enemies. Christianity as the illumination of the human condition is not a Christianity at war with the world. Liberal Christianity, of course, has enemies; but they are everyone's enemies — sexism, racism, homophobia. Yet liberal versions of Christianity,

4. Frank Lentricchia, *Modernist Quartet* (Cambridge: Cambridge University Press, 1994), pp. 112-13.

which can be both theologically and politically conservative, assume that what it means to be Christian qua Christian is to have no enemies peculiar to being Christian. Psalms that ask God to destroy our enemies and their children, such as Psalm 109, can appear only as embarrassing holdovers of "primitive" religious beliefs. Equally problematic are apocalyptic texts that suggest that Christians are part of a cosmic struggle.

"Cosmic struggle" sounds like a video game the children of the middle class play. Most do not go to church because they are seeking a safe haven from enemies, but rather to be assured that they have no enemies. Accordingly, ministers are expected to exemplify the same kind of bureaucratic mentality so characteristic of modern organizational behavior and politics. I sometimes think that there is a conspiracy afoot to make MacIntyre's account of the manager in *After Virtue* empirically verifiable.[5]

That the manager has become characteristic of liberal politics should not be surprising, but I confess I continue to be taken aback by the preponderance of such character types in the ministry. Of course, I should not be surprised that a soulless church produces a soulless ministry devoid of passion. The ministry seems captured in our time by people who are desperately afraid they might actually be caught with a conviction at one point in their ministry that might curtail future ambition. They, therefore, see their task to "manage" their congregations by specializing in the politics of agreement, by always being agreeable. The preaching such a ministry produces is designed to reinforce our presumed agreements since a "good church" is one without conflict. You cannot preach about abortion, suicide, or war because those are such controversial subjects — better to concentrate on "insights" since they do so little work for the actual shaping of our lives and occasion no conflict.

I confess that one of the things I like about the Southern Baptists (and most things about the Southern Baptists I dislike) is that they have managed to have a fight in public. At least fundamentalists believe they are supposed to have strong views, and they even believe they are supposed to act on their convictions. The problem with most of the mainstream churches is that we do not even know how to join an argument — better to create a committee to "study the issue."

If postmodernism means anything, it means that the comforting illusion of modernity that conflict can and should be avoided is over. No unbiased viewpoint exists that can in principle insure agreements. Our difficulty is not that we have conflicts, but that modern people have not had the courage to force the conflicts we ought to have had. Instead, we have comforted ourselves with the ideology of pluralism, forgetting that pluralism is but the peace treaty left over from past wars that now benefits the victors of those wars.

---

5. Alasdair MacIntyre, *After Virtue* (Notre Dame: University of Notre Dame Press, 1984), pp. 73-76.

God may be using this time to remind the church that Christianity is unintelligible without enemies. Indeed, the whole point of Christianity is to produce the right kind of enemies. We have been beguiled by our established status to forget that *to be a Christian is to be made part of an army against armies.* It has been suggested that satisfaction theories of the atonement and the correlative understanding of the Christian life as a life of interiority became the rule during the long process we call the Constantinian settlement. When Caesar becomes a member of the church, the enemy becomes internalized. The problem is no longer that the church is seen as a threat to the political order, but that now my desires are disordered. The name for such an internalization in modernity is pietism, and the theological expression of that practice is called Protestant liberalism.

In contrast, I am suggesting that our theology and our preaching should presume that we are writing and preaching to a church in the midst of a war — a position you may find odd to be advocated by a pacifist. I hope the oddness, however, might encourage a reexamination of the dominant understanding of Christian nonviolence, an understanding probably shaped by Reinhold Niebuhr. Who more than the Christian pacifist knows Christians are in a war against war? Moreover, as a pacifist, I do not need something called the human condition illumined when I am preparing to face the enemy. Rather, I need to have a sense of where the battle is, what the stakes are, and what the long-term strategy may be. Yet that is exactly what most preaching does not do. It does not help us locate our enemy because it does not believe that Christians should have enemies. In the name of love and peace, Christian preaching has but reinforced the "normal nihilism" that grips our lives. We have a difficult time recognizing the wars that are already occurring or the wars that should be occurring because we think it so irrational that some should kill others in the name of "values."

James Edwards has argued in his *The Plain Sense of Things: The Fate of Religion in an Age of Values* that nothing characterizes the nihilism that grips our lives better than the language of "values." Nihilism is not a philosophical conspiracy designed by Nietzsche and some French intellectuals to undermine the good sense of liberal Americans — indeed, Nietzsche was the great enemy of nihilism. Rather, nihilism is now the normal condition of our lives to the extent that we all believe that our lives are constituted by what Edwards calls "self-devaluating values." All our values are self-devaluating because we recognize their contingency exactly because they are values. As Edwards puts it, "normal nihilism is just the Western intellectual's recognition and tolerance of her own historical and conceptual contingency. To be a normal nihilist is just to acknowledge that, however fervent and essential one's commitment to a particular set of values, that's all one has: a commitment to a particular set of values."[6]

---

6. Edwards's book is soon to be published by the University of Florida Press. I am quoting from a manuscript copy.

Normal nihilism is not, however, a condition that grips only intellectuals, but rather forms everyone in liberal social orders. Edwards, for example, suggests that one could not want a better exemplification of normal nihilism than the regional shopping mall.[7] In the mall, one not only sees alternative values tenuously jostling one another, but our very participation as consumers means we also indirectly act as the creator of those values. "In air conditioned comfort one can stroll from life to life, from world to world, complete with appropriate sound effects (beeping computers; roaring lions). Laid out before one are whole lives that one can, if one has the necessary credit line, freely choose to inhabit: devout Christian; high-tech yuppie; Down East guide; great white hunter. This striking transformation of life into life-style, the way in which the tools, garments, and attitudes specific to particular times and places become commodities to be marketed to anonymous and rootless consumers: they are the natural (if also banal) expressions of our normal nihilism." Nihilism is the result of having so many compact discs from which to choose that no matter which ones we choose, we are dissatisfied because we cannot be sure we have chosen what we really wanted.

The moral challenge is not consumerism or materialism. Such characterizations of the enemy we face as Christians are far too superficial and moralistic. The problem is not just that we have become consumers of our own lives, but that we can conceive of no alternative narrative since we lack any practices that could make such a narrative intelligible. Put differently, the project of modernity was to produce people who believe they should have no story except the story they chose when they had no story. Such a story is called the story of freedom, and it is assumed to be irreversibly institutionalized — economically as market capitalism and politically as democracy.[8] That story and the institutions that embody it are the enemies we must attack through Christian preaching.

I am aware that such a suggestion cannot help but be met with disbelief. I surely cannot mean that the enemy of Christianity is liberal democracy. Such societies, after all, are so wonderfully tolerant. Surely you are not against tolerance? How can anyone be against freedom? Let me assure you that I am serious. I am against tolerance; I do not believe the story of freedom is a true or good story. I

---

7. The shopping mall is almost a perfect image to suggest Frederic Jameson's analysis of postmodernism in his *Postmodernism: or, The Cultural Logic of Late Capitalism* (Durham: Duke University Press, 1991). As Jameson suggests, our postmodern condition is the phenomenon of late capitalism, so "if the ideas of a ruling class were once the dominant (or hegemonic) ideology of bourgeois society, the advanced capitalist countries today are now a field of stylistic and discursive heterogeneity without a norm. Faceless masters continue to inflect the economic strategies which constrain our existences, but they no longer need to impose their speech (or are henceforth unable to); and the postliteracy of the late capitalist world reflects not only the absence of any great collective project but also the unavailability of the older national language itself" (p. 17).

8. For a more developed account, see my *Dispatches from the Front: Theological Engagements with the Secular* (Durham: Duke University Press, 1994).

do not believe it is a good story because it is so clearly a lie. The lie is exposed by simply asking, "Who told you the story that you should have no story except the story you chose when you had no story?" Why should you let that story determine your life? Simply put, the story of freedom has now become our fate.

For example, consider the hallmark sentence of the *Casey* decision by the United States Supreme Court dealing with abortion — "At the heart of liberty is the right to define one's own concept of existence, of meaning, of the universe, and of the mystery of human life." Remember that was written by political conservatives. Moreover, it is exactly that view of freedom that John Paul II so eloquently condemns in the encyclical *Veritatis Splendor*. A view of freedom like that embodied in Casey, according to John Paul II, assumes we must be able to "create values" since freedom enjoys "a primacy over truth, to the point that truth itself would be considered a creation of freedom."9

In contrast, John Paul II, who is not afraid to have enemies, reminds us that the good news of the gospel, known through proclamation, is that we are not fated to be determined by such false stories of freedom. For the truth is that, since we are God's good creation, we are not free to choose our own stories. Freedom lies not in creating our lives, but in learning to recognize our lives as gift. We do not receive our lives as if they were a gift, but rather our lives *are* gift. We do not exist and then God gives us a gift, but our *existence* is gift. The great magic of the gospel is providing us with the skills to acknowledge our life as gift, as created, without resentment and regret. Such skills must be embodied in a community of people across time, constituted by practices such as baptism, preaching, and Eucharist, which become the means for us to discover God's story for our lives.

The very activity of preaching — that is, the proclamation of a story that cannot be known apart from such proclamation — is an affront to the ethos of freedom. As a church, we stand under the Word because we know we are told what we otherwise could not know. We stand under the Word because we know we need to be told what to do. We stand under the Word because we do not believe we have minds worth making up on our own. Such guidance is particularly necessary for people like us who have been corrupted by our tolerance.

The liberal nihilists are right, of course, that our lives are contingent, but their account of contingency is unintelligible. Contingent to what? If everything is contingent, then to say we are contingent is simply not interesting. In contrast, Christians know that their contingency is a correlative to our status as creatures. To be contingent is to recognize that our lives are intelligible only to the extent that we discover we are characters in a narrative we did not create. The recognition of our created status produces not tolerance, but humility. Humility derives not from the presumption that no one knows the truth, but rather is a virtue dependent on our confidence that God's Word is truthful and good.

9. *Veritatis Splendor*, ¶35.

Ironically, in the world in which we live, the minister with such humility will more than likely be accused of being arrogant and authoritarian. To be so accused is a sign that the enemy has been engaged. After all, the enemy, who is often enough ourselves, does not like to be reminded that the narratives that constitute our lives are false. Moreover, the church in which such preaching takes place had better be ready for a fierce counter-offensive as well as be prepared to take some casualties. God has not promised us safety, but rather participation in an adventure called kingdom. That seems to me to be great good news in a world that is literally dying of boredom.

God has entrusted us, God's church, with the best damn story in the world. With great ingenuity we have managed to make that story, with the aid of much theory, as boring as hell. Theories about meaning are what you get when you forget that the church and Christians are embattled, in particular embattled by subtle enemies who win easily by denying that any war exists. God knows what God is doing in this strange time between "worlds," but God is inviting us again to engage the enemy through the godly weapons of preaching and sacrament. I pray that we will have the courage and humility to fight the enemy, in Walter Rauschenbusch's wonderful words, with "no sword but the truth." According to Rauschenbusch, such truth "reveals lies and their true nature, as when Satan was touched by the spear of Ithuriel. It makes injustice quail on its throne, chafe, sneer, abuse, hurl its spear, tender its goal, and finally offer to serve as truth's vassal. But the truth that can do such things is not an old woman wrapped in the spangled robes of earthly authority, bedizened with golden ornaments, the marks of honor given by injustice in turn for services rendered, and muttering dead formulas of the past. The truth that can serve God as the mightiest of his archangels is robed only in love, her weighty limbs unfettered by needless weight, calm-browed, her eyes terrible with beholding God."[10] May our eyes, our preaching, and our theology be just as terrible.

10. Walter Rauschenbusch, *The Righteousness of the Kingdom*, ed. Max L. Stackhouse (Nashville: Abingdon Press, 1968), p. 92.

The Travail of Theology
in the Modern Academy

Nicholas Wolterstorff

I write about the future of theology with some reluctance. Though by no means ignorant of theology in general nor of Professor Moltmann's theology in particular, I am by profession a philosopher rather than a theologian. Who am I, then, to talk about the future of theology — a discipline with its own history, its own texts, its own controversies, its own patterns of thought, its own standards of excellence, its own intellectual giants, its own needs of the day? Would I relish having a theologian instruct me on the future of philosophy?

It would all depend on what the theologian had to say and how he said it. It has been my experience that persons looking in on my discipline from the outside sometimes notice things that have escaped the attention of those of us on the inside — and sometimes remind us of things we have not so much overlooked as pushed to the side as features of our discipline we would rather not face up to. Of course, philosophers seldom allow the comments of outsiders, no matter how perceptive, to go without critique: there's some ignorance to be dispelled here, a formulation to be sharpened up there, and so forth. Still, insight into the practice of philosophy is not confined to its practitioners.

No doubt my reflections on the future of theology will at many points betray my outsider status. I offer them in the hope that, once they have undergone appropriate critique and correction by those on the inside, they will prove of some use. And I offer them as someone who, while not himself a theologian, cares intensely about the future of theology. There are many like me.

§1. Why is that? I daresay there aren't many outside the field of, say, mathematics, who care intensely about its future. We all know enough about the role of mathematics in the development of the wonders of the modern world to be thankful that mathematics has flourished. But there aren't many among those of us who are not mathematicians for whom the future of mathematics is a matter of *care* — not to mention, *intense* care. Why is theology different? By "theology" I mean, *sustained reflection about God*. Why is it a matter of intense care to a great many of us that theology, thus understood, flourish? And who are that "great many?"

I should make clear that it will be about *Christian* theology that I will be speaking. For one thing, it is Christian theology that I know much the best. But also it is my clear impression that quite different things would have to be said about Jewish and Muslim theology. Indeed, a good many Jews and Muslims insist that if one's paradigm of theology is *Christian* theology, then there is not much among them that very closely resembles that.

Theology as "sustained reflection about God." I spoke above about the insider to philosophy characteristically wanting to sharpen up the formulations of the perceptive outsider. Is this one of the formulations of an outsider to theology that the theologian will want to sharpen up? Will the theologian insist that sustained reflection about God, if it is to be theology, must have a theoretical or scientific character — something of that sort?

Perhaps so. But I'll have to turn down the proffered revision; otherwise I won't be able to say what I want to say. Within some segment of the Christian church there arises the felt need for sustained reflection about God. That which evokes that sense of felt need has always been highly diverse and will no doubt continue to be so. Perhaps that segment of the church is living under oppression and longs to understand better the causes of that oppression and God's role in it and what God wants done about it. Someone then emerges from within the community who leads the community in reflecting in a sustained way on its question. Though it often also happens that no one emerges; the felt need for sustained reflection goes unsatisfied. Perhaps someone from outside the community undertakes to impose on the community his or her own answer to their question. We should not regard it as part of the nature of things that persons emerge from the community to engage in sustained reflection on God when the community feels a need for that. We should not even, in my view, regard it as part of the nature of things that a given segment of the Christian community would desire sustained reflection about God that goes beyond what is already available to it.

I can now state the line of thought that I wish to develop. The Christian church in the modern world has felt an urgent need for theology, understood as I just explained it: sustained reflection about God. The felt need has been evoked by a wide variety of developments: the collapse of a unified church, the need for a new social order capable of incorporating significant religious diversity within a single polity, the rise of a new science aimed at discovering connections of efficient causality, the rise of modern historiography, the prevalence of oppression, and so forth, on and on. Many persons have emerged to make a contribution to answering this need. And a good many of those — but by no means all — have conducted their reflections and their research within the institutional context of the public academy. However, as modernity has advanced, the work of these latter displays less and less the stamp of Christian conviction, and proves less and less useful for the life of the church. There are striking exceptions. It would not occur to anyone to say of Karl Barth and Jürgen Moltmann that their work does not display much of the stamp of Christian conviction and that it is of little use to the church. But when I speak nowadays to theologian friends and acquaintances working within the public academy, *they* will often make exactly the generalizations that I formulated above.

The question I wish to pursue, then, is this: What accounts for this increasing travail of Christian theology in the public academy of the modern world? Why is it that sustained reflection about God that clearly displays the stamp of Christian conviction and answers some felt need of the church does not thrive in the public university of late modernity? What is it about the way in which Christian theology has fitted itself into the public academy — or the way in which it *has been* fitted — that accounts for this? And what of the future?

Those who disagree with my judgment that there is this travail — those who view theology within the public university of late modernity as continuing to be distinctly Christian and useful to the church, not to mention intellectually imaginative and rigorous — will regard what follows as much ado about precisely nothing, and will dismiss it as of no interest to them. On that last, they would be mistaken. Most of those inclined to respond in this fashion would insist that the root of the alienation of university theology from the church lies in the modern church wanting the wrong things of its theologians, and that the theologians of the modern academy are often nothing short of heroic in refusing to give the church what it wants — forcing it to ask the questions it *should* ask rather than those it prefers to ask, forcing it to accept the answers it *should* accept, rather than those it would like to accept. But if we asked why it is that academic theologians so often think along these lines, we would find ourselves pursuing exactly the same line of thought that I will be pursuing in answering my question. It doesn't matter which end of the stick one picks up; it's the same stick.

§2. Any university, be it medieval, Renaissance, or modern, operates with an understanding of what sort of learning is appropriate for this particular institutional setting — and with an understanding of what, within the appropriate, is better and worse. Learning is not some eternal essence that happens to enter history at particular times and places, but a long-enduring social practice whose goals, methods, standards of excellence, and legitimating and orienting frameworks of conviction change drastically over history and are often deeply contested. To undertake to be an institutional locus for this practice is thus unavoidably to be confronted with choices on such matters. The university may talk as if it is doing no more than insuring that the abiding essence of learning will be found within its halls, and the eternally valid standards of excellence, applied with rigor. What it is actually doing is lending institutional support and preference to just some versions of that malleable, often-changing, long-enduring social practice that is learning — and excluding others.

The understanding of acceptable and preferred learning with which a university operates is typically not something that it has firmly in hand and simply applies; it is itself the subject of contest within the university. One aspect of this contest is especially important to keep in mind for our purposes. The university of the modern world emerged out of the universities of the Middle Ages and the Renaissance; and often the modern university continues its support of modes of learning no longer in fashion, on the ground that to abandon them would be for the university to repudiate an important part of its own tradition. Of those universities in the modern world that include faculties of theology, how many would now decide to *introduce* such a faculty if they had never had one?

It follows from the above that to practice theology within the institutional setting of the university is to be under pressure to conform one's practice to whatever be that university's operative self-understanding of acceptability and excellence in learning. I suggest that one of the most important causes of the travail of theology in the modern university is to be found at precisely this point. The discipline under which the modern university places its members, by virtue of its judgments as to acceptable and preferable scholarship, has indisputably promoted the flourishing of the natural and social sciences. It has, by contrast, inhibited the flourishing of a theology that exhibits the stamp of Christian conviction and answers to felt needs of the church.

Let me characterize, all too briefly and selectively, what I see as the understanding of learning that has come increasingly to dominate the universities of the modern world — without ever subduing all modern competitors, and without even to this day entirely squeezing out traditional understandings. I should mention that when I speak of "the modern" university, I mean to exclude the contemporary university of the past twenty-five years or so. About that, I will shortly be saying something different.

Perhaps the deepest component in that understanding of university-appropriate learning which came to dominate the modern university is that such learning is to be a *generically human* enterprise. To put the point pictorially: Before entering the university halls of learning we are to strip off all our particularities — particularities of gender, race, nationality, religion, social class, age — and enter purely as normal adult human beings. If I have failed to strip off some particularity, and my fellows in the hall of learning notice this, they are to call it to my attention and order me back into the entry, there to remove the particularity which, unintentionally or not, I kept on. Black history, feminist sociology, Muslim political theory, and liberation theology, whatever may be said for their practice in other contexts, have had no place within the halls of the modern public university. It is true, of course, that particularities develop *within* the halls of the university — in particular, those that accompany academic specialization: the physicist possesses concepts, skills, habits of discrimination, frameworks of conviction, etc., that are both indispensable to the practice of the discipline and almost entirely alien to me as a philosopher. But physicists are to have acquired these particularities *within* the hall of learning, *after* they have stripped off all that does not belong to them *qua* normal adult human beings. Within the hall they learn and inquire not *qua* American, *qua* black, *qua* Christian, *qua* female, *qua* proletarian — not *qua* any particularity whatsoever, just *qua* normal adult human beings. It was assumed that the results of learning so practiced will, over the long haul, gain consensus among all normal adult human beings knowledgeable in the discipline. When academic learning, *Wissenschaft,* is rightly conducted, pluralism in the academy is an accidental and temporary phenomenon.

Another fundamental component in the dominant understanding of university-appropriate learning was a certain hierarchy of esteem among the academic disciplines. The paradigmatic disciplines are the physical sciences and mathematics, with everything else ranged down from them. At the bottom is theology, though the humanities in general are not much better; and the social sciences occupy a position somewhere in between the physical sciences and the humanities. What underlay this hierarchy of esteem was a certain notion of *true science,* which had its origins in the medieval notion of *scientia,* but was then significantly revised in the seventeenth century, most influentially by John Locke and his cohorts in the Royal Academy. The thought was that mathematics and the natural sciences have attained the status of true sciences, whereas the other academic disciplines have not yet done so. When their Newtons appear and their revolutions take place, they too will become true sciences. Accordingly, in speaking of "the logic" of the sciences, we are not speaking of something unique in principle to the natural sciences and mathematics; we are speaking of the logic that any academic discipline will exhibit once it attains the status of a true science. As it so happens, that logic is now exhibited only in mathematics and the natural sciences. But that is happenstance; we hope for the day when all the disciplines will have become true sciences exhibiting "the logic" of science. In the meanwhile, we can compose a hierarchy of the disciplines in terms of how far they appear to be from meeting that ideal.

Thirdly, the dominant understanding of "the logic" of science was the foundationalist understanding: The theorist collects a body of evidence consisting exclusively of the deliverances of perception, consciousness, and reason; and his or her conclusions are to be deductively, inductively, or abductively (abduction = inference to the best explanation) based on that evidence.

This, I say, is the understanding of university-appropriate learning that came to dominate the universities of the modern world — though never, let me say again, to the exclusion of other understandings of university-appropriate learning. In particular, the interpretation of texts, so prominent in the universities of the Middle Ages and the Renaissance, was never entirely squeezed out;

it was, in fact, given a significant boost by the Romantics and by the emergence in this century of a body of theory to accompany the practice — namely, hermeneutics.

§3. It takes no special insight to surmise the effect on university theology of the dominance, within the modern university, of this Enlightenment understanding of university-appropriate learning. It placed powerful pressure on the theologian to cast the argumentative structure of theology into a new, distinctively modern, mold. What is novel about the mold can best be appreciated by contrasting it with the quite different argumentative structure of medieval university theology.

The understanding of university-acceptable learning with which Aquinas worked was also a foundationalist understanding. But it was a different version of foundationalism — yielding correspondingly different results. On the Aristotelian concept of *scientia* of Aquinas and all the medievals, for a proposition to be the premise of a *scientia*, it had to be or have been evident to someone or other — the "someone or other" including God and the blessed. Now notice, says Aquinas, the following feature of the academic disciplines: there are pairs among them, such that one member of the pair is subordinate to the other in the sense that those who work within the subordinate discipline accept, on the say-so of those working in the superordinate discipline, that such-and-such propositions have been evident to them or proved from such, and they (in the subordinate discipline) then, without further ado, use those propositions as premises for work in their own discipline. Aquinas's favorite example of such a pair was that of mathematics and physics, physics being subordinate to mathematics.

Now revelation consists of God telling us what is seen by God to be true. The theologian *qua Christian* accepts the Scriptures as God's revelation and their contents as true on God's say-so; and as a Christian *who is a theologian*, he or she uses the contents of Scripture as premises for the construction of sacred theology. In the course of developing sacred theology, thus based, Aquinas was more than happy to insert arguments that did not appeal to God's say-so in sacred Scripture, but only to the deliverances of reason, perception, and consciousness; but he understood such arguments exactly as *inserted* into that more general, scripturally based, enterprise. And he offered next to no argumentation for his operating assumption that Scripture was God's revelation.

Theology in the modern university is under pressure to cast its argumentative structure into a very different mold. Natural theology can no longer occur as an occasional insertion into the framework of scripturally based sacred theology. Conducted as a generically human enterprise, it must *precede* scripturally based sacred theology, as the necessary foundation thereof. Until that foundation is firmly laid in the deliverances of our human nature, there can be no going beyond. And the "going beyond," from natural theology to scripturally based sacred theology, can occur only if the theologian, appealing solely to the deliverances of our human nature, has succeeded in establishing that the Christian Scriptures are indeed the revelation of God. Natural theology, conducted as a generically human enterprise, is thus to be followed by inquiry into the revelational status of Scripture, also conducted as a generically human enterprise. If the result of this last inquiry is that Christian Scripture is likely to be (or include) God's revelation, then one can construct the remainder of one's theology on the basis of that revelational content — with the proviso that one's interpretation of the meaning of Scripture is also to be conducted as a generically human enterprise.

That is the argumentative form into which the theologians of the modern university were pressed to fit their inquiries. I submit that one of the major causes of the travail of which I spoke is exactly that pressure. In the late seventeenth century, when the view of learning that I have sketched first emerged, there was widespread confidence — though even then not universal — that the content of classical Christian theology could be successfully cast into this new mold. Then doubt began and spread: the doubt that belief in the occurrence of miracles could be adequately supported by evidence of the generically human sort; the doubt that the claim that God had been uniquely revealed to one ancient Near Eastern ethnic group could be adequately supported by evidence of the generically human sort, in the face of the a priori improbability of the claim; the doubt that the claim that the Christian Scriptures are a reliable report and record of revelation could be adequately supported by evidence of the generically human sort, when biblical criticism practiced in a generically human way shows that they have been stitched together by "interested parties" from preexistent fragments; and so forth, on and on. Theology all but lost its scriptural basis. And over and over it felt itself forced to trim its sails to match the evidence.

One can make a rough-and-ready distinction between three ways in which theologians have trimmed the sails of theology so as to make it a university-acceptable discipline. Some have adopted the strategy of simply assigning to *faith* those parts of traditional Christian belief which could not be foundationally grounded, thus removing those parts from the scope of university theology. Some have adopted the strategy of keeping the words in which traditional Christian belief has been expressed, but giving to those words a new content, until the newly devised content meets the demand for groundedness. Often nowadays that new content is an anti-realist content, constructed in the spirit of either Kant or Wittgenstein. And some have adopted the strategy of reconceiving the very project of theology, arguing that theology ought to be thought of as reflections about the God-talk of the Christian community rather than as reflections about God, and then developing theology thus reconceived so as to meet the demand for groundedness.

My description has necessarily been highly schematic. But whichever of these three strategies the university theologian adopts, it is most unlikely that the result will display very much of the stamp of Christian conviction, and most unlikely that the church will find within it very much by way of those sustained reflections about God that it feels it needs.

Someone might respond by saying that university theology has its own integrity, and that the "travail" of which I speak is a wholly irrelevant category. Why ask of university theology that it bear the stamp of Christian conviction? Why ask of it that the church find in it the sustained reflections about God that it desires? If we are to speak about the "travail" of university theology, it had better be of travail within the university that we speak — not of travail vis-à-vis the church.

Surely the position of theology within the modern university can also be described as *travail*. But on this occasion it is precisely of the relation of university theology to the needs of the church that I have wanted to speak. And that cannot be dismissed as irrelevant to the concerns of those who practice university theology, on the ground that university theology does its own university-relevant thing and should be judged solely by reference to that. Such dismissal would be suicidal. If persons did not *come* to the modern university with convictions and questions about God, shaped and evoked in them by religious experience and religious communities, university theology would wither on the vine; those three revisionary enterprises of which I spoke above would die out for lack of interest. What keeps them alive, insofar as they are alive, is persons turning up who for one and another reason want sustained reflection about God. If no such persons turned up, some of the old theological texts might still be read by students of the humanities, but the only point at which one would find reflections about God occurring in the university would be among the more speculative free-thinking cosmologists — and among some of the philosophers. Only there do the dynamics operating in the modern university themselves lead to the question of God — which, interestingly, is also approximately where Aquinas thought that natural theology, in its own right, would occur. Were university theology to ignore the felt need in religious communities for sustained reflection about God, it would cut itself off from that which sustains it.

§4. Let me now turn to a second dynamic operating within the public universities of the modern world that contributes to the travail of university theology. My discussion of this dynamic will have to be brief. At the heart of the classically liberal solution to the problem posed by diversity of religions within a single polity is the distinction between the public and the private spheres and the insistence that in the public sphere we legitimate and orient our actions by reference to what is neutral as among the diverse visions of God and the good found within that polity. There has always been pressure to have a good deal, at least, of the academy located in the public sphere — with the consequence that it is expected of that segment of the academy that it offer an education grounded in what is neutral as among the diverse religious groups in society. As long as the

42

members of the polity were all Christian, what transpired in the public sphere could at one and the same time express the heart of the liberal solution and exhibit the traits of Christendom. But as non-Christians began to appear in significant numbers, Christendom gradually had to be left behind. First, people spoke of "Christian values" as constituting the basis of the university; then, of "Judeo-Christian" values; then, of "religious and moral" values; then, of the values of "the Western tradition." Now even that answer is unacceptable in many places. All along there were those who insisted that *reason* is to be the basis of the public university; the public university is where rationality is at work. But that answer, too, has fallen on hard days.

The pressure that the liberal solution places on theology in the public university is obvious. Theology has to be taught in a manner that betrays no religious partiality; and when theologians address the public in their capacity of university academics, they must speak in a way that betrays no religious partiality. Nowadays they will have to content themselves with appealing to "spiritual values." And even that will evoke dissent in some quarters. The only saving virtue of the situation is that the liberal solution, for all its power, has never succeeded in securing full acceptance in the modern West.

§5. What for the future? What should be noted, in the first place, is that there is no imperative laid on the Christian community to see to it that the sustained reflections about God that it needs for its life as a community of fidelity, obedience, and hope take place within the public university of the modern world and under the discipline that university imposes upon its members. Very early in the history of Christian theology, a significant number of theologians made the decision to cast their reflections into the mold of theoretical inquiry as delineated by the classical Greeks; and from the very time that universities arose in the Middle Ages, there were theologians who believed that these would be appropriate institutional bases for theology. But those decisions were not the obedient response to some abiding imperative; they were, at bottom, prudential. And in any case, there have always been and there continue to be serious Christian reflections about God occurring outside the setting of the public university — outside the setting of *any* university, and even bearing only distant similarities to the tradition of *scientia* and *Wissenschaft*. Were Christian theologians now to make the judgment that the public university of late modernity is not an institutional setting in which sustained reflections about God that bear a Christian stamp and respond to the needs of the church can flourish, they would be sacrificing certain things of worth. I have, on this occasion, spoken only of the travail of theology in the public academy, not of the benefits of theology being there. But leaving the public university would most certainly not mean abandoning Christian theology.

What makes the future fascinatingly open-ended, however, is that the public universities of the Western world are now undergoing deep changes — some of such a sort as to hold out the promise of becoming institutions in which Christian theology may once again thrive as it has not in the public universities of late modernity. There is indeed one development that is threatening to theology, and to very much of the rest of academia as well. A large number of the public universities of the Western world are more and more orienting themselves toward serving the professional and technological needs of modern society. What bread does philosophy bake, they ask — and literary studies, and history, and musicology, and art history, and theology? If the answer is "None," then a cloud of suspicion forms above them, no matter how eloquently it be argued that human beings cannot live by bread alone.

The more promising developments, and in my judgment the more profound, are the following two. It is now widely accepted that the assumption that the university, with minor exceptions, was engaged in *generically human learning,* was deeply erroneous. Perhaps it makes sense to regard mathematics and the natural sciences as engaged in such learning — though even that is controversial. But if so, they are peculiar in exactly that regard. What traditionally passed for generically human learning in the rest of academia is now widely perceived as having been, in good measure, the learning of Western males belonging to the upper middle class of society. I myself would add that those characterizations only begin to state the particularities reflected in that learning.

The response to this now widely shared perception could, in principle, have taken various forms. The response might have been that the characterization is correct and that that is how things should be: academia should be in control of Western males belonging to the upper middle class of society. Or the response might have been that the characterization is correct, and that we must accordingly work much harder than we have in the past at making academic learning a generically human enterprise. In fact, the response has almost always been, if not that the characterization is incorrect, that fairness requires that space be opened up in the public academy for other sorts of particularist scholarship as well: for avowedly feminist interpretations of texts, for an avowedly native American perspective on the history of North America, for an avowedly Jewish perspective on the Holocaust and factors leading up to it, for an avowedly Palestinian perspective on the conflict in the Middle East, for an avowedly liberationist perspective on theology, for an avowedly black theology.

Simultaneously with that development there has occurred the death of the notion that there is such a thing as *the* logic of *Wissenschaft* and that we know what that is; and the death, as well, of the notion that there are *two logics* of *Wissenschaft* and that we know what those are. The decisive cause of this death was scholars trained in natural science, philosophy, and history alike, looking closely at important episodes in the history of modern natural science and concluding that it simply was not true that natural science obeyed the "logic" outlined by Locke and his Royal Society associates.

The response to these results might in principle have been, "So much the worse for natural science." If it had been theology that was under scrutiny, and it was concluded that theology did not measure up, the response certainly would have been, "So much the worse for theology." And as a matter of fact theology often has been under scrutiny, and the conclusion often has been that it did not measure up, and the response always has been, "So much the worse for theology." But the prestige of natural science in our society made it impossible for anyone to say: "So much the worse for natural science." The universal response was, "So much the worse for the supposition that fully reputable learning must exhibit that logic." Over the past twenty-five years there have been a number of attempts to do a better job at digging out and formulating "the logic" of natural science on the assumption that there is such. None has enjoyed wide acceptance. And I think it is safe to say that there is now near-consensus around the view that there is no such thing as *the* logic of natural science — in other words, the logic of reputable natural science is multivarious. But once that conclusion is accepted, then other components in the Enlightenment understanding of university-acceptable learning lose their support — in particular, the old hierarchy of esteem among the academic disciplines. If there is not some true logic of the *Wissenschaften,* which has already been well-embodied in mathematics and the natural sciences but at best poorly embodied in everything else, then why exactly are those others to be judged inferior?

We are still in the very early stages of the playing out of these new dynamics. The postmodern scholarship that we have in hand thus far is in good measure resentful in tone and anti-realist in assumptions. In my judgment, there is no reason to think that that will continue. I fully expect that shortly we will see scholarship emerging that, though it, too, has broken sharply with the epistemological assumptions of modernity, is neither resentful nor anti-realist. But as to how the public university will cope with these new developments, of that we have few clear indications. It is hard to see, however, how the university of the future could be anything else than much more tolerant of particularist, perspectival scholarship than it has been throughout modernity — thus, much more fundamentally pluralistic.

In such a university, the factors I have identified as causing the travail of Christian theology in the academy would no longer be present. In such a university, Christian theology might well flourish. It might once again deal, in intellectually rigorous and imaginative ways, with the questions that impel Christians and others to desire sustained reflection about God; and the results might once again bear the stamp of Christian conviction. Though let me add that Christian theology of this sort will be *tolerated* in the new academy only if it firmly renounces the legacy of Christendom and the attempts at hegemony that have accompanied that.

§6. As we are all walking the road to that new university which lies still over the hill, we must be in conversation on two fundamental issues: How can the perspectival pluralization of academia, which justice demands, be secured without sacrificing peace and coherence of purpose? And what would an epistemology that gives up on foundationalism without sinking into relativism look like? To be in conversation on these issues, we will have to practice the virtues necessary for dialogue with those with whom we disagree, resisting the temptation to adopt the arrogant posture of announcing to our fellow wayfarers that we have discerned that there really are no substantive disagreements among us about God and the good — that what appear to be substantive disagreements are nothing more than equally valid responses to Mystery.

I hope that our theologians will join the conversation, *qua* Christian theologians, on those two questions. And I *very much* hope that they will assist in the cultivation of the virtues needed for true dialogue among people who genuinely disagree about God and the good. If we do not cultivate and exhibit those virtues, Bosnia is everybody's future.

The Last Universalists

Johann Baptist Metz

What can one say reliably about the future of theology? Who knows for sure? Even Jürgen Moltmann, the friend and masterful thinker of hope to whom the following gesticulation is addressed with uncertainty, probably does not know. This uncertainty, after all, derives from the fact that the question of the future of theology must be concerned not only with content but also with the disposition and self-understanding of what it means to engage in theology. Hence the first question to ask would be just what kind of theology, which subjects, places, and addressees of theological activity are at issue here; and whether the professionalization and specialized division of labor that has hitherto characterized theology should not itself be called into question or complemented if one is to speak in any promising fashion at all about the future of theology. I have already presented my own views and suggestions on this topic on frequent occasions. It is not without a tinge of resignation that I take as my point of departure here the basic situation of theology that almost exclusively predominates in this country, namely just this division of labor and professionalization. Hence I am inquiring primarily concerning the significance in the future of traditional, professional theology.

So let us proceed on the assumption that the status of theology in its academic particularity will retain into the next millennium this division of labor already familiar to us, that it will continue to be a discipline at our German universities, and that the latter, too — amid the anonymous and diffuse pressure for accommodation coming from Europe and the United States — will not be robbed of their familiar identity. What would be the task, and — to formulate it a bit more emotionally — what would be the fate of theology in the future world of the university disciplines? Let us not examine this question in a fashion too far removed from the ultimately practical significance of theology, nor too far removed from its basic Christian and ecclesiastical task of defending a certain type of hope and of formulating in a manner capable of mediation a "new manner of living" deriving from that hope. For the world of the sciences has long been part of the determinative definition of the world of our own lives, and has long influenced our views regarding civilization, culture, and religion, and as far as we can see will increasingly do so.

This question can no doubt be addressed with some degree of reliability and without vague, meandering conjectures only if the answer itself tries to key on that which is already emerging as the risky task of theology in the university. And what I have to say regarding this is something allegedly quite simple and apparently quite traditional: Theologians will be the last universalists in our highly differentiated world of the sciences and scholarly disciplines, and they will have to remain such — for the sake of both God and human beings — whether this is convenient or not. And they will always have to deal with the suspicion of being somewhat out of date. (After all, the life of the spirit — *sit venia verbo* — includes forms of being out of date that are not only behind the times and sectarian, but also productive, just as it includes unproductive forms of overly diligent contemporaneity.)

Even today, our universities are "universities" without universalism and without universalists. Nothing seems more suspicious than the universal. It is generally considered to be the deceptive intellectual and moral trap *par excellence,* one that should be eliminated precisely in the name of universities themselves, supported by postmodern sensitivity toward the continually lurking dangers of universalistic concepts and their cognitive degradation of plurality and difference. In the meantime, this specialization of our scientific and scholarly world manifests itself not only in the disciplines of the natural and technological sciences, but also in the so-called humanities and in philosophy, which has long seemed to have lost its trust in the unity and universality of human reason. So today theologians are probably already the last remaining universalists at the university. And not infrequently, when they do not surrender their unavoidable universalism in a postmodern, aesthetic, or psychological manner, they pay for it with increasing cognitive loneliness and isolation within the ensemble of sciences.

The universalism of theology is, I would assert, indispensable — precisely in view of its own future, since the theologian who would not engage in both self-deception and deception of others, the theologian who engages in theo-logy, and does so not as just this or that, but rather as the ever new attempt at speaking about God — this theologian is and remains obligated to universality. God is either a universal theme, a theme of all humankind, or is no theme at all. I do realize that such a statement can be horribly misused and can degenerate into theological and ecclesiastical totalitarianism. *Historia docet.* At the same time, however, this statement properly understood is also a statement about the self-delimitation of theology — namely, that God is never the private possession of the church or of theology.

But what does all this have to do with today's and tomorrow's world of the sciences and the scholarly disciplines? And what does that world in its own turn have to do with talk about God? Is this world of the sciences, to say the least, not already shaped in all its areas, and thus also in those of the humanities and of philosophy, by methodological atheism? God no longer makes an appearance in the modern sciences. Fine. But then — I would ask, thereby bringing my first point to a head — do we ourselves, does the "human being" still appear in any of these modern disciplines? Or has discussion of the "human being" not in the meantime become the primary, real anthropomorphism within the world of our sciences — including in the increasingly subjectless, technomorphic system language of the humanities? Not even those engaged in the humanities still appear in their own discipline. Hence the entirety of academic and scientific language is gradually becoming a secondary language of fate from which the "human being" is increasingly disappearing, or in which that human being is at most dealt with as a gloomy "phantom." Anyone who in the meantime engages in theology, both today and tomorrow, anyone who tries to speak about God, must always also speak about a human being who is not only his or her own experiment, not only his or her own objectivization, but rather — in a more fundamental sense — his or her own memory as well, someone discernible not only from the perspective of that person's attendant structures and functions, but of the person's history as well.

Is this merely a helpless postulate, or can it be universalized from the perspective of reason endowed with memory and thus rendered accessible to the scientific and scholarly world? Wherever in a human being's self-knowledge nothing more is missed, it is not the "human being" that is known, but rather nature, or rather the human being as memory-less, subject-less nature, as that particular piece of nature that has not yet reached the end of the experiment. It may well be that in the future ensemble of sciences and scholarly disciplines this view may not be possible without a certain measure of metaphysical civil courage. Theology will then need just such courage — not for the sake of its own self-assertion, but rather in order to thwart the emerging scientific-technological over-determination of our future world. And if I am not completely mistaken, theology will have to acquire the spiritual resources for this resistance a bit less from the world of ideas associated with Athens and a bit more from the anamnestic culture of Jerusalem.

As regards the future of theology, I am also concerned with another universalism and with encouraging theologians to bear with equanimity here, too, the onus of being the last universalists. I am referring to that particular universalism which I also consider indispensable in the age of postmodern sensitivity over against the undeniable dangers of all universalistic orientations. I am referring to that particular universalism of responsibility in the face of the moral exhaustion of Europe, an exhaustion that is everywhere lamented and obviously everywhere acquiring ever clearer contours, in the face of the increasing over-individualization and diffusion of the world in which our lives take place, a world that seems increasingly less structured by or oriented toward any "binding" memory. Even today, binding universal connections are discussed — if at all — only in an extremely formalistic sense, that is, exclusively in the sense of procedural universalism. Is there then any responsibility at all deriving from a concrete historical ethos, responsibility that might be universal or at least capable of universalization without becoming imperial or totalitarian, that is, without ignoring the new (postmodern) sensitivity for plurality and difference, for the inherent differences of those who are indeed different?

Now, those particular traditions to which theology is indebted do describe a kind of universal responsibility born of the memory of suffering. This memory of suffering becomes the basis of universal responsibility by always also considering the suffering of others, the suffering of the stranger, and — in an unconditionally biblical sense — even the suffering of one's enemies, and by not forgetting this other suffering when evaluating its own history of suffering. This remembrance of the suffering of others is not only the moral basis of intersubjective understanding, but it extends deep into the political landscape of our world as well. One scene I will never forget is that in which the Israeli Rabin and the Palestinian Arafat shake hands and mutually assure one another that in the future they will not only pay attention to their own suffering, but will also be prepared to consider the suffering of the other, the suffering of those who were previously their enemies. I do realize that this peace, concluded in this way, is extremely fragile, and that it will demand great sacrifices from both sides; and it may well be that when these reflections concerning a "weak" and wholly endangered universalism appear in print, this vision of a future emerging from a remembrance of the suffering of others may already have foundered. But it will remain exemplary for a politics of peace from the perspective of the biblical *memoria passionis*, and will also remain exemplary for a universal moral stance that in its own turn is not guided by any myth of freedom from suffering.

This universalism of responsibility will not emerge on the basis of any laboriously accrued minimal consensus in which the consenters ultimately no longer even recognize themselves, but rather on the basis of a basic consensus to be achieved ever anew between peoples and cultures. There is, in my opinion, one authority that is acknowledged in all the great cultures and religions and that is not obviated by any criticism of authority: the authority of those who suffer. Respect for the suffering of others is the precondition for any great culture. And to bring to expression the suffering of others is the prerequisite for any universalistic claims, including and especially those of theology. This simultaneously contains the antidote against the dangerous diseases and temptations presented by possible types of universalism, including the one guided ultimately not by a remembrance of the suffering of others, but by the myth of freedom from suffering.

Christianity — and precisely Jürgen Moltmann's work obliges us to this reference — is not primarily morals, but rather hope; its theology is not primarily ethics, but rather eschatology. Yet precisely here does that particular power reside that might prevent it from surrendering or from prematurely diminishing the standards of responsibility even in its allegedly or genuinely powerless and diffused state. I realize that the content of this universal responsibility can hardly be freed from the suspicion of overreaching abstraction, and I would do better to formulate it as a question: Is there any suffering at all in the world of which we might say that it does not concern us all? Is there a single cry of suffering that is not meant for every ear? Anyone who takes these questions seriously is not simply falling for some theological fantasies of omnipotence; that person is merely taking seriously the fact that these questions articulate nothing more than the simple moral version of the statement about the universality of the children of God. In its political version, this statement addresses the equality of all human beings, and is thus a statement to which not only the biblical traditions with their own remembrance of suffering are indebted, but also the basic laws of modern constitutional states. Democracies, too, are not without this universalism. Previously, this universalism was given by "tradition." But how can the modern constitutional democratic state assure itself of this universality, and how can it preserve it in the stage of the so-called posttraditional societies?

The consistent success or failure of attempts at the kind of universalism of responsibility portrayed here will thus determine not only the future of theology, but also whether Europe itself will be a landscape of peace or, as many fear, one of escalating civil wars — whether it will be a blossoming or burning multicultural landscape. Theologians are the last universalists. Wherever they do not surrender the universalism portrayed here, they by no means must become sectarian fundamentalists or hardened traditionalists. The future of our own human world, a world whose conflicts are apparently being displaced increasingly into the spheres of cultures and civilizations, depends too greatly on preserving just this universalism,.

It may well be that Jürgen Moltmann will find this small contribution to be "typically Catholic." That will not bother him unduly, however, for we have always been bound by an ecumenical friendship that, instead of seeking its common features by way of some minimal consensus, struggles for a common basic consensus in which the characteristic features of each person, rather than disappearing, assert themselves ever anew and ever more vigorously.

Is There Anything "New" in Theology?
Reflections on an Old Theme

Dietrich Ritschl

I. The Question

The question concerning what is "new" in theology will be equated here with the question concerning "progress." Although there may well be differences between these two questions, I am ignoring them here. By theology here I understand primarily systematic theology as characterized by English-speaking usage. Is there any progress in this theology? Can its books become obsolete? Can anything "new" be clearly discerned and as such also be ecumenically assimilated? Or put concretely: Are the books of the person to whom this *Festschrift* is dedicated new in the sense of "progress" in comparison to Barth, Schleiermacher, Thomas, Athanasius?

Progress can certainly be discerned — this is one's first impression — in the *stricte dictu* nontheological subdisciplines found within theology as such as a scholarly discipline. These are largely "nontheological" because the historians and exegetes involved here take neither their methodologies nor their criteria for judgment from theology. Neither do they want to do so. Although theological interest may well prompt them to turn their attention to the Bible or to a specific historical topic, or the object of their study may be of a theological nature — nonetheless, their questions, methods, and judgments are not theological. In exegetical and historical disciplines, one can earn a doctorate or be appointed as a professor on the basis of accomplishments containing not a single theological idea. Although this may be the exception, it does illustrate what in principle is the case: Neither the methodologies nor the criteria in these disciplines are theological. (I in no way intend these observations to be polemical; they merely reflect precisely that which scholars of ancient Oriental studies observe and appreciate in Old Testament scholars, classical philologists in New Testament scholars, historians in their colleagues in church history, as well as that which is the sole determining factor in faculty meetings considering new faculty appointments.)

But is there any "progress" in these disciplines? Can books here clearly become obsolete? Certainly, if one does not allow oneself to be irritated by the plethora of contradictory results and perspectives admittedly characteristic of progress in all the humanities. In New Testament studies, for example, the great theological questions of Jesus' resurrection, God's actions, Jesus' death on the cross as atonement, eternal life, God's providence and salvific plan, and so on, have all been answered so unsatisfactorily and contradictorily during the past 250 years that one hardly really looks forward to the next publications on these topics. A similar situation now also applies to Old Testament studies, which after a long period of fairly homogeneous instruction and aid for preaching now offers something "new" all too often merely as a contradiction to something else "new." And church historians? Something new probably can be found in the numerous detailed results of diligent research. Or is it found in new interpretations, in altered perspectives, or even in conscience-struck historical writing with respect to the horrible deeds and omissions of Christians through the centuries? I hope so, but I fear this is only rarely the case. Do our students today really know "more" and something "new" about the ancient church than did the students of Hans Lietzmann during his day, or more about the Reformation than did the students of Karl Holl? Although I certainly do not want to deny them what they have accomplished through their sincere efforts, I do fear that in the lectures of many church historians one still hears the old cliches about the abstract character of the doctrine of the Trinity or of Chalcedonian Christology, about emperor and pope during the Middle Ages, about Thomas and Calvin. In any event, this is what is reflected in the innumerable tests I administer — and all of it shaped by an alarming national constriction and with perpetually imposed Protestant blinders.

The following discussion will thus inquire whether and how there can be anything "new" in theology understood as systematic theology (dogmatics and ethics).

II. Merely New Ordering, Weighting, Comparing

Edward Farley at Vanderbilt University, at the time my colleague in Pittsburgh, once spent an entire vacation considering how many genuine innovations could be observed in systematic theology. He found eight or ten, though I unfortunately have forgotten just what they were. In the meantime, Farley, along with David Tracy, Peter Hodgson, and several others, has come to distinguish quite distinctly between "constructive theology" on the one hand, and purely descriptive theology on the other. Naturally, only the former is able to exhibit any "progress." And this is indeed the case: in most of our books and lectures we merely order and evaluate anew what has long been known and said. We merely shift the stones back and forth again. And all too often we merely report what others have said, and add our own critical or assenting commentaries. Dogmatics is then theological history extended into the present. Given this situation, our own students naturally do not learn how to think theologically for themselves, how to say something constructively new about the great questions that concern congregations as well as people on the periphery of the church. Instead, we hear in concluding theological examinations — an institution that in any case, coming as it does after a course of study that is itself already too long, is utterly obsolete and wholly in need of reform — in these examinations we hear that Barth said this, Moltmann that, Pannenberg yet something similar, but then Tillich something quite different concerning this or that topic. And to make a bad situation worse, the bibliography of this list of things learned by heart almost always includes only German-speaking sources. Compared to the social and human sciences (comparison with the natural sciences is not appropriate), we in theology fare in a bad way. In this connection one might even ask whether we are really engaged in a "science" or discipline [*Wissenschaft*] in that sense. To the chagrin of several colleagues, I have already long doubted that (systematic) theology really constitutes such a *Wissenschaft*. In any case, in reality it usually does not; ideally, it is wisdom that employs scientific or scholarly methods.

III. Should There Be Something "New"?

Can our American colleagues' call for "constructive theology" be fulfilled at all? And if so, is it to be addressed only by some particularly creative professors, and not also by local pastors? Admittedly, pastors are not supposed to be preaching "theology," but rather the gospel itself with its news that God's grace is new each day, and that God's spirit will lead us to the whole truth. *Stricte dictu,* theology belongs at a person's desk during the preparation of sermons, and not in the pulpit — excepting genuine doctrinal sermons — but could something "new" then not also be conceived there? And if something constructive and new thus can be conceived not only among theological authors, but also among preachers, then the same question remains whether there can be anything genuinely new in theology — that is, in reflection on how one is to speak about God and in the interpretation of the world from within the God-perspective — something new in the sense of surpassing, of a corrective and completion of what has gone before. Can this really come about? Is this not a dilemma?

I cannot speak for others, but I, as an ecumenical theologian who initially spent many years teaching patristics and the history of dogmatics, cannot get away from the image of the tree or of a river delta when I consider the church as a whole. Of course, these metaphors, too, have their limits; a river or the branch of a tree does not precisely reflect the multiplicity of biblical traditions. These metaphors can, however, very well describe the great branchings of the church into Byzantine and Oriental orthodoxy, into the Eastern and Western church, into the churches of the Reformation and the subsequent emergence of the various denominations and groups. What marks the beginning of these branchings? Was it a coagulation of what went before, a self-delimitation from others? Was this new element — for example, among the Reformers — so powerful that it defined everything that came before as something old, and restricted it in the name of the new within its old boundaries, perfecting thus the coagulation itself? This is one possible view. It can be applied not only to revolutions in church history such as the Reformation, but also quite well to new initiatives in theology — for example, Irenaeus's new concept of salvation history; Athanasius's and the Cappadocians' development of the doctrine of the Trinity; Augustine's rediscovery of the Pauline doctrine of grace and justification; Thomas's understanding of God through analogues as well as his reintegration of nature into theology; and so on — all the way up to Schleiermacher, to the so-called new departure of theology in the 1920s, to Karl Rahner and Vatican II, to the advances in the ecumenical movement, to a new view of eschatology and a new emphasis and development of the doctrine of the Trinity in the work of Jürgen Moltmann, to the constructive reception of the recent philosophy of language and theory of knowledge, to the new understanding of social ethics in the United States, to the new understanding of spirit Christology, the doctrine of the Holy Spirit, and the initiatives toward a new biblical theology, to the various forms of liberation theology, of feminist theologies. . . .

The revealing elements in these enumerations are the unavoidable expressions such as "new initiatives," "new concept," "rediscovery," "new departure," "advances," "new view," "new emphasis," "new doctrinal understanding." Does this mean that what is new is always only relatively so, and is ultimately merely a reformulation of what has gone before, whereby actual divisions in the church also result — that is, along with these new elements — only in crass instances or because of special historical circumstances and accidents? The latter assertion is supported by the observation that today the acceptance of "the same new thing" often cuts straight across confessional boundaries without altering those boundaries. Apparently, it is not only the "new" in theology itself that is merely relatively new compared with what has gone before, but also the confessions themselves that once emerged through coagulation and resolute self-preservation or through the power of assertion exhibited by the "new." Even if, so to speak, these confessions have "had their day," and even if the reasons for their emergence or persistence at the time have largely disappeared, they nonetheless continue to exist. The boughs of the tree rarely grow together — to remain a moment with the metaphor — and the arms of the river delta unite only when they flow into the sea itself and cease to exist.

The "range" of the new should also be considered. Perhaps oral theology is the primal locus of the emergence of the new; perhaps by successfully breaking through and surpassing a thousand theological and ecclesiastical cliches, oral theology is the real, living theology before coagulation into written form. Its range, however, is for just that reason correspondingly more restricted.

We must apparently pose the question of the new in theology at various levels.

IV. Liberated and Imprisoned in Language

I find the numerous studies on language and theology undertaken during the past three decades on the whole to be extraordinarily interesting. I do not intend to discuss them here, and want rather only to refer within the context of the present discussion to a single basic situation: theological truth is "freed" from the "hiding place" of the implicit — from the biblical books, the prayers and experiences and hopes of the congregation — to become linguistic expressions that can be appropriated, are capable of communication, and function as aids for believers. A loquacious example is the doctrine of the Trinity. It is contained implicitly in the biblical texts and in the early liturgies, and in its articulation in language not only acquired a full and mature form to the great joy of theological specialists, but also offers an irreplaceable aid for believers in the larger sense, enabling them to experience and understand something new and meaningful about God, and to understand in a completely new manner larger connections. Without a doubt, the classical doctrine of the Trinity and its implicit, temporally subsequent Christology — Harnack back and forth — should function as an aid to believers, and should function as such not only for their thinking, but also for their doxology. Truth was freed into language. (The same applies to other doctrines — for example, the Reformation doctrine of justification, or maxims such as *sola scriptura*.)

At the same time, however, this process of liberation also creates a prison for truth. The tiny, almost incalculable period of time between the liberation of the implicit into helpful, true theological articulation and — after this "blessed second" of theology — its tipping over into linguistic imprisonment: this is the tragic irony inhering in all theological effort.[1] What we experience in daily life is also crassly true in theology: truth can become the prisoner of language. In the case of steep formulations — those especially far removed from what is narrated or that try in a daring fashion to summarize it — language even of necessity becomes a prison. The repetition of truth in formulaic struc-

---

1. I have elsewhere expanded this to include everyday language use; see my contribution to *Language, Theology, and the Bible. Festschrift for James Barr*, ed. S. E. Balentine (Oxford: Clarendon, 1994).

tures becomes a lie. A terrible dilemma arises here, since liturgy is, after all, precisely this. We avoid the dilemma only if we strictly differentiate between doxological and explicative language. One important task of theology is to remind us of this difference. It must protect both itself and the church against the erroneous equation of declarative or "is-statements" whose validity actually applies only at different levels.

If theological language helps loosen what has become encrusted, if it cracks linguistic prisons and thus, as I unabashedly like to put it, behaves "therapeutically" toward the church, then without a doubt it does bring us something new, albeit only relatively with respect to earlier "blessed seconds" when truth once flashed before us.

This, then, would be a fine and helpful activity for theology, and I can hardly imagine a theological author who would not agree. All of them want to loosen what has become encrusted, to help explain obscure doctrines, terms, and maxims in a meaningful fashion. It is all the more depressing that many of them — or many of us, I should say — usually offer a hybrid of clarification and reencipherment. I must admit that today — after working in theology for over forty-five years, and equipped with all possible linguistic-philosophical tools — I still understand only with great effort or not at all many passages in books and essays, especially by German authors. (I also fear that students only momentarily understand what these authors say in lectures — that is, in a way that does not endure — and that they are unable to integrate it in any enduring fashion into what they already know and understand. In examinations we find proof of this in the fashionable and cliche-ridden use of excessively complicated concepts, or in the retreat to utterly simple, pre-stamped formulae.) But this is not just a matter of the excessively complicated language of theological professionals; rather, the language of the church itself, with its infinitely repeated, undeciphered formulae, is equally a factor in the stabilization of such linguistic prisons. New wine is constantly being poured into old bottles.

V. A New Paradigm?

Konrad Kaiser has applied to the ecumenical sphere the notion of a "paradigm change" in theology (or in the world religions) as presented by David Tracy and Hans Küng.[2] Hans Küng portrays in vivid colors his own path from traditionalism to the "postmodern paradigm."[3] These authors no doubt saw that Thomas S. Kuhn's concept of the paradigm change, which he developed over against Karl Popper's understanding of research characterized by steady prog-

---

2. David Tracy and Hans Küng, eds., *Paradigm Change in Theology* (New York: Crossroad, 1989).

3. Hans Küng, *Theology for the Third Millennium* (Eng. trans., New York: Doubleday, 1988).

ress, actually derives from the natural sciences, and that its application to the humanities and to theology is problematical. It presupposes a methodological homogeneity that really cannot exist in theology in this way. Nonetheless, they are intent on using this concept of a paradigm change.[4] What can be learned from this with regard to our present question?

The concept of the paradigm has a more complicated history than an acquaintance with its contemporary theological use might suggest. It begins with Aristotle's analyses, and then acquires a complex shape in N. R. Hanson and S. E. Toulmin, as well as in Wittgenstein's *Blue Book*.[5] The concept contains several distinct components referring to the various methodological, theoretical, and exemplary aspects obtaining within research, and showing how these aspects are related to the actual "new" element discerned. Certainly no one in theology should be talked into this differentiated view, but if indeed the concept is to be used, then it must be made clear just what is to be accomplished with it.

Although one can understand how Konrad Raiser finds a new "paradigm" in the new model of the conciliar process and of a theology focused on the entirety of "God's household," it is unclear whether there is more here than merely a new selection of biblically possible themes, a new perspective in the light of these themes. Something similar might be said of Hans Küng's expansion or new coupling of central themes, although in this case it is not yet clear to what extent his double theses that the theology of world religions must be simultaneously "christocentric" and directed toward the entire earth with all its cultures and religions, and must be both practical-pastoral and scientific-theoretical — to what extent this is something more than merely an agenda.

Have there not always been — and especially in the second half of our own century — monothematic theologies along with the "comprehensive," all-encompassing (but not necessarily fully "systematic") theologies? It is just these monothematic theologies that often enter the scene with the claim of novelty or newness. They offer a single theme or a collection of related themes concerning the perspective of the interpretation or overall portrayal of theology — often successfully (measurable in ecumenical influence) and often also justifiably (discernible in sound theological argumentation). Their advantage over against the traditional, comprehensive theologies is their relevance in a specific time and their interpretative power in a specific situation, though their limitations also derive from precisely such temporal or situational determination. The various liberation theologies are the most loquacious example in this respect.

---

4. I have said more about this in *Ökumenische Theologie* (Stuttgart: Kohlhammer, 1994), ch. 2.

5. The best source for information on this subject is W. Stegmüller, *Theorie und Erfahrung* (Berlin: Springer-Verlag, 1973).

It would be a bit more daring to mention also the Reformation doctrines of justification as an example: We are perhaps yet too much under their control to realize that they, too, were monothematic theologies that in another time and another situation might be replaced.

New paradigms — if this word must be used — doubtless bring forth something new, perhaps even a new overall view; but their legitimate claim to relevance is bound to a limitation of their temporal and situational validity. What is "new" in them is the composition of a chain of theological concepts in view of new themes, themes that — in a fashion similar to that in ethics — either were not there at all earlier or were not seen, yet are now relevant, and perhaps even significant in terms of life and survival itself.

VI. Marriages with New Philosophies?

The various marriages into which theology has entered with philosophical systems have at various times doubtless contributed to the production of something new. This is abundantly clear with respect to middle- and then neo-Platonism in the ancient church, and then also with respect to Aristotelian philosophy in the high Middle Ages, and so on. Something could be conceived and articulated that previously remained unconceived and unarticulated. New cognitive-theoretical and thus linguistic conditions were disclosed and shown to be applicable to theological articulation. What is new resides initially not in the content of theological statements, but rather in the parameter function of the philosophical partner, a function that — even given the distinction between "manifest" and "latent" parameters — always exhibits the character of a variable. Except in the case of dogmatic representatives of Christianized philosophy, in principle this always includes the concession that one might say the same thing in a different form; that is, with a different philosophy. Hence in the best sense, philosophy is a ladder that — as Wittgenstein put it — can be put aside after it has been used. Although this particular dynamic has not always proceeded quite this peacefully and objectively in the history of theology, one can nonetheless usually reconstruct in retrospect the translation process that took place. We are able to extract interpretatively the theological content of Chalcedon as if the Fathers of 451 had not had the philosophical concept of "nature"; or Thomas's doctrine of God as if he had not been an Aristotelian; or Luther, as if he had not been rooted in nominalism; or — to leap forward — as if Jürgen Moltmann had never heard of Ernst Bloch, or Wolfhart Pannenberg of Hegel. This process of subtraction is thus theoretically possible, and it illustrates — this is, of course, merely a game — that at least in retrospect the ladder might well be put aside in the case of a given theological author.

These speculations do not intend to assert that the "isolation" of theological elements — and that then also means: of new elements — is possible in every case. As far as process theology is concerned, one can hardly say that the subtraction of A. N. Whitehead and Charles Hartshorne from the theological edifices of the process theologians leaves behind a "hard core" of "new" theology. In any event, this has not yet been demonstrated persuasively.

Moreover, one should also keep in mind that there are certain types of philosophy that theology will not precipitately embrace, since their themes and questions initially seem alien to theology. Although these do not include all of Kant's works, they do include his cognitive theory, and certainly also analytical philosophy. These philosophies sooner assume a threatening and warning posture toward the traditional theology of their age. When theology nonetheless does engage them, it subjects itself voluntarily, so to speak, to the cleansing fire of self-criticism, something that wholly benefits it — in any case, history illustrates that this has been the case. I definitely believe that something new has emerged from the purgative fire of analytical philosophy, and that — if I may be permitted to say this — German-speaking systematic theology has until now largely avoided this cleansing clarification, much to its disadvantage.

VII. Something New through an Interpretation of the Old

Viewed formally, something "new" can manifest itself (a) in a new way of expressing the old, (b) in new knowledge transcending the old, and (c) in a rediscovery of the old through the prism of the new, ultimately in a discovery of God.

In theology, of course, the "old" includes two things: the Bible and tradition. If the new that emerges through interpretation is new only in reference to the current situation, if it merely renders possible new applications, then — *stricte dictu* — it is not really new. We are then dealing with an ultimately deistic understanding of God; truth is fixed, already articulated, and repetition and application are the only remaining tasks. The creative God has paled, the *creator spiritus* merely illuminates now, and does not create anything new. We have, of course, already had such theologies, and still have them. The principle of *sola scriptura* has repeatedly cast us into this prison even though this is, of course, not at all its real purpose.

Now, as we asserted above (§IV), interpretation is the art of breaking open this prison. It fails only as long as it merely reconstructs the paths of the old — for example, in the biblical books, or in church history — and does so with methodology drawn from the humanities whose purpose is to determine who influenced whom. To return to the metaphor of the tree or river delta: Interpretation reveals nothing new if it merely pursues the number and form of boughs, or the course of the tributaries. But if it inquires concerning why these boughs, tributaries, and blockages emerged and entered the scene, if it asks how this or that was not seen at all, and how in this way God was missed, and if it helps free us — the descendants — from the consequences of mistakes and omissions, if it can make its way to "conscience-struck historiography" in solidarity with the ancestors — and probably also to thankful doxology — if indeed it can do all this, then it will not only place the present in a relevant relationship with the past, but in this relationship with the old will also discover the new, namely, God.

One cardinal example of this sort of new discovery, indeed, of the emergence of something genuinely new, is the discovery of the "Judaeo-Christian reality" (to use Paul van Buren's expression) for Christian theology. Since the emergence of this new element, Christian theology — at least for many of us — has not been the same. Just as when we turn a kaleidoscope, a completely new picture emerges even though the number of glass particles remains the same.

The significance of this example is so central because in this case what is new is not simply brought forth through a deduction from old texts; much more is at work here than derivation from biblical texts and "application" to the present. The interpretation of the present has been applied to the old texts. Is it too daring to say that the connection between the old and the new would have to reside ultimately in God, for our recognition in the Holy Spirit? I prefer this theological (trinitarian) solution to the question of the connection to the old instead of the initially attractive, but too easily misunderstood ecclesiological solution. Only penultimately, and only in an extremely broken fashion, is it the church that represents among us, the descendants, this connection with the ancestors in faith. (To take and even press the metaphor of the tree and river one last time: it is, after all, the church that has to answer for the shriveled boughs, and that repeatedly has poured the new wine into old bottles.)

We must wait to see what new fruits our efforts at finding a new biblical theology (for example, the *Neukirchener Jahrbücher für Biblische Theologie*) will yield, and whether one can successfully discover in the old books something new such that a full departure is made from the traditional methods of unavoidably arbitrary selection and shallow deduction from biblical passages, and such that the interplay between an analysis of the present in the God-perspective on the one hand, and a search for God in the old texts on the other, determines the process itself.

Furthermore, we must also wait to see — and this does constitute waiting for conscious theological decisions — whether this search for the connection between the presence of God as it is experienced anew today, and the old in the biblical books, can be expanded without hindrances to the interpretation of the postbiblical Jewish and Christian liturgies and writings. If this becomes possible, it can also lead to a completely new and profoundly theological manner of research and teaching in the discipline of church history. One can then also speak about genuine "progress," that is, about cognitive gains in theological interpretation, if the interpreted texts come from the postbiblical period —

despite the old Protestant warning that we should not speak about two "revelatory sources." This might also lead to a reinterpretation of the Fathers and teachers of the church — and of the synagogue as well — not merely to a reconstruction of their ideas, but to new ideas about God, ideas that those whom we interpret did not yet themselves have. Someone might write a book about the doctrine of the Trinity that produces something quite new over against Athanasius and Gregory of Nazianzus, something that would, however, have greatly pleased both of them had they been able to read it.

There are theologies — unfortunately, only the published academic products can be evaluated, and not the countless sermons that might demonstrate this even more beautifully — in which this interplay between a present experience of the new in God on the one hand, and the search for the implicitly new in the old writings of the Bible and in the postbiblical witnesses on the other, are determinative. Among these I include — as one-sided and personally colored as such an enumeration doubtless is — such completely different publications as the books of Edward Farley, the ethical writings of James M. Gustafson, parts of F. Mildenberger's "Biblical Dogmatics," the dogmatic and sacramental theological works of Theodor Schneider, Michael Welker's *God the Spirit*, and especially Jürgen Moltmann's book (which appeared one year earlier) *The Spirit of Life*,[6] which among all his books seems to me to be most exemplary and to be saying something genuinely new. To him I dedicate this small series of reflections with cordial congratulations and with a sentence from his previously mentioned book (p. 287): "The experience of 'flowing light' of course does not deny the transcendent source of light, and the experience of the 'living water' does not forget the inexhaustible wellspring; but the important thing is not the distinction between source and river. The whole weight lies on the connection. In this experience of God, the Spirit is known as a 'broad place' and a 'flooding light' in which those touched by it can discover themselves and develop."

---

6. Moltmann, *The Spirit of Life: A Universal Affirmation*, trans. Margaret Kohl (Minneapolis: Fortress Press, 1992).

Is There Such a Thing as
Being Ready for Another Millennium?

John H. Yoder

It has long been evident that one major dimension of Jürgen Moltmann's omnivorous ecumenical openness has been the attention he has given to those positions that historians used to call "sectarian" and now designate more descriptively as belonging to the "Radical Reformation." We see this in his republishing Otto Weber's tract for congregationalism, *Versammelte Gemeinde*. We see it in the many ways he led in the renewal of understanding for the centrality of the Christian peace witness.[1] We see it in his investment of time in actually visiting and conversing with the small communities of the Radical Reformation tradition.[2] We see it in the importance of his personal friendship with the Russian-born Mennonite literary critic, teacher of *Sozialpädagogik* and congregational elder Johannes Harder.[3] It would thus be quite proper to project, as I was once invited to do concerning the theological trajectory of Karl Barth,[4] that Moltmann "has been moving toward" a central vision that could be identified

---

1. *Das Bekenntnis zu Jesus Christus und die Vriedensverantwortung der Kirche* (Gütersloh, 1982), a declaration of the Moderamen of the (German) Reformed Alliance. It may be significant that the specifically Reformed communities furthered this agenda in Germany in the nuclear debate slightly more rapidly than the more Lutheran Evangelische Kirche in Deutschland. In 1983 the World Council of Churches joined this "nuclear pacifist" stream.

2. The substance of his lectures at Mennonite institutions in Winnipeg (Manitoba) and Elkhart (Indiana) in the fall of 1982 was published in *Following Jesus Christ in the World Today* (Institute of Mennonite Studies, Occasional Papers No. 4, 1983). He also conversed with the ecumenical European study group Church and Peace. The picture would be still fuller if we were to attend to his contacts with Baptists, Congregationalists, etc.

3. Moltmann contributed a paper entitled "Dostojewski und die 'Theologie der Hoffnung' " to the Harder Festschrift *Entscheidung und Solidarität*, ed. Hermann Horn (Wuppertal: Peter Hammer Verlag, 1973).

4. "Karl Barth: How His Mind Kept Changing," in *How Karl Barth Changed My Mind*, ed. Donald McKim (Grand Rapids: William B. Eerdmans, 1986), pp. 166-71.

as a retrieval of that of the Radical Reformation. That could be described as an especially fitting response to the end of the age of Christendom.

Yet such an effort to co-opt would be banal. It would also be inaccurate, since Moltmann has at the same time and in analogous ways been moving acceptingly toward Marxists, toward Jews, toward the Eastern Orthodox, toward feminists. . . . His breadth of concern and of relationships forbids any such "type" identification. More importantly, to try to find the meaning of theology in the fact that the discipline as a whole, or one of its leading voices, is "evolving" in a particular direction, whose history the next generation will write, would be to fall prey to one of the very temptations of which the discipline should be wary.

The Temptation to Discern the Direction of History Immanently

Our ordinary style is to seek to manage the future by projecting how it can be an extension of our past. We mark landmarks in time, especially the big round numbers like millennia, as if their meaning were both evident and binding.

This very preoccupation with discerning direction is at once a part of the biblical vision and a temptation. It is part of the biblical vision in that the meaningfulness of the historical process is part of the promise to Abraham whereby the covenant faith moves beyond the stabilizing function exercised in all cultures by religion in general.[5] Yet concern for not being surprised by the future is also a temptation. It is a kind of sovereignty claim that seeks to escape the vulnerability of contingency and the dignity of the Other. It seeks to make one's survival or prospering the object of one's own manipulation, rather than of trust. Should we succeed in charting the future surely, we trust that that would make us secure against the threats of ignorance, creativity, and conflict. That is why our generation has created the new social pseudo-sciences of futurology. We state our support for some contemporary idea we like by predicting that in the future it will be remembered.

Karl Barth responded rightly to the epoch-making rise of Nazism when he wrote that his task would be to go on "doing theology as if nothing had happened." It was the "German Christians," whom he led in denouncing, who thought that a new epoch had dawned, to which theology had to adapt. Yet in order to discharge that perennial task "as if nothing had happened," at the same time he plodded away at writing the century's greatest *Summa*, Barth never ceased to speak to current events, and created a literary instrument called "Theological Existence Today." So in 1995 our task is to articulate, in loving and patient dialogue with the course of events, but without fundamental respect

5. This is the kernel of truth in the contrast sometimes made between the "cyclical" quality of many religious worldviews and the "linear" mode of Hebrew and Christian thought.

for the revelatory authority some ascribe to them, what will not be different, except superficially, about the twenty-first century.

The most impressive transitory change underlying our common experience, one that some thought was a permanent forward lunge in salvation history, was the so-called Constantinian shift.[6] The Renaissance, the Enlightenment, the Industrial Revolution, and numerous important changes since then have changed our immediate agenda, but without setting aside the foundational challenge of the confusion between the Good News and the establishment for which the son of Constantius Chlorus and a Serbian barmaid was partly the agent, partly the beneficiary, and mostly the symbol.[7] Our unending concern to reassure ourselves that what we are about "has a future" is constitutive for our cultural style, formed as it is by the way in which our common Western story has taught us to identify socio-political flourishing with validation.

This commonality is represented by the current debates in some circles between "liberation" and "conservation." On both sides of that debate, what has happened to the governments that controlled Eastern Europe for forty years is being read as proving something Christians should affirm about the course of history. We do not watch with equal perceptiveness the "signs of the times" in southeast Asia or central Africa. Why do we take the modest progress made recently toward forms of political democracy in Eastern Europe or southern South America as more representative of where the world is going than the resilience of capitalist dictatorships in China or Indonesia, or the massacres and failures of Western nerve in Bosnia, Somalia, Rwanda, Chechnya? I submit that we do that because, since the Western story has been told to us by the heirs of the winners, we have learned to discern meaning where there is success. We associate "meaning" with observable continuities.

We are not able to discern the meaning of the far more numerous cultural "bubbles" that did not survive. The archaeologists who retrieve the traces of older "lost civilizations," which in some ways were superior to our own, tickle our curiosity, but at the same time our admiring them ratifies our confidence that our own line is that of history properly so called, since it led to us.

---

6. This is not to suggest, as much critical but naive historiography tacitly does, that until about 300 Christianity had not changed in important ways. There were other basic changes in some of the churches and in Christian thought, which may also be discerned to have betrayed something of the original message. The rise of supercessionist anti-Judaism and the turn toward some "apologetic" modes of thought may have been just as basic, and may have prepared the way for being insufficiently critical when the fourth century's privileges came along.

7. I summarized a few of the major changes that the shift introduced to Christian moral thought in my paper "The Constantinian Sources of Western Social Ethics," in *The Priestly Kingdom: Social Ethics as Gospel* (Notre Dame, Ind.: University of Notre Dame Press, 1985), pp. 135-47. Moltmann has frequently taken account of the difference "Constantine" made; see, e.g., *The Experiment Hope*, trans. M. Douglas Meeks (Philadelphia: Fortress Press, 1975), p. 105; and *The Theology of Hope: On the Grounds and Implications of a Christian Eschatology*, trans. James W. Leitch (New York: Harper & Row, 1976), p. 306.

What Constantine did once for the world from Britain to Babylonia by sharing the credit for his victories over Maxentius and Licinius with the God of the Christians, has been done again in the last two centuries by the military and commercial dominion of the globe by European markets and technology. The world has become one, but not because the Jewish and Christian vision of the oneness of the Creator and Provider behind the cosmos convinced people. The world is one because the sailing ship, gunpowder, the internal combustion engine, the limited liability stock company, and electronic communication have created a global culture of control stronger than any of the states that it still uses to keep order. The other subhistories and local cultures have been left in the dust not because they were less moral, or less wise, or because their religious practices were less ennobling, but because even Kuala Lumpur has a stock market, Coca Cola, and Japanese electronics. The demonic autonomy of the world as unity was well represented in March 1995, though on a very small scale, when an ancient British bank collapsed because it had let a bright young technician in Singapore gamble on the future of the Tokyo stock exchange.

The world of the twenty-first century will not be able to back away from having become one world. It is thus fitting that I take this one likely trait of our common future (there would be many more) as an exemplary instance of the critical task of theology. What does theological discernment say to the world's having become one?

Making Sense of/within/against Global Oneness

a) That the world is one under God as Creator, and that it is called to become unified under God the Provider, has come about thanks to the work of Jesus the Risen, Crucified, Anointed One. This is what Paul presupposed and proclaimed when to the Lystrans in Acts 14 and the Athenians in Acts 17 he described the wholeness of a divine plan that would supersede or transcend their past cultural plurality (14:16) and religiosity (17:23-24).[8] It is what Jeremiah projected when he called the immigrants in Babylon to seek the peace of the city where Yahweh had sent them (29:5ff.). That the world is one is therefore not immaterial to us.

b) Yet it is our task to discern the myriad ways in which the unification of the world in our time, from the top down,[9] fails to incorporate most of

---

8. Paul did not base that affirmation on an empirical reading about the relative success of the *pax Romana;* it arose from the intersection of his Jewish monotheism and his messianic witness to the Resurrection.

9. "Top down" is not only a metaphor for social power; air travel and satellite communications are both the symbols and the agents of the most recent cultural homogenization. Paul's locating the rulers of the cosmos in the "heavenly places" (Eph. 6:12) has taken on an odd literalness.

humanity. The millions who crowd the slums of Calcutta, Mexico City, or Cairo are farther from sharing in global "civilization," and farther from basic human prospering, than were their grandparents, or than their contemporary cousins who are still out in the country. The resource depletion and pollution that it takes to fuel our planes and satellites and air conditioners decreases even more our chances of survival. The vision of world unity thus tantalizes more than it serves.

c) The unity vision of diaspora Judaism was borne by the synagogue; that is, by the decentralized, nonclerical structure whereby any ten households were qualified to gather in prayer and praise around the scrolls that linked them in memory and hope to God's humanizing work. Sociologically, the synagogue was the alternative to Gentile "religion," whether it celebrated (for example, with Marduk) the unity of an empire or (with Baal) the fertility of an agricultural economy. Theologically, Hebrew monotheism was the alternative to polytheism because the same Name and the same scriptural stories could be carried anywhere. Already well before Jesus, those synagogues were open to Gentiles.

d) That same unifying vision was carried around the Mediterranean world by messianic synagogues with the same structure (later to be called "Christian"), except that now the incorporation of the Gentiles, and thereby potentially the global reach of the communities, had become part of their self-definition. It is of the reconciling of Jew and Gentile in the messianic synagogues that the "Paul" of Ephesians wrote that the very existence of these empirical communities proclaimed God's unifying or peacemaking purpose to the cosmic powers. Those powers, in other words, had a stake in human dividedness.

Then the core process that matters most, if the Good News is to be retrieved for our twenty-first century, is the formation and maintenance of concrete human communities, the "congregation from below" that Jürgen Moltmann evoked most simply in his chapter by that name in *The Passion for Life*.

e) Yet the cunning of the powers has repeatedly shown its capacity to divert both the prophetic judgment and the world-making creativity of the gospel witness. The Church (that is, the hierarchy) after Constantine was ready to accredit and co-opt the mendicant and the monastery, cutting the edge of their critique, making the radical life of the gospel a complement rather than a challenge to the "mainstream" structures of empire. Prophetic Protestant voices from Jan Hus through Luther and Zwingli to Cromwell were accredited and co-opted by the new territorial polities arising out of the collapse of the vision of the Holy Roman Empire. The *collegia pietatis* of continental pietism and the prayer cells of Zinzendorf and Wesley drove their critique deeper into society and deeper into the individual psyche, yet sociopolitically they, too, hoped to renew Christendom rather than to leave it behind. In ever new incarnations, the Constantinian ethos accredits and co-opts the critics, thereby updating a hope correlated with socioeconomic flourishing more than with crossbearing and servanthood, and leaving most of the Gentiles outside. These updated forms of Christendom retrieve the unity of church and state,[10] lordship and worship, in one place, while accepting the sacrifice of the panethnic and global unity.[11]

f) James (3:1ff.) warns his readers in the "tribes of the dispersion" not to have many teachers, since language tends to destroy. "The tongue," whose obstreperousness he warns against, does not mean merely speech as an individual capacity, so that this stoic-like image would be a warning against the individual's impulsiveness. Language as such, attending intensely to defining terms and using language games on each other, what we call the sophomoric style, is the threat. Similarly, the author of 2 Timothy commends "the pattern of sound words which you heard from me" (1:13) and forbids "disputing about words" (2:14). The task of theology must then be the vocation of linguistic criticism, disciplining discourse by testing its aptness for its object, and refusing any definition game that would rule out (or rule over) any part of the heritage.

This job description suffices to affirm reasonable doubt about some of the word games that are called "fundamental" or "programmatic." Any claim to restructure from scratch the thought life of the community, without taking account of interlocutors down through the canonical texts and the history since then, is working at what Timothy was told to avoid.[12] The *didaskalos* (teacher), who has this task of being careful about the common language in the fear of God, is only one of many bearers of charisma in the community, and numerous of the charismata are verbal.[13]

Here we have had to move beyond the questions raised by the "one world" vision of messianic Judaism, to other questions concerning the communities' internal integrity. Yet the subject has not changed; for the internal microcosm (how to make sense of the group's inner life) mirrors the macrocosm (whether God is unifying the world). Whether, in a given congregation in Ephesus or Corinth, Jew and Greek, male and female, slave and free are being reconciled is

---

10. Both in interpreting Constantine and in interpreting the "Radical Reformation" witness, many center almost exclusively on the issue of the morality of violence. That issue is prototypical, but only one specimen. When taken alone, it gives inordinate weight to the issue of the state as actor.

11. For a survey of the resilience of the Christendom mind-set, and the way it skews our efforts to discern the direction of history, see my essay "Christ, the Hope of the World," in *The Royal Priesthood: Essays Ecclesiological and Ecumenical* (Grand Rapids: William B. Eerdmans, 1994), pp. 198-203.

12. There are, of course, various ways to interpret this deviation. Some may seek to review the whole field with a view to catechetical integrity, in order not to leave anything out, or to be consistent. Others claim that they both can and should "found" the theological task by determining its validity as if from scratch. This "foundationalist" mode of "programmatic" purpose is the mistaken one.

13. See my *Fullness of Christ* (Elgin, Ill.: Brethren Press, 1987). The case I needed to make there, in the context of the congregation, against the monarchical pastorate, is analogous to my case here against the academic theologian.

the microcosmic counterpart of whether the Creator of the globe is making global *shalom.*

All of the above simple descriptions of how the Christian thinker should watch over the language of the community, locally wherever there are ten households, in the light of the heritage show what it means to build the church from below. Rather than ask what new power structure seems destined to replace the state or the theater or the Japanese auto industry or the media or Wall Street as the next elect bearer of the meaning of the next wave of history's progress, so as to celebrate that new surrogate for Constantine, we are called to vigilant attentiveness to the perennial simple questions, watching our language in the fear of God. Such a scaling-down and focusing of our sense of mission is neither naive nor anti-intellectual.

PART II
PERSPECTIVES

Christian Theology:
What Direction at the End
of the Second Millennium?

Michael Welker

Christian Theology: Crisis at the End of the Second Millennium!

In many parts of the world, churches deriving from the Reformation and Counter-Reformation seem paralyzed. Bad moods — characterized by helplessness and fatigue — are spreading. Faith seems empty and incapable of articulation. Love is taken back into the private sphere, where it often suffocates in the struggle for self-assertion. Hope has no goal, no clear perspectives, and has even become extinct. Many worship services are sterile, joyless, and poorly attended. Scholarly theology has the reputation of being either elevated and incomprehensible, or banal and boring.

On the other hand, general religious questions abound. At least in a vague way, people are questioning and searching for enduring inner stability, for supportive surroundings filled with a consciousness of responsibility, with trust, and with shared joy. They are searching for consolation in the face of the finitude and perilous nature of life. And they are asking about the meaning of existence. Similarly, genuinely real distress also abounds, distress that obviously cannot be overcome merely politically, economically, legally, and morally. This includes the tormenting consciousness of guilt and complicity in the oppression and miserable circumstances of weaker people both near and far; or the perception of spreading indifference and brutality toward foreigners, toward the socially disadvantaged and excluded, toward weak elderly people, helpless children, and dependent young people; or the realization that humankind is systematically and rapidly damaging and destroying air and water, earth and forests, animals and plants; or the dull feeling that a life spent in individual striving for success, in orientation toward entertainment and consumption, and in narcissistic selfishness to the point of addiction — that such a life is vapid and false.

There seems to be hardly any escape from this distress. The more incisive and pressing the situation is recognized to be, all the more futile do all the suggestions, admonitions, and offers of direction seem to be. Amid apathy and an attitude of doom, perplexity, and cynicism, people settle into a rut of simply going on.

Under the spell of such perceptions of the world and self, many theologians in the Western industrialized nations find themselves confronted by the question: What direction can theology take in the third millennium? At the same time, Christian theology must ask itself whether and to what extent it has itself contributed to this crisis in orientation.

Has theology taken seriously its task of bringing to people's attention God's vitality and love for human beings, God's creative and delivering power? Or has it rather directed their thoughts and feelings to some rigid authority in the beyond that has merely formal "relations" to the world and to human beings? Or has it directed them to mere projections of deliverer and deliverance amid the various problems and crises?

Has it, in its questions concerning God, assiduously exhausted the biblical sources of knowledge of God, sources that grew for more than a millennium and that for more than two millennia have shaped "world culture" for both good and bad? Or has it contented itself with theological abstractions that are seductive because they offer simple, integrative syntheses, thereby offering to common sense simple impressions of God and of salvation?

Has it developed forms enabling people of different cultural and social spheres to organize their various searches and questions concerning God as well as their various experiences of God into a critical and creative framework? Or has it become specialized in "the God–human being relation" characteristic of abstract, imperial modern thinking, or in those particular contextual experiences of God that maintain their immunity against any enrichment and questioning by other experiences of God?

Has it released the powers of distinguishing between experiences of God and images of idols, between illusions of self-redemption and an orientation toward God's saving acts? Or has it largely specialized in strengthening religious claims of immediacy and religious moralism?

Has it found forms for critical discernment that do justice both to the vitality and *doxa* of God on the one hand, and to the creative freedom of creatures on the other? Or has it stabilized old, long-transparent forms of dominion and self-preservation in order to avoid the difficulties of real joy in God's vitality, genuine fear of God, and the vitality of human experiences of God?

These self-critical questions about whether theology has not contributed to the present crisis in religious orientation direct our attention to a religious form that has long dominated the Western world, and that now is deteriorating. At issue is classical bourgeois theism. Its collapse strengthens the present crisis in normative and religious orientation just as much as does half-hearted, immature searching for alternatives.

The Collapse of Classical Theism:
A New Beginning for Christian Theology?

In many parts of the world today, churches deriving from the Reformation and Counter-Reformation are facing the collapse of a religiosity shaped by classic bourgeois theism. This theism, characterized by the idea of a God who in absolute dominance and control brings forth and maintains both himself and everything else, is crumbling.[1] The evocation of a transcendent personality that brings forth both itself and everything else hardly counts now as "true faith" and "true worship." The abstract notions of God's "omnipotence" and "omnipresence" are no longer theologically tenable. For many people, such notions perished in the Holocaust, in the world wars, in global environmental destruction, though also in the countless events characterized by suffering and injustice that are reflected daily and made public on a worldwide basis in the media. Monotheism needs a new theological understanding.[2]

God's "omnipotence" and "omnipresence" must be understood theologically anew.[3] God cannot possibly be self-evidently and enduringly present at or focused on every point in the time-space continuum. We must understand anew what the biblical traditions call God's invisible and hidden nature. We must understand what those traditions understand by God's face turning away, lowering itself, and being concealed. We must make clear just what they mean by God's Spirit becoming weaker, attenuated, and ultimately extinguished, and what they mean by the Spirit being chased away and fleeing. We must pose anew — and not only and not for the first time only with regard to the cross of Christ — the questions concerning the relationship between God's revelation and God's mighty acts in the world on the one hand, and God's absence and the world's distance from God on the other.

There are no doubt experiences of suffering, crises in orientation, and feelings of meaninglessness that prompt the suspicion that God is absent, at

---

1. Concerning theological criticism of classical theism, see Jürgen Moltmann, *The Crucified God: The Cross of Christ as the Foundation and Criticism of Christian Theology*, trans. R. A. Wilson and J. Bowden (New York: Harper & Row, 1974), pp. 207ff.; Eberhard Jüngel, *God As the Mystery of the World: On the Foundation of the Theology of the Crucified One in the Dispute between Theism and Atheism*, trans. Darrell L. Guder (Grand Rapids: Eerdmans, 1983), esp. §B.

2. For many theological conversations that strengthened my persuasion in this regard I owe thanks to my colleague and friend William Schweiker, and to the interdisciplinary group "Bible, Theology, and Cultural Critique."

3. Cf. in this regard Wilfried Härles's suggestion that we understand God's omnipotence and omnipresence as characteristics of that particular *love* that is essential to God: *Dogmatik* (Berlin/New York: de Gruyter, 1995), 258f., 264ff.

least temporarily, in certain parts of the world. And yet God's relative absence cannot be discerned in these situations of distress themselves. It must rather be perceived and portrayed in the light of God's revealed presence in this world. The question acquires contours only in view of the challenge of discerning God and God's presence in this world, and of discerning this presence — in the light of God's revelation — in the face of the collapse of classical theism and of the contemporary crisis in religious and normative orientation: What direction can theology take in the third millennium? In the following answers I draw on conceptual initiatives of the Reformation in describing directions for its further development, oriented toward contemporary developments in the theology of the Western world that have persuaded and shaped my thinking in this regard.[4]

The Renewal of Reformation Initiatives as a Future Task of Christian Theology

By "Reformation initiatives" I am not referring to the insurance of confessionalist incumbency. I am trying rather to pick up some of the most important impulses of the Reformation renewal of the church, impulses that even Counter-Reformation and non-Reformation churches have appropriated, and some of which have, to be sure, paled in parts of Reformation churches.

In my opinion, such impulses include:

1. The search for the living God and the inquiry concerning God's intervention in this world, and trust in that intervention (an impulse that in Christian theology must be taken up by a theology of the Trinity).
2. Biblical orientation as the basis and measure of any tenable Christian theology.
3. An understanding of the church as the congregational church *and* as ecumenically based Christendom.
4. Concentration on a theology of the cross, as well as a resistance to even subtle notions of self-redemption.
5. The challenge of distinguishing between "law" and "gospel" as an unfinished task for theology, one whose realization should also realistically determine the relationship between church and culture.[5]

---

4. Throughout this undertaking, programmatic and divinatory features are unavoidable. As hesitant and with as much justification as the theological guild may well react to such features in the sphere of the scholarly disciplines, just as much does the theme of this volume call for a consideration of precisely these things.

5. In my reference to "Reformation initiatives" I am cognizant of the fact that many of the Reformers developed merely pale trinitarian theologies, that the Reformation was unable to overcome the medieval doctrine of satisfaction, and that in the distinction between "law" and "gospel" they often operated with a distorted understanding of "law" and with extremely vague notions of

1. Tasks for a Theology of the Trinity

At the end of the second millennium, theology stands before the task of explicating anew the doctrine of the triune God. This will call into question traditional totalitarian, personalistic, or moralistic notions of God. Theology must illuminate the relationship between God and creatures, between human beings and God, and must seek to promote its various forms for the sake of arriving at a realistic knowledge of the unity, vitality, personality, efficaciousness, and *doxa* of the triune God. In the process, it must take as its orientation the complex weave of witnesses of the biblical traditions and allow modes of perception to emerge that are shaped by differentiated social, cultural, scholarly, and other considerations.

The most influential conceptual initiatives in trinitarian theology during the past few decades have emerged either from hybrids of christological orientation and classical theism (employing the doctrine of the two natures), or have been appropriated from notions of "divine sociality" (adopting the doctrine of the perichoresis as its basis). Both of these initiatives for developing a theology of the Trinity contributed to the dissolution of classical theism, though they still failed to satisfy both theological thinking and Christian devotion. Instead of developing a consistent doctrine of the triune God, these initiatives either bogged down in binitarian thinking (with at most vague perspectives on the Holy Spirit), or they were diluted in quasi-mystical notions of mutuality (the "sociality" of God and of all things) offering no really persuasive basis for a faith seeking understanding and support.[6]

Fully developed alternatives are not yet clearly discernible, though those particular well-worn paths down which an escape from these difficulties has repeatedly — and futilely — been sought are easily identifiable. Neither the conceptual game with derivatives of the "Unmoved Mover" nor the theological "application" of modern conceptions of subjectivity and person have provided any persuasive gains for a theology of the Trinity. Neither is any progress discernible in the continuing increase and variation of linear relational figures that still dominate many current trinitarian theologies today (lover — love —

"gospel." Similarly, the conceptual dichotomies of the Reformers are still in need of correctives. Finally, their understanding of a believer's immediacy to God was often formulated such that personalism, individualism, and subjective feelings of right could appeal to such an understanding and could also religiously transfigure themselves in an often fatal fashion. All these forms are in need of theological critique and revision. My attempt at a constructive and critical appropriation of Reformation impulses has learned a great deal and been enriched by Berndt Hamm, "Einheit und Vielfalt der Reformation — oder: was die Reformation zur Reformation macht," in B. Hamm, B. Moeller, and D. Wendebourg, eds., *Reformationstheorien. Ein kirchenhistorischer Disput über Einheit und Vielfalt der Reformation* (Göttingen: Vandenhoeck & Ruprecht, 1995), pp. 57-127. I would also like to thank him for helpful suggestions concerning the following reflections.

6. For a criticism of these dilemmas, see M. Welker, *Kirche im Pluralismus* (Gütersloh: Kaiser, 1995), pp. 42ff.

beloved; I — address — thou; God comes from, to, as God, etc.). Rather, there is reason to doubt that with the initiatives of Reformation theology (and with a continually growing number of theologians in the present) any genuinely tenable and persuasive doctrine of God can be developed on the basis of "top down" speculation. A new trinitarian-theological initiative "bottom up" must address anew Eberhard Jüngel's pertinent insight that the gospel "cannot be maintained as a *joyful* word" where theology and piety allow "God's *earthly* existence among us to be denigrated and allow God to be God only *above* us."[7]

In the Gifford Lectures of 1993/94, the theoretical physicist and Anglican theologian John Polkinghorne asserted that "many theologians are instinctively top-down thinkers." He warns: We in the natural sciences "have learned so often in our own explorations of the physical world that 'evident general principles' are often neither so evident nor so general as one might at first sight have supposed."[8] Polkinghorne thus advocates inquiring whether and how the great theological speculations consistently reflect "what we know of the process and history of this present world." This initiative corresponds not only to the scientifically fruitful initiative of modern thinking, one that countered the rationalism and intellectualism of the Middle Ages by pledging itself in a thoroughgoing fashion to examination and support derived through observation,[9] but also to the origins of Reformation thinking that in 1518 already connected the demand for a binding of all theology back to Scripture on the one hand, with the planning of an anti-Scholastic reform of universities and scholarly disciplines on the other. Not only criticism of Scholastic philosophy and theology, but also the adoption of humanistic concepts of education (a study of the sources, philological competence, etc.) serve such reorientation in the theological search for knowledge — from the "bottom up."

This initiative from the "bottom up" by no means excludes the discovery of christological, creation-theological, and pneumatological forms of power, forms whose differentiated interplay it is trinitarian theology's task to disclose. Quite the contrary. But it does work to counter any mistaking of these forms of power for merely metaphysical accomplishments and simple, highly abstract commonsense notions. It prompts the discovery of these forms of power through an orientation toward the complex relationships among the multifarious witnesses of Scripture. It stands in perpetual conflict with all artificially constructed attempts — attempts guided by a single fancy, by an impression of

---

7. E. Jüngel, "Thesen zur Grundlegung der Christologie," in *Unterwegs zur Sache. Theologische Bemerkungen* (Munich: Kaiser, 1972), pp. 274ff., 278: "The gospel of Jesus Christ cannot be had as a *joyful* word without the *skandalon* of the earthly existence of God and the doctrine of the Trinity that reflects upon this *skandalon*."

8. John Polkinghorne, *The Faith of a Physicist. Reflections of a Bottom-Up Thinker: The Gifford Lectures for 1993-4* (Princeton: Princeton University Press, 1994), p. 4, cf. pp. 4f.

9. See Alfred North Whitehead, *Science and the Modern World* (New York: Macmillan, 1953), esp. ch. 1.

plausibility, or by a variously demonstrated conceptual figure — to perceive God's divinity or to find orientation in questioning and searching for God. Neither can such conceptual figures and procedures be sanctified by even a long tradition and a history of success. They acquire validity not just through the constructive development of their internal rationality, but rather only in proving themselves within the weave of witnesses of the biblical traditions, traditions that have taken centuries to develop. A theology of the Trinity must distinguish God's "unity" from the abstract simplicity of an "ultimate point of reference" (G. Kaufman), from the diffuse complexity of an "ultimate reality," or from the alleged coherence of an "all-determining reality" (R. Bultmann and W. Pannenberg). Similarly, it will have to replace the abstract and dualistic attempts to distinguish between God and creatures with distinctions that bring to expression both christologically and substantively/creation-theologically and pneumatologically God's relationship with creation.

A theology that thinks "bottom up" and allows itself to be measured against the witnesses of the biblical tradition will not only have to pick up and deepen the Reformation insight that "Jesus Christ is not without his own,"[10] but will also have to realize that the creative God does not wish to be and act without the creatures, and that the Spirit is not attested without those who are seized and animated by the Spirit.[11] This puts before us the extraordinarily far-reaching questions: (a) whether we will not have to develop equivalents for the christological doctrine of the two natures for the first and third articles of faith,[12] and (b) whether it is not precisely the theology of the Trinity that must develop a nondualistic *distinction* between God and creature that does justice to the complexity of the relationship between the triune God on the one hand, and creation on the other.

2. Biblical Theology, Polycontextual and Inductive Thinking

In the third millennium, the crisis of classical theism and the need of churches in pluralistic societies for orientation will confront theology with new urgency

10. Cf. M. Welker, "Resurrection and the Reign of God," in *The 1993 Frederick Neumann Symposium on the Theological Interpretation of Scripture: Hope for the Kingdom and Responsibility for the World. Princeton Seminary Bulletin. Supplementary Issue,* 3, ed. Daniel Migliore (1994), pp. 3-16.

11. Cf. M. Welker, "What is 'Creation'?: Rereading Genesis 1 and 2," *Theology Today* 48 (April 1991): 56-71; idem, *God the Spirit: A Theology of the Holy Spirit,* trans. John H. Hoffmeyer (Philadelphia: Fortress, 1994).

12. Here one should be aware of the difference between the total entry into creaturely existence in the Incarnation on the one hand, and the Creator's and Spirit's relationship with creation on the other. Neither would I advocate maintaining the concept of "nature" in this context. It would, however, have to be replaced on the basis of a trinitarian-theological foundation. For fruitful discussions on trinitarian-theological "bottom-up" conceptual initiatives, I am extremely grateful to the "Consultation on Science and Theology" at Princeton.

with the Reformation task of examining and renewing their dogmatic forms and content on the basis of the biblical traditions. In this regard, theology must develop conceptual forms and methods that — differently than in many traditional concepts of "biblical theology" — allow one to proceed multisystematically, historistically, "bottom up," inductively. In the process, theology can no longer "despise the day of little things."[13]

In his article "Why Jews Are not Interested in Biblical Theology,"[14] John Levenson, a Jewish Hebrew Bible scholar at Harvard, not only criticizes the "intense antisemitism" found in many of the classical works of leading Protestant exegetes,[15] but also rejects any form of "biblical theology" that imputes or tries to demonstrate a specific conceptual form or a specific theoretical nexus as *the* form and systematic framework of *the* biblical traditions. He similarly criticizes all so-called "biblical theologies" that emphasize a single theme (for example, reconciliation, covenant, God's dominion, God's holiness, etc.) as "*the* content" of the biblical traditions, or that try to impose such a theme on those traditions. Levenson finds that "the effort to construct a systematic, harmonious theological statement out of the unsystematic and polydox material in the Hebrew Bible fits Christianity better than Judaism because systematic theology in general is more prominent and more at home in the church than in the yeshivah and the synagogue." Over against this, as he puts it, "inclination of Christians to systematize," he emphasizes the "stubborn Rabbinic resistance to losing the particular in the general."[16]

But does this characterization of "biblical theology" really correspond to the discussion and interdisciplinary cooperation that has taken place under the auspices of this programmatic formula since the 1980s, especially in the United States and in Germany? Is the issue really a search for the pan-integrative form, for the all-encompassing theme, for the "one great idea" informing all the biblical traditions? As Rolf Rendtorff has already suggested in his discussion with John Levenson,[17] this is hardly an adequate description of leading Christian exegesis today. And it certainly does not describe the enduring concerns and forms of research and of interdisciplinary exchange presented under the rubric of "biblical theology" or "new biblical theology" in, among other places, the *Overtures to Biblical Theology* (since 1978), in the periodical *Horizons,* in the *Frederick Neumann Symposium on the Theological Interpretation of Scripture* (since 1986), in the *Jahrbuch für Biblische Theologie* (since 1987), or in the

---

13. Phyllis Trible, *God and the Rhetoric of Sexuality* (Philadelphia: Fortress, 1978), preface (with reference to Zech. 4:13).

14. John Levenson, "Why Jews Are Not Interested in Biblical Theology," in J. Neusner et al., eds., *Judaic Perspectives on Ancient Israel* (Philadelphia: Fortress, 1987), pp. 281-307.

15. Levenson, "Why Jews Are Not Interested," p. 287.

16. Levenson, "Why Jews Are Not Interested," pp. 296, 298.

17. R. Rendtorff, "Wege zu einem gemeinsamen jüdisch-christlichen Umgang mit dem Alten Testament," *EvTh* 51 (1991): 431ff.

project *Bible and Theology* (since 1989) or *Bible, Theology, and Cultural Critique* (since 1995). Similarly, many initiatives undertaken during recent years toward feminist and liberation-theological scriptural interpretation do not fit Levenson's description. On the contrary, those particular examples of research, discussion, and documentation consciously associated with the programmatic formula "biblical theology" are incisively different from the initiatives toward an "absolute way of looking at things" critically presented by Levenson.

Rather, these examples take the Bible seriously as — to take Heinz Schürmann's formulation — a "remarkably pluralistic library with traditions spanning more than 1500 years."[18] Their own systematic initiatives are consciously "pluralistic." For them, the different biblical traditions with their differing "settings in life" are important precisely in those differences. It is just those differences that point toward a reality of God that every age and culture try to comprehend in their own way and that nonetheless cannot be "conceptualized" definitively by any single age or culture. The conceptual and research initiatives of theology under the title "biblical theology" take seriously the fact that the biblical traditions bring to expression experiences and expectations of God that are both continuous and discontinuous, both mutually compatible and at least not directly capable of being mediated between one another. They take seriously the fact that not only the appropriations that have accrued throughout church history, but also the biblical traditions themselves offer distortions and dissimulations of perspectives on God and on the reality intended by God.

This pluralistic initiative in biblical theology is shaped — from a systematic-theological perspective — by the realization that important, indeed even central theological concepts in our cultures often function now only as ciphers. Complex key religious terms and conceptual frameworks of the biblical traditions (for example, creation, world, sin, atonement, sacrifice, righteousness, God's reign, God's Spirit) that once functioned to a high degree as points of orientation have been worn away to the point of incomprehensibility through repeated accommodation to culturally imposed conceptual habits and to specific conceptions of rationality and morals. Hence the content and forms that these "great theological words" conceptualize must be recognized anew in their "settings in life" and in their *complexity and coherence.* "Seek simplicity — and distrust it!" is the basic scientific-theoretical guideline formulated by A. N. Whitehead. Since theology has for so long forced the search for "simplicity," for simple, highly integrative abstractions and for quick plausibility, it is now time to rediscover the substantively adequate complexity and the complex substantive adequacy of the content of faith. This theological content can be regained only through biblical-theological reorientation that assumes a critical posture toward quick and selective "systematization." Only on the basis of an acknowledgment of the differentiated reality attaching to this content can it again

---

18. H. Schürmann, *Gottes Reich — Jesu Geschick* (Freiburg: Herder, 1983), p. 246.

demonstrate its multifarious fruitfulness and inherent vitality. Through inter-disciplinary cooperation, theology must counter a mediocre reductionism that boasts of its "universal" clarity and its unobtrusive accommodation to general culture. It must offer guidance in learning to distinguish deceptive reductionist clarity from substantively adequate clarity, as well as in addressing the difficult distinction between the creative presence of religion within culture and religion as "systemic distortion."[19]

3. Recognition of the Fundamentally Local and Ecumenical Disposition of the Church and of Creative Pluralism

Theology that takes seriously God's vitality, and that pledges itself ever anew to a reorientation toward the biblical traditions — traditions that developed over a period of one and a half millennia — should be characterized by a "freedom under the Word"[20] that is formative not only for theological work but also for church life. The richness of "God's Word" and the multiperspective accessibility of the "pluralistic library 'Bible'" make it necessary for theology and the church to arrive at an understanding of its content, at self-understanding, and at organizational forms capable of mediating this inherent complexity and coher-ence. The non-monohierarchical and yet clear disposition of a creative-plural-istic church must be both recognized and tended (whereby pluralism is not — as is often the case — to be confused with relativism and individualism). On the one hand, the church emerges from the authentic communication nexus of the congregation assembled and united through God's Word and the celebration of the Eucharist. On the other hand, in its orientation back toward Scripture — an orientation common to all churches — it has ecumenical scope. The theology of the third millennium will have to develop forms that allow the "freedom of the church under the Word of God" and the authority of Scripture to be related such that the development, testing, and transformation of con-fessional, organizational, institutional, and other forms of the church can be implemented and followed from both a congregational and an ecumenical perspective.

Historically, the church's most efficacious conceptions either were based on stratified organizational forms tying the church to the clear form of a specific hierarchical figure, or were shaped by "congregationalist," "social," or "primary congregational" concepts that emerged from the elementary process of free association and then tried dogmatically or morally to justify, guide, and shape

---

19. Some initial suggestions can be found in the volume *Power, Powerlessness, and the Divine,* W. Schweiker et al., eds. (forthcoming); cf. also M. Welker, "Auf der theologischen Suche nach einem 'Weltethos' in einer Zeit kurzlebiger moralischer Märkte. Küng, Tracy und die Bedeutung der neuen Biblischen Theologie," *EvTh* 5 (1995): 438-56.

20. Karl Barth, *Church Dogmatics,* I/2 (Edinburgh: T. & T. Clark, 1956), pp. 695ff.

just this dynamic. This tension between hierarchical systemic conceptions of form and an orientation toward associative forms can still be observed today. It manifests itself in the noticeable uneasiness attaching to contemporary sociological discussion that tries to understand the church either as a subsystem of a secondary system within a functionally differentiated society (N. Luhmann), or as an ensemble of "civil-social" associations (J. Habermas). Whereas the one side is unable to determine the specific system quality of the church, the other is unable to distinguish clearly the association "church" from other civil-social associations.[21]

This fails to recognize the special disposition and public nature of the church that necessarily connect systemic and associative forms. This one-sided perspective fails to see that the ecumenical church, at all times and in all parts of the world, is subdivided into numerous confessions with all their accompanying, particular perspectives on the content of faith, and that every day and every week, the church can be generated and renewed from within this concentration on Word and sacrament, especially in the millions of congregational "associations." Until now we have lacked (both inside and outside theology) the conceptual means for understanding and consciously cultivating the interplay and dynamic tension between systemic forms and associative forms. In its own turn, this lack made the church inclined to take "counter entities" as its point of orientation for self-description, entities that with respect to universality and authenticity were actually beneath it. It did this in order to understand itself in a delimitation from such a "counter entity," in Europe especially with respect to the relationship between "church and society" or "church and state."[22]

In the third millennium, theology will have to develop a self-understanding of the church as an ecumenical entity in congregational form, or as a congregation with ecumenical consciousness and ecumenical efficacy. In this way, it might counter false notions of powerlessness and irrelevance. It might also be in a position to replace false notions of homogeneity both in view of the church itself and in view of its cultural and social surroundings with a "nuanced historical sense" and a "subtle social analysis."[23] Such ecumenical self-understanding from a congregational perspective will make it difficult to

---

21. In this regard see the discussion with Habermas conducted by D. Tracy and F. Schüssler-Fiorenza, in Don S. Browning and Francis Schüssler-Fiorenza, eds., *Habermas, Modernity and Public Theology* (New York: Crossroad, 1992); E. Arens, ed., *Habermas und die Theologie. Beiträge zur theologischen Rezeption, Diskussion und Kritik der Theorie kommunikativen Handelns* (Düsseldorf: Patmos, 1989), esp. pp. 115-44. See also M. Welker, " '. . . And Also Upon the Menservants and the Maidservants in Those Days Will I Pour Out My Spirit.' On Pluralism and the Promise of the Spirit," *Soundings* 78/1 (1995): 49-67; cf. further M. Welker, "Niklas Luhmanns Religion der Gesellschaft," *Sociologia Internationalis* 29/2 (1991): 149-57.

22. See the issue *Kirche-Staat-Gesellschaft* (*EvTh* 54/2 [1994]).

23. Concerning the development of these forms also independently of "biblical theology," see C. West, *Prophetic Thought in Postmodern Times. Beyond Eurocentrism and Multiculturalism*, I (Monroe, Me.: Common Courage Press, 1993).

maintain provincial, regionalist, chauvinist, and similar distortions of church and faith. The congregational disposition of the church at all times and in all parts of the world, however, is indispensable for authentically living and maintaining the freedom of the church under the Word of God. Here the churches will have to develop more intensively than was previously the case interactive forms for regular proclamation in ever new scriptural interpretation and an ever new understanding of the present.[24] Similarly, churches will have to develop a more differentiated understanding of the interplay among the various "offices" as well as corresponding organizational forms in order to do justice to the multiplicity of charismatic phenomena that in the classical high churches of the West in the present must be persistently "muted," not least because of the internal and external (structural) disposition of churches.

Finally, it must become clear that freedom of scriptural interpretation does not simply serve a regional strengthening of faith within a congregation, but rather the ecumenically significant question concerning knowledge of God, the reality intended by God, and the truth of such knowledge. This *ecumenical responsibility* characterizing the search and inquiry concerning God, the responsibility manifesting itself in every proclamation, in every assembled congregation, and in a reverse fashion the concrete congregational authenticity in which this proclamation itself is supported and defended — are of significance for any serious search for God's Word as well as for the church's own vitality. Both in this search and in the engagement of its vitality, the church must continually deal with its own self-endangerment. In the classical high churches of modernity, this great self-endangerment of the church has been veiled by massive but false religious claims of immediacy toward God, and by a no less massive religious fascination with various forms of morality.

4. Confronting Religious Moralism and Religious Claims of Immediacy toward God: The Theology of the Cross and Hamartiological Considerations

In the third millennium, Christian theology — beginning with itself — must more clearly and realistically disclose the threatening and destructive powers of individual and collective life. It must identify the strategies of concealment and assuagement and help uncover the illusions and lies that veil such self-endangerment and destruction. Without precipitating and inciting the "moral struggle of all against all" (Karl Barth), it must promote a culture of sober individual and public recognition of sin. It must promote this recognition of sin in order to make clear to people in a differentiated fashion the enormous earthly power of their own capacity for destruction. But it must also promote this recognition

---

24. Cf. Welker, "Auf der theologischen Suche," 438-56.

of sin in order to reveal the fatal consequences and vanity of the use of this power. It must promote this recognition of sin in order to work toward multiform change and renewal. Christian churches can reacquire this beneficial recognition of sin ever anew only by taking as their point of departure the recognition of the cross of Christ and its evocation in proclamation and celebration of the Eucharist.

In his book *The Crucified God*, Jürgen Moltmann draws attention to the fact that the event of the cross must be comprehended in a differentiated fashion in both its religio-critical and its politico-critical dimension. Jesus of Nazareth is killed both as a "blasphemer" and a "rebel."[25] This conceptual initiative should be taken up and developed further. Jesus of Nazareth was condemned to a shameful and agonizing death and executed in the name of religion, in the name of two kinds of law, in the name of predominating politics, and supported by "public opinion." The cross thus confronts us with the horrible realization that religion, law, politics, morality, and public opinion — all of which are advances designed to serve piety, public order, justice at large, the promotion of the good, and the community — that all of these can work together to drive people who make use of these advances away from God, into untruth, a breach of the law, compassionless behavior, and lawless disarray. The systemic form of sin in its multifarious forms and the entanglement of individuals in this demonic power are revealed "beneath the cross."

Retrospectives on world history sufficiently attest the fact that a community of human beings can be thoroughly blind, corrupt, and incapable of recognizing what is good, just, liberating, and commensurate with God. Very few people would deny that the "Third Reich" or Stalinism created utterly rotten societies with utterly false orientations in which the very powers providing orientation were employed in a conspiracy against life itself. Over against such ravages, the cross of Christ refers us to an exemplary and horrible expansion of this, since according to the witness of the biblical traditions, both natives *and* foreigners, the occupied *and* the occupiers, Jews *and* Romans, Jews *and* Gentiles worked together to bring Jesus to the cross. The entire representative world worked together, cooperated, and conspired in this abysmal "will to be distant from God" (H.-G. Geyer). The "final correctives" of world opinion, of a different system of justice, of a different religion, or at least of "the enemy" — all these are eliminated here. Not only the elite, but also the general public, and even Jesus' most intimate associates cooperated here. The cross of Christ confronts us with an unsurpassable depth of destructive and self-destructive human power. It confronts us with chaos and horror. It confronts human beings with the abyss of their own power to disseminate meaninglessness and hopelessness.

In the third millennium, theology must guard against relating such insights solely to the simple self-relation of "human being" and "world," both of which are

---

25. See Jürgen Moltmann, *The Crucified God*, ch. 4.

allegedly *"incurvatus in se"* and "self-centered" with respect to God. Instead of approaching human beings with religiously embellished moral appeals, theology must comprehend these systemic normative forces and forms of power in their destructive interplay, and learn how to recognize them in their fruitful interdependence. From theology we should expect orientation aids for distinguishing between destructive and beneficial normative forms and developments. Theology can fulfill this task, however, only if it does not assign such recognition of sin to mere morals alone. Rather, it must make it clear that morals — the communication of mutual acknowledgment, the interplay of giving and withholding respect — can be occupied and guided by the most varied forms of ethos. Theology must contribute to a recognition of the ambivalence and corruptibility of morals, though it must do so without engaging in a blanket denigration of moral communication (which is, after all, indispensable). Quite in accord with this, it must provide initiatives for critical and self-critical dealings with legal, political, mass media–related, and other forms of normative entities. This enlightenment of transindividual formative forces affecting life, and the corresponding transindividual recognition of sin, both presuppose that theology will have at its disposal an intensified willingness to engage in education. It also presupposes a willingness to be subject to criticism — criticism from the perspective of a theology of the cross and on the basis of hamartiological considerations — the religious admixture of piety and self-righteousness that has in modern times largely made theology a matter of individual religious and moral feeling. To prevent this basic theological posture from generating what in its own turn is a destructive, self-righteous, power-hungry theology, all believers must be taught the basic theological distinction between law and gospel.

5. Realistic Theology and the Distinction Between Law and Gospel

In the third millennium, theology will have to rediscover the significance of the basic Reformation distinction between "law" and "gospel." In the process, it will have to reject the common abstractions and caricatures of the law, its reduction to the Decalogue, as well as numerous airy notions of the gospel. In place of the pairs "indicative and imperative," "demand and gift," "promise and claim," it must provide more differentiated insights into the inner disposition of the law and its "sublation" (its relativization accompanied by a preservation of its intention) by the gospel. Only a theologically and substantively appropriate understanding of the law and of its potential for being perverted through the power of sin will reveal the tense but fruitful alliance of hope involving both the church and Israel. An understanding of the culturally formative dynamic of the law's own normative nexus of form, and of its dialectical relationship with the gospel, however, will put interreligious dialogue back on a substantive basis, and will reestablish theology's "cultural competence."

This distinction between law and gospel confronts theology with the power of demanding normative relationships, with their destructive deformation (under the power of sin, revealed in an exemplary fashion in the cross of Christ), as well as with their liberating and creative transformation (through the gospel, the coming reign of God, and the outpouring of the Spirit). These normative relationships are conceptualized as "the law" both by and in connection with many biblical traditions, and although they do exhibit inner structures and developmental dynamics that seem to transcend culture, these structures and dynamics are for now only partially transparent in their powerful interdependencies.[26]

All the biblical traditions relating to the law contain norms serving to secure justice, to protect the weak, and to promote mercy, and norms serving the publicly regulated relationship with God, namely, the cult. The interdependence of these relationships generates developmental dynamics in which the norms themselves are progressively completed and refined, and at the same time an effort is made to thwart their dissolution (which is, of course, the threat attaching precisely to such continued development). Hence — to take only a few examples — the ethos of mercy and similar notions secure the universality of striving for reciprocity before the law. In its own turn, the law works counter to paternalistic and therapeutic inclinations in morals shaped by mercy. The cult secures a basis for this normative thinking in collective recollection and expectation, whereas justice and mercy also focus on the general accessibility of the cult, securing thereby its supportive function.

The biblical traditions, however, demonstrate not only that deficits arise in the various subdivisions pertaining to keeping the law, but also that the entire complex of the law itself can be perverted. Mercy can be ignored, justice bent, and worship misused — again, in mutually supportive ways. Christian theology must on the one hand make clear at all times the revelation of the lost human condition under the perverted law; and, on the other hand, it must draw attention to the saving power of the coming reign of God and to the new creative presence of the Spirit, with which God, by taking human beings themselves into service, counters this particular situation of distress and perversion. Precisely this basic orientation is served by (1) trinitarian-theological concentration on God's vitality, (2) a preeminent orientation toward the witnesses of the biblical tradition, (3) freedom lived under the Word of God in both the congregational and ecumenical church, and (4) the ever new reflection back to the revelation of the lost condition of the world beneath the cross.

More intensively than has hitherto been the case, theology should show that law and gospel have become formative forces not only of church life, but

---

26. My own persuasions in this regard were strengthened by a seminar in the Heidelberg *Graduiertenkolleg,* "Religion and Normativity," conducted with Jan Assmann, Klaus Berger, and Bernd Janowski, and by the ensuing discussions.

at a different level also of culture at large, and are forces that can be ignored only at the price of enormous insecurity in orientation.

One recent example is the intensive debate concerning literature and morals, a debate at least strongly stimulated if not actually generated by Harold Bloom's book *The Western Canon*.[27] Bloom polemicizes against the invocation of a practical ethical function for art and literature, against a critical view of the canon for the sake of representing "voices" within national, ethnic, sexual, and other differentiations. He attacks the moralization and politicization of literary texts, and tries to maintain a canonical collection of literature that is to be kept out of the reach of what he considers to be such "relativization." Here Bloom fails to recognize — fixated as he is on the dimension of the cultic (or on a subdivision of the cultic) — the tension-filled, dynamic relationship between cultic, legal, and mercy-related forms that culture has activated with its own "pluralistic" differentiation of various "contextual" and social-moral movements. According to the systematic insights generated by the distinction between law and gospel, a "canon" can maintain itself only in a continual, vital complementary relationship with forms that guarantee equality of access, and forms that continually strive to include outsiders, minorities, and repressed perspectives. Only such mutual support between forms can guarantee a vital and living normative condition, one toward which canonical literature, in its own way, is working. Anyone who one-sidedly laments dissolution, and reviles a critical posture, fails to recognize the relationships of form to which our culture owes a decisive dynamic of depth within its own development.[28]

"Realistic" theology will have to preserve these insights in a constructive and creative cultural critique and in an analysis of systemic distortions in culture and society. The avoidance of such prophetic and critical objectivity can only result in serious damage to both culture and society.

---

27. Harold Bloom, *The Western Canon* (New York: Harcourt Brace, 1994).

28. An additional current example is the virtually desperate search for a "world ethos" (for example, H. Küng), along with the problems of orientation it unintentionally generates. See in this regard M. Welker, "Auf der theologischen Suche nach einem 'Weltethos' in einer Zeit kurzlebiger moralischer Märkte. Küng, Tracy und die Bedeutung der neuen Biblischen Theologie," *EvTh* 5 (1995); W. Huber, *Die tägliche Gewalt. Gegen den Ausverkauf der Menschenwürde* (Freiburg: Herder, 1993), pp. 150ff.

Back to the Future

Geoffrey Wainwright

Facing the Past

In the heyday of the lexical and grammatical approach to biblical theology, the certainty of God's coming reign was thought by some to be reflected in the way in which, in the Hebrew language, the end could be spoken of as behind us, so that one apparently walked backward into the future.[1] However that may be as linguistic and locomotive theory, several of the most important movements in the twentieth-century history of the church and of theology have, as a matter of fact, looked toward the past in order to gain their bearings in the present and get guidance for the ongoing journey. My modest thesis is that we shall have to continue in that direction — looking back with and through those movements into the full depth of God's history with the church — if their full benefits for ecclesial life and theological thought are to be drawn in the twenty-first century. As examples, I will take the cases of liturgy, ecumenism, dogmatics, and hermeneutics. Moreover, it will emerge that work in each of these areas has demonstrated a strong interest in God's future and definitive reign.

Liturgy

From very different starting points in Roman Catholicism and Protestantism, the modern liturgical movement has looked toward the early church for help

---

1. Thus graphically, in terms of railway travel and oarsmanship, J. N. Schofield, *Introducing Old Testament Theology* (London: S.C.M. Press, 1964), p. 26: "The Hebrew pictured himself as riding with his back to the engine, or as one of a rowing eight, not the cox. The past, he thought, lay in front of him." Cf. Thorleif Boman, *Hebrew Thought Compared with Greek*, trans. Jules L. Morean (Philadelphia: Westminster Press, 1960), pp. 149-50, but also the sharp criticism of James Barr, *The Semantics of Biblical Language* (London: Oxford University Press, 1961), p. 77.

and inspiration in the renewal of Christian worship. On the Roman Catholic side, it has been a matter of docking excrescences and concentrating on the essentials. On the Protestant side, it has been a matter of recovering the rich diversity of symbolic communication. In either case, the church of the first centuries has provided the models. At a time when Western Christendom has been in decline, and both the identity and the relevance of Christianity have become problematic for many in the West, it is significant that the exemplary period in the search for renewal has been found to lie in those early centuries in which the church was first finding its identity and showing its relevance by seeking the conversion of the world.

The key witness from the second century has been Justin Martyr and his outline description of Sunday worship in the Church of Rome around the year 150. In his *First Apology,* Justin describes how all the Christians gathered together from town and country to hear readings from "the writings of the prophets" and "the memoirs of the apostles," to listen to those Scriptures expounded, to offer prayers, to present the bread and wine, and then, when thanks had been said over them, to receive them as the communion of the body and blood of Christ; and a collection was made, from which the president saw to the needs of orphans and widows, the sick, the imprisoned, and strangers. Justin explains that Sunday is the day for the worship assembly, "because it is the first day, on which God, having transformed the darkness and matter, made the world, and Jesus Christ our Savior rose from the dead the same day."[2] In his *Dialogue with Trypho,* Justin reveals that Sunday is also known as "the eighth day," for Christ's resurrection is the beginning of a regenerated humanity and the start of the age to come.[3] On the verge of the twenty-first century, Protestant Christians in particular still have far to go in regaining in eucharistic practice the gathering of the Lord's people for the Lord's Meal on the Lord's day.

From the third century, the modern liturgical movement picked up the sense of the new exodus, of the paschal mystery of Christ's death and resurrection at the heart of God's redemptive work. Commemorated and celebrated in the church at Easter (which is the presumed date of the baptismal vigil in the so-called *Apostolic Tradition of Hippolytus*) and at every Eucharist *(memores igitur mortis et resurrectionis eius),* Christ's Passover is the effective revelation of God's all-embracing plan of salvation to be fully achieved in the end times. At our present juncture in history, the churches stand in need of a strengthened confidence in the final completion of God's universal purpose.

From the fourth century, from the testimonies of Cyril of Jerusalem and Ambrose of Milan, of Chrysostom and Augustine, the modern liturgical movement has extracted the lesson of a serious doctrinal, moral, and ritual catechu-

---

2. Justin, *Apology I,* 67.
3. Justin, *Dialogue,* 138; cf. the contemporary *Epistle of Barnabas* 15:8-9.

menate for the making of Christians. The finest flower has been the Roman Catholic *Order for the Christian Initiation of Adults* (1972), which stretches from evangelization, through instruction in the Scriptures, the faith, and ethics, to baptism on profession of faith, first communion, and postbaptismal instruction. The *Catechism of the Catholic Church* (1992) provides a standard for instruction to converts and learners. In their respective ways, various Protestant churches are rediscovering the necessity of solid catechesis. On all sides, the process of evangelization and incorporation will have to be prolonged if a people is to be prepared for the advent of the Lord.

In sum, the modern liturgical movement has drawn from the early church the vision of the evangelized and evangelizing church as a company of baptized and believing people, assembling on the day of the Lord's Resurrection to "proclaim the Lord's death until he comes" and thence scattering week by week to bear witness to God's transforming presence and power. That vision has still to be embodied and enacted in the next century.

Ecumenism

The modern ecumenical movement took as its motto the prayer of Jesus for his disciples on the eve of his passion, "that they all may be one." The unity of Christ's followers was to be a testimony "so that the world might believe" in the divine mission of the Son (John 17:21). In Pauline terms, the unity of the church as Christ's body is the beginning of the realization of God's purpose to sum up all things under the headship of Christ (Eph. 1:3-10). The common embodiment of Christ's mind is both an anticipation of, and a witness to, the day when every knee shall bow, and every tongue confess that Jesus Christ is Lord, to the glory of God the Father (Phil. 2:5-11). Reconciled to God through Christ, Christians are to be Christ's ambassadors — preachers and ministers of the divine reconciliation in the world (2 Cor. 5:17-21). It follows that dissension and division among Christians are a counter-testimony to the gospel. The mission of the church requires its unity.

Twentieth-century endeavors to "live in harmony with one another, in accord with Christ Jesus" (Rom. 15:5) have looked back to times before the occurrence of the lasting great schisms in Christian history in order to find the ground plans for a common dwelling place. This was the procedure adopted in the convergence document on *Baptism, Eucharist and Ministry* produced by the Faith and Order Commission of the World Council of Churches (1982).[4] The method was recognized and appreciated in the official response of the Roman Catholic Church to the so-called Lima text, and the generally positive evaluation

---

4. *Baptism, Eucharist and Ministry,* Faith and Order Paper No. 111 (Geneva: World Council of Churches, 1982).

made by that church of the eucharistic section of *BEM* in particular is one measure of its success. Moreover, this response makes a point of the future orientation of the sacrament as it is found in the early texts:

> The sources employed for the interpretation of the meaning of the eucharist and the form of celebration are Scripture and Tradition. The classical liturgies of the first millennium and patristic theologians are important points of reference in this text. . . . The presentation of the mystery of the eucharist follows the flow of classical eucharistic liturgies, with the eucharistic theology drawing heavily on the content of the traditional prayer and symbolic actions of these liturgies. The text draws on patristic sources for additional explanation of the mystery of the eucharist. . . . There is a strong eschatological dimension. The eucharist is viewed as a foretaste of Christ's parousia and of the final kingdom, given through the Spirit. It opens up the vision of the kingdom and the renewal of the world.[5]

Before the ecumenical convergence can reach the degree of consensus required for eucharistic communion, more work needs to be done in refining the agreement on still debated points and in the reception of the agreement into the doctrinal, catechetical, and liturgical practice of the churches. Those tasks await the twenty-first century.

Such work now fits into the broader study of WCC Faith and Order on the Apostolic Faith. When it started on its project "Towards the Common Expression of the Apostolic Faith Today," the Faith and Order Commission, after long and hard debate, made the decision to take as its "theological basis and methodological tool" the Nicene-Constantinopolitan Creed.[6] If the divided churches were to regain "visible unity in one faith" and be able to "confess their faith together" in a "common witness to the saving purpose of the triune God for all humanity and creation" and in a "common mission and service to the world," they needed to "re-appropriate their common roots." The "apostolic faith" was "expressed in Holy Scriptures and summarized in the creeds of the early church." In particular, the Nicene-Constantinopolitan Creed constitutes "an exemplary and authentic summary of the apostolic faith." In that capacity, it "served as an expression of unity in the Early Church and is, therefore, also of great importance for our contemporary quest for the unity of Christ's Church." The Creed is already "officially recognized and used by many churches within the ecumenical movement," and its content is "present in the thinking and life" also of some churches that do not accord it such status. An explication of the Creed is needed in order to determine the degree and form in which "the

---

5. *Churches Respond to "BEM,"* vol. 6, Faith and Order Paper No. 144, ed. Max Thurian (Geneva: World Council of Churches, 1988), pp. 16-17.

6. *Confessing One Faith,* Faith and Order Paper No. 140 (Geneva: World Council of Churches, 1987), pp. 1-5.

fundamentals of the apostolic faith as witnessed to by the Holy Scriptures, proclaimed in the Tradition of the church, and expressed in the three articles of the Creed, can be commonly understood and expressed by churches of different confessional traditions, living in different cultural, social, political and religious contexts." To help the churches recognize their "common basis" for a "common witness" to "God's salvific action in creation, redemption and fulfilment," their representatives in WCC Faith and Order have placed at their disposal a study document on *Confessing the One Faith: An Ecumenical Explication of the Apostolic Faith as it is Confessed in the Nicene-Constantinopolitan Creed* (381).[7] Once again, the task passes into the twenty-first century: a continued revisitation of the apostolic and patristic church remains vital to the ecclesial reconciliation without which the credibility of the message of cosmic reconciliation is impaired and its final realization frustrated.

Dogmatics

The twentieth-century revival of dogmatics was launched by Karl Barth. Barth declared that "a Christianity which is not entirely and utterly eschatology has entirely and utterly nothing to do with Christ."[8] Barth's eschatological orientation and his christological concentration were mutually conditioning. Since the church was living "between the times" of Christ's first coming and his return, the whole history of the believing community was caught in a single tension that allowed for a theological conversation across the generations. Church dogmatics had a diachronic as well as a synchronic dimension. Although Barth's Anselm book marked an important point in his own development, it was chiefly to the Reformers of the sixteenth century and to the Fathers of the early church that the Barth of the *Church Dogmatics* looked in their common engagement with the scriptural witness to the Christ who had come, comes, and is to come. It remains significant that Jürgen Moltmann's "gekreuzigter Gott" should have been adumbrated in Gregory of Nazianzen's "theos stauromenos," Martin Luther's "deus crucifixus" (WA 1:614), and (a Methodist may add) Charles Wesley's "crucified God."[9]

In the Roman Catholic Church, the theological and dogmatic renewal that

---

7. Faith and Order Paper No. 153 (Geneva: World Council of Churches, 1991).

8. "Christentum, das nicht ganz und gar und restlos Eschatologie ist, hat mit Christus ganz und gar und restlos nichts zu tun" (Karl Barth, *Der Römerbrief,* 2nd ed. [München: Chr. Kaiser, 1921], p. 298; Eng. trans., *The Epistle to the Romans,* trans. Edwyn C. Hoskins [London: Oxford University Press, 1933], p. 314).

9. Jürgen Moltmann, *Der gekreuzigte Gott* (München: Chr. Kaiser, 1972); Eng. trans., *The Crucified God,* trans. R. A. Wilson and J. Bowden (New York: Harper & Row, 1974). Gregory Nazianzen, in Migne, *PG* 36:661. Luther, in *WA* 1:614. Wesley, in *The Poetical Works of John and Charles Wesley,* ed. G. Osborn, vol. 9 (London: Wesleyan-Methodist Conference Office, 1870), p. 362.

prepared the way for the Second Vatican Council owed much to patristic studies, and (a fact of considerable ecumenical importance, both to the Orthodox and to Protestants) particularly to work in the Eastern Fathers. Nor is it unimportant that monographs should have been devoted to patristic theologians with strong, if problematic, interests in eschatology: Jean Daniélou wrote on Origen and on Gregory of Nyssa, Hans Urs von Balthasar on Maximus the Confessor. Yves Congar's majestic surveys of the entire Tradition brought to light broad ranges of historical diversity that justified a more generous orthodoxy than had been characteristic of post-Tridentine Catholicism.

As we move into the twenty-first century, it may well prove that the most valuable acquisition of twentieth-century dogmatics to accompany us will be the rediscovery of a vital doctrine of the Trinity. Here again it was, on the Protestant side, Karl Barth who led the way; on the Roman Catholic side, Karl Rahner; and once more the Western Churches have profited from the Eastern, through such ecumenical intermediaries as Georges Florovsky, John Meyendorff, and John Zizioulas, who have drawn with ease on their patristic inheritance and its liturgical mediation for their widely read dogmatic and theological contributions. With an acknowledged debt to Dumitru Staniloae, Jürgen Moltmann's writings over the years took on a more intrinsically trinitarian cast, and more pervasively than simply in the works entitled *Trinität und Reich Gottes* (1980) and *In der Geschichte des dreieinigen Gottes* (1991).[10]

Trinitarian doctrine will retain its importance for keeping the churches faithful to the identity of the self-revealing God, Father, Son, and Holy Spirit, and to the triune work of redemption, reconciliation, and consummation. Here the next generations should be served by Thomas F. Torrance's *The Trinitarian Faith: The Evangelical Theology of the Ancient Catholic Church* (1988), which both contains a lucid historical account of the early development of trinitarian doctrine and its establishment under Athanasius and the Cappadocians, and offers a powerful exposition of what was and remains at stake dogmatically in the ecclesiastical decisions then taken and the faith confessed. A similar intention characterizes Catherine M. LaCugna's *God for Us: The Trinity and Christian Life* (1991), although her historical survey reaches further, and she is critical of some of the theological directions in which some avowedly orthodox classic figures have taken the primary doctrine.

Then, too, a firmly trinitarian perspective will be necessary as the church and theology of the twenty-first century tackle some questions that have already emerged and that appear likely to grow in importance on the intellectual, cultural, social, and religious planes. With regard to the philosophy and practice

10. Jürgen Moltmann, *Trinität und Reich Gottes* (München: Chr. Kaiser, 1980); Eng. trans., *The Trinity and the Kingdom: The Doctrine of God,* trans. Margaret Kohl (San Francisco: Harper & Row, 1981); and *In der Geschichte des dreieinigen Gottes* (München: Chr. Kaiser, 1991); Eng. trans., *The History and the Triune God* (New York: Crossroad, 1992).

of the natural sciences, T. F. Torrance, again, in a series of books from the 1960s through the 1980s, has argued, historically, for the biblical and patristic foundations of Western science; and he has given, systematically, a trinitarian grounding to the "logical" structure of reality and of the matching investigation into it, and to the "spiritual" character of the divine workings and of creation's participation in them. trinitarian understandings of history have been displayed, in their quite different ways, by Wolfhart Pannenberg and, again, Jürgen Moltmann. Social correspondences to trinitarian doctrine have been set out by theologians as diverse as Leonardo Boff (*Trinity and Society,* 1986), John Zizioulas (*Being as Communion,* 1985), and John Milbank (*Theology and Social Theory,* 1990). If, amid the increasingly obvious religious variety of the world, Christians are in both a critical and a constructive way to maintain the uniqueness and the universality of Christ, they will need to draw on the full resources and possibilities of a strong doctrine of the Trinity.

The abiding significance of the trinitarian faith for the ultimate future is captured by John Wesley in the peroration to his sermon on "The New Creation": "And, to crown all, there will be a deep, an intimate, an uninterrupted union with God; a constant communion with the Father and his Son Jesus Christ, through the Spirit; and a continual enjoyment of the Three-One God, and of all the creatures in him!"

Hermeneutics

The modernity of the Enlightenment was characterized by a rejection of the presumptive authority of the past. While some so-called postmodern trends represent in fact a *reductio ad absurdum* of modernity in that they dismiss authority altogether, other postmodern movements have revitalized the sense of Tradition that had never quite disappeared from liturgical, ecumenical, dogmatic Christianity.

In philosophy, Hans-Georg Gadamer, in *Wahrheit und Methode* (1960), already sought to counter the Enlightenment's "prejudice against prejudices" and argued that, in the shared moral world of humankind, we can be enriched by engagement with texts that reach us along the track of their *Wirkungsgeschichte.* Alasdair MacIntyre, in *Whose Justice? Which Rationality?* (1988), showed how inquiry, argumentation, and practical reasoning are both tradition-constituted and tradition-constitutive, located in particular though permeable historical communities. In theology, George Lindbeck, in *The Nature of Doctrine: Religion and Theology in a Postliberal Age* (1984), drew on both the anthropological studies of Clifford Geertz and the philosophical insights of Ludwig Wittgenstein into language in order to present the church as a cultural-linguistic community both diachronic and synchronic, a traditional form of life with its characteristic rules of speech, ritual practices, and behavioral patterns.

Andrew Louth, in *Discerning the Mystery: An Essay on the Nature of Theology* (1983), took not only from Gadamer and from Michael Polanyi, the philosopher of "personal knowing" and "tacit knowledge," but also from the Eastern Orthodox theologian Vladimir Lossky, according to whom the divine Word is always accompanied by a margin of silence when God addresses humankind and, as the Holy Spirit, lives the life of the church. From these influences Louth advocated a "return to allegory" as a way of reading the Scriptures.

There we rejoin the work of Henri de Lubac, which could prove an invaluable vade mecum for the church and theology as they journey into the twenty-first century. If, exploiting the title of the opening chapter in Gerhard Ebeling's *Wort Gottes und Tradition* (1964), we view "Church History as the History of the Exegesis of Holy Scripture," then there is guidance to be found for present responsibilities in the interpretative practices of the patristic and medieval periods that de Lubac recounts in his four volumes on *Exégèse médiévale: Les quatre sens de l'Écriture* (1959-64). A look into that earlier history offers the chance to appreciate what has been called "the superiority of precritical exegesis" for the sake of renewing a Tradition whose life has been threatened by a historical-critical approach to the Bible that was willy-nilly incompatible with certain vital ingredients in the Scriptures and Christian dogma and experience.[11]

The "four senses of Scripture" are set out in a quatrain found in Nicholas of Lyra:

> Littera gesta docet,
> Quid credas allegoria,
> Moralis quod agas,
> Quo tendas anagogia.

The mighty deeds *(gesta)* of God in history are the foundation of the Christian faith (and it is only a mechanistic naturalism that excludes "miracle"). Faith then seeks to formulate its understanding in doctrine *(allegoria)*. Right belief finds moral expression in action ("what we are to do"). The fourth sense is the aim and goal of God's redeeming activity and of the responsive "faith that works by love": the human destiny in God's loving purpose is "onwards and upwards" *(anagogia)*, not in the modern sense of progress, but in the sense of Wesley's vision of "The New Creation" already quoted.

Jürgen Moltmann's *Theology of Hope* contained a full-range reading of the Scriptures that reached from history through faith and works to glory: The Exodus and the Resurrection are divine promises that mobilize believers for a praxis that anticipates God's final kingdom.[12]

---

11. David C. Steinmetz, "The Superiority of Pre-Critical Exegesis," *Theology Today* 37 (1980-81): 27-38; reprinted in his *Memory and Mission* (Nashville: Abingdon Press, 1988), pp. 143-63.

12. Jürgen Moltmann, *Theology of Hope: On the Grounds and Implications of a Christian Eschatology*, trans. James W. Leitch (New York: Harper & Row, 1967).

The Eternally New

To seek *ressourcement* by way of retrospection was more than a methodological device for the twentieth-century church in its continuing pilgrimage. That Jürgen Moltmann, with others, could call theology back to the future as a theme for reflection and action gained its full legitimacy only because God's future has already, in Christ and in the Holy Spirit, broken into history; and so we may know, albeit as "puzzling reflections in a mirror," the *not yet* through the *already.* "Christ was raised from the dead by the glory of the Father" (Rom. 6:4), and "if the Spirit of him who raised Jesus from the dead dwells in you, he who raised Christ Jesus from the dead will give life to your mortal bodies also through his Spirit which dwells in you" (8:11). Now the entire creation waits "to be set free from its bondage to decay and obtain the glorious liberty of the children of God" (8:21). While awaiting "the redemption of our bodies," "we have the first fruits of the Spirit" (8:23).

Having thus been inaugurated by the Father through the Son in the Holy Spirit, the "new creation" (2 Cor. 5:17) and its "new covenant" (1 Cor. 11:25; 2 Cor. 3:6; Heb. 9:15) are permanent and definitive in their qualitative and unsurpassable singularity. The new covenant is in fact "eternal" or "of the world/age to come" (*aionios;* Heb. 13:20). As the community of the new creation and the new covenant, the church also is perennially new; her youth and strength are perpetual like the eagle's (Ps. 103:5; Isa 40:31). There is, therefore, a communion of the saints that spans the generations and transcends time. To look back is also to see our contemporaries.

In the twenty-first century, the ecumenical task will still be to identify the church. Scriptural hermeneutics will be needed to test whether the liturgical anamnesis truly proclaims the things of Christ and the liturgical epiclesis effectively produces the fruit of the Spirit. Dogmatic reflection will be needed to aid pastoral and magisterial judgment in discerning where the voice of the Beloved Son is heard and the Holy Spirit flourishes.

The determinative nature of God's reign is such that at the very end, in a final retrospection, it will be seen to have informed the life of the faithful church and indeed to have governed the whole of history.

Theology, Meaning, and Power

Miroslav Volf

Introduction

A sense that academic theology has lost its voice is widespread today. Many observers note, as Jeffrey Stout did in *Ethics after Babel*, that theology is unable "to command attention as a distinctive contributor to public discourse in our culture."[1] Equally disturbing is the loss of interest in academic theology on the part of the church; as scholars write for scholars and students, the ear of church folk is tuned in elsewhere. Helped by the mass media, popular preachers and a diverse chorus of social critics are dominating the discourse in the church and in the wider culture. Theologians are on the sidelines. Like the street-corner preachers of yesterday, they find themselves talking to a crowd too hurried to honor them with more than a fleeting glance.

Seeking to redress the inability to get a hearing, theologians have increasingly turned into methodologists. Before addressing the church and the wider culture, we think it salutary to talk to ourselves about the conditions of plausibility and intelligibility of our speech. The trouble with this strategy is that the longer you stick with it, the more self-defeating it becomes. Jeffrey Stout has put it starkly: ". . . preoccupation with method is like clearing your throat: it can go on for only so long before you lose your audience."[2]

Though vivid and fitting, the image of clearing the throat is also misleading on two counts. For one, theological method is more analogous to the strategy of an oration than to the clarity of a speaker's voice; learning proper method is more like taking lessons in public speaking than like clearing the throat. Second, method is never just method; "method is message." I do not mean this in the trite sense that the way you communicate also communicates. More

---

1. Jeffrey Stout, *Ethics after Babel: The Language of Morals and Their Discontents* (Boston: Beacon Press, 1988), p. 163.
2. Stout, *Ethics after Babel*, p. 163.

profoundly, all major methodological decisions have implications for the whole of the theological edifice; and inversely, all major theological decisions shape theological method. Like many things in life, reflection on method is good if there is not too much of it.

Since the publication of *The Nature of Doctrine: Religion and Theology in a Postliberal Age* over a decade ago, George A. Lindbeck, a key ecumenical figure, has established himself also as a major authority on "theological throat-clearing," if I may be permitted to return to Stout's somewhat misleading metaphor. As a good theologian and methodologist, Lindbeck is more interested in the act than in the "endless methodological foreplay," to use another of Stout's metaphors. Hence Lindbeck's methodological proposal "to renew . . . the ancient practice of absorbing the universe into the biblical world"[3] is intended both to instruct and to empower theologians to perform — to speak authentically to the church and to the culture at large.

After reading *The Nature of Doctrine*, however, I found myself wanting not only to do theology, but also to engage Lindbeck about how theology ought to be done. That he has had a similar effect on many others is a testimony to the power of his methodological vision. Though I critically examine Lindbeck's proposal here, my goal is not so much to clear Lindbeck's throat as my own. To change the metaphor, partly with his materials and partly with my own, I am beginning here to lay methodological foundations for a different theological house.

Absorbing the World

In his short study of the relationship between New Haven (standing for the so-called Yale school) and Grand Rapids (standing for neo-Calvinism), Nicholas Wolterstorff has suggested that there is "no deeper guiding metaphor" in the thought of theologians like George Lindbeck than "reversing the direction of conformation."[4] Instead of translating the biblical message into the conceptualities of the social world we inhabit as modern theology was prone to do, Lindbeck tells us that Christians should redescribe this world with the help of biblical categories. Before the dawn of modernity Christians did theology "intratextually"; now at its sunset they should relearn doing the same, though in a posttraditional and postliberal mode.

Lindbeck's proposal has an edge. It is directed against "liberal" theology, which has elevated conformation to the "extrabiblical realities" to a theological

---

3. George A. Lindbeck, *The Nature of Doctrine: Religion and Theology in a Postliberal Age* (Philadelphia: Westminster Press, 1984), p. 135.

4. Nicholas Wolterstorff, *What New Haven and Grand Rapids Have to Say to Each Other* (Grand Rapids: Calvin College, 1993), p. 2.

program under the guise of "translating" the biblical message. Though such translations may "have made easier the continued commitment to the faith of the would-be believers," in Lindbeck's view the translations tended also "to replace Scripture rather than lead to it"[5] as well as to make Christians "accommodate to the prevailing culture rather than shape it."[6] The time has come to reverse the direction of conformation: instead of the world absorbing the text, the text needs to absorb the world; instead of being guided by contemporary plausibilities, we need to be guided by the inner logic of the Christian story.

Good reasons speak in favor of Lindbeck's critique of the liberal pattern of conformation. In contemporary de-Christianized, pluralistic, and rapidly changing Western cultures, only those religious groups that make no apologies about their "difference" will be able to survive and thrive. The strategy of conformation is socially ineffective in the short run (because you cannot shape by parroting) and self-destructive in the long run (because you conform to what you have not helped shape). A good deal of courage in nonconformity is needed both to preserve the identity of Christian faith and to insure its lasting social relevance.

Lindbeck's methodological proposal is attractive from afar, if one concentrates on the contours of the polarity he sets up between "the text absorbing the world" ("redescription") and "the world absorbing the text" ("translation"). Strange things happen, however, if one draws near. The sharp contours of the polarity blur and one is no longer sure who is doing the absorbing and who is being absorbed. Consider the examples Lindbeck gives of the text absorbing the world. We are not surprised to find him pointing to Augustine's relation to Platonism and Aquinas's relation to Aristotelianism to demonstrate that "a scriptural world is . . . able to absorb the universe,"[7] though even here we would expect both more awareness that "the universe" did a good deal of absorbing, too, and more willingness to let the presence of such countermovements shape the methodological proposal. But when Lindbeck places Schleiermacher (in his relation to German idealism) alongside Augustine and Aquinas, we begin to wonder whether the polarity between "the text absorbing the world" and "the world absorbing the text" is not vacuous. Finally, when we are told that Thomas Huxley was carrying out the scientific enterprise "in an imaginatively biblical world" because he was operating with the contrast between justification by verification and by faith,[8] we are left perplexed. Has not Lindbeck's program of absorbing the world become yet another form of the criticized "fusion of a self-identical story with the new world within which it is retold," only motivated

5. George Lindbeck, "Scripture, Consensus, and Community," in *Biblical Interpretation in Crisis: The Ratzinger Conference on Bible and Church*, ed. Richard John Neuhaus (Grand Rapids: Eerdmans, 1989), p. 87.

6. Lindbeck, *The Nature of Doctrine*, p. 130.

7. Lindbeck, *The Nature of Doctrine*, p. 117.

8. George A. Lindbeck, "Barth and Textuality," *Theology Today* 43 (1986): 371.

this time by the nostalgia for a long-lost cultural dominance of Christianity? Is his "ecumenical sectarianism," born out of the insight that religion no longer creates and permeates the very fibers of the social world, just a tactical move calculated to maneuver the church once again into the center of society?

The point I wish to make here is not that Lindbeck is not sectarian enough. Rather, I want to underline that he is trading on the inherent ambiguity of metaphors such as redescribing the world, seeing it through scriptural lenses, or absorbing it. *Since it is difficult to say who is absorbing whom at any given moment, Lindbeck can programmatically claim to be absorbing extratextual realities into the world of the text while at the same time clandestinely allowing extratextual realities to shape profoundly the textual world he claims to be inhabiting.*

The problem of ambiguity arises because of a deeper problem with the metaphors of "reversing the direction of conformation" and "absorbing the world." They suggest a general way of relating to the culture as a whole: you either absorb it, or are absorbed by it; you either conform it to yourself or conform yourself to it. For two reasons such a general approach to the wider culture will not do: first, since you are never outside the wider culture, that culture is part and parcel of who you are; second, the wider culture is not a monolithic whole but a differentiated network of beliefs and practices. On the ground that culture is not monolithic, John H. Yoder has rightly refused to set up a new typology of Christ and culture after his devastating critique of Niebuhr's classic *Christ and Culture*. He explicitly rejects "the kind of total formal answer around which the entire Niebuhr treatment is oriented, namely, the call for a global classification of all of culture in one category."[9]

Once you accept that "culture" is not "monolithic" (as Yoder underlines) and that being a Christian is a way of inhabiting a culture (as I would add), then you must reject the Niebuhrian assumption that "culture" as "a whole must be responded to somehow as a monolith, either affirming it all, rejecting it all, synthesizing with it all, or paradoxing it all," or as Lindbeck would put it, absorbing it all. *There is no single correct way to relate to a given culture as a whole, or even to its dominant thrust; there are only numerous ways of accepting, transforming, or replacing various aspects of a given culture from within.*

Location 1

Lindbeck proposes that a theologian should inhabit the "intrascriptural world." How else could she absorb the universe into the world of the text? How else could she see the world with scriptural eyes? Will the proposal work, however?

---

9. John Howard Yoder, "How H. Richard Niebuhr Reasoned: A Critique of *Christ and Culture*," *Authentic Transformation: A New Vision of Christ and Culture*, ed. John Howard Yoder et al. (Nashville: Abingdon Press, 1995), p. 38.

On extrascriptural grounds, I would suggest that if he tried consistently to explicate "religion from within" and then from that standpoint to describe "everything as inside, as interpreted by the religion,"[10] he would fail.

Let me start my argument by examining one aspect of the thought of Clifford Geertz, the person to whom Lindbeck's proposal owes probably more than to any other single thinker. Religious symbols, claims Geertz, offer a "perspective," a "mode of seeing," a "framework of meaning," a "world" to live in. Notice, however, how he qualifies this living in the world of religion. He writes:

> But no one, not even a saint, lives in the world religious symbols formulate all the time, and the majority of men live in it only at moments. The everyday world of common-sense objects and practical acts is . . . the paramount reality in human existence — paramount in the sense that it is the world in which we are most solidly rooted. . . .[11]

Instead of simply inhabiting the world of religion, as Lindbeck suggests, in Geertz's view we move "back and forth between" religious and nonreligious worlds. This movement effects change in a person, and with change in a person a change also takes place in "the common-sense world, for it is now seen as but the partial form of a wider reality which corrects and completes it."[12] As the transformation of a person suggests, the temporal sequence of habitations is the outward dimension of their inner "spatial" differentiation. A person lives in a complex cultural world and, at the same time, she lives in the world of religious symbols. Both worlds live in her and, in a profound sense, she is these worlds. What one can learn from Geertz is that the world of a Christian is never simply intratextual, but always "intratextual-cum-extratextual" (or rather "extratextual-cum-intratextual").

Yet even Geertz is one-sided. It will not do simply to note the movement back and forth between the two worlds, the coexistence of the two in the same person, and the shaping of the commonsense world by the religious world. Talal Asad has argued that Geertz's understanding of the relationship between religious and nonreligious worlds is deficient because there is no suggestion anywhere in Geertz "that the religious world (or perspective) is ever affected by the commonsense world";[13] the shaping is unidirectional, from the religious world to the commonsense world. Lindbeck follows Geertz's unidirectional construal of the relationship between the two worlds and, in correspondence with his

---

10. Lindbeck, *The Nature of Doctrine*, pp. 114f.

11. Clifford Geertz, *The Interpretation of Culture: Selected Essays* (New York: Basic Books, 1973), p. 119.

12. Geertz, *The Interpretation of Culture*, p. 122.

13. Talal Asad, "Anthropological Conceptions of Religion: Reflections on Geertz," *Man* 18 (1983): 250.

own strong notion of inhabiting religious symbols, emphasizes the need for religion to absorb the world. We get no sense in Lindbeck that the intratextual and extratextual worlds crisscross and overlap in a believer or a community, or that the religious world is being shaped by the nonreligious world as well as shaping it.

What Lindbeck gains by construing the influence between religious and nonreligious worlds unidirectionally is a strong sense of Christian identity within changing cultures. Yet the gain in religious and theological security comes at the cost of hermeneutical simpleness. We can look at our culture through the lenses of religious texts only *as we look at these texts through the lenses of our culture.* The notion of inhabiting the biblical story is hermeneutically naive because it presupposes that those who are faced with the biblical story can be completely "dis-lodged" from their extratextual dwelling places and "re-settled" into intratextual homes. Neither dis-lodging nor resettling can ever quite succeed; we continue to inhabit our cultures even after the encounter with the biblical story. Hence it is not enough to recognize, as Lindbeck does in a good postliberal fashion, that there is no neutral standpoint, that we are always shaped by traditions of beliefs and practices. An adequate methodological proposal must also take into account *that there is no pure space on which to stand even for the community of faith.* Ecclesial nonneutrality is always already shaped by the culture that the church inhabits.

Location 2

Let us assume that Lindbeck is persuaded. He is comfortable with the claim that Christians always inhabit more than the intratextual world and is willing to make required adjustments in the program of absorbing the extratextual world. Is the notion of "textuality" on which his methodological proposal rests theologically plausible? Is Lindbeck's description of religion as a "cultural-linguistic system" adequate?

The "text" Lindbeck invites us to inhabit, stands for "a kind of cultural and/or linguistic framework or medium that shapes the entirety of life and thought." As a cultural-linguistic medium, religion consists both of a language and of its correlative form of life. The language of religion is the "doctrines, cosmic stories or myths, and ethical directives"; the forms of life are "the rituals it practices, the sentiments or experiences it [religious tradition] evokes, the actions it recommends, and the institutional forms it develops."[14] To be a religious person means to inhabit such a cultural-linguistic system; to be a Christian means to interiorize "the language that speaks of Christ" and behavior correlative to such language.

14. Lindbeck, *The Nature of Doctrine,* p. 33.

How are "language" and "forms of life" related, however? Lindbeck does not give us a precise answer, but it seems clear, as James J. Buckley has noted, that "the analogy of religions to languages . . . controls the analogy to cultures, ways of living, and forms of life."[15] Following Geertz explicitly, Lindbeck is primarily (though not exclusively) interested in religion as a "semiotic system,"[16] as a "system of meanings embodied in the symbols which make up the religion proper."[17]

If we accept a Geertzian interpretation of Lindbeck — and he himself has summarized his position in thoroughly Geertzian terms — a significant contrast emerges between how Lindbeck and how the New Testament (and the Christian tradition) speak of the location of Christians. In the New Testament, of course, we read nothing of inhabiting a "cultural-linguistic system" or "texts." Much more prosaically, we are told that Christians live, on the one hand, "in Corinth" or "in Rome" and, on the other hand, in some mysterious way also "in God" or "in Christ"; they inhabit both "Corinth" and "God," "Rome" and "Christ," at the same time. It is not that the New Testament is ignorant of the relation between Christians and the language of faith. But the relationship is exactly inverse of the one Lindbeck postulates between Christians and the Christian "story": the "word of Christ" is supposed to "dwell in them richly," not they in the word of Christ (Col. 3:16); they, "the saints and faithful brothers and sisters," dwell in that peculiar double habitation described with the unusual phrase "in Christ in Colossae" (Col. 1:2).

Someone could object that my argument is naively biblicistic. Lindbeck, the objection could continue, is saying the same, just one step removed and in a more contemporary philosophical and anthropological jargon. Yet behind the difference in language lies a difference in perspective. Consider the obvious. Both "Corinth" and "God," both "Rome" and "Christ" are more than cultural-linguistic systems, more than symbols and corresponding patterns of behavior. "Rome" is also political power and economy; "Corinth" is also drives and desires. To live in Rome or Corinth means to be inserted into the nexus of political and economic interests and powers, to struggle with drives and desires that form one's personality structure. And what does it mean to live "in God"? According to Christian tradition, God undergirds both "semiotic systems" (even those that are necessary to access God!) and the multiple relations of power in which semiotic systems are always involved. God's relation to us and ours to God are therefore always more than the model of "language and signs" can express. To say that one inhabits "a semiotic system" and that one inhabits "Corinth" and "God" at the same time is to say two different things (even if cognitively both "Corinth" and "God" are accessible to us only through a system of signs).

---

15. James J. Buckley, "Doctrine in Diaspora," *The Thomist* 45 (1985): 449.
16. Lindbeck, *The Nature of Doctrine*, pp. 27-28, n. 16.
17. Geertz, *The Interpretation of Culture*, p. 125.

What the talk about inhabiting a cultural-linguistic system tends to hide from us (and what the talk about inhabiting "Corinth" and "God" implies) is that Christians are always shaped by more than just the Christian cultural-linguistic system. As citizens of "Corinth" we are shaped by structures of our political and economic life and by the structure of our personalities. Though the system of signs that our culture represents shapes these, they are partly independent factors, shaping both who we are and how we practice our faith. As those who dwell in God, we are touched by God not simply through the language and behavioral patterns we learn, but at the depths of our souls. God is there "touching" us before we inhabit the Christian cultural-linguistic system, and God continues embracing us if we choose to move out of it. All this amounts to saying that at different levels we need to talk about structures, forces, and experiences when we talk about Christian faith in the world, not just about "cultural-linguistic systems" and their influence on how we see the world and behave in it.

The same forces that shape us as Christians, shape also our cultural-linguistic system. One way to get at my point here is to ask an innocent but I believe profound question: "If I am supposed to be located in a Christian 'cultural-linguistic system,' where is that 'system' itself located?" Like some blimp fashioned out of a canvas of religious intersignifications, Lindbeck's cultural-linguistic system seems to float in mid air: we get into it and see the whole reality anew from within it; we behave differently because we are in it. "Cultural-linguistic system" is connected to the rest of the social reality, but only, so to speak, at the back end of the it, rarely at its front end. Lindbeck explores what the "culturallinguistic system" does *to the world* (and occasionally what *people as agents do* with the semiotic system to the world), but *not what the world does to the semiotic system.*The movement is all in one direction: the cultural-linguistic system does something to the larger social reality — it lets us see social reality from a different perspective; it lets us behave in it differently. Questions such as: What does it take for the semiotic system to emerge, to be kept alive, to do things we see it do? What keeps the blimp of religious intersignifications and their corresponding behavioral patterns in the air? remain unexamined.

If in the previous section ("Location 1") I pushed Lindbeck to take more seriously the hermeneutical tradition, here I want to push him not to disregard some important Marxian and poststructuralist insights. Though I believe that Michel Foucault slights the "domain of signifying structures" and elevates unduly the "relations of force,"[18] he is right in warning against reducing the relations of power to relations of meaning;[19] "semiology" may indeed be a way

---

18. Michel Foucault, *Power/Knowledge: Selected Interviews and Other Writings, 1972-1977,* trans. Colin Gordon et al. (New York: Pantheon Books, 1980), p. 114.

19. Michel Foucault, "Afterword: The Subject and Power," in *Michel Foucault: Beyond Structuralism and Hermeneutic,* 2nd ed., ed. Hubert L. Dreyfus and Paul Rabinow (Chicago: The University of Chicago Press, 1982).

of avoiding the violent character of social conflict "by reducing it to the calm Platonic form of language and dialogue," as he suggests.[20] If we grant that the distinction between the relations of force and signifying structures that Foucault is making is significant, we need to ask what is the interplay of semiotic elements and nonsemiotic forces involved in the construction and enduring power of the Christian semiotic system.

Truth

Lindbeck contrasts his own postliberal and postcritical cultural-linguistic account of religion with a traditional precritical "cognitivist" account on the one hand, and a liberal critical "experiential-expressive" one on the other. One way of reading the previous section is to see it as an attempt to retrieve the experiential dimension of Christian faith that got swept away by the force of Lindbeck's legitimate critique of the liberal experiential-expressive model. In the present section, I want to examine briefly some ambiguities of his critique of the cognitivist account of religion. As "a comprehensive scheme or story used to structure all dimensions of existence," religion is, claims Lindbeck, "not primarily a set of propositions to be believed, but is rather the medium in which one moves, a set of skills that one employs in living one's life."[21] The trick in interpreting a sentence like this is to know what "not primarily" means. How secondary is the propositions-to-be-believed side of religion?

The question is not easy to answer. Lindbeck does claim that in the case of some religions, such as Christianity, truth is "of the utmost importance." Yet we are never told what work the propositional side of religion does; it seems idle. When he compares religions, for instance, the focus is not on truth claims, but on the power of religion to conform people "to the ultimate reality and goodness that lies at the heart of things."[22] Since a given religion defines the ultimate reality and goodness, religions end up being tested in terms of their capability to make good on their own promises. What matters is the performative side of religion. A religious utterance "acquires the propositional truth of ontological correspondence only insofar as it is a performance, an act or deed, which helps create that correspondence."[23]

Important in Lindbeck's stress on performance is the insight that religious language aims at correspondence not only of the mind, but of the whole human being to the reality of God. What is deeply troubling, however, is the small word "only" (repeated in a similar context): religious utterance "acquires the propo-

20. Foucault, *Power/Knowledge*, p. 115.
21. Lindbeck, *The Nature of Doctrine*, p. 35.
22. Lindbeck, *The Nature of Doctrine*, p. 51.
23. Lindbeck, *The Nature of Doctrine*, p. 65.

sitional truth of ontological correspondence *only* insofar as it is a performance," he claims. This seems to imply that propositionally or ontologically true claims (such as "Christ is Lord") are *propositionally false* when they do not produce or are not accompanied by corresponding performance. Conversely, proposition-ally vacuous claims (such as "God is good," according to Lindbeck) are *propositionally true* if through them we commit ourselves "to thinking and acting as if God were good."[24] Lindbeck seems to consider religious sentences primarily connected with other religious sentences, and all of them together and singly are true not because they are adequate to reality, but because and insofar as they make reality adequate to them. If I see correctly, this would be the epistemo-logical side of religion as a free-floating semiotic system that seeks to absorb the world.

Bruce Marshall has argued that such an interpretation of Lindbeck (shared by many other interpreters) rests on a misunderstanding: adequate performance does not make a statement ontologically true, but provides the conditions "under which one can state a sentence which is a true proposition."[25] Lindbeck has endorsed Marshall's interpretation.[26] Though I have some reasons to remain obstinate, it would be foolish from my perspective not to grant that Marshall and Lindbeck are right on Lindbeck. For if they are, then one can speak of the ontological truth of religious utterances apart from the concrete performance of what they affirm. Then the cognitive aspect of religion is no longer idle, which is what I think one ought to assert.

Whatever the proper interpretation of Lindbeck is, it would seem curious to downplay the propositional side of religion. Phenomenologically, at the level of the self-perception of religious actors, propositionality seems built into the very fiber of religious belief. Geertz, at any rate, maintained that religion constructs meaning under two conditions: it must affirm something, and what it affirms must have "an appearance of objectivity."[27] "What any particular religion affirms about the fundamental nature of reality may be obscure, shallow, or, all too often, perverse; but it must . . . affirm something."[28] And what it affirms must be portrayed not "as subjective human preferences but as the imposed conditions for life implicit in a world with a particular structure."[29] That is to say that the "meaning" acceptable to religious actors cannot be seen by them as constructed out of arbitrary signs, but (at least in part) out of true propositions.

It could be that I am mistaken about "religion." Perhaps in some postcritical age religious semiotic systems will flourish. We will know that they are not true in the ordinary sense of the word, and we will still let them shape our lives because

---

24. Lindbeck, *The Nature of Doctrine*, p. 67.
25. Bruce D. Marshall, "Aquinas as Postliberal Theologian," *The Thomist* 53 (1989): 364.
26. George A. Lindbeck, "Response to Bruce Marshall," *The Thomist* 53 (1989): 403.
27. Geertz, *The Interpretation of Culture*, p. 131.
28. Geertz, *The Interpretation of Culture*, pp. 98-99.
29. Geertz, *The Interpretation of Culture*, p. 131.

they project a world we would like to inhabit. Just perhaps. But in such an age, should we be content with adding our own Christian religious cultural-linguistic system to many others? I think not. Earlier my argument was that the purpose of the Christian story is not to make us inhabit that story. Instead, the story witnesses to the re-creation of the world that God brought about when Jesus Christ entered the networks of significations and of powers proclaiming and enacting the kingdom of God; when he was crucified, resurrected, and seated at the right hand of God. Hence the *truth* of the Christian story consists in adequately pointing to the "performance" of Jesus Christ and the Spirit of God, not in eliciting our performance, though that is what this story aims for. If *God* and *God's grace* are the proper objects of religion and theology (rather than religion and theology being just efficacious talk about the talk about God), then religion and theology must be at their core propositional.[30]

Power

Whether religious language is true because it corresponds to who God is and to the history of Jesus Christ or because it creates this correspondence, it is essential for theologians not to be simply interested in the propositional side of religious language. As Lindbeck rightly underlines, religious language is meant to *do* something. This brings us again to the question of power — that nonsemiotic something that undeniably shapes our individual and social behavior.

In his complex analysis of truth and power, Michel Foucault insists on a reciprocal relationship between the two (though tending to dissolve truth into a product of power). On the one hand, each society with its own network of power relations and power techniques develops its own "regime of truth"; on the other hand, "truth" also induces "effects of power."[31] Through mechanisms of power, a society creates and "conveys its knowledge" as well as "ensures its survival under the mask of knowledge."[32] Power produces truth; truth exerts power. Lindbeck, I suspect, would be comfortable with the idea of truth exerting power, for he insists that the true story creates correspondence with the divine reality. But how about the other side of the relation? I think it is incumbent on theologians to think about the way power is involved in the creation and maintenance of "truth."

If we clearly distingish between what is "true" and what is "made to function as true" — a distinction Foucault does not seem overly eager to embrace — the idea that *knowledge never functions outside power* seems theologi-

30. See Walter Kasper, "Postmodern Dogmatics: Toward a Renewed Discussion of Foundations in North America," *Communio (U.S.)* 17 (1990): 189.

31. Foucault, *Power/Knowledge*, p. 131.

32. Michel Foucault, *Language, Counter-Memory, Practice: Selected Essays and Interviews*, trans. Donald F. Bouchard and Sherry Simon (Ithaca: Cornell University Press, 1977), p. 225.

cally very significant. In Foucault's thought, this idea is closely related to the claim that power is not simply localized here or there or possessed by this or that person (say, a sovereign). Instead, power is " 'always already there', and one is never 'outside' it."[33] Power is "co-extensive with the social body; there are no spaces of primal liberty between meshes of its network."[34] As a consequence, one possesses knowledge or even truth always *within* multiple relations of power.

It would not be difficult to show how some such (though modified!) account of power and knowledge could be defended on theological grounds. Assuming that it can, I wish here only to draw attention to the consequences of such a view concerning the interrelation of power and knowledge for the understanding of Christian faith and the task of theology. As theologians we could be tempted to dismiss Foucault's contention and seek refuge in the reaffirmation either of the cognitive power of our "sets of beliefs" (if we are traditionalists) or of the semiotic power of our system of intersignifications (if we are postliberals). To do so would be a mistake, however, and a serious one — the fact that it is frequently made notwithstanding. Though the question of power is almost absent from the writings of theologians, in the Bible it figures prominently. We need to pay careful attention to the biblical discourse of power and explore what kind of power Christians should exercise. The answer, I suggest, is neither "worldly power" nor "no power," but *the power of the crucified Christ."*

Consider the interrelation between wisdom and power as Paul addresses the "foolishness" and the "weakness" of the cross in 1 Corinthians 1–2. The "rulers of this age" (2:8), the "strong" (1:27), do not understand the cross; it is foolishness and weakness to them. But to those who are "called" by God (1:24), the "word of the cross" (1:18) — or rather "Christ crucified" himself (1:23) — is both the power and the wisdom of God. The nature of the Christian church and its proclamation, Paul argues, must correspond to the life of the one who is proclaimed. The crucified Christ must be proclaimed "in weakness and in fear and in much trembling" (2:3), not with "plausible words of wisdom, but with a demonstration of the Spirit and of power" so that the faith of the hearers "might rest not on human wisdom but on the power of God" (2:5).

Notice that the crucified Christ is not a Messiah without power; he is a Messiah with a new kind of power — the power of "what is weak" that puts to shame "the strong," the power of "the things that are not" that reduces to "nothing the things that are" (1:28). Theology as reflection on the word of the cross must be embodied in the community of the cross *whose particular kind of weakness is a new kind of power inserted into the network of the powers of the world.* That new network of power does not create Christian truth and cannot

33. Foucault, *Power/Knowledge*, p. 141.
34. Foucault, *Power/Knowledge*, p. 142.

109

therefore be a substitute for it. Instead, it sustains the truth, not so much by providing plausibility structures as by providing a space within networks of power in which the truth about Christ — which is always a truth about power — can be lived out; the new network of power sustains truth by providing, if you wish, livability structures. The new network of power, which Christian community should be, sets the truth free to exercise its own specific kind of power.

Center and System

If I am reading Lindbeck correctly, what drives his project at least in part is the desire to retrieve the unity of Western culture lost in the wake of progressive de-Christianization. The mission of the church in the postmodern world is to supply the wider culture with "the conceptual and imaginative vocabularies, as well as grammar and syntax, with which we construe reality."[35] The language of Christian faith must become again "the tongue," the medium of the larger cultural conversation about the great issues of the day. In his hand, outstretched to the culture, Lindbeck holds the scriptural world, and he is issuing an invitation to come inhabit it. His missionary program is: re-Christianize the de-Christianized Western culture.

If I am reading contemporary societies correctly, the re-Christianization of the culture will not succeed, not because the world is worse than it used to be, but because it is structured in such a way that it must reject all hands that want to help it the way Lindbeck seemingly does. Whereas in traditional societies there was a symbolic center that held them together and through which influence on the whole could be exercised, in contemporary societies this is no longer the case. What sociologists call the functional differentiation of society — the fact that various subsystems specialize in performing particular functions, such as economic, educational, or communication activity — implies (relative) self-sufficiency and self-perpetuation of those social subsystems. And self-perpetuation means resistance of the subsystems to the values brought to it from the outside.[36]

It is not easy to know what the social role of Christian faith can be under these conditions. One of the major challenges for theology today is to rethink Christian social responsibility in a functionally differentiated world. What is

35. George A. Lindbeck, "The Church's Mission to a Postmodern Culture," in *Postmodern Theology: Christian Faith in a Pluralist World*, ed. Frederic B. Burnham (New York: Harper & Row, 1989), pp. 39-40.

36. For a brief summary of this argument see Niklas Luhmann, "Paradigm lost: Über die ethische Reflexion der Moral. Rede anläßlich der Verleihung des Hegel-Preises 1989," in *Paradigm lost: Über die Ethische Reflexion der Moral*, ed. Niklas Luhmann and Robert Spaemann (Frankfurt a. M.: Suhrkamp, 1991), pp. 23-24.

certain, however, is that re-Christianization will not work for the simple reason that Christian faith cannot locate itself at the center in order to exercise from there an integrative function; a social center no longer exists. Should the impossibility of re-Christianization of the Western culture trouble Christians? It can be persuasively argued that the center is not the place where Christian faith should be anyway. That faith was born on the margins to serve the whole humanity. The Messiah of the world was crucified outside the gate; the resurrected Lord, with all authority on heaven and earth, appeared to a few, charging them with a mission. Social marginality is not to be bemoaned, but celebrated — not as a ghetto protected from the rest of the culture by a high wall of private communal language and practices, but as a place from which the church can, speaking its own proper language, address public issues, and holding fast to its own proper practices, initiate authentic transformations in its social environment.

Closely related to the functional differentiation of contemporary societies is their insuppressible cultural plurality, reinforced by rapid social change. As a consequence, we inescapably inhabit a multicultural or multilingual world. It would be a mistake in such a situation to seek to retrieve the language of faith as some kind of universal metalanguage, unifying all other languages we speak, a Christian version of the universal Esperanto of modernity or a post-Christian version of a premodern cultural Christianity. Robert Bellah suggested that instead we need to become "genuinely multilingual, speaking the language of science and psychology where they are appropriate, but also speaking the language of the Bible and of citizenship unashamedly and well."[37]

A theology appropriate to multilingual people living in functionally differentiated and culturally pluralistic societies should be conceived primarily as a nonsystemic and critical intellectual endeavor — a proposition Lindbeck would certainly not disagree with. In a time of "increasing interdependence, cultural diversity and historical change," Stephen Toulmin argued, the intellectual task before natural and social scientists is "not to build new, more comprehensive systems of theory with universal and timeless relevance, but to limit the scope of even the best-framed theories, and fight the intellectual reductionism that became entrenched during the ascendancy of rationalism." We should "pay less attention to *stability* and *system*, more attention to *function* and *adaptability*."[38] The same, I would argue, holds true of theology. The more systemically rigorous and timeless our theologies are, the less useful they will be in the diverse situations of our fast-changing cultures (which by no means entails the claim that the *least* systemically rigorous theology — a haphazard conglomera-

37. Robert N. Bellah, "Christian Faithfulness in a Pluralist World," in *Postmodern Theology: Christian Faith in a Pluralist World,* ed. Frederic B. Burnham (New York: Harper & Row, 1989), p. 89.

38. Stephen Toulmin, *Cosmopolis: The Hidden Agenda of Modernity* (New York: The Free Press, 1990), pp. 184, 192-93.

tion of theological assertions — will be the most useful). Does theology so conceived forfeit its universal claim? To the contrary: It is *because* "Jesus Christ is the same yesterday and today and forever," it is *because* Christian faith is for all times and all places, that our theologies need to be nonsystemic, contextual, and flexible.

Theology between Pain and Delight of God

Jürgen Moltmann — who offered his public both beautiful and complex theological melodies, reserving most of his throat-clearing to the privacy of his study — started his keynote address at the American Academy of Religion in Chicago (1994) with the following words: "It is simple, but true, to say that theology has only one, single problem: *God.* We are theologians for the sake of God. God is our dignity. God is our agony. God is our hope."[39] But, he asked, who is this God? Both the subject of God's own existence and a passionate lover of the world, he answered. And then, turning from the vision of God to the character of theology, Moltmann continued:

> For me theology springs from a *divine passion:* that is the open wound of God in one's own life and in the tormented men, women, and children of this world. . . . But for me theology also springs from God's *love for life,* the love for life which we experience in the presence of the life-giving Spirit, and which enables us to move beyond our resignation, and begin to love life here and now. These are also Christ's two experiences of God, and because of that they are the foundation of Christian theology too: God's delight and God's pain.

Because God's delight and God's pain are not circumscribed by the walls of ecclesial communities and universities, theology can neither just feed the pious souls in the church nor just delight the inquisitive minds in the academy. Beyond the church, beyond the academy, the horizon of theology is the world as the place of the coming reign of God. For the sake of the future of the world, that object of God's pain and God's delight, theology must be a public endeavor, Moltmann insisted, "a public theology for the public gospel."[40]

The purpose of my critical conversation with Lindbeck was to rethink public theology in a post-Christian, post-industrial, and post-modern context. I argued that Christians and their theologies are always situated in a given culture; we understand Christian faith as we do because we see it with spectacles tinted by our culture ("Location 1"). At the same time, I insisted that the truth

39. Jürgen Moltmann, *Theology and the Future of the Modern World* (Pittsburgh: ATS, 1995), p. 1.

40. Moltmann, *Theology and the Future of the Modern World,* p. 3.

Christians are called to proclaim and theologians to guard is a public truth, addressed to all and accessible in principle to all ("Truth"). I argued that Christians and their theologies are always situated in a given field of personal and social forces — drives, desires, and interests, struggle for goods and for power ("Location 2"). At the same time I insisted that Christian faith does not entail renunciation of relations of power, but insertion of a different set of relations of power — the power that is set free when people walk in the footsteps of the crucified Messiah — into the larger field of forces ("Power"). Finally, I argued that theology in a post-Christian and post-industrial context should celebrate the social space it was forced to inhabit — the margins — and shed all traces of nostalgia for the life in the center. It is from the margins, in the form of a nonsystemic, contextual, and flexible critical reflection, that Christian theology should exercise its role of addressing public issues in the light of the coming universal reign of God.

Here, then, is a vision of a public theology for a public gospel: looking through the spectacles of its own culture, it sees the city whose builder and architect is God; situated in multiple relations of power, it advocates the weakness of the Crucified as a new form of power; dwelling on the margins, it seeks to bring the reign of the triune God to bear on all domains of life.

Without a vision people perish, said the prophet. But without people whose hearts throb with the pain and delight of God, the vision will remain nothing more than fading ink on a sheet of paper, sound waves disappearing in space.[41]

41. For helpful comments on previous versions of this chapter I am greatly indebted to Professors Robert Cathey, Philip Clayton, and Robert H. Gundry, to the members of the Fuller Restaurant Group (in particular, Professors Judith Gundry-Volf and Nancey Murphy), and to my research assistant, Richard Heyduck.

Reviving Theology in a Time of Change

Ellen T. Charry

I. The State of the Problem

As the second Christian millennium draws to a close, theology is caught in a power struggle between two models, one academic and one activist, neither of which bears strong resemblance to what Paul, the first Christian theologian, was doing in his letters that laid down the tracks for the theological task. Paul reflected on events that transpired in his own time and tried to persuade Jews and pagans that life grounded in knowing, loving, and giving glory to God is the highest human calling. Such a grounding required a radical personal re-orientation: new modes of behavior and standards of community, and the crafting of a new self modeled on Christ himself.

Subsequent reflectors built upon their predecessors' opera as they, too, sought to persuade people, mostly pagans, to accept the new vision of the good life and to find salvation and happiness within the new people of God. The church muted national and ethnic rivalries as a result of reformation in God, positioning Christianity to receive the multicultural mantle from Roman civilization under the binding power of the cross of Christ. The moral and social transformation commended by theologians shaped the church as a transcultural community ordered toward purity of life and adoration of God.[1]

Today both academic and activist theological models disregard central features of that pastoral heritage. The academic model has turned from en-couraging personal reform through attachment to God toward articulating the logic of Christian doctrines, unearthing the history of Christian texts and politics, and analyzing ethical reasoning. It posits an autonomous self, formed in advance of engagement with God, whose reason and knowledge manipulate

---

1. Charles Norris Cochrane, *Christianity and Classical Culture: A Study of Thought and Action from Augustus to Augustine* (New York: Oxford University Press, 1944).

the ideas of the tradition. The multicultural-deconstructionist strand of activist theology embraced a secular politics of identity and power based on an ethic of self-expression in support of a sociologically, rather than a theologically formed self.[2] It thereby set aside God's power to transform cultural and ethnic differences through the cross of Christ.

The academic model cultivates and employs the intellectual virtues for the correction and interpretation of the tradition; the political model draws attention to the social virtues inherent in the Christian life. Both pursued these interests without regard for their grounding in the basic Christian exhortation: God wants people to know, love, and glorify him in an embrace of Jesus Christ. Both the academic and political models have thus lost their moorings and gone their own ways.

This chapter is written in hopes that a way may now be sought to reclaim life with God as the primary theological task, to be undertaken with intellectual rigor and social sensitivity. Although the task needs no justification, I will begin by arguing that this is an opportune moment for reclaiming theology's pastoral task. I will then suggest that, in spite of itself, the deconstructive moment opens an epistemic door to precisely that reclamation.

II. Specifying the Context

To commend theology's pastoral calling is to bring the discipline back to itself. If Christians believe God to be God, no other argument need be made. God should be glorified with our bodies and our souls because God alone is worthy of adoration, and we humans constantly need to be recalled from wandering.

Still, the dominance of the modern models calls for a case to be made for this retrieval. One practical reason to retrieve theology is that society needs Christians to express their joy in life with God — not to impose it on others. Modern secularism, lacking a doctrine of sin and the hope of salvation, cannot offer an ethic deeper than acquisition, a model of achievement other than skill, or a notion of self more engaged than "I'm OK, you're OK."

The "culture war," amidst moral and intellectual decline in the United States, suggests either that the democratic vision of equal rights, progress, and opportunity requires a deeper grounding than secularism can provide, or that democracy has become captive to such an extreme anticommunitarian rights

---

2. What I refer to as the multiculturalist-deconstructive model in theology is my impression of an academically popular ideology that runs together the deconstructive position of Jacques Derrida and Michel Foucault and their followers, including literary critics like Stanley Fish, with the multiculturalist agenda promoted by feminists and ethnic writers. In the field of theology, the feminist position is ably represented by Elisabeth Schüssler-Fiorenza and Rosemary Ruether.

orientation and outright economic greed that it is in danger of collapse.[3] The notion of community as diverse groups working together for the common good has been replaced by that of co-location: diverse groups competing for power and wealth in a common and shrinking space. It is not clear how such an ideology could be compatible with Christian teachings. But it is clear that the Christian church offers an alternative model of community, one that transforms individuals — even former adversaries — into companions who enjoy God together.

While liberal theology embraced democratic values, it is not clear that political theologies in the United States ever did. James Cone patterned black theology on the nationalist Black Power movement, not the careful amalgam of Christian, democratic, and nonviolent teachings forged by Martin Luther King, Jr. Subsequently, feminist and other political ideologues, following Nietzsche, Derrida, and Foucault, synthesized identity politics — with Marxist undercurrents — with a radical critique of beauty, truth, and goodness in the name of power. The resultant multiculturalist ideology trusts in the ability of power to enhance specific groups on the secular assumption that there is no other reality on which to rely. Again, Christianity offers another way, because at its center lie alternative visions of power, community, salvation, goodness, and truth as given to us by God. These are understandings that we must be given because we are unable to envision them on our own.

The multiculturalist ideology contains no narrative that commends the compromise or joint action that is needed in order for diversity to promote peace. Since the current epistemic breakdown admits no overarching narratives, the culture lacks a framework for cohesion. Untempered special interests, whether religious, cultural, political, or economic, promote conflict and, if unmoderated, social breakdown, because they carry with them no moral responsibility beyond one's own interest group.

Perhaps nothing illustrates the present state of affairs so well as the society's inability to civilize its children. School and family are unable to hold children's attention long enough to rear them; or perhaps the decline of civility and propriety is so great that school and family can no longer identify standards for educating and nurturing children. The lack of a national will to eliminate drugs and guns and to set limits on popular culture and individual rights speaks to the breakdown of civil society, precisely the goal of the postmodern academic assault on Western civilization.

This climate reminds religious communities of their civilizing function. Such communities uphold social cooperation; attending to the needs of others; compromise for the sake of ends larger than personal or group needs; attending

---

3. Amitai Etzioni, *The Spirit of Community* (New York: Crown Publishers, 1993); and James Davison Hunter, *Culture Wars: The Struggle to Define America* (New York: Basic Books, 1991); Jean Bethke Elstain, *Democracy on Trial* (New York: Basic Books, 1995).

to texts, history, and trained leadership; and, at least once upon a time, hope for life with God. In short, religious life orders, identifies, and directs one's personal narrative beyond oneself and one's circle of intimates. And that is the crux of civilized societies. Religious communities that experience themselves as marginalized or misunderstood should recognize the important role they play in a fragmented and morally confused society simply by being present in the lives of their members.

This decline calls Christians to serve society by strengthening the churches; it invites theology to reclaim its task of helping people attend to God. What is wanted is theology that can assist in the formation of persons who learn from God that forgiveness, repentance, self-control, humility, compassion, and compromise enhance human happiness and ground genuine community. The church, a community of those who know, love, and give glory to God, is well-accoutered to form just such persons. In short, the society does not need Christians to take it over by political cunning — Christians are notoriously inept governors — but it does need them to live Christian lives in public, to let their light shine, perhaps more in action than in words.

A second reason for reviving theology at the moment is more positive. Old doctrinal debates that pitted loving God against having faith are weakening. This is partly due to good scholarship and to the ecumenical movement (for example, the Lutheran-Episcopal Concordat and Catholic-Lutheran consultation), but also to the fact that some theological issues have taken on different coloration with the passing of centuries and as a consequence of Vatican II.

For example, while the issue of adult versus infant baptism may still arouse the ire of some, the general theology of baptism has changed. First, the low incidence of infant mortality in North America means that baptism is no longer an urgent need here. But more significantly, since Vatican II, baptism is increasingly understood as the divine grafting of an individual into the body of Christ rather than the washing away of original sin. This places baptism in a public and communal rather than a private and individualist context. Within a "body of Christ" or "people of God" ecclesiology, the point at which baptism is administered may still be of interest, but these ecclesiologies allow for various practices without disagreeing on the objectivity of divine action in the act. The new ecclesiology invites a rethinking of baptismal (and more generally of sacramental) theology that focuses on the nature and formation of Christian identity rather than on individual salvation through the sacramental system.

Another troublesome intra-Protestant division has been over high and low doctrines of grace: Augustine versus Pelagius, Synod of Dort versus Arminius. Patient scholarly work is nuancing our vision of the past and helping us to see that harsh theological rhetoric may have served more to strengthen one's position than one's argument. Thus, medieval positions at one time dismissed as Pelagian are recognized as grounded in a doctrine of grace; while the theology of Martin Luther is being reclaimed as deeply Catholic.[4] This rapprochement paves the way for Protestants as well as Catholics not only to elucidate the logic that animates Christian doctrines, but also to cultivate the virtue of loving God.

Reclamation of patristic and medieval theology by Protestant scholars also changes the theological landscape. Recent scholarship and ecumenism are bringing to Protestant attention the riches of the Catholic and Orthodox heritages, where reform of the self through devotion and deification are central. It is essential that the current wave of moral criticism being leveled at the tradition not be allowed to deter this movement by training a generation of scholars that irresponsibly dismisses the classical tradition without reading it.

A third reason to reclaim premodern models of theology, especially in theological schools, is that the modern theological disciplines no longer attend to Christian formation. Biblical studies and church history are largely responsible to the disciplines of secular history or literary theory. Historians are not trained to pursue normative questions, or to promote knowledge and love of God. Today these secularized disciplines are being taken over by poststructuralist scholars for whom Christian commitments are a form of tyranny, perhaps a natural outgrowth of some themes in Voltaire.

This circumstance vividly points up the notion of the autonomous self that lies beneath both modern models. The academic paradigm places the self outside and in control of the theological enterprise on the grounds that human cognition properly judges the adequacy of the truth of God. The political paradigm, following J. J. Rousseau, assumes a whole self oppressed by external forces and not ultimately in need of the transforming power of God's grace, beyond encouraging one to fight those with power.

A fourth reason to consider alternative models for theology is really a subset of the third. The key critical theological discipline, systematic theology, is dying as a result of the postmodern epistemic crisis. Modern systematic theology attempted to organize Christian beliefs and practices within a modern epistemic framework in response to the assault on theological knowledge by the Enlightenment. Within this school, Karl Barth may represent its finest and perhaps final hour. In an important sense, Barth broke with the modern tradition by rejecting the need for a secular epistemic framework by which to judge the adequacy of Christian claims, reconstructing the discipline instead on its own intellectual foundation — revelation — and unfurling it around a single christological principle. The magnificent "cathedral" that Barth constructed undertook more and deeper corrective and reconstructive theological tasks than perhaps any before it. Barth finally proclaimed God's freedom from every human construction of self, culture, and philosophy.

---

4. Tuomo Mannermaa, "Theosis as a Subject of Finnish Luther Research," *Pro Ecclesia* 4 (1995): 37-48.

It may be that Barth's magisterial accomplishment was the last stand of academic theology, at least for a good while. For now the very notion of general knowledge, be it through non-Christian philosophy or revelation, is heavily criticized. As is often the case following periods of great intellectual synthesis, epistemology is in disarray. So theology is again left lurching in the dark for epistemic support — only this time it is not only theological claims that must be defended, but claims to any objective knowledge at all. Nietzsche's children now train their guns at all the academic disciplines, not only at theology. The deconstructive moment names all attempts at beauty, truth, and goodness as social constructions of reality for the sake of manipulating power. Ironically, in this nihilistic, or more precisely solipsistic move, ostensibly against the manipulation of power, the will to power finally opposes all comers. Knowledge is no longer to be discerned, since texts have no rights. Truth is no longer disclosed by revelation or reason, for "truth" is only the attempt of one cultural system to impose itself on another. Indeed, cultural relativism claims that intellectual endeavor is no longer worthwhile because truth has been traded in for opinion. Thus, the multicultural-deconstructive project hopes to bring the very possibility of truth and knowledge to a grinding halt.

The argument for reclaiming theology that aims to form Christians, then, is as follows: The church's primary task is to help people know and love God. In addition, and through this responsibility, it has a social responsibility; and, if able to reclaim its original calling, it is equipped to exercise it at a time when the general culture is in crisis. The success of the ecumenical movement provides an opportunity to reclaim the pastoral task of the apostolic faith: to know and love God. The secularization of the theological disciplines prevents them from speaking about attending to God, and the fragmentation of the disciplines makes it impossible for them to cooperate in this task even if they could articulate it. Additionally, politicization of theology, along with the Nietzschean assault on knowledge and morality, makes it impossible for theological disciplines grounded in Enlightenment forms of rationalism and empiricism even to find grounds on which to make Christian claims, let alone commend life centered in God.

III. Beyond the Impasse

The nihilist version of the deconstructive moment claims that knowledge, at least to the extent that it implies publicness, is dead — therefore all is permitted. But just what is the knowledge that is claimed to be dead, and what is offered in its place? What is hailed as dead is basically the same understanding of knowledge that the Enlightenment claimed to discredit: knowledge taken on trust, accumulated from one to another, or acquired by training and practice; in short, any knowledge that the individual does not personally oversee. The popular deconstructive move, like many before it, wants knowledge put in the hands of each interpreter in the name of freedom, regardless of the mind's cultivation for it. That is, it wants to deny the traditional assumptions that reasoning is a skilled reflective practice that requires training and that knowledge has a centripetal binding function among individuals across time and space. This fear of the colonization of the mind by alien forces is based upon an Enlightenment assumption of the autonomous self that needs no help.

Taken to its logical conclusion, however, such personally controlled "knowledge" is no longer public, no longer transmissible, and therefore, finally, not socially helpful. A society could not survive on a private rather than public notion of knowledge, for there would be nothing but impulsive solipsism. Indeed, it is unclear whether the word *knowledge* is appropriate any longer on this view, because the word itself implies publicness, transmissibility, and re-flection.

What is criticized is not only any public understanding of knowledge, but also, when the multicultural element is added, any claim to truth — that is, any overarching frame of reference that claims to be cross-cultural. General frames of reference are characterized — or caricatured — as thinly veiled power manipulations. Those who have contributed to the advancement of knowledge have been parochial while claiming to be universal, prejudiced while claiming to be objective, and self-interested while claiming to be rational. For what is wanted is supposedly interpretive freedom — freedom to construct one's men-tal and social world autonomously — so that one is protected from external influence and exerts one's identity against received authorities who may mute one's individuality. Yet to pit freedom against knowledge in this way does not really respond to the notion of knowledge in the modern sense, because knowl-edge and the reasoning on which the modern university is founded have always and only had an open-ended and progressive view of knowledge — one that builds upon, enhances, corrects, and modifies knowledge upon subsequent reflection. Framing the argument as the pitting of knowledge taken on trust against knowledge discerned by the autonomous individual is a caricature of the modern understanding of knowledge.

Despite the desire of deconstruction to create an anti-epistemology of no knowledge, no reason, no truth, no goodness beyond self, it nevertheless claims authority for itself, a kind of "truth" for its claims. How so? I want to suggest that deconstruction, joined to the multiculturalist claim, is an odd amalgam of two interpretations of the self: an autonomous self deriving from Descartes and Rousseau, and a culturally embedded self deriving from Piaget with help, perhaps, from Aristotle. Rousseau's romantic view, relied upon — perhaps inadvertently — by feminists, is that the good, natural self is distorted by civilization; it flourishes when isolated from it or by repudiating its influ-ence. This stands in tension with Piaget's cognitive developmental psychology that views the self not as unfolding against civilization, but as formed by and in learning, through interactions with experience and with the environment, that is, with culture.[5]

The deconstructionist aspect of the postmodern self follows Rousseau; the multiculturalist aspect offers a biocultural twist on Piaget. From one perspective, the romantic self posited by the feminist version of the hermeneutic of suspicion is a self-formed, self-directed, self-confident self of modernity that interprets reality and the texts it encounters in subjective terms. But to speak of a self-created, self-directed, autonomous self is itself, at best, a sketchy undertaking. Is there really such a thing as an autonomous, self-directed self that takes nothing on authority, trusts nothing but its own judgments, and stands over against the world and the text in freedom? Is not the idea of such a self a naive notion that neglects the cultural, social, and religious formation of which Descartes himself was, albeit unconsciously, a perfect example, and which the multiculturalists themselves celebrate?

Yet this is not the whole story. For in addition to the autonomous self, the multicultural liberationists make precisely the opposite claim: that the self is formed by experience in a tradition, a subculture; only it is an alternative one having practices, texts, companions, and needs that are not identical to those that inform the judgments made by the dominant authorities. The point, then, is not really freedom from determination of the self on the modern model, but rather a preference for certain influences that enable perspectives missed by the dominant group to be spotlighted by another.

But even these two tensive elements, one seeking freedom from determination, the other seeking parochial forms of cultural influence, do not circumscribe the deconstructive multiculturalist self. For some versions of the position also claim a natural element that hopes to screen out influences deemed undesirable because alien: for example, women are naturally nurturing and compassionate; men, domineering and controlling. These precultural features of temperament are meant to act as a screen so that the self can be encouraged in accord with its nature. Feminists in this camp want women only to read literature written by feminists who share their views of feminism, so that they can be reinforced in their "own" identity. But the range of options turns out to be narrow indeed, limited as it is to certain strands of feminist thought. And what are claimed to be temperamental predilections for mutuality, cooperation, and compassion in women turn out to support a double-standard anthropology with women having the morally superior temperament. (Ironically, the claim for women's temperamental moral superiority is made using "male" strategies that argue for power and dominance of women or a women's ethic or ways of knowing!)

What seems to be at work, then, is a contradictory view of how persons are formed that now prefers freedom over temperament, now temperament over culture, and now certain cultures and temperaments over freedom. The

5. Robert Kegan, *The Evolving Self* (Cambridge: Harvard University Press, 1982).

position thus does not really claim freedom for the individual as the modern self does. It pleads for freedom to form the self by socialization into a narrow subculture that in some cases is guided by temperament, in which case the cultural and social dimensions of the claims to self-determination are muted — and cognitive formation is peripheral.

At the same time, such feminists select a carefully controlled subculture in which the self is to be healed by withdrawal from the dominant culture and immersion in the subculture that perhaps nourishes what is believed to be a natural temperament. A still narrower view would suggest that within temperamental limits, further socialization is yet desired. There would appear to be little freedom in any of these options, even were such an impractical, theoretical framework realistic. And perhaps most disturbingly, this counsel of retreat from "foreign" ideas, companions, and cultures finally discourages women from energetic participation in nonfeminist texts and ways of thinking, confining them instead to a feminist ghetto. This sectarian vision of self and knowledge is as divisive as the private view, as various groups seek to create knowledge for their own political purposes with no basis for cross-cultural communication. Each cultural group is deemed to be self-sufficient and, since each culture claims autonomy and immunity from influence, each conceives itself to be beyond criticism. Perhaps the term *multicultural* is a misnomer. For what is sought is really serial uniculturalism.

This multicultural/deconstructive "corrective" of modernity claims that there is no universal knowledge, but only parochial knowledge, knowledge constructed by the interpretive capacities and temperament of the group. It has difficulty moving between groups precisely because the peculiarities of formation of each group are unique. Thus the mistake Kant made in describing the conditions of the mind that construct knowledge, according to these postmoderns, is that he failed to account for the cultural determination and cast of mind that construct knowledge. Ironically, he presumed a freedom within the limits of universal reason that the postmodern multiculturalists deny. Perhaps they have a point.

If the postmoderns wish to offer a humble corrective to modern epistemology and Christian theology, it ought not to be in the name of further privatization or sectarianism, but in the name of recognizing particular types of *accompaniedness* — that is, embeddedness in ways of being in the world that affect how and what we see and think. What is wanted, rather, is the thoughtful prioritizing of sorts of accompaniedness through careful discernment. On this view, it is easy to make an argument for the retrieval of Christian formation not only as a legitimate way of knowing, but also as a desirable form of accompaniedness. For Christians trust in a self both created by and ready to be reformed by God: they *want* to be accompanied. And so they embed themselves in trusted and desired company for the sake of influence. This puts Christians in tension with the autonomous self of the Enlightenment. The Christian view is not satisfied, however, in the company of a preselected, enclosed cultural or temperamental identity; but rather it desires the company of God who is not a Feuerbachian projection of one's own culture or biology, but who comes to us as, of all arbitrary things, an ancient Jewish peasant, to remake our temperament and reshape the context of our socialization. A Christian is formed in the same way as a child is formed. The child models what she sees, becomes what she experiences, learns the language she hears and the culture she absorbs. Her ability to absorb new information and data informs her personality as these are assimilated into patterns of cognition and affect already in place. So, too, the Christian thinks and knows Christianly by being formed by knowing, loving, and worshipping precisely a God who is different from ourselves in the company of others who share that commitment.

The point that the serial uniculturalist and the Christian share with one another, but not with the modern self, is that we become what we know. We become the company we keep with guidance from our DNA. That is why parents are concerned about their children's friends, teachers, and entertainments. For it is easy to see how impressionable children are. Are adults impervious to influence as the Enlightenment model would suggest? Or has the myth of autonomy created a macho shield against the notion of accompaniment and influence, lest the fragile self be given away?

Put in these terms, Christians are those who do not fear giving themselves away. Rather, they are mature enough to embed themselves in God over against competing formative influences of culture, whether dominant or subdominant, for the shaping of their minds and behavior, that is, their selves. Thus, while the structure of the brain may vary slightly from individual to individual, the self varies greatly depending on how it is developed.

On this view, multiculturalist-deconstruction could offer a helpful corrective to Western Christians who have been so blinded by the Constantinian establishment that they became arrogant about their epistemic hegemony. But whether the insights gained are helpful or harmful depends upon how the issue is framed. If the argument is that cultural polytheism is morally superior to monotheism because it is more tolerant, or celebrates our natural selves, then it will be difficult for Christians to grasp the benefits to be gained from embracing the multiculturality of the circumstance. But if the insight is that multiculturality — not serial uniculturalism — is a circumstance of which Christians need to take more pastoral cognizance, it may be hearable, for it may enable Christians who once were supported by the culture to gain a broader perspective on how selves are formed and the ways God reaches out to us to conform us to himself.

The difference, then, between the serial unicultural-deconstructionist and the postmodern Christian comes at three points of judgment: (1) whether, as Feuerbach put it, God is a strategic tool that we form after our image and likeness, or whether God is real and humans need God to form us; (2) how to determine which set of influences will be desired and which disfavored; and,

(3) as Nietzsche put it, whether the framework of influence selected should aggrandize or moderate individual cultures.

By now we have brought ourselves back to the world of Origen, Athanasius, and Augustine with its understanding of the formation of the self as a delicate and graceful process in which the self is reformed by what it knows, by the tradition and community in which it places itself. We moderns have lost the dynamic that they knew, that a self is in constant process of formation, and that it must struggle throughout life, not just through adolescence, against temptations to be formed by lesser goods than God. They also knew that to be formed by God, one had to become skilled at knowing, to be still and know that God is God. On the simple principle that we become what we know, by training ourselves to know God, indeed to know God deeply and truly, we become as like to God as possible. This is the patristic doctrine of *theosis*. In principle it is no different from formation in any other tradition, culture, gender, or racial identity. And in this regard, like the serial uniculturalists, Christianity, too, is parochial, yet in a decisively multicultural way because it embraces all cultures in God.

Now admittedly it is frightening to put oneself in God's hands. We think we have so much more control when we remain within the cultural categories that are already so familiar. St. Paul knew this only too well from dealing with the Corinthian and the Roman Christians. And the Fathers, seeking to turn pagans into Christians, understood this vividly. Our struggle is no different from theirs; only we are conscious of a long history of Christian mistakes, mistakes that deformed rather than reformed persons in the image of God. And perhaps it is well that we proceed with fear and trembling on such heavily plowed ground. For giving oneself to God requires resisting formation by competitors such as possessions and power, but also by exclusive nationalisms or by suffering; and it means deferring to an authority higher than ourselves. This makes the reclamation of theology frightening because it curbs our power.

The postmodern moment offers Christian theologians an opportunity to return to theology's original task of making Christians out of pagans. The need is to encourage persons again to allow themselves to accede to God, by placing themselves in God's company, so that God's grace and power can heal and transform them. This is the original task of interpreting the violent events that took place in first-century Palestine and the Christian texts and doctrines that resulted therefrom. Perhaps the setting, going into the third Christian millennium, offers enough similarity to these days that the possibility of knowing and loving God is again a joyous option.

IV. The Return to Knowing and Loving God

If Christians are again to claim that knowing, loving, and enjoying God are the foundation of a happy life, they will need to find a way to talk about it. Alasdair

MacIntyre's and Martha Nussbaum's work of retrieving the Aristotelian insight into formation through practice, skill, and affection, guided by a moral tradition and its literature, suggests one way of understanding what is involved in the formation of Christians.[6] A retrieval of the Platonic understanding of love and knowledge, dominant throughout the Patristic age, has yet to be undertaken, although Charles Taylor has hinted at what would be involved.[7] The resources on the theological side are vast in both East and West. Tracks have already been laid down by theologians and historians of both traditions that lead in this direction. Gerhard Ladner, Rowan Williams, and Rowan Greer are but three writers who have elucidated the pastoral dimensions of the Western heritage.[8] And Vladimir Lossky and John Meyendorff have done the same for Byzantine theology.[9]

The constructive challenge will be to translate theological insights of the past into theological language that speaks to contemporary readers. This will necessitate some deconstruction of modern secularism, which will have to be recognized as a time-bound construction rather than simply as the truth unmasked. Within this large task, it will be necessary to engage the anthropology or psychology of modernity and secularism that cannot acknowledge that we need help. A postmodern pastoral Christian theology will need to argue that dependence on God's power to build and reform the self is more realistic and freeing and is therefore truer than the secular insistence on self-formation.

Under any discussion of the retrieval of divine guidance lies the central modern stumbling block to theology: skepticism about the reality and power of God. To address this problem, it will be helpful to reclaim a cautious, critical realism, an epistemology that can argue, minimally, that it is not silly to believe in the reality of God, and can argue, maximally, that believing in God's reality is as sensible as believing in the reality of other things, say, in the reality and power of psychotherapy, or other healing arts and sciences that rest on accumulated bodies of knowledge thoughtfully considered and applied.

Of course, Christianity stakes its truth claims not only on the reality of God, but also on the involvement of God in historical events. The modern struggle over

6. MacIntyre, *After Virtue: A Study in Moral Theory*, 2d ed. (Notre Dame, Ind.: University of Notre Dame Press, 1984); Nussbaum, *The Fragility of Goodness: Luck and Ethics in Greek Tragedy and Philosophy* (Cambridge: Cambridge University Press, 1986); *Love's Knowledge: Essays on Philosophy and Literature* (New York: Oxford University Press, 1990); and *Therapy of Desire: Theory and Practice in Hellenistic Ethics* (Princeton: Princeton University Press, 1994).

7. Taylor, *Sources of the Self: The Making of the Modern Identity* (Cambridge: Harvard University Press, 1989).

8. Ladner, *The Idea of Reform: Its Impact on Christian Thought and Action in the Age of the Fathers* (New York: Harper, 1967); Williams, *The Wound of Knowledge* (Cambridge: Cowley, 1979-90); Greer, *Broken Lights and Mended Lives: Theology and Common Life in the Early Church* (University Park, Pa.: Pennsylvania State University Press, 1986).

9. Lossky, *In the Image and Likeness of God* (Crestwood, N.Y.: St. Vladimir's Seminary Press, 1985); Meyendorff, *St. Gregory of Palamas and Orthodox Spirituality* (New York: St. Vladimir's Seminary Press, 1974).

revelation and Scripture as reliable, and now as helpful rather than harmful, will continue whatever emphases theology attends to. Christians may have to be content with less than utter certainty in such matters. After all, there never was a time when Christian claims about God's intervention in history, the truth of the incarnation and resurrection, did not have to be accepted on faith. Jews and pagans always scoffed at Christian claims. This should come as no surprise.

What is needed to call Christians back to knowing, loving, and enjoying God is the same courage and reasoning that enabled Christians and Jews to challenge the gods of Greece and Rome. In our day this may require some modest expansion of the rather narrow construal of reason constructed by Descartes, Locke, Hume, and Kant. But it will certainly not require the assault on rationality proposed by the anti-moderns. For the Enlightenment stood in continuity with the Christian tradition's appreciation of human reason, even though it greatly constricted its limits. It may be necessary to recognize ways of knowing that extend beyond reductive rationalism and empiricism. This is to suggest that the modern dualism between reason and affect is probably misplaced, and that an understanding of knowledge that takes account of the affections is truer than accounts that confine knowledge to cognition alone. Without this broader and, I would argue, more realistic understanding of knowledge, it will be impossible to speak again of enjoying God. Other theological doctrines will also have to be rethought, the doctrines of grace and sin among them.

This suggestion of a way ahead for Christian theology will be difficult. It is important to see that a return to the tradition need not perpetuate the abuses committed by the church. The claim made here is that Christianity is not exhausted by its errors and that it contains within itself the seeds of its own correction. Doing theology is more like the children's game "Whisper Down the Lane" than like "Go Fish." Christianity's truth becomes readily distorted in transmission from one to the next, so that its integrity must be guarded; the point is not to fish one's wish. It will not be easy to return to a theology that seeks to know, love, and enjoy God. But some people pine for God. Surely theologians have a responsibility to them too.

Time for God's Presence

Ingolf U. Dalferth

I

We live in a fast-paced time. No other generation has experienced as many new departures into the future as we have, and no other has had to correct and revise such new beginnings in as quick succession as we have. Will what holds true today still be valid tomorrow, when what held true yesterday is hardly still valid even today? The past recedes ever more quickly, and it is increasingly difficult to draw lessons from it either for today or for the future. We have become skeptical, and we no longer trust our own traditions since they increasingly prove to be of little use in comprehending or, especially, in solving the problems of our present, grounded as they are in life experiences that are not those of our own age and epoch. Hence, they have less and less to say to us, and daily become more and more alien.

This applies in a disconcerting way to the Christian faith in its traditional form. Both inside and outside the various churches, the ever more pervasive mood is that of living in an age of epilogue, of fading memories, and of a futile clinging to yesterday. God, many believe, has had his time, and here at the end of the second millennium that time seems to have run out. Although traces of God's memory can indeed be found in the lives of an increasing number of people, this seems to perturb only a few. Nietzsche was yet able to confirm, to the horror of his own age, that we have killed God. A hundred years later we have forgotten how to be horrified. God has largely become a matter of indifference for us; we live as if God did not exist, or at least many people do, and increasing numbers are joining them.

Of course, this is not the whole picture. We can still find traces of the past everywhere, including churches, congregations, and Christians; and new departures and new beginnings no doubt are also taking place both inside and outside the established churches. Yet the influence of the churches is unmistakably diminishing, and the objections of Christians increasingly fade away unheard.

127

One no longer expects much of Christians, at least not regarding anything determinative for today. One no longer really knows what to do with them, and one has neither time nor interest for them. Who, indeed, is still really familiar with the churches and the faith they represent? Who still finds in them the binding framework of orientation for one's own life? And who really goes to the trouble to come to terms with the substance of their views? It is not the critical objections of enlightened reason, but rather quite simply the accelerating velocity of our own daily life that is causing the Christian churches in Europe to founder. Their Waterloo is life, not thought.

Precisely this is what makes the whole situation so difficult and so theologically awkward. The teachings and practices of the Christian churches simply do not seem up to the sheer tempo of our age. Their influence is rapidly fading because an increasing number of people here expect less of them, and find less of substance for their own lives through and in them. Increasingly, people are living quite as a matter of course without these churches. Although churches and cathedrals and basilicas are appreciated as cultural and tourist monuments and concert halls, they are largely avoided in their real functions as the setting of worship assemblies of Christian congregations. A person is believed to have come of age when he or she no longer has contact with them. And one has the feeling of keeping up with the pulse of the age when one ignores the Christian faith, criticizes the church as an institution, and turns one's back on it in either aggravation or indifference.

The churches themselves react with uncertainty. They rigidly retreat — as has not only the Catholic church — back to their legal and doctrinal positions, positions which they then try to assert and defend with authoritarian or fundamentalist tactics. Or — and this is true not only of the Protestant churches — they try to check the exodus by dissolving, virtually to the point of self-dissolution, into a multiplicity of undertakings focusing on group-specific interests, wishes, and needs. A mere defense of traditional positions, however, as little represents a genuine path into the future as does chummy accommodation to the quickly changing currents of the *Zeitgeist*. Indeed, both these options accelerate the very trend against which they are trying to assert themselves to begin with. Hence it is no surprise that the public at large, shaped as it is through the media, perceives churches either not at all or merely as the object of criticism, polemic, or satire. Both internal and external distance predominate. Fewer and fewer people expect from them or from their message any life orientation with a genuine sense of reality.

It would be a mistake to attribute this merely to the commonly evoked social processes of pluralization and individualization, as considerable as their roles may well be. The churches themselves also bear some of the guilt in this development. With virtually unsurpassable ineptitude, they avoid not a single topic that might open them to public criticism. Synods, commissions, and ecclesiastical leadership busy themselves in an almost grotesque way with peripheral topics such as homosexuality, feminism, church asylum, birth control, pastoral care in the military, the collection of church dues, or Penance Day — grotesque not because these topics are not of significance in and of themselves, but because these seem to be the only things with which churches yet deal intensively and the only things with which they yet appear publicly. These become the central questions both for the internal perception and for the external societal perspective on churches because the churches' own view of what is essential has been distorted by relevant topics of the day (though also by their own traditions and didactic structures). Secondary questions dominate church discussion, while in reality the foundations themselves are in question.

II

It has been noted often, and unfortunately not without some justification, that it is above all the churches themselves who, with their traditions, didactic structures, and traditional practices, set up their own obstacles. Hence liberation from the ballast of traditional doctrine has repeatedly been advanced as the way to renew the spiritual life of the church and to reestablish its social relevance in the present. The preferential position accorded life, however, as correct and important as it certainly is, poses the questions of doctrine rather than avoids them. Sooner or later, practical decisions must be made that require substantive clarification and distinctions and lead to the theological formation of doctrine.

Life, including the life of a community, consists of a series of decisions that determine our historic identity precisely because they often might have taken different forms. We are what we have become. Although we neither must nor will remain what we have become, it would be foolish to believe that we might exit this history and live as if it were not a factor. Even the decision to begin completely anew and to live in a completely different fashion is connected to preceding decisions made by both us and others — decisions that have actually made us into what we are. There may be perfectly good reasons not to remain or to continue as we are, and we must then try to give both our life and our history a different direction. We can do this only by assuming a critical posture toward our own history, by picking up on what is worth preserving, and by not preserving what is detrimental or obstructive. Just what that is may well be the object of dispute and critical discussion. In any case, the presupposition is that we both are familiar with our own previous history and take that history into consideration. For if we ignore it, we allow ourselves to be further determined, without differentiation, by the decisions shaping that history and by their consequences, and we gamble away what chance we may have for self-determination.

In a reverse fashion, however, this also means that our lives are never completely self-determined. Self-determination is an operation of critical differentiation in view of all the determining factors that are already shaping our lives. We neither can nor want to internalize all these ourselves such that they all enter into our conscious decisions concerning the path our lives take. Rather, we choose. We pick up certain decisions and try to correct others. We concentrate our efforts on certain areas of our lives, and in others give ourselves over more strongly to tradition. We decide where our own decisions are necessary and where we are better advised to trust in decisions that have already been made. For we recognize that one cannot always find and discover everything anew, yet also that one must not continually merely repeat and carry forward what one finds at hand. Hence we try to learn from earlier decisions, and not to repeat all the mistakes of the past. This is true of a person's individual life, of the life of communities, and also of churches.

Hence to forget and bid farewell to those particular past clarifications that have entered into the doctrinal structures and traditions of churches simply because they have nothing more to say to our own age, is as false as to defend them stubbornly and to implement them even to their ultimate, absurd consequences over against an increasingly uncomprehending public. They must prove their relevance for decisions that are now on the table, and must do so in such a way that people are inclined to appropriate them because they can see how this will enhance their own lives. Churches must be concerned with precisely this *appropriation,* and not with some merely abstract defense of principles. Attention should be directed toward people's lives, not toward an apology of ecclesiastical doctrine and practices. It is the *gospel* that they are to bring to people, not the doctrinal statements and behavioral norms with which they have protectively fenced it in. And they must bring the gospel to them in such a way that they can perceive it as present reality, and not misunderstand it as some doctrinal matrix that has been passed down, or as a merely traditional practice, both of which come from an age that is no longer theirs.

What is sacrosanct is not the doctrinal structures and devotional forms of tradition, but rather that which these tried to protect and to practice in their own age: the gospel and faith. Thus if churches really want to take their own doctrinal and life traditions seriously, and if they do not want simply to relinquish either those particular experiences that have shaped them or their historic identity, then they are not permitted to defend the temporally dependent formulations, situationally determined emphases, and historic forms of these traditions as timeless truths and norms void of any context, or to misuse them as unquestionable premises of deductive argumentation. Rather, they must understand their teachings and practices historically. They must distinguish their actual consequences from their content and intention, critically evaluate their substantive appropriateness in view of Scripture, determine the extent to which they can be translated into the problem contexts and formative possibilities of our own age, and thus in a larger sense evaluate theologically the functional validity of every doctrinal structure and practice. Finally, they must preserve in its uniqueness, clarity, and truth through all the changes of the ages, and must practice in the actual business of life that which is always the essential concern of any serious doctrine and ecclesiastical guidance: the gospel and faith.

As certainly as, for the sake of the fellowship of life, the church cannot do without doctrine, just as certainly doctrine is never an end in itself within the church, even if it repeatedly threatens to become such. Precisely because it develops its own intellectual dynamic, conceptual fascination, and institutional significance, it constantly runs the risk of going astray from its practical character, of being misunderstood as a system of theoretical truths, and of being misused for legitimizing ecclesiastical power claims. Thus it is the task of theology constantly to refer it back to and check it from the perspective of that which alone is essential: the gospel and faith. It is these that all doctrine is to serve, and these alone are never at issue. Hence in the case of conflict — this is the basic insight of the Reformation — the gospel and faith are to be asserted against ecclesiastical doctrine, not in order to dismiss the latter, but rather in order to remind it of its essential concern, and thus to reformulate and formulate it anew in a more appropriate form that is itself more beneficial to life. For the gospel is not a doctrinal system, but rather a life force disclosing reality and altering life. And correspondingly, that particular faith elicited by the gospel is more than doctrine, moral persuasion, or religious orientation: It is the perception or observing of the presence of God's love, and as such is an all-encompassing (that is, both individual and collective) enactment of life by human beings before and with God. This enactment of life is the goal of all church activity and doctrine, and only that which serves this practical goal is relevant.

Hence if ecclesiastical and theological interest in doctrine is not directed toward this faith, but rather to doctrinal development in and of itself, then it misses life and with it its own real task. Faith, however, is not some complicated doctrinal edifice that only theological experts are able to fathom in all its theoretical and practical consequences. It is to be understood as the observing — in the double sense of the word — of the simple life truth of the presence of God, a truth both available to everyone in some way and yet equally unfathomable to everyone: *God is present.* He is present as the love disclosed in Jesus Christ. And this love is at work here and now, and is engaged in creating something new, in changing the world into creation, and in overcoming our own blindness toward God. That is the gospel[1] to which the church owes its

---

1. Of course, the gospel can also be formulated differently: as the liberation to freedom, the enablement to truth, the redemption from sin, and so on. But the formulation I have given above has the advantage of being not only simple and straightforward and without weighty theological terminology, but also sufficiently capable of differentiation so as to avoid excluding from the outset certain types of human existence (children, the elderly, senile, handicapped, etc.) from that which the gospel promises. For however one formulates the gospel, it must be conceived in a fashion encompassing all the spheres, levels, and types of human life, since it concerns — both qualitatively and quantitatively — *all* of human life.

own existence and for whose sake it exists. It is the truth of this gospel that the church and all Christians are to proclaim and probe and verify with all their speaking and thinking and doing. It is a matter of this alone, and thus it is a matter of everything. Nothing is added to this simple truth; rather, everything further emerges from it.

God is present and is at work here and now in his love — faith lives from this insight, and this and only this is the genuinely essential thing that churches today are obliged to say to human beings in a completely unequivocal fashion. This is no harmless message, for this faith is never without that particular permanent *temptation* posed by the often unbearable contradiction of our own tangible experience of reality: If indeed God is efficaciously present as love, then how can our world and our lives be the way they are? Faith's perception of the present power of God's love cannot be publicly justified without speaking of sin and of a creation that quite frankly is not yet what it should and will be. Whoever would renounce the discussion of sin, guilt, and fate renders faith harmless and denies it precisely that which sets it apart, namely, that on the basis of its own perception of the presence of God's love, it renders a person extraordinarily sensitive (or should do so) to the multifarious open and concealed contradictions against God's love in the world of our experience. Believers suffer from these contradictions, try to eliminate them, and yet realize that they cannot rid the world of these contradictions through their own actions, since they neither adequately control the consequences of their actions nor are able to get comprehensive control of the presuppositions of their own lives. Hence neither is faith ever without *hope* in God's own completion of that which is perceived as the presence of his love and yet which often can be perceived only contrafactually. Christians are thus characterized by both real hope in the capacity of God's love to bring about this completion — a love whose present reality they do indeed perceive — and the critical-realistic view of created reality and of our own human possibilities and capabilities — a view struggling equally against fatalistic lethargy on the one hand, and false hopes on the other. For if God is indeed present, then for long stretches our own present lives do not at all exhaust the possibilities available to him. Much to our own detriment, we are living beneath our own possibilities. And we will find our way out of this condition only if by perceiving the presence of God's love here and now we recognize what we can and must do, and what we cannot do and need not do.

Making this clear and working toward it is the duty of churches, of all Christians, and not least also of theology. Each of them, in its own way, stands before the task of awakening a sensibility for God's presence, and thus of working toward heightening the capacity for perceiving and addressing God's presence in our own present. The central practical challenge to the churches of our time is to make this possible and not to themselves constitute a hindrance. And one of the most important theoretical tasks of theology today is to provide the conceptual clarification necessary for this task, that is, to develop, probe, and critically investigate what *God is present* means.

III

The basic presupposition for this task is that theology cease to behave as, and to misunderstand itself as, a social or human science. It is as little such as is natural science. Theology is neither an empirical nor a historical science. And neither can it be a guiding science for some religious system or for the church if it is not first something different and much more basic, namely, *critical knowledge of God,* knowledge that develops argumentatively the various perceptions of God's efficacious presence and evaluates the various religious symbolic renderings of such perception regarding their truth, validity, and reasonableness. The theme of theology in all its variations is *God* — God in his multifarious presence in the varied contexts of our own world and of all possible worlds that owe their existence to his presence. This theme is accessible to theology through a critical reconstruction of the *perceptions of the presence of God* available to it in the life of faith of concrete communities of faith and in their symbolic renderings of God's perceived presence. The standard for this critical reconstruction is the *knowledge of God's reality* that either manifests itself in these symbols of the perception of God and in the accompanying understanding of self, world, and reality posited in these symbols, or can be derived from these symbols analytically.

Theology formulates this knowledge of God's reality — knowledge that, even when those who perceive it hold it to be certain, is never finished or beyond question for thought itself, but rather always pushes for more depth, more clarity, and for argumentative verification — in theological *conceptions of God* that are always preliminary, are always open to further determination and correctives, and above all are to be distinguished from *God himself,* since it is not our own knowledge of God that is the measure of God.[2] Only where this critical-realistic

2. That *God* is the theme of theology, and not any *notions, ideas,* or *conceptions of God,* is also and precisely the case when theology has access to this theme only by way of a critical reconstruction of present *perceptions of God* and their perpetually contextually bound rendering in symbols. Precisely because *God* is never directly and immediately accessible to theology, it can approach this theme epistemologically only by way of critical-hermeneutical analyses by reconstructing the symbolic renderings of God's perceived presence accessible to it, and do so such that it then critically focuses at every point on the very real, fundamental distinction between *God* and the *perceptions/notions/ideas of God.* This does not mean that it concerns itself only with notions of God and the like, but not with God: its theme is *God,* not some notion of God. Methodologically, however, theology can address its theme only by dealing with the concrete historic ways in which God is discussed and faith in God is lived. From these it then derives the understanding of God that shapes the corresponding perceptions of God's presence and their symbolic renderings, as well as the understanding of self, world, and reality posited in these symbolic renderings. Through

orientation toward *God* is placed unmistakably in the center of theological efforts, where the referential accomplishments of religious speech about God are not theologically suppressed, and where realistic talk about God is not, because of its alleged offensiveness to reason that fancies itself enlightened, left over in shame to religious praxis and to the life of faith, but rather comes to bear in theology itself in the form of this critical differentiation and self-differentiation of God himself from all perceptions, notions, knowledge, and ideas *about* God — only there has theology something to say and thus also a future, since it is speaking about a reality that concerns everyone always and everywhere.

---

a systematic development of these contexts of understanding, it derives criteria with whose help it then is able to test the symbolic renderings of the perceptions of God that it is trying to reconstruct and think through. Hence both methodologically and epistemologically, theology is moving in a critical circle. Yet precisely in so doing, theology resembles other disciplines that are concerned with examining a reality that is not itself first constituted through just this attempt at examination. It cannot a priori decide or decree what is true or false here, what is adequate or inadequate, but rather must discover and learn this through experience and through constant correctives to its own findings.

The realism of this critical hermeneutical procedure becomes clear in an exemplary fashion in theological dealings with the Christian faith. The precise concealed quality (to be developed on the basis of a theology of the cross) of God's efficacious presence underscores that for Christian faith there can be no knowledge of God without a perception of the specific *concealed quality of God:* God's presence can be perceived only along with a consideration of his concealed quality, and God's concealed quality only along with a consideration of the *different* presence *and* concealment of God *in the cross and resurrection of Jesus Christ* and *in the world.* The result is that our understanding of God — though also our understanding of both the world and human beings — is characterized by irreducible differences. Yet these evince not a static juxtaposition, but rather an eschatological dynamic insofar as the *deus revelatus* has priority and will keep the upper hand over the *deus absconditus,* the *new* creation over the *old world,* the *homo iustus* over the *peccator.* Theology, too, can neither circumvent nor avoid these differences. It, too, does not have any direct, immediate, or special access to its theme that might circumvent God's precise concealment. Hence it can deal with its theme only by way of faith and its historic manifestations in which the differentiated modes of God's presence and concealment along with their cosmological, anthropological, ethical, etc. consequences come to expression. Thus, methodologically theology is not (immediate) talk of God, but rather talk of "God," though not in the sense of a mere description of the empirically and historically accessible circumstances and conceptual content of a specific religious praxis, but rather in the form of a critical reconstruction of this praxis oriented toward the perceived reality of God's presence and expressed in basic distinctions such as that between *God* and *notions of God, faith in Jesus Christ* and the *faith of Christians,* the *church* and *empirical churches, the truth of faith* and the *content of Christian convictions of faith at a given time,* and so on. Without these distinctions, theological talk of God would be exposed without any criteria to the unclear admixture — one also in need of clarification — of faith and superstition in any given extant religious praxis. On the other hand, neither can it acquire such distinctions through some concept of reason, however articulated it might be, or derive them from some concept of rationality, but rather must procure them itself from the historic manifestations of Christian faith as it is genuinely lived. Precisely because its theme is God, and because it is able to deal with this theme only by way of a critical explication of existing perceptions of God and their symbolic renderings, theological talk of "God" belongs methodologically to a critical *grammar of the life of the Christian faith,* a grammar that claims to be normative because it is aiming at God whenever it speaks of "God."

God is unique, and for just that reason cannot be restricted to any partial sphere of our reality or reduced to any partial function of our social realities. God is not the *tribal deity* of Christians or of any other religion or tradition; and faith in God is not a special religious faith that one might — as its enlightened contemporary — safely ignore simply because, though it may well retain some function for believers, it possesses no significance at all for anyone else. The meaning of faith is its truth, and this truth is valid for all or for no one. If God is as present as Christians believe, then everyone is dealing with God, whether everyone acknowledges this or not.

Objections focusing on the contextuality of the Christian faith, to the alleged relativity of its truth, or to the authoritarian character of its absolute claims, confuse elements that should be clearly distinguished. The fact that Christian faith can be lived only concretely and thus as something contextually determined does not render its validity dependent on specific contexts: The truth of the life of Christian faith depends on the truth of the gospel to which faith owes its existence, not vice versa. Neither does it make any sense to say that faith is "true for me," but not necessarily for others as well. Whatever one may understand by "truth," anyone who says "this is true *for me*" is at the same time saying "I believe that it is *true*," and precisely in so doing is asserting its validity not only for himself or herself, but for others as well. The truth of faith depends not on it being believed, but rather on reality indeed being the way faith believes. But if it is true that God is present in the way faith confesses (namely, as the compassionate love that makes everything new), then this is the case universally, everywhere, and always, regardless of what we may think of it or how we may respond to it.

In this sense, faith in God implies a realistic attitude toward reality. This posture is fundamentally different from the postmodern attitude that pretends it is unable to distinguish meaningfully between construction and reality, between God and our imaginative images and notions of God. Whatever the case, whenever a half-truth is declared to be the whole truth, everything becomes false. The correct insight into the unlimited discursive potential of language seduces us into taking leave of a realistic attitude toward the realities in which we live. People generally fail to see that this increasingly undermines one of the central accomplishments of enlightened thinking, namely, the critical *distinction between truth and power*. However, ever since Socrates made it clear to the Sophists that knowing truth is something different from allowing oneself to be persuaded of something, the distinction between truth and power has been fundamental to European thought. It governs not only science, philosophy, and theology in the sense familiar to us, but also ethics, politics, and the functioning of democratic societies. Even if hardly a single area offers completely dependable methods for acquiring the certainty of truth, this in no way means one might relinquish the critical question concerning truth, that which among all that is possible is actually real and can justifiably claim validity amid the multiplicity of referents.

Wherever the distinctions envisioned here are no longer made, responsible action and thus also human life as such become impossible. Wherever actions are taken, such distinctions are also implemented, and in all the areas relevant to life we do indeed know how to use them more or less effectively, regardless of what constructionist theoreticians may try to tell us. Yet if we do not ourselves try to distinguish according to proven criteria between true and false, valid and invalid, possible and actual, and rather allow others to do that for us, then truth becomes equated with the opinion of those in power, or — as in our own societies — with that which the majority believes or which the media make the majority believe. And we should thus not be surprised that in our societies it is no longer efforts concerning truth and knowledge that count, but rather above all the ability to use language and the media so that the majority is won over to one's own opinion or interests. Wherever the power of language to disclose truth is disputed, and wherever language is denied the capacity to refer to reality that is independent of language, we must fear that truth is made dependent on majority opinions and on market considerations. Even religions are increasingly viewed according to this model: as a market for possibilities of meaning and sense from which we choose according to our own individual wishes and needs, but not from the perspective of truth and untruth.

The theology of the past few decades has made a not inconsiderable contribution to this development. It has largely appropriated the methodological dogma that it is not God's reality and efficacious presence, but rather only the religious phenomena of human existence and history that can be researched in a rationally justifiable and academically respectable fashion; and it has also — often without even noticing it — appropriated, along with the methodologies of the corresponding sciences, their prejudices as well. Whatever cannot be addressed thematically in an empirical and historical fashion is allegedly a matter of private convictions, individual desires and ideas, or perhaps even social needs; in any case, it might at most be the object of the social sciences, not of theological investigation.

It is high time for theology to take leave of this misleading methodological dogma. There is nothing for it to discuss or investigate if there is no God. There is no religious use of language and no other religious or nonreligious activity if God is not present. And there is no faith and no serious objects of theological reflection if God's presence cannot be perceived. It is not the essential task of theology to explain why people believe what they believe, and how they (might) acquire or preserve their faith, but rather to explain what makes their faith true, valid, and reasonable; and no matter what practical, psychological, or social functions faith in God may well fulfill, it is true and valid only if God exists, and it is reasonable only if there are reasons to believe that what is believed of God is indeed true, or is at least more probable than the contrary. Theology is concerned with truth, more specifically with a truth that is not exhausted by that which is accessible through the operational modes of historical and empirical science. The truth of faith cannot be grounded historically or empirically, and theology is not a historical or anthropological science of meaning, but rather *critical knowledge of God* (in the sense explained above).

This by no means disputes that our own perceiving and thinking of God depend in many respects on earlier perceptions, experiences, and thought. We all live in a world into which we were born. But we cannot live in it without forming it. This applies to our physical surroundings as well as to the social and societal realities into which we grow, and to the languages we learn and whose grammars dominate our speaking and thinking. We live in a world that we have not ourselves created. But we cannot live in it without creating it. We have been created in order to create both ourselves and our world.

It is not for us to choose whether to do this. We cannot decide not to decide. We cannot choose not to choose. We cannot not create ourselves and our world. Whatever we do, we could also have done it differently. But we must of necessity decide, choose, and act, and whatever we do indeed decide, choose, and do will always take place under conditions that do not allow all possibilities to be a genuine option for us. We must decide in view of what has been decided for us. Our lives and our thinking stand under a double contingency from which we cannot extricate ourselves.

It is precisely the contingencies of our existence that thus constitute the necessities under which our lives take place and which do not stand at our disposal. Much could have been different, but since it is not, we must realistically reckon with its reality. By contrast, we must reckon with God's reality because God could not have been different: God is God precisely because he is as he is. If theology takes this seriously, then it must speak realistically about God's reality. It is not yet doing so if it misuses the contingencies of our lives as premises from which to conclude the necessity of religion by way of the postulate of an allegedly unavoidable praxis of overcoming such contingency. Such attempts at rendering religion functionally plausible, and at turning notions of God into anthropological and social-psychological instruments, leave open the decisive question of whether such worship of God is genuinely directed toward God, or whether it exhausts itself in the psycho-social, civil-religious, and metaphysical accomplishments of the corresponding notions of God and their attendant cults and fellowship structures. Hence neither are they immune from the various attempts at shaping one's notion of God according to the standard of our own current needs, desires, expectations, and demands in order to make it more capable of fulfilling those particular functions we ascribe to it and expect from it. *To each man his own God, to each woman her own Goddess,* and *an appropriate deity for every life situation* cannot be the postulates of a theology that seriously wants to be realistic and as such insists on being taken seriously. For either God's reality is something not dependent on our (religious or theological) thematization, but rather is something that itself decides concerning the latter's truth or falsity, its sense or nonsense; or God's reality does not deserve to be so called, regardless of what functions this reference to God may well play in the life of believers.

Hence theology is not *realistic* merely because it takes religious diversity seriously, allows for the religious views of others, does not make its own opinions the standard for all things, and advocates the equal rights of all religious opinions. As certainly as freedom of religion does indeed imply the right and obligation to follow one's own consciousness of truth precisely with regard to God, just as little does it assert that every faith is equally valid, every religious opinion equally correct, or that no (religious) consciousness of truth might be subject to the criticism of another. Rather, theology becomes realistic only when it searches for criteria allowing it to decide concerning the truth, validity, and reasonableness of a particular faith, *and* when it does not consider these criteria adequately justified by the function of this faith in the life of the corresponding community of faith, but rather first and foremost grounds those criteria in God's reality, which itself precedes and grounds the community. Its efforts must be directed toward the critical knowledge of God focusing on the distinction between *God* and *notions of God,* and not merely toward a knowledge of the various understandings of God entertained by various communities. Only then will it develop the critical capacity for avoiding over the long run the sad alternative between withholding judgment — because of its own inadequate orientation — concerning the truth or falsity of religious views on the one hand, and the fundamentalist equation of its own opinion with truth on the other. For it knows that each situation demands that everyone (itself included) is to move forward from the confusing admixture of unclear and vague perceptions of God's presence to a clearer, more unequivocal and complete perception of God's presence and reality.

Only a theology that realistically wagers that God is perpetually present in a real and efficacious way can with good reason look everywhere for God's reality, and inquire of everyone concerning the perception — in however fragmentary a form — of his presence. For as little as we can decide not to decide, just as little can we decide without actually doing it in the present, or decide in the present without doing it in God's presence. It is not necessary for us to know or perceive this to make it true, for it would not be true if it were not valid utterly independent of what we may or may not do, what we may or may not know. But this does not at all mean that we should not put forth an effort concerning this perception or utilization of God's presence. It is a trivial truth that asserts we cannot live and act except in the present; and it is equally true, if not trivial, that we cannot live and act in the present without living and acting in God's presence. Although we need not be aware of both in order to live and to act, acquiring this awareness helps us give our lives and actions a realistic orientation. The first makes it clear to us that we are living in the present rather than in the past or the future, and that we thus should not expend our energy, time, and money trying to win the Napoleonic Wars, or doing something that actually can only be done tomorrow. Correspondingly, the second makes it clear to us that we should refrain from any attempt to acquire complete control over our own lives and over the conditions of our lives: We cannot choose our parents, we cannot control the unintentional consequences of our good deeds (not to speak of our bad deeds), and we cannot circumvent the reality (if it indeed is one) that we all live in God's presence.

IV

It is this and nothing else that theology is to plumb, develop, and deepen. In the confusion of the present, theology is to call the church to its essential concern by persistently recalling the gospel of the efficacious presence of God's love. God is present for everything that is present for itself, something else, or others. God is present for every presence and for the presence of every single being in the way that is most beneficial for this being in its relationship to God and to its fellow creatures. For God is not vague and indeterminate for every presence, but rather is present in the way he defined and proved himself in the cross and resurrection of Jesus Christ: as the inexhaustible, creative love that effects life, brings about righteousness, liberates, and makes everything new. As the evocation of creative love, God's presence is a perpetually efficacious presence that leaves nothing as it finds it. God's love is efficaciously present because here and now it seeks what is best for those to whom it directs itself. What is best for the addressees of this divine love, however, is that which actualizes in the most perfect fashion the potential of their own possibilities for existence in relationship with God, and what that is in any concrete instance depends on the actual condition in which the addressees of God's love variously find themselves.

The concrete manner in which God's love exerts its influence is thus always determined by two conditions: by the unalterable will of God's love to make possible for his creations the unrestricted realization of their talents and capabilities in the perception of and response to the presence of his love among them, *and* by the current condition in which God's love encounters its addressees, a condition that it tries to bring forward into a more appropriate condition with regard to the envisioned goal. Yet because its addressees are infinitely different and their conditions also extremely varied, God's love is not always the same, but rather is efficacious in an infinite variety of ways. Although it is indeed always God's love that as the ultimate reality does determine every presence, this love works in every case in a new and underivative fashion because it enters into the condition of its addressees in the most sensitive way possible and in each case seeks what is best for them. The actual form of God's love perpetually orients itself to its addressees, whose differences it respects, whose possibilities it picks up, and whose various capabilities it keys on. Hence God's love works in the nonhuman part of creation differently than in situations where it is cooperating with creaturely freedom. Because God reckons with our freedom and tries to attain what is best for us by respecting rather than by excluding it, he does not assert himself in an authoritarian fashion, but rather in such a way that as creator, redeemer, and perfecter he makes it possible for us to correspond to his love in free acceptance.

Trinity, Christology, and pneumatology are the doctrinal contexts in which Christian *theology* reflects upon and works through this truth. These doctrines, however, are not the object of Christian proclamation, but rather the theological attempt to define this object clearly and to protect it against misunderstanding. The only object of Christian proclamation is *the present efficaciousness of divine love disclosed in Jesus Christ.* It is not for Christians, as it were, to put this love into effect, that is, to bring God to human beings (and how could they in any case!), but rather to refer human beings to this love and to draw their attention to the fact that God's love is already variously at work in their lives. Hence the essential, core concern of the Christian church is nothing other than to sensitize the human beings of its own age to the hidden ways in which God's love is at work, and to guide them to a perception of and response to God's presence. It is this upon which theology should anchor the church again and again when it threatens to lose itself in the noise of the world. And this is why theology has a future worth discussing only if it does not lose sight of its central theme, namely, the *presence of God's love.*

It is high time for theology to take the time necessary for this again. Theology is not important because it is able to say something about all possible topics by employing all possible methodologies currently in vogue, but rather because it possesses its own theme. Only because of this theme itself do theology's contributions to the themes of other disciplines deserve to be heard. Theology should not be satisfied with acquiring from other life contexts or sciences the problems with which it concerns itself. Neither does it become more important by contributing an additional, theological commentary to every nontheological problem, whether or not this contributes to actually solving the problem under discussion. If theology relinquishes its claim that faith perceives reality and in an unmistakable way discloses reality, it renders itself superfluous. If it accepts being reduced to a second-class interpretative discipline that merely subjects to a secondary religious interpretation that which the analyses of the social sciences have disclosed as the complex reality of our lives, then one can do without theology as a scholarly discipline. This kind of theology does not need a future, since it has nothing to say of any real significance.

Many people have the impression — and not without some justification — that precisely this is the case: Theology does indeed have a past in which it was important, but it neither has nor needs a future, since today its topics and problems are better addressed in other disciplines. Its time has run out. It belongs to a cultural epoch that is sinking into the past, and has fulfilled its obligations. Whatever was to be learned from theology, other disciplines have long appropriated into their own spheres of competence. One can do without theology in the future because today it no longer contributes anything original to the comprehension of reality, but rather restricts itself wholly to that which it was always inclined to be in the first place: group ideology.

Anyone who argues thus is insinuating that theology has nothing to contribute to the methodical or scholarly comprehension of that which is empirically and historically the "case," that is, nothing that is not already or might not be also and better comprehended in other disciplines. This is completely correct. But it has always been incorrect to expect this sort of thing from theology. It is time for theology to counter such false expectations and their attendant, unavoidable disappointments, and to make clear that it is not an empirical or historical science, nor merely a secondary organizational form of social problems and claims regarding meaning, but rather is concerned with a single, unique reality: God's presence. *Our reality is more than what is merely the "case," because God is present in it.* The permanent task of theology is to make this clear over against science, society, and the church.

Theology is concerned with something singular and unique: the efficacious presence of God's love. It cannot comprehend this singularity through any scientific simplification, abstraction, and generalization. It must proceed down its own methodological path in order to take God's reality as its theme.[3] As long as it allows its problems and methods to be served up by other disciplines, it will miss its own theme. It errs equally regarding both itself and these sciences if it presents itself as one science among others through an imitation of scientific methods and an adaptation of empirical theories, instead of pursuing its own distinctive task: to take as its theme God's presence in his creation, and thus the world in all its variety as the creation of the triune God. It is high time that theology takes the time necessary for this. For the more it concentrates unmistakably on *God,* the more will it have to say, and the less it will need to worry about its own future.

---

3. Cf. I. U. Dalferth, "Der Eine und das Viele," in J. Mehlhausen, ed., *Pluralismus und Identität: Veröffentlichungen der wissenschaftlichen Gesellschaft für Theologie,* 8 (Gütersloh, 1995).

Pneumatic Nudges: The Theology of Moltmann, Feminism, and the Future

Catherine Keller

To envision a future, we step back into the shaded recesses of the present. There, what is past wrestles endlessly, passionately, with what is possible, like Jacob with the angel. What is frantic and finite craves the blessing of a future, a promise of the fulfillment of itself, not of just any *futurum* but of its specific *adventus*. At the end of the millennium, we strain after the glimmering of a decent collective life for the future. We doubt its probability. And stubbornly, like parents, we protect its possibility — against the odds, the trends, the projections; against our fears. Of course this struggle for a future that blesses the present belongs under the heading of Christian eschatology as redefined once and for all by the early Jürgen Moltmann. But we all stand now at the end of this century of battered aspirations and obscene satisfactions. We can no longer merely proclaim the future and command hope. Everywhere — among the sort of Christians who care about the creation and its creatures — *that* eschatology seems to collapse into incredulity.

In the face of this utopian burnout, we might best lift up not hope itself or its ultimate objects, but the *sources* of hopeful life in the present. These modalities of faith — as that which resists the odds and persists in the struggle — proliferate into many theological re/sources, many means of access; and recognizing their multiplicity has become itself a source. Their differences incite the angelology of struggle. The sustaining sources I am after here will reveal a character at once intersubjective and indeed, in a certain sense, trinitarian. Rather than presenting us a commanding vision of "the future," they wrestle and nudge and bless.

My own ever-feminist means of access will articulate themselves here as the germ of a Wisdom pneumatology in more or less Jürgen Moltmann's sense. *More*, because of the hints of his transformation of neoorthodoxy into compatibility with what I will evoke as feminist theology; *less*, because these gestures remain uncertain, tentative, subject to being ignored both by the feminists and the antifeminists among his readers, and in danger of being eclipsed by the nearly exclusive masculinity of his own rhetoric.

But first I want to step back — *reculer pour mieux sauter* — into the memory of my own theological present, where Moltmann's influence has both a past and a future.

Some memories will not let the angel go: they stand out as Virginia Woolf's "moments of beings," they hold out for a possibility that could not have been grasped consciously at the time. Such is the memory of my first encounter with Jürgen Moltmann two decades past. Already among the Great Theologians, Moltmann was especially important at my seminary. So his visiting lectureship — along with the gift of Elisabeth Moltmann-Wendel's lecture — was a matter of great local excitement. Yet I was in an inner state of revolt: to me at that time, Moltmann embodied the theological orthodoxy cum political progressivism that dominated the seminary ethos and that disappointed and disapproved my own theopoetic instincts. *The Theology of Hope,* I appreciated even then, did retrieve the future from a static liberal presence, did lift eschatology out of the mire of "afterlife" back into historical *life.* It did so, however, by pitting "hope" against "experience," and so "future" against "present" as the essence of Christian faith. This polemical tendency, as dogmatically amplified within an almost all-male institution polarized along precisely those lines, put me in a foul mood. The patriarchy, as I was beginning to recognize it, had no more effective tool than the delegitimizing of (women's) experience. My emergent feminism, impatient of the Sunday school kind seeking mere "inclusion," had nurtured itself on a variety of philosophical, psychological, mystical, pluralist discourses. Overwrought and immature inclinations guided my syncretistic attractions, to be sure; but they were mine, they were spirited, they lent me breathing room over against the suffocating masculinity of the Father, Son & Co., and provoked my first conscious experiences of the patriarchal repression of me.

Yet there was Jürgen Moltmann, lecturing in the chapel with his cheerful vitality. I could not make out the suppressive antinomies I was steeled against: no *Verbot* against experience, against interiority, against spirituality. Moltmann was not lecturing in prohibitive polarities, but in inviting complexities. So I approached him during the reception to indicate something of the polarization in which his work was here held captive. With that sweet intensity of his he declared, "But no! Messianism and mysticism are twins!"

Blessed by a generational movement bubbling into a wholesale reformation of Christianity, I have since been able to walk in community and in commitment, or in b. hooks's famous image, to move between center and margin; in theological parlance, between *ekklesia* and *eschaton.* Drawn through the likes of Ruether to a feminist appreciation of the messianic-prophetic heritage, I was no longer lured by the goddesss-dream of pure immanence. Moreover, its assertions of a female empathic continuum seemed to me distorted not only by romanticism, but by simplistic polemics against "Christianity." Drawn through Cobb and Whitehead to an irreducible rhythm of inner and outer, of immanence and transcendence, nature and history, my mystico-philosophical impulses no longer tempted me to forsake the disciplines of extraversion. I wanted that feminist mysticism which embraces the body of the world and the world of the body, not the apolitical piety that flees finitude and flesh. But the point of spirituality is not mysticism as such, but rather the transformation and refreshment of subjectivity in its relation to its source.

Feminism itself, as a particular theological work, now demands the mature metabolism of a pluralist social justice prophetism and an eco-cosmological reconstruction of subjectivity. In other words, a certain Jewish-Christian messianism and a certain ecumenical mysticism — or, rather, spirituality — cooperate within the constructive feminist theology that has taken root at the threshold of the next millennium. Happily, Moltmann's own maturation over these decades of his prodigality gives aid and solace to this work of feminists within the church.

It is under the heading of "pneumatology" that Moltmann now pursues the field of experiences and meanings with which I am concerned. But of course the terms for cooperation remain contested. Let me not imply any dawning consensus among feminist theorists in or beyond theology, let alone of Moltmann with feminist theology. The very notion of "consensus" lacks legitimacy, and the pluralizing, problematizing power of postmodern influences makes it an increasingly daunting task to conjure either "nature" or "subject," let alone "spirit" or "Spirit," among academic feminists.

The lack of any developed engagement of feminist theory in Moltmann's otherwise widely intertextual works poses a special obstacle. Those allusions that do appear seem veiled, defensive, or politely sublimated. I am aware, therefore, that by highlighting areas of overlap between feminist theology and Moltmann's messianic pneumatology, I may not be doing him the honor I intend. To the degree that such an effort bears up, it works toward that theology of the future which I would consider conducive to any faithful rather than fundamentalist future of Christianity.

Because Moltmann, like a gigantic magnet, has the power to draw with him multifarious aggregations of tradition (neoorthodoxy, postliberalism, narrative, and moderate evangelical theologies), certain insistent moves, however understated, deserve special feminist consideration. This is not just a matter of rhetorical strategy, but a case of the dynamics by which the energies of the Christian past are transformed constructively rather than conserved backlashingly. Thus, for instance, there is special drama in Moltmann's arrival at the phrase "immanent transcendence" as the lynchpin of his pneumatology.[1]

1. Jürgen Moltmann, *The Spirit of Life: A Universal Affirmation,* trans. Margaret Kohl (Minneapolis: Fortress, 1992).

"Immanent transcendence" presents itself in the midst of his radical retrieval of the concept of "experience" — radical in the context of a German tradition of Protestant and Kantian orthodoxies for which *Erfahrung* has been an unacceptable source for theology — as the basis for any doctrine of the Holy Spirit. Criticizing the Enlightenment subjectivisms that would hold experience subject to a merely individual and anthropocentric self-experience, and by implication I presume his own younger anthropocentrism of "history," he breaks the subject open to a startling width of embodied cosmic relations. This anthropological move had been anticipated in the argument for "the greater Christ" of his prior book, *The Way of Jesus Christ.*[2] Claiming now on the basis of pneumatology that "we can discover transcendence in every experience, not merely in experience of the self," he goes on to proclaim the "transcendence which is immanent in things and which can be inductively discovered."

We are invited *"to experience God in all things"* and *"to experience all things in God"*: to perceive the "infinite in the finite" and conversely to appreciate the particular things of the world in the light of "the all-embracing horizon (his emphasis)."[3] This is nothing other than what Hartshorne dubbed "panentheism" to distinguish Whiteheadian theology both from the classical theism of mere transcendence and the pantheism of mere immanence. Yet Moltmann, while at last acknowledging in passing the affinity to Whitehead, has largely insulated himself, Barthian style, against such ontological influences.[4] By the same token, he has arrived at this rhythmic pneumatology very much from *within* his own evangelical process. In other words, the concept of immanent transcendence performs here a kind of methodological version of itself — an act of transcendence from within its own theory.

This pneumatological experientialism in itself represents a theological breakthrough. Its alignment with that which has attracted so many to process theology, and in a more popular vein to creation theology, allows healing allegiances between the varieties of theological progressives. But more importantly, it discloses divine immanence from *within* the trajectory of a tradition that had sorely overemphasized the transcendence of God and of the future, at the expense of any existentially credible (not merely "believable"!) doctrine of incarnation or spirit.

Both Christology and pneumatology have functioned within the mainstream theology since Nicea-Chalcedon as the exceptional moments of immanence that prove the rule of transcendence — "the rule of the Father." Thus Christology until the last century had lost both its historical and its creational dimensions: no matter how much Christolatry was committed in every liturgical

---

2. Jürgen Moltmann, *The Way of Jesus Christ: Christology in Messianic Dimensions,* trans. Margaret Kohl (Minneapolis: Fortress Press, 1990).

3. Moltmann, *The Spirit of Life,* pp. 35-36.

4. Moltmann, *The Spirit of Life,* pp. 33-34.

act and theological text produced, "Christ the Lord" eclipsed both the historical Jesus and the cosmic Christ. Quite a disappearing act — of infinite convenience to the patriarchal forces of Christian empire and to its modern nature-destroying heirs. At the same time, pneumatology had drifted into a ghostly afterthought, relegated, as Moltmann argues so pointedly, to the status of a mere function of the relation of Father and Son by the *filioque* clause. In other words, no matter how much pious insistence on the three persons, two thirds of the Trinity had its underpinnings knocked out from below.

Moltmann's *"holistic doctrine of God the Holy Spirit"* as "God *in, with, and beneath* each everyday experience of the world," that is, as a holism of the soul with its body and of the human being with the cosmos, heals the sibling rivalry of those twins, messianism and mysticism. For while messianism focuses on the transcendent dimension of the divine work, as creating a transhistorical future that judges and transcends the status quo, mysticism dwells on the holism in, through, and toward which transcendence is always already immanent. But is it only, as he argues christologically, in the body that ecological concern meets the individual faith? In the testimonial such as that which he makes with and against Augustine this "holism" can be experienced by the reader. Augustine posed the question "What do I love when I love you?" to his God, and answered in negations of the beauty of the world. Moltmann answers instead: "When I love God, I love the beauty of bodies, the rhythm of movements, the shining of eyes, the embraces, the feelings, the scents, the sounds of all this protean creation."[5]

Attunement to the divine in the world and the world in the divine does not inspire flight from the world or absorption into the self: such a spirituality heightens sensitivity to the beauty and thus accountability to the suffering and yearning of all the other finite creatures — human, animal, vegetable, and mineral. At the same time, it revitalizes the flagging spirits of the faithful, ever prone to burnout in the face of the dystopic trends, that they may take delight in life already and thus remember the fragments of a beloved future. Hence the power of Moltmann's identification of "spirituality" as "vitality." While he takes pains to distinguish his construction of God's Spirit as "the life-force of created beings" from the Nietzschean "will to power" so lethal within the German context, he has taken quite a risk. He awakens spirituality from its sleepy haze of organic repressions. Yet by defining "vitality" as "*love of life* (his emphasis)"[6] he directs it to the ends of Christian ethics. To the ends, that is, of what feminist theology calls "mutuality" or "right relation."

Linked with a revolutionary messianism, mysticism's sense of immanence becomes a force for historical transcendence. Perhaps, to keep faith with the pneumatological project and with Moltmann's trinitarian relationalism, we

---

5. Moltmann, *The Spirit of Life*, p. 98.
6. Moltmann, *The Spirit of Life*, p. 86.

might refer to this mysticism as a "spirituality of relations." This term, which I gratefully (re-)received from a Salvadoran church activist working with youth through the war and its disappointing aftermath, suggests at once the flow of self into relations and of relations through the Spirit — and back. Only as pneumatological relations do relations have the tendency to heal from the structural deformations by which history has reneged on the promise of "justice and mercy."[7]

It goes without saying, I hope, that this relationalist move in theology, especially with its panentheist depth, resonates profoundly with feminist theology. Rosemary Ruether, Elizabeth Johnson, Sallie McFague, Carter Heyward, Rita Nakashima Brock — in short, a critical mass of those Christian feminists who are willing to construct metaphors of the divine do so out of their analysis of subjectivity as co-constituted by its relations: for good or for ill, I become part of you as you become part of me. This analysis took on its singularly feminist flavor by way of revisionist psychology (Chodorow, etc.), examining the formation of gender through the earliest, most formative relations within our social order: *perichoresis* begins at home. The social formation of the psyche within modern patriarchal Western families formed males oedipally, painfully severed from the mother and thus from access to the matrix of relations; and it formed females strong in empathy and weak in agency, tending to fuse rather than to relate. Hence Simone de Beauvoir, with no theological intention, judged traditional femininity as "mere immanence" (but unfortunately uncritically celebrated the male-identified "transcendence"). The feminist relationalist ideal has sought to avoid both deformations, that is, to build the strengths latent within our empathic connectivity into the public agency of intersubjective vitality for males and females. Indeed, Moltmann tries, albeit hesitantly, as though anxious at any relations that come too close, to take serious account of this web-working feminism.

A more recent, deconstructive wave of feminism challenges the relationalist as well as the experiential premises. Its critique of the danger of "fusion" and homogenization has been useful. Yet constructive work in feminist theology will, I suspect, revise rather than reject radical relationalism: that is, the fluid interdependency of relations as the matrix of our experience and the starting point for theory.[8] The antirelationalist animus in feminism, however postmodern in intention, unfortunately suggests a reversion to the entrenched modern habit of thinking an isolated subject transcending its object. This subjectivity mirrors faithfully, if inadvertently, the *imago dei* of classical theism. To think of ourselves and all other selves, including those of the nonhuman crea-

---

7. Michael Welker, *God the Spirit*, trans. John Hoffmeyer (Minneapolis: Fortress Press, 1994).
8. See Seyla Benhabib, *Situating the Self: Gender Community and Postmodernism in Contemporary Ethics* (New York: Routledge, 1992); Iris Marion Young, *Justice and the Politics of Difference* (Princeton: Princeton University Press, 1990).

tures co-constituting our worlds, as submerged in and emergent from a ceaseless flux of interdependent energies, threatens both Enlightenment humanist autonomy and the theology that prefigured it. Poststructuralists would argue that relationalism threatens "difference." I would respond that only "difference" predicated on autonomy is threatened. It may be the critics rather than the proponents of relationalism who have been unable to distinguish between relationship and "fusion." This inability parallels rather precisely classical theism's inability to distinguish between panentheism and pantheism.

But — granted the contestations of relationalism — how are we to understand the deformations and the reformations of relations in the Spirit as *gendered?* Hence the inquiry into the gender-imagery of God: not because any thinking person believes that God is male or female, but because Christianity, like Judaism, has figured God as personal, and thus, within the patriarchal matrix of language and culture, as overweeningly male. The matter of "inclusive language" becomes theologically interesting, indeed unavoidable, once one recognizes that what Moltmann calls "immanent transcendence" does not work without it. The experience of God in all things and of all things in God will confine itself to rare moments of speculation or ecstasy, will not issue in a pneumatological praxis of embodied social life *without* the shift toward solidarity and equality in our gender relations. The ongoing formation of selves as either insulated from relation ("masculine" and "rational") or lost in relation ("feminine" and "mystical") — emulating merely transcendent or merely immanent God-forms — has hypnotic, stereotypic, force. If indulged, it will continuously sabotage the solidarities and coalitions by which we might work out our differences in responsible relation.

Alternatively, human creatures might find themselves satisfied by their creative interconnections with each other and with all the other creatures and with the source of creation itself. Before it is too late for this planet? Before the new creation becomes an impossibility for a creator who does not create, who does not exist, apart from relationship to the creatures? In other words, *if* the new creation is to *take flesh* in our gendered, raced, classed, cultured relations; *if* right relation is a work which faith demands and not merely a matter for endless postponement by post-imperial Christendom, *then* we must reform our bodily-emotive habits. Formed along with our gender and reinforced by our theology, our self-destructive habits cannot be reformed merely by politically or doctrinally correct belief. These habits of masculinity and femininity, of violence and masochism, of arrogance or self-abnegation, incorporate patterns of "sin" and thus require holistic and transgenerational processes of healing — of redemption.

If the language of faith matters — and for people of the incarnate Word it had better matter — then it is not enough to claim that "God does not have a sex" and at the same time insist that "because we have always spoken of God as a male we will continue to." Theology at the edge of apocalypse pertains, after all, to the issue that seemed trivial, that of inclusive God-language. Enlarging the pool of images for the divine does not contradict any biblical claims. Yet the anti-inclusive language movement, increasingly defensive in a period in which a plethora of female images, some biblical, some not, have become available, would forbid the Spirit to work beyond the Bible.

Far be it from me to accuse the perpetrators of sexist language of the dreaded "sin against the Holy Spirit"; however, I do concur with Michael Welker that the work of feminist theology represents an instance of the work of the Holy Spirit in our time.[9] To criticize arguments within feminist theology may be responsible; to brace against its anger, inevitable; but to deny its world-historic invitation to lift the biblical tradition into a relationship of honor with its own women threatens the spirit of Christianity. For there has nowhere been more life-loving vitality apparent in church and theology in North America. Because how we *image* God is precisely the revelation of God that we access, expanding our language to honor the equality of women in the image of God by imagining female metaphors of God is more than a matter of forced correctness. It is the symbol and symptom of a collective work of *metanoia.*

Moltmann's argument that Jesus' Abba-mystery represented a repudiation of patriarchy in his time is perfectly plausible; indeed, Elizabeth Schüssler Fiorenza's reconstruction of Christian origins concurs. After Jesus' century, however, the insistence upon Father imagery has functioned to reinforce patriarchy in church and society, and with it the entire apparatus of a dominative "God of Power and Might" whose transcendence trivializes "His" immanence. As my appreciation of Moltmann has grown, along with his opus, I feel less irritation than mournfulness that he has not wanted to adjust even the gender pronouns of God to a postpatriarchal life of Christianity (not even the minimal strategy of repeating "God" rather than using any pronoun). Though I experience this language in the text of a contemporary theologian as a rejection, not an oversight, I have not joined most women colleagues in their aversion or indifference to him. This dismissal threatens to abandon Moltmann to those conservatives who conserve the Bible's sexism more faithfully than its messianism or its mysticism. I persist in reading him with my students in context and at multiple levels. But this is so only because certain unmistakable, if perhaps inadvertent, gender signals accompany his discovery of God-in-all-things and all-things-in-God.

Now to my context: as I write, the ecumenical Protestant churches of the United States are recovering from the stunning backlash against feminism that answered the Re-Imagining Conference of 1993. Orchestrated by the right wings of the United Methodists and Presbyterians in conjunction with the Institute for Religion and Democracy (the think tank designed to counter liberation, feminist, and other theologies that pose a challenge to the capitalist agenda),

9. Welker, *God the Spirit.*

this controversy is forever symbolized by the name *Sophia*. That conference spun an ecumenical, female, and flesh-affirming liturgy around the biblical *Hokma/Sophia* tradition. The liturgy became the ammunition for a heresy hunt, spearheading a campaign to discipline and intimidate "liberating" seminaries and pro-feminist or womanist church leaders.

The forcefulness of the backlash pays tribute to the established strength of the feminist and womanist transformation of Christianity. In this century, perhaps only the debate between fundamentalists and evolutionists has reached this level of involvement. Moreover, in the formal document prepared in response by the Bishop's Task Force Report on the Study of Wisdom, something like an ancient conciliar settlement has been reached: a *wiser* settlement than many ancient ones — if wisdom implies justice, peace, and the integrity of dialogue.[10]

Moltmann, ever the prophet, had already prepared the way for a firm response to such "sophiaphobia." It is hardly insignificant that at precisely the moment Moltmann offers up the concept of immanent transcendence, he appeals to the Wisdom tradition as his biblical warrant. Indeed, the text that justifies the book's entire argument is drawn from the Wisdom of Solomon, extracanonical for Protestants and Jews: "God's spirit fills the world and he who holds all things together knows every sound" (Wisd. 1:7).[11] On the basis of this book, he claims that "*ruach* and *hokma*, Spirit and Wisdom, are so close to one another that they are actually interchangeable."[12] Moltmann had already established the interchangeability of Spirit and Sophia in *The Way of Jesus Christ*, in which he laid down the criteria for the return to the early Christian Spirit Christology, which prepared the way for his full-fledged pneumatology. "Spirit and Wisdom are incidentally feminine modes of the divine appearance. Spirit or Wisdom christology is the premise of every Son of God christology; for according to messianic tradition, the messiah who is anointed with the Spirit of God is 'the son of God.'"[13]

The "feminine mode of the divine appearance" signified by Sophia has been lost on neither feminists nor their foes, who would deem such claims heretical if uttered by a woman. What is "incidental" is Moltmann's own oblivion to the cosmological importance of gender. I am not suggesting a "cosmic" sex or gender; I do not wish to ontologize human socio-biological constructions. It is a matter of how we *construct* our cosmos. Because of the deep gender structures of our capacity to perceive our creaturely interdependence discussed above, I would argue that it is no coincidence that his systematic leap into the dimension of divine immanence could only occur under the sign of a transcendent woman.

10. "Bishop's Task Force Report: The Study of Wisdom," *The Circuit Rider*, March 1995.
11. Moltmann, *The Spirit of Life*, p. 34.
12. Moltmann, *The Spirit of Life*, p. 46.
13. Moltmann, *The Way of Jesus Christ*, p. 74.

The key issue remains the cosmological link provided by Moltmann via *Hokma/Sophia:* "What the psalms have to say about the presence of the Spirit in the depths of the human heart is developed by Wisdom literature in the wider context of the natural cosmos."[14] This female Wisdom is "an ordering power immanent in the world" and at the same time is "certainly transcendent in origin." While some of us in the wake of the backlash, cowed by accusations of "Goddess worship," rushed to insist that Sophia was a mere attribute, Moltmann insists that Wisdom, like Spirit, is no mere attribute of God but, in the language of the Fathers, a hypostasis. This is what he means by "counterpart." "In the form of Wisdom, the Spirit is a kind of counterpart in God himself [*sic*], and is at the same time the divine presence in creation and history." From this claim it is a short move to the *Shekinah*, the Jewish concept of the divine counterpart, always personified as feminine and sexualized in cabalistic tradition. The Shekinah names another aspect of God's self-manifestation crucial — by any other name — to Moltmann's thought since *The Crucified God.* She is "the God who suffers with us." Thus the Shekinah reveals that "the Spirit is *God's empathy.*"[15]

Given that access to empathy is systemically repressed in males and by the same token cultivated, often at the expense of any self-transcendence, in females, the gender identification of this pneumatological mode does not come as a surprise. This is not to claim some sort of feminine privilege for the kenotic gift of empathy or for its spiritualization as a theological modality. In abstraction from creative agency, it merely reifies femininity, albeit apotheosized, in its traditional functions. But because Spirit-Sophia-Shekinah do not, in Moltmann's work, ever symbolize immanence in isolation from its own transcendence, gender stereotypes are evaded: no danger of identifying femininity with immanence, masculinity with transcendence, however historically they are yoked. The Spirit nudges from within.

Note the movement: in the margins, at the edges, the *eschata*, of Moltmann's systematic opus, a new trinitarian revelation is occurring. Veiled, but not unrecognizable in its femaleness, this trinity of Shekinah, Sophia, and Spirit does not replace the Father-Son version. History cannot be erased. Interchangeable with each other and with their masculine code names of Yahweh-Father, Christ-Logos, and Spiritus, these Jewish female persons of the Trinity at once playfully, almost parodically, mirror and shift into motion the static triangle hammered out by Christian orthodoxy. The double triangle of the Jewish star comes to mind. Presence, Wisdom, and Spirit: they tenderly affirm the creaturely metaphors of a nonpatriarchal *abba* and a vulnerable boy-child, while exposing its distortion into the greatest patriarchal tool in history. In other words, this new trinitarian image at once reveals/veils the masculinized trinity for what it is, *Apo-kalypso.*

14. Moltmann, *The Spirit of Life*, p. 46.
15. Moltmann, *The Spirit of Life*, p. 51.

The woman-coded trinity dis/closes the earlier and *coming* pneumatological dimensions of Christianity itself. It is not a matter of girls versus boys seeking apocalyptic vengeance for millennia of boys versus girls. Rather, it is precisely a matter of the life-and-death struggle to keep *open* the future. The forces of economic and ecological closure within the patriarchal *oikonomia* of modernity is formidable. The patriarchal household of faith laid the foundations for the structures of ecocidal, genocidal modernity. To dis/close the possible is to refuse the aberrant apocalypses of the end of this millennium. The ecumenical and ecological resonances of God's suffering Shekinah, of God's incarnate Wisdom, and of God's indwelling Spirit at once transcend and embody the matter of justice for human women. It is as though the Spirit has picked up a path left behind back when Christianity shut down its gender ambiguities, its communalizing complexity, and its perichoretic nuances in order to provide the empire with the kyriarchal service of Oneness.[16]

But perhaps such a claim to return to one's own preferred version of primitive Christianity rings too familiar. Every new movement reverberates with the sense of its own apocalypse — its unveiling of the corruption of the old, the imminence of the new. Those of us committed to the "New Reformation" now underway in the multiple and mutually contested global guises of postcolonial, liberation, womanist, feminist, ecological, and pneumatological Christianities must not sever our future from the past. In other words, the theology of the future must paradoxically root itself in the past without repeating the tendency to romanticize the past. Most especially, we must not privilege that past form of futurism which dissociates itself from any prior past. We must, in other words, not literalize the apocalypse. We recognize in the broken communities and destroyed ecosystems mounting up all around us the effects of a literalized apocalypse: the end of worlds with no sign of the new creation.

A theology for the next century is a theology of counter-apocalypse. It is not anti-apocalypse, for to merely oppose the vision of John and its history of effects is to join the whole conservative chorus of anti-utopians and their elite accompanists who would purge themselves of all "grand narratives." Yet the metanarratives of progressive movements, derived as they are from the melodramatic and self-destructive dualisms of good and evil, also predicate an elite of the saved. So the theology of the future does not jump on the bandwagon of liberation apocalypse and its secularized revolution: that vehicle crashed at great cost to the very future it pursued. For all its materialist atheism, its driving force remained perilously transcendent of the earth and our relations within it.

Counter-apocalypse suggests a dialectical eschatology of wisdom: "those who miss me injure themselves," she declares; "all who hate me love death" (Prov. 8:34). Her church of the future embraces a future that is a possibility

---

16. Cf. Elizabeth Schüssler Fiorenza, *Jesus: Miriam's Child, Sophia's Prophet* (New York: Continuum, 1994) on kyriarchy and the patriarchal household codes of patristic Christianity.

"subtle and manifold" — to be realized in empathy with the suffering at the root of all apocalypses and thus in ancestral connection to our past. The suffering, like that of John of Patmos's martyrs under the altar, needs vindication through the transformation of the habits of injustice that caused it. But then we do not merely perform a transcendent judgment. We enact the immanent transcendence of a healing vision.

Only so do we keep our access to the formidable energies of life and death that flow from our past. By transforming rather than dismissing and repressing these energies, we may recycle them. But such an ecology of tradition and text requires, precisely because the past has such an overwhelming grip on the present, the future-tilted vitality of Spirit. Only along this widely ecumenical but narrowly discernible pneumatological path can a theology of the future flourish in our own foreseeable future. It is my guess that progressive churches will either die out, leaving Christianity to the reactionaries; or the church will overcome its fear of immanence, of webs and women and wisdom, and only thereby transcend itself into the future that needs it. But then this Christianity will have worked out new modes of mutuality with the other religions and social movements inasmuch as they share the Great Spirit of its *eschatos:* its renewal in justice, peace, and the integrity of creation.

Let us then proceed, as I think Moltmann's revised eschatological rhythm of immanent transcendence would have us proceed, with the lively bounce of a messianically and mystically charged present — that is, of a present suffused and exceeded by the sacred: an immanent transcendence. The God who is the Shekinah, suffering and staying with the victims of history; who is the Sophia whose "paths are peace," the "tree of life to those who lay hold of her," makes Godself available only in and through the Spirit.

Spirit — at once ours and not ours, mine and not mine — accesses possibilities that may attract our energies toward the New Creation: toward, that is, the renewal of *this* creation — not the deadly expectation of the end of this one. If we ruin this one, there is no Daddy to make us a new one. Moltmann might not agree with that last point. But he agrees that we write the theology of the present, which at the end of the millennium must be the theology of the future, "under end-time conditions."[17] However, this is no cheerless task. On the contrary, a counter-apocalyptic theology eschews the self-indulgent cynicism of so much progressivism. Its spirit, no longer the odd one out, does not calculate the odds. The confluence of past energy and future possibility upon which we draw for the presencing of our sources, the wisdom of our words, and the inspiring of our spirits is dis/closed only in and as "the love of life."

---

17. Moltmann, *The Way of Jesus Christ*, p. 45.

Otherwise Engaged in the Spirit:
A First Theology for a Twenty-first Century

D. Lyle Dabney

What must we speak of *first*, if we would speak of God? That is the fundamental problem of prolegomena to theology that has captivated the theological debate for much of the twentieth century and that remains unresolved as we approach a new millennium. In the following essay, I want to briefly rehearse the development of this problem, summarize the state of the question, and then examine how a parallel philosophical question concerning "first philosophy" has recently been addressed. I will then draw upon that parallel discussion for a suggestion as to how we might seek to open up the theological debate and move toward a "first theology for a twenty-first century," that is, a theology that begins with the notion that we are "Otherwise engaged in the Spirit" from the very first.

Karl Barth, of course, was the theologian who early in this century brought this issue to the fore in his unremitting attack upon the thought of Friedrich Schleiermacher. It was with this "father of modern theology" in mind that Barth formulated the underlying question of modern theology, and intimated his own answer to it:

> We ought to speak of God. We are human, however, and so cannot speak of God. We ought therefore to recognize both our obligation and our inability and by that very recognition give God the glory. This is our perplexity. The rest of our task fades into insignificance by comparison.[1]

Thus, to the question: How can the human speak of the Divine, or the finite of the Infinite? Barth responded that the only true answer leads humanity to turn from all things creaturely and to look to the Creator and Redeemer and so "give

---

1. Karl Barth, "The Word of God and the Task of Ministry," *The Word of God and the Word of Man,* trans. Douglas Horton (Boston and Chicago: Pilgrim Press, 1928), p. 186.

God the glory." It was precisely that contention that led him into conflict with Schleiermacher. For it was to that great nineteenth-century churchman that Barth traced the practice in modern Neo-Protestantism of prefacing dogmatics, or theological discourse, with anthropological prolegomena, of claiming, that is to say, that in order to speak of the Divine, we must *first* speak of the human.

Writing in a time that boasted of itself as the *Neuzeit*, Schleiermacher had envisioned a new theology for a new age, a *Glaubenslehre* or "doctrine of faith" that was to be properly related to, and ultimately grounded in, the new, modern scientific understanding of the world and humanity's place within it. In an open letter to his friend Dr. Lücke in 1829, he described his theological program as follows:

> Unless the Reformation from which our church first emerged endeavors to establish an eternal covenant between the living Christian faith and completely free, independent scientific inquiry, so that faith does not hinder science and science does not exclude faith, it fails to meet adequately the needs of our time. . . . Precisely this position, my dear friend, represents that of my *Glaubenslehre*.[2]

To ensure that "faith does not hinder science and science does not exclude faith," Schleiermacher began his chief theological work, *The Christian Faith*,[3] with an introduction or prolegomena that, drawing propositions from fields of science other than theology, "since the preliminary process of defining a science cannot belong to the science itself,"[4] sought to relate science and faith to one another in a twofold manner. On the one hand, he emphatically disclaimed that his *Glaubenslehre* sought to establish "on a foundation of general principles" the doctrinal substance of Christian faith or to "prove the propositions of the Christian Faith to be consonant with reason."[5] Faith and reason or science were thus separate, and the one did not hinder, nor was itself hindered, by the other. On the other hand, if faith and reason were indeed separable, they nevertheless were not to be thought of as unrelated, as if the second excluded the first. Thus the main task of the introduction had to do with a "scientific," that is, rational examination of religion or piety, which Schleiermacher took to be the root reality of all forms of faith. His analysis yielded a definition of the essence of piety that was to lay a foundation for all that would follow:

> The common element in all howsoever diverse expressions of piety . . . or, in other words, the self-identical essence of piety is this: the consciousness of

2. F. D. E. Schleiermacher, *On the Glaubenslehre*, trans. James Duke and Francis Fiorenza (Chico, Calif.: Scholars Press, 1981), p. 64.

3. F. D. E. Schleiermacher, *The Christian Faith*, ed. H. R. Mackintosh and J. S. Stewart (Edinburgh: T. & T. Clark, 1928).

4. Schleiermacher, *The Christian Faith*, p. 2.

5. Schleiermacher, *The Christian Faith*, p. 3.

being absolutely dependent, or, which is the same thing, of being in relation with God.[6]

In the introduction, therefore, Schleiermacher grounded Christian theology in a claim about universal human God-consciousness, an awareness of being "absolutely dependent," that is, of being "in relation with God." All historical religions, including Christianity, he argued, are to be seen as concrete determinations of that one universal reality. That reality is therefore the foundation and the norm for all theology: the foundation in that every particular expression of piety is but one specific form of the universal, the norm in that theology itself is reflection upon one particular expression of the universal. In that way, Schleiermacher pointed to human consciousness as that which served as the proper prolegomena to all talk about God. The anthropological category of God-consciousness, he believed, is that which makes it possible for humans to speak of the Divine. Then and only then, but just then and precisely then, when the anthropological foundation is *first* made sure, can the theological superstructure be erected in which the human can speak of the Divine and the finite of the Infinite. Thus, if we would speak of God, claimed Schleiermacher, we must *first* speak of the human.

To this, as we have already noted, Barth was unalterably opposed. We cannot speak of God, he declared early on, "simply by speaking of man in a loud voice";[7] for God is the "Wholly Other" and is not to be read off the assumed givenness of human God-consciousness in any of its purported historical forms. Above all, this is not to be attempted in the name of the Christian church. He subsequently developed this response to Schleiermacher in the first volume of his *Church Dogmatics,* published in 1932, entitled *The Doctrine of the Word of God: Prolegomena to Church Dogmatics.*[8] There Barth argued that Schleiermacher's introduction was not an innocuous set of propositions borrowed from other disciplines, "since the preliminary process of defining a science cannot belong to the science itself," which served to offer only preliminary orientation for the dogmatics that were to follow. Rather, as many of Schleiermacher's nineteenth-century disciples had themselves recognized, the introduction in reality belongs to the theological substance of the *Glaubenslehre* itself. Indeed, it is the very basis of the doctrine of faith, and as such it controls and defines that which is built upon it. Thus, over and against the claim that prolegomena were merely neutral introduction, Barth proposed the course that he would take in his *Prolegomena to Church Dogmatics:*

. . . prolegomena to dogmatics are possible only as part of dogmatics itself.

---

6. Schleiermacher, *The Christian Faith,* p. 12.

7. Karl Barth, "The Word of God and the Task of Ministry," p. 196.

8. Karl Barth, *Church Dogmatics.* Vol. I, *The Doctrine of the Word of God: Prolegomena to Church Dogmatics,* trans. G. W. Bromiley and T. F. Torrance (Edinburgh: T. & T. Clark, 1975).

The prefix *pro* in prolegomena is to be understood loosely to signify the first part of dogmatics rather than that which is prior to it.[9]

And as an integral part of the theological enterprise, prolegomena are not to control and define dogmatics, but are rather to be themselves subject to the same determinative criterion as all other theological statements. For Barth that criterion was clear: "In the prolegomena to dogmatics, therefore, we ask concerning the Word of God as the criterion of dogmatics."[10] Thus it is that the first volume of Barth's *Church Dogmatics* is a prolegomenon treating the doctrine of the Word of God. For according to Barth, we can only speak of God when we have *first* spoken of God's self-revealing Word.

As was noted at the beginning of this essay, the issue of prolegomena to theology, of what must be said *first*, if we are to speak of God, has dominated much of the theological discussion in the twentieth century and still remains unresolved today, and that despite the fact that many theologians on the American side of the Atlantic have attempted to beg, ignore, or finesse the question. But the question remains unanswered; indeed, the two rival solutions that have been proposed are now part of the problem itself. For we find ourselves at the end of the twentieth century confronted with a set of mutually exclusive approaches to theology that appear to brook no compromise: either we begin with the human, or we begin with the divine; either we pursue an anthropological "theology of ascent," or a strictly theological "theology of descent"; either we assume talk about God to be grounded in creation, or we declare such speech to belong solely to the realm of redemption; either we claim there exists a demonstrable continuity between the creature and the Creator, or we proclaim absolute discontinuity between God and world in the name of the one who is "Wholly Other." It may very well be that one of the primary reasons that theological discourse has come to its present confused and unhappy state is that we literally no longer know what to say *first*.

Fortunately, it is not only modern theologians who have debated the question concerning what we must say first. The issue has also arisen among philosophers, and in a way that may be helpful for the theological discussion of the problem of prolegomena. In *The Concept of the Spiritual. An Essay in First Philosophy*, published in 1988, Steven G. Smith has taken up the question of what is the most fundamental of all philosophical questions and has offered a suggestive analysis of and solution to the problem. Smith notes that the Western philosophical tradition has put forward three ways to approach the issue of a *philosophia prima* or "first philosophy."[11] The first is that of ontology, which asks whether we can rightly claim to understand anything that exists if

---

9. Barth, *Church Dogmatics*, p. 42.

10. Barth, *Church Dogmatics*, p. 43.

11. Steven G. Smith, *The Concept of the Spiritual: An Essay in First Philosophy* (Philadelphia: Temple University Press, 1988), pp. 3-4.

we have not first of all come to grasp what existence, that is, "being itself," is. The second way of approaching the issue is the question of epistemology, which asks how we can claim knowledge about being until we have clearly laid out the grounds and limits of the human capacity to know anything whatsoever. And the third approach to a first philosophy in the West is that of language, which asks how we can possibly define knowing or grasp the nature of being without having first gotten clear as to the conditions and rules determining all our statements about being or knowing. Having rehearsed that history, Smith then goes on to argue that even the third approach, the twentieth-century shift to the question of speech, is not properly basic. For that which sets language apart as the starting point for philosophy, according to Smith, is: "that it is essentially interpersonal, or to be more specific, essentially an activity of creating and maintaining forms of commonality among persons. Interpersonal commonality is not just what language is *for*; it is *in* language, and in it more than in anything else."[12]

And therein it becomes apparent that hidden in the approach of language to the problem of a first philosophy is a question yet more basic — indeed, prior to all other questions: the question of relationship. The language of relationship is, Smith suggests, the language of "spirit"; and in the book he sets himself the task of demonstrating that "the term 'spiritual' remains uniquely suited to bear an adequate conception of the original situation where the order of priority in questions begins."[13] In other words, he sets out to show that the question of the spirit or the spiritual is, in point of fact, the proper theme of first philosophy and in just what such a *philosophia prima* would consist.

Now, at another place and time, I intend to offer an analysis and response to Smith's understanding of the concept of "spirit," but in the context of this brief chapter I simply want to consider his suggestion that even the modern philosophy of language is not properly basic, but rather assumes something even more fundamental. For I believe this philosophical insight has important implications for the question of what we theologians must say *first*, if we would speak of God, especially for all who take seriously Barth's concern that the only proper prolegomena to theology must arise out of the inner necessity of dogmatics itself, which for this twentieth-century father of the church consists alone in a doctrine of the Word of God, God's self-revealing speech. What would be the result if we took Smith's illuminating observation that "word" or "speech" or "language" is not properly basic, but rather assume an even more fundamental relational reality, "spirit," and applied that to Barth's account of theological prolegomena? What kind of *theologia prima* or "first theology" would result if the "Wholly Other" who is revealed alone through the Word was seen to be, in fact, not that which is ultimately basic, but as itself assuming an even more

---

12. Smith, *The Concept of the Spiritual*, p. 4.
13. Smith, *The Concept of the Spiritual*, pp. 4-5.

fundamental reality, a relational reality, the Holy Spirit? What would it look like if we began a theology with a prolegomenon giving an account of "interpersonal relationship in the Spirit" instead of "identity in the continuity of God-consciousness" or "otherness in the discontinuity of the Word"? Initially it can be said that such a first theology would have *pneumatology,* the doctrine of the Holy Spirit, as its theme and a theology of *continuity in creation and re-creation through the discontinuity of sin and death* as its end. In the remainder of this chapter, I want to begin the process of thinking through a few of the possibilities raised by these questions.

First, in the Christian theological tradition, the Holy Spirit is understood as precisely this sort of relational or interpersonal reality. Whether it be Augustine's definition of the Spirit as *donum,* the common "gift" of the Father and the Son to the faithful, Aquinas's identification — so similar to another pneumatological formula of Augustine's — of Spirit and love, or the Reformation's definition of the Holy Spirit as the "Spirit of faith," in each instance the underlying notion is of that which relates Creator and creature, the one to the Other.

This theological usage is implicit in that of the biblical traditions themselves. The Spirit-terms found in the witness of the Old and New Testaments, *ruach* in Hebrew and *pneuma* in Greek, are each rooted in the metaphor of air in motion as breath and as wind. In moving air there was perceived to be an invisible power effecting visible results, often dramatic and having great consequences. Thus in the "east wind" that parted the waters, dried the seabed, and thereby effected Israel's deliverance from the armies of Egypt (Exod. 14:21ff.) the Old Testament identifies the "blast of [Yahweh's] nostrils" (Exod. 15:8), that is, the Spirit of God, the invisible power of a divine wind resulting in God's visible redemptive effects. Likewise, living things are said to have within themselves just such a wind, the "breath of life," a special instance of God's Spirit that, like the movement of air into and out of the body, results in life and energy in the creature, and thereby the possibility of creaturely movement and efficacy itself. Correspondingly, just as the presence of God's Spirit creates life, so its absence means death: "When you take away their breath, they die and return to their dust," the Psalm intones (104:29). Precisely as such, Steven Smith comments, "a breathing being is more fundamentally dependent on air than on food."[14]

But breathing does not only bring about life and movement in the creature, it also relates all living things to the otherness of a reality outside of themselves, to that which is other than themselves, in the most concrete way possible. For air is not simply the condition of our creaturely existence; it is the all-encompassing element in which we, as in God, "live and move and have our being" (Acts 17:28). Therefore, just as the east wind drives the various waters

14. Smith, *The Concept of the Spiritual,* p. 10.

westward or bends the many different plants of the field in a common direction, thereby effecting in the many a common result without in any way reducing their individual differences, so in like manner the divine wind of God's Spirit can move among a people and bend their lives to a common purpose and a distinctive social existence. Again, as such commonality-in-difference is generally brought about through human words, all this is accomplished according to the biblical witness above all in and through the divine Word, which is itself closely related to Spirit or breath. For just as the human word is born on the breath of the mouth and moves through wavelike motion of the air and thus is perceived by another, so it is that from the very first the Word of the One who is Wholly Other has implied God's breath or Spirit: "By the word of the LORD the heavens were made, and all their host by the breath of his mouth" (Ps. 33:6).

If, therefore, the question at the end of the twentieth century is what must we say *first*, if we would speak of God, then before we can simply assert with Barth, *Deus dixit*, "God said" (Gen. 1:3), we must *first* say that the "divine wind" or the "Spirit of God" was sweeping over the chaotic abyss (Gen. 1:2). And before we can say that "the LORD God commanded the man" (Gen. 2:16), we must *first* say, God "formed the man from the dust of the ground, and breathed into his nostrils the breath of life; and the man became a living being" (Gen. 2:7). For the Word presupposes the Spirit. Thus, in the order of questions to be asked in theology, we must *first* ask about the Spirit of God if we would speak of the self-revealing Word of God.

Asking that *first* question in the order of questions concerning how it is that the human can speak of the divine, we are led to the realization that from the very first, human beings are "Otherwise engaged in the Spirit." Indeed, according to the biblical testimony, from the very inception of our lives we live "out of" the presence of God's spiritual breath, borne away from ourselves on the winds of the Spirit to the "other" of our neighbor and to the "Wholly Other" of our Creator. At no point in our existence are we abandoned or left alone, but rather at every moment we are "Otherwise engaged" by the God whose Spirit is the source and the maintenance of our very being. We live therefore, literally, "eccentric" lives — lives, that is, having their center not in themselves, but in an Other. For there is a relationship in the Spirit from the very beginning between Creator and creature from God's side that permits the speaking of the Word to another and the hearing of the Word of the Other.

Now that is not to say with Schleiermacher that the ground of all religion is "piety" and the root of all piety is God-consciousness, and therefore that what we must say first if we would speak of God has to do with the human rather than the divine. For if, on the one hand, we must insist against Barth that it is the *Spirit* of God and not simply the *Word* of God that is properly basic to Christian theology, then against Schleiermacher we must maintain that it is the Spirit *of God* and not *human* spirituality that is the proper subject matter for an appropriate prolegomenon to theology. To claim, therefore, that speech about God needs to begin not simply with transcendence is not necessarily to turn to claims of divine immanence. The notion of the Spirit of God in whom we are "Otherwise engaged" from the first does not fit neatly into either category. It is rather precisely that which is intended to help us escape the either/or of a "theology of ascent" versus a "theology of descent" — a theology, that is to say, that takes the human as its subject and the divine as object versus one that asserts that God is the sole subject of theological discourse over and against every human object. The Spirit of God is not human spirit aspiring to the divine, but neither is it the subjectivity of God making an object of the human. Indeed, rather than *subjective* or *objective*, the Spirit is better conceived as *transjective*; that is to say, that by which we as individuals are transcended, engaged, oriented beyond ourselves, and related to God and neighbor from the very beginning. As such, the Spirit is never simply immanent. For even in the "giving" of the Spirit portrayed in the New Testament, in which the risen Jesus appeared to his disciples and "breathed on them and said to them, 'Receive the Holy Spirit'" (John 20:22), the wind of the Spirit remained its own and thus "ungiven," freely the One who, in the words of Jesus, "blows where it chooses, and you hear the sound of it, but you do not know where it comes from or where it goes" (John 3:8).

Furthermore, as the One in whom we are "Otherwise engaged with God" from the first, the Holy Spirit is that which makes possible the genuinely o/Other. Contrary to what one might initially assume, the concept of *otherness* presupposes and demands not only a difference between two persons or things, but also their relatedness. To say that x is other than y, for example, is not simply to make a statement about x alone. For implicit in those words is the notion of comparison and the relation of x to y. The sentence "x is other than y" means, therefore, that x is different *as compared to, in relation to y*. Thus, while the statement certainly *denies* identity between x and y, it also implicitly *affirms* relationship between the two. Only that which is both different and related is other. That with which we are identical is not other; it is simply a repetition of ourselves. That to which we have *no* relation, on the other hand, is likewise not other; it is, as far as we are concerned, simply "not." The otherness of God is to be understood in precisely this manner. How is it that the Creator can relate to the creature as the Wholly Other, the One who is truly and utterly other than ourselves? How is it that the Word of God can be the Word of the Wholly Other and not just our own word "spoken in a loud voice"? The answer is to be found in the Spirit of God in whom we are "Otherwise engaged" from the first, in that we are established and maintained in relationship with the One who is truly Other, the Wholly Other with whom we are not identical and yet with whom we are always related.

That engagement with the Other endures even as we wander breathless and dispirited "east of Eden." For the estrangement of the creature from the Creator is not to be construed as the absence of God from the midst of humanity. If that were the case, then the temptation in the garden would be judged to be true, for we creatures would indeed "be like God" (Gen. 3:5), self-existent and not like the radically contingent beings that we are, ever dependent upon the Wholly Other who condescends ever and again to bend down to our side and breathe the breath of life yet once more into our nostrils. Even in our faithlessness, God remains faithful, for the Spirit of God joins us in our estrangement and accompanies us in our wandering in the wilderness.

It belongs, therefore, not to the nature of the creature, but to the nature of the "Spirit of grace" (Heb. 10:29) to relate creation to the Creator. Thus it is not to be taken as another claim for the nature of the creature, but rather the proclamation of the grace of the Creator who has been faithful to creation even in its sin and death. For even "east of Eden," God is present in and with creation as the source of its every breath and the infinite hope of its every finite aspiration. As such, the Spirit in whom we are "Otherwise engaged" is that which haunts our dreams and disturbs our sloth, the source of our every broken intimation of an o/Other as it constantly drives us out of our self-centered existence, and the object against which we struggle as we lean into the wind, holding our breath, "grieving the Spirit." Thus, like the divine wind of old, the Spirit broods over the abyss of our broken lives, effecting our engagement with the Other, anticipating the day when God will breathe anew into the dry bones of the peoples.

That now brings us to a final point. If it can be demonstrated that Spirit is more basic in the order of theological questions than Word, and if it is taken to be the task of a proper prolegomenon to theology to lay out the pneumatological conditions by which we are "Otherwise engaged" with God from the very first, then that pneumatological orientation will also bring about our understanding of the substance of the gospel itself. What would be the result if we were to consider the center of Christian proclamation, the person and work of Jesus Christ, from the standpoint of the doctrine of the Holy Spirit?

To begin with, we should not be surprised to find in the testimony of the New Testament to Jesus Christ, that it is first said to the woman, "the Holy Spirit will come upon you, and the power of the Most High will overshadow you" (Luke 1:35; cf. Matt. 1:18), before the birth of the Son of God is proclaimed, or, as the Gospel according to John presents it: "the Word became flesh" (John 1:14). Just as in creation, so in re-creation the Spirit is once again portrayed as that which is presupposed by the Word.

But beyond that, we must explore the implications of the fact that the Word that becomes flesh in the person of Jesus of Nazareth is himself defined by the Spirit: he is the *Christ*, the Spirit-anointed One. Indeed, Vernon Neufeld has made the case that "Jesus is the Christ" was the earliest confession of faith in the first-century church.[15] And furthermore, we must explore the nature of

15. V. H. Neufeld, *The Earliest Christian Confessions* (Leiden: E. J. Brill, 1963), pp. 108-26, esp. 125-26.

the reconciliation that Christian theology claims to have been accomplished by that Christ. For in the New Testament, we hear the witness that God, who as Spirit is the *source* of all life, becomes then the *re-source* of all life in and through Jesus Christ, the One who from all eternity is defined by God's Spirit, of whom all four Gospels proclaim: "He will baptize you with the Holy Spirit" (Mark 1:8 par.). Here, too, the investigation of this pneumatological definition of the salvation wrought by Jesus Christ remains to be undertaken. But it is perhaps precisely a doctrine of the Holy Spirit as prolegomenon to Christian theology that will make that both possible and necessary.

If it is indeed the case, as Stephen G. Smith argues, that "one question may be called prior to another if we necessarily make an assumption about its meaning in addressing the other,"[16] then we must say that in the discipline of Christian theology, the question of the Spirit is prior to that of the Word. For the notion of the self-revelation in the Word of the God who is Wholly Other makes an assumption about the relationality of the Spirit both for the reality of its own otherness in relation to the creature and in the possibility of its relation to the creature that is itself an other. The doctrine of the Spirit of God is, therefore, the proper *theologia prima* or "first theology" of a properly conceived Christian theology. As such, it is the challenge of developing this sort of "first theology for a twenty-first century" that lies ahead for theological discourse as it attempts to move beyond the either/or of the theologies of modernity represented by Schleiermacher and Barth.

Such a first theology, I would suggest, would be both a true *theology* and truly *first*. It would be a true *theology* in that it would concern itself not with an anthropological account of God-consciousness, but rather solely with the wonder and mystery of the condescension of the Holy Spirit to the broken creature, a condescension that results in humanity being "Otherwise engaged" with God from the first to the last and each moment in between. In doing so, such a theological prolegomenon to dogmatics would lay the foundation for what Barth late in life referred to as a true evangelical theology, a relational theology, what he called a "theoanthropology" that was "concerned with God as the God of *man*, but just for this reason, also with man as *God's* man."[17] Furthermore, such a first theology would be truly *first*, for it would plumb the fundamental questions of the relationship of God to world as that which establishes the creation as "Otherwise engaged" in the Spirit from the very first. In the history of theology in the West, as has often been observed, pneumatology has played a secondary, perhaps it would be more appropriate to say, a tertiary role. But if in the past the first has been last, in the theology of the twenty-first century it may very well be the case that, finally, the last shall be first.

16. Smith, *The Concept of the Spiritual*, p. 3.
17. Karl Barth, *Evangelical Theology: An Introduction*, trans. G. W. Bromiley (Grand Rapids: Eerdmans, 1970), pp. 11-12.

Theology from amidst the Victims

Jon Sobrino

We do not know what theology will be like in the future. Sociocultural paradigms are changing too quickly. In terms of the changes occurring in Latin
America, we are witnessing the closing of the circle that began with Vatican II
and Medellín and that has been expressed in the popular communities and in
such an exceptional generation of bishops (Dom Hélder Câmara, Proaño, Don
Sergio, Archbishop Romero), attaining its greatest splendor in numberless martyrs — and all of this shot through with hope and a praxis of historical liberation. During this period, liberation theology has been (as it continues to be)
the theoretical moment in the Christian dynamization of the process.

The question we now ask is: Which of the realities just cited will be present
in the future that is dawning for us? And what ought Christian theology to be
like on the Latin American continent? Basically, we think that it ought to
continue to be a theology of liberation, and the reason for this consists in the
fact that the ever more dense element of reality continues to be the oppression
that generates *victims*. These victims are real, and as real, they call theology into
question. But they also offer the opportunity for the performance of theology's
task.

Victims are not the sole *reality* of our world, of course. But unless they
are given a central place in our accounting, we shall fail to grasp the fundamental
element of our historical reality, and theology will be in serious danger of
becoming unreal: of falling into a kind of *docetism of reality* — the docetism
that, in any of its forms, has always been the greatest threat to theology.

Others in this book will analyze the future of theology from other perspectives. But on the basis of what we have just said, and because perhaps this
is what someone living in a world of victims would wish to see, we are going
to concentrate upon how we see the future of theology *from amidst the victims*
— from the standpoint of the victimized. This includes, directly, their reality
of crucifixion — but also their longing for life and hope of resurrection.

And I should like to say, by way of concluding this introduction, that in these reflections I keep the work of Jürgen Moltmann constantly in mind, not only because this book is dedicated to him, but also because his reflection on the victims — their cross and their hope, so central to his theology — has been such a help to me in my own reflection.

1. The Victims and the Primacy of Reality

May I be permitted to begin with a personal recollection. On November 16, 1989, in San Salvador, in the courtyard of our house, six Jesuits — all members of my community — along with two women who worked with us, Julia Elba and Celina, were murdered. I was in Thailand giving a course in Christology, and so did not meet with the same fate. Now, it happened that, after the murders, those who had committed them dragged the corpse of one of the six victims, Juan Ramón Moreno, back into our house. And in all the bumping and pushing, there fell from the bookcase a book — one book — that would now lie there covered with blood. The book was Jürgen Moltmann's *El Dios crucificado* — "The Crucified God." Some years later, in 1994, Moltmann himself passed through El Salvador, to see the place where the Jesuits had been murdered and lay buried. He had not come to teach; instead, he spent a long while in silence, meditating in the courtyard and in the chapel.

One might wish to dispute the theology of Moltmann's *The Crucified God,* but one thing is beyond discussion. And that is that in our historical reality, there is massive, cruel crucifixion — what Archbishop Romero and Ignacio Ellacuría referred to in terms of "the crucified people." The blood that covered Moltmann's book expresses that crucified reality. And the fact that the book was precisely *El Dios crucificado* supplies objectively theological depth: in concrete historical crucifixion is ultimacy, and in that ultimacy, very God.

This is where I should like to begin. Reality continues its irruption, and cannot be concealed. It is unfortunate that it makes that irruption in bloody and crucifying fashion. It does so for every human being. It does so for every theologian as well. The massacres in El Mozote, Haiti, Bosnia, and Rwanda, and the poverty of Chad, Bangladesh, and Nicaragua eliminate the suggestion of the purely metaphorical. And while any theology can demand theoretically that reality be assigned the primacy in the theological enterprise, it is the victims who force theology to make that demand absolute, and who seal off all hope of escape from it.

1.1. The Victims and the Signs of the Times

Assigning the primacy to reality means taking the "signs of the times" seriously — which, in my opinion, is not done very often. Let us remember, then, that this is called for by Vatican Council II, which, in a first step, understands by "signs of the times" the characteristics of an era (*Gaudium et Spes*, no. 4). The concept is a historico-pastoral one, then, in which a discernment of these signs is necessary in order for theology to have relevance. In these terms, the problem consists in how to know these signs, and especially, how to order them hierarchically. For example, a characteristic of our time is the religious dialogue, with the questions that dialogue poses for Christian theology regarding ecumenism, or regarding the uniqueness of Christ. Other characteristics of our world are ecological destruction, and the death by starvation of twenty or thirty million human beings a year. The task before us, then, is, to hierarchize the characteristics of our age (while not ignoring any of them).

In Latin America, the theology of liberation has regarded the fundamental sign of the times to be "the irruption of the poor" (Gustavo Gutiérrez), "the crucified people" (Ignacio Ellacuría) — realities that express at once unjust death, longing for life, and the possibility of offering salvation to others. And the problem for the theology of the present and of the future is whether this continues to be *the* sign of the times. Yes, it is indeed hierarchically the most important sign of the times, in our opinion; and in any case it ought to be, and continue to be. And we emphasize it because "poor," "victims," "crucified people," are elements of language relegated to oblivion today by so many intellectuals and theologians, as if their reality were overcome today, or as if the corresponding concepts were by now sufficiently integrated into theology.

Of course, to the initial analysis of poverty implemented by liberation theology, other forms of poverty and oppression must surely be added (race, gender, culture, caste, destruction of nature, etc.). But this in no way militates against the central thesis, which, formulated globally, runs as follows: Up until today, as well as for the foreseeable future, *the* sign of the times continues to be the crucified people, deprived of life and dignity. And we emphasize it, again, because this is precisely what some theologies would like to bypass, lest they have at last to face up to injustice and death. Accordingly, let us briefly recall how matters stand in our world.

A. If we ask ourselves how things are with the human *species* (noting that we do not yet speak of the human *family*), perhaps the answer would be that it is doing well — even too well, since, far from being in danger of extinction, it is enjoying a growth that is precisely part of the problem. And yet, in this species — to give only a single datum — 1,500 children an hour die of hunger or of illnesses related to hunger — more than thirteen million a year. And a new language has begun to be developed in order to speak no longer of exploited human beings merely (a cheap workforce), but of human beings not taken into account at all, human beings who do not exist. The human *species* can survive, badly, and even grow, but with a great part of it belonging practically to another *subspecies*, the one that does not count. The

First World needs the Third World's geography in order to dispose of its toxic waste and its raw material. "What it no longer needs is the greater part of its population" (Franz Hinkelammert).

B. If we ask how things stand with the human *family,* the answer is terrifying. The United Nations knew that answer in 1989, but delayed its publication for months and years due to the gruesomeness of the specifics. While in 1960 there was one rich person in the world for every thirty poor ones, now, thirty years later, there is one rich person for every sixty poor. Eduardo Galeano has put it graphically: "One citizen of the United States is worth fifty Haitians." And he wonders, as if to shake our civilization metaphysically, "what would happen if one Haitian were worth fifty United States citizens?" And here is another recent datum:

> In 1960, the poorest 20% of the population of the planet shared 2.3% of the world income — a percentage that dropped to 1.7% in 1980 and to 1.4% in 1990. Meanwhile, the richest 20% climbed from [a] 70.2% [share of the world's income] in 1960 to 76.3% in 1980 and 82.7% in 1990. (J. M. Mella Vázquez)

However much it might be ignored — even in theology — the parable that best describes the situation of our current world is that of the rich person and the poor Lazarus. It is very doubtful that the crumbs — the promised "trickle down" — will satisfy the hunger of all the poor. But what is beyond any doubt is that the policy in question rejects the reality and even the concept of the human family.

C. And to all of this must be added that the *solution* offered us for the future is inhumane. Inherent in that solution is having to make a decision as to which peoples shall live and which not, what percentage of the population in the poor countries — 40%, 50%, or 60% — are going to survive and what percentage not. And who decides this? No one. The life and death of human beings would have to be left to the coldness of the market — which is precisely what is occurring, and this is what is meant today when we hear, in all of the harshness of the term, of the "idolatry of the market."

This cannot be a solution even for the human *species,* let alone for the human *family.* And so we must unmask the proposition made to us. We must show that it is a bad solution masquerading as a good solution — or else, blackmail to the effect that, good or bad, it is the only solution. What we are being asked to accept is "the geoculture of despair and the theology of inevitability" (Xavier Gorostiaga) as our cultural substratum. In other words, the powers of this world have managed to prevent or crush not only objective radical changes — revolutions — but their subjective premise: any hope that change is possible and that it is worth the trouble to work for it.

Finally, let us observe that this inhumane solution is now foisted on us as a Christian solution, and Jesus' language is even misappropriated to this end: the neoliberal solution is said to further the coming of the reign of God for the poor! (M. Camdessus).

1.2. The Presence of God in the Victims

The crucified people are not the only characteristic of our age, but they are the fundamental, and in our opinion the central reality of that age. Furthermore, that which is positive in our world — hope, advances in humaneness — must be understood from their capacity to seize the history of the crucified people by its lapels and "turn it inside out," in such a way that the lining appears — utopia, where prophecy abides. It is in this sense that utopia will be a "minimum that is the maximum," which is what Archbishop Romero used to call the gift of life. But when all is said and done, it will be genuine utopia for the victims!

We have not yet mentioned, however, the most important thing about the crucified people for theology, and to this purpose we must recall that, in Vatican II, the "signs" have a second meaning. The Pastoral Constitution on the Church in the Modern World makes this surprising declaration: "The people of God . . . labors to decipher authentic signs of God's presence and purpose in the happenings, needs, and desires in which this people has a part along with other men of our age" (*Gaudium et Spes*, no. 11). The signs of which this text is speaking are historical realities, as in the earlier, historico-pastoral sense of the term, but now are understood sacramentally, besides: not only do they describe what is thickest or most dense in reality, but now we are told that God becomes present in them. They are signs of the times in the historical sense of God's intervention in history.

The question — the most important question for theology — is where these signs occur, and whether the historico-pastoral sign coincides with the historico-theological sign. In other words, the question is not only whether the sign of the crucified people is the most characteristic sign of our world, but whether it is also the privileged locus of the presence of God. Scripture, Medellín, Puebla, Archbishop Romero, and the theology of liberation have taken this fundamental question seriously. Moltmann did so too, in another context, many years ago now, when he wondered whether the *true* church subsisted "in the manifest community, through word and sacrament, or in the latent siblingship of the universal Judge hidden in the poor."

The answer that liberation theology has given is that the crucified people are also the privileged place of God's presence — which, of course, explains Moltmann's daring formulation, "the crucified God." And let us add that this theological reading of reality not only does not trivialize the historicity of that reality, but actually radicalizes it. And at the same time, it is this crucified reality that enables us, and demands of us — with all the cautions to be observed in the application of human language to God — to speak of God crucified.

What is at stake here are the furthermost depths of the faith — honesty with reality and with God, without our deciding beforehand that we already know the most profound reality of both things. This is why we have begun with that which is most able to lead theology to historical reality, and to lead it mystagogically to God: the victims, the crucified people.

This explains another important point of the theological undertaking as well, as that enterprise has been understood from the outset by the theology of liberation: that theology is "second act," occurring after a spiritual experience and a praxis. After all, it is the presence of God in the crucified people that enables us to speak logically of the possibility of a spiritual experience in the poor and that adds urgency to the praxis of taking the crucified down from the cross.

2. Doing Theology from amidst the Victims

From all that has been said, we discern the need for theology to assign the primacy to the reality of the victims, and to do theology in service of that primacy. This is what we intend to analyze next. To be sure, our analysis will stand in need of correction and complement in light of the changes that occur in history, but we do not think that it can be eliminated or relativized as long as the victims constitute the sign of the times.[1]

2.1. *"Elevating Reality to a Concept"*

A. In accordance with what we have said, theology should assign logical priority to *reality* over *text*, and to the *present* over the *past* — which, in principle, it can do in confronting any reality, but which is far more urgent (and theology has recognized this urgency, and acted accordingly) when it confronts the victims. And that stands to reason, since it is the historical reality of the cross and its theological correlate, the crucified God, that unsettles the intelligence, without the possibility of any text, however important it be, offering solace. Thus, it is

---

1. We have presented liberation theology's *modus procedendi* — which we summarize here — in the following writings: "Teología en un mundo sufriente: La teología de la liberación como intellectus amoris," *Revista Latinoamericana de Teología* 15 (1988): 243-65; "¿Cómo hacer teología?" *Sal Terrae* 5 (1989): 397-417; "Los 'signos de los tiempos' en la teología de la liberación," in *Fides quae per caritatem operatur*, by various authors (Bilbao, 1989), pp. 249-69; "Epílogo: Los pobres, crucificados y salvadores," in *La matanza de los pobres*, by María López Vigil and Jon Sobrino (Madrid, 1993), pp. 355-70; "De una teología solo de la liberación a una teología de martirio," *Revista Latinoamericana de Teología* 28 (1993): 27-48; "Ignacio Ellacuría: El hombre y el cristiano," *Revista Latinoamericana de Teología* 32 (1994): 131-61; 33 (1994): 215-41.

good and necessary that theology utilize texts of the past clarifying the relationship between God and victims, in this case like the Pauline and Markan traditions regarding the victim Jesus and the presence and silence of God on the cross — Hegel's "speculative Good Friday," Bonhoeffer's "Only a suffering God can save us." All of this is important for situating today's questions in the context of the best *tradition,* and for finding concepts in that tradition that will assist us in selecting the right path toward a response. But, while it is good and necessary, it is not sufficient, and this for a twofold reason.

The first reason is that it is a matter of texts of the *past,* while the question of the victims continues to echo in the present, and does so, specifically, as a question of the *present* — that is, a question that has never been silenced despite the fact that there have already been responses to similar questions in the past. And the second reason is that not even the most vigorous *texts* — be they of the past or of the present — have, as texts, sufficient capacity to mobilize the human and believing spirit in adequate ways in the quest for a response. The strength to ask and to answer comes only from *reality* itself.

B. Accordingly, in doing theology, while one must take the texts seriously into account — to do theology is, formally, to elevate reality to a theological concept in the element of that reality that manifests God and can occasion a faith response to its manifestation of God. This does not, of course, militate against the obligation to refer time and again to Scripture, which functions as a criterion of truth lest we deviate from that truth, and positively as the reserve of a totality that is inexhaustible at any one point along the course of history. And let us note that the theology of liberation, which insists so much on reality in the present, is probably also the theology that most insists on the past of Christ: seeing Christ as Jesus of Nazareth in his concrete reality.

And if this comprehension of what it is to do theology seems frightening, then let us ask ourselves whether the contrary conception would not be more frightening: the reduction of theology to an explanation of reality and God's revelation in the past, and the interpretation of texts in which this revelation has been handed down to us, without ever coming to grips with today's word of God as God, but only as word already interpreted by the magisterium and by other theologies. To put it another way: not to take seriously the possibility of God's self-manifestation in the present would mean accepting either that God no longer speaks today or that the divine word is not heard by theology. If the latter should occur, theology would vitiate its essence, or would be reduced to interpreting the history of theology. If the former were to occur, all theology would have to keep a long, respectful silence.

C. From this it follows that one can, and ultimately must, appeal to reality as well — and not only to the texts — as a theological argument. The proposition is delicate and dangerous, and therefore any theological argumentation from reality must dovetail with God's revelation. The argument from reality is, evidently, defenseless, but it is also necessary and fruitful.

And it likewise follows that, precisely by virtue of its "theological" attitude toward historical reality, this way of doing theology is exposed — more than other ways are — to the problem of theodicy. After all, for a theology that, even without explicitly recognizing it, actually presented a "deist" God, if we may put it that way, the problem of theodicy would not arise very forcefully. But if we accept a God present in the (tragic) reality of history, a God who furthermore will be specified as a liberating God, a God of life, the God of the victims, then the question of theodicy is inevitable and trenchant. But it has the advantage of keeping the question of the reality of God-today ever alive. And this *today* of God's is essential in a theology done from amidst the victims.

2.2. Intellectus Amoris

Obviously the world of the victims calls for a reaction in the form of an effort to eradicate and transform the victimhood, and this reaction should shape theology as well. A like reaction on theology's part will presuppose that theology make the reign of God, in its totality of transcendence and history, its central object. And it will presuppose that the finality of addressing that reign will not be primarily only to understand it, but also to build it.

This is central in the theology of liberation, which understands itself as "the adequate theory of the praxis of the oppressed and believing people" (Leonardo Boff), and as "the ideological moment of ecclesial and historical praxis" (Ignacio Ellacuría). This means that theology must be shot through with mercy — that, in its theoretical thinking, it be moved by the suffering of the victims, and that this suffering direct the praxis of taking the crucified down from the cross. To say it another way, within the triad *fides, spes, amor,* theology can — and in our opinion must — be understood as *intellectus amoris,* which in turn must be concretized as *intellectus misericordiae, justitiae, liberationis.*

This approach to theology's self-understanding is novel. It is possible, however, because it is real: this is how liberation theology understands itself. Furthermore, we do not know of any dogmatically binding assertion according to which theology should have to be understood exclusively or primarily as *intellectus fidei* — and Moltmann proposed years ago that theology be understood as *intellectus spei,* in correspondence with *spes quaerens intellectum.* Finally, this understanding of theology is justified, and even required, by the ultimate finality of all Christian activity: the building of the reign of God. We have, then, *amor quaerens intellectum;* and the *intellectus* that responds to this quest of love, mercy, and justice is theology.

But above and beyond the justifying precisions that we have just offered, we believe that in a suffering world, a world of victims such as we have described it, it is essential that theology understand itself as *intellectus amoris.* Surely it must rethink the mediations of which it makes use: it must be self-critical, it must "look itself in the face" (Hugo Assmann). It must rethink with what spirit praxis ought to be pervaded. That spirit could well be described in the following terms: *radicalness* (since what we are about is "turning history inside out"), *objectivity* and *realism* (since it is crucial that praxis be effective), and *prophecy* and *utopia* (in order to know what must be rejected and toward what we ought to tend and advance). But we must make no mistake about what is fundamental: we live in a world in which Christian faith may not abdicate its responsibility to transform it — and accordingly, neither may theology abdicate that responsibility. We fail to see, then, that the theology of the future ought to be praxis in a lesser way. On the contrary, it ought to be more so.

In view of all this, the reader will understand that it is not pure rhetoric when liberation theologians repeat that they are more interested in liberation than in theology; or that therefore they also wonder whether theology really liberates or whether, on the contrary, it presents an obstacle to liberation (by glossing over oppression), or even worse, whether it actually fosters oppression. Hence the permanent value of the task called for by Juan Luis Segundo: the liberation of theology.

2.3. "Taking on the Burdensome Element of Reality": Persecution and Martyrdom

The world that theology ought to try to transform is fundamentally sin, anti-reign, and negativity, and all of this in active form: those acting against that world ought to expect that world to act against them. Put simply: in doing theology as *intellectus amoris* we must be prepared to take upon ourselves the onerous element of reality.

Experience shows that, in order to uproot negativity, one must struggle against it, defeating a certain kind of excessively tolerant postmodernity. But one must also defeat a certain optimism inherent in modernity. In order to eradicate negativity, it is not enough to struggle against it from "without." The struggle must be waged "from within" as well: one must take on the burden of negativity under the presupposition that sin will discharge its force upon those who take on its burden.

In Latin America, this conviction is not solely or principally the upshot of conceptual theoretical analyses (although R. Girard's theses do shed a great deal of light on the subject). It is the product, rather, of a conviction whose ultimate root is in a combination of an honest view of history and of Christian faith. And so we side with Ignacio Ellacuría, who so frequently cited the songs of the Suffering Servant of Yahweh, and made of them a central element in his theological approach. Not that he was "doloristic" or "sacrificialistic." But he did see the figure of the Servant as something central: in order to uproot sin, it is a necessary condition, although not a sufficient one, to take it upon oneself.

In the Zubirian terminology that Ellacuría frequently used, in order "effectively to take upon oneself the reality" that generates victims, one must be prepared to "pick it up" — one must allow oneself to be affected by the sin of the world. There is something in sin that is not reversed by combating it only from without: it must be struggled against from within. This is a way of formulating the *mysterium iniquitatis,* which affects the theologian as such, too, and, in a greater or lesser degree, leads to persecution and martyrdom.

These reflections may seem to some to be out of place in a composition on how to do theology, but in our opinion they are crucial. In the first place, there have been theologians who have confronted reality and have sought to transform it, but who, besides, likewise as theologians, have been prepared to take it upon themselves — and they have been put to death. In the second place, not to consider this possibility seriously would imply an acceptance of the world in which theology is done as a *tabula rasa* world, and not an active anti-reign that acts against all those opposing it, though they be intellectuals. In my judgment, such a view of the world would constitute a serious error — and not only a practical one, but a theoretical one as well. And conversely, if theology (and theologians) never suffer any kind of attack at the hands of the powers of this world (however they may suffer it at the hands of the church hierarchy), then that theology will be open to the suspicion that it is not a theology that faces reality — the reality that generates victims, especially — but a theology of concepts in the reductionistic sense.

And if I may be permitted a bit of irony, it will be well to recall that, in the first Christian centuries, there were martyr theologians, who unified their existential and theological reflection on martyrdom. So we had an Ignatius of Antioch and a Justin. After all, in our days, an Ignacio Ellacuría is also both a theologian and a martyr, and he reflected, *as a theologian,* on the relationship between the two. Persecution and martyrdom were foreseeable things for him, if it is true that the theologian "picks up reality" and shoulders it.

2.4. *"Allowing Oneself to Be Picked up by Reality": Theology and Grace*

Reality is not only negativity, but positivity as well, and therefore theology must not only take it up, but can also allow itself to be taken up by it. Playing with the word "take on" or "pick up," Karl Rahner said: "The gospel is a heavy charge and a light one: the more one takes it on the more it picks one up" and carries that person forward. Something analogous could be said of the relationship between theology and reality.

The premise is that reality contains not only negativity, but positivity as well. Not only does sin exist, but grace as well. In taking up reality, theology takes up as well the element of grace in that reality, and thereby reality takes on theology. And this is verified in experience.

When we take on victims, the latter take us on — offer us *light* to know content and to recognize that which has always been in revelation but has gone unperceived. It is the sort of light that the Servant of Yahweh offers when he is "set . . . as . . . as a light for the nations" (Isa. 42:6). The victims are like a light we carry when we are looking for something. No one looks at the lamp, and yet, in its light, we find what we are looking for because we can see it. And furthermore, the victims offer content to the intelligence. The concepts of this content may have long existed, but may frequently have been ignored, or been unknown in terms of their actual weight.

This means that the victims are transformed into a theological locus, understanding the latter not primarily as a categorical *ubi* (academic department, seminary, university, curia, community), but as a substantial *quid*. And experience shows that, when theology is done on the basis of the reality of this locus, important truths of God's revelation, hitherto unknown or glossed over, are rediscovered and become central. The most crying example of this is the rediscovery that liberation is a central reality in revelation, as both Vatican Instructions of 1984 and 1986 came to recognize, but which had been unknown in theology for centuries, even in progressive theology. And the same will have to be said of many other themes, especially when they are focused dialectically: reign of God and anti-reign, God and idols, greater God and lesser God, grace and sin, beatitudes and woes, martyrs, church of the poor, and so on. All of this has been shown by the world of the victims. If we may be permitted a bit of paraphrase and paradox, the victims are the *Sitz im Tode* that has helped bring it about that any *Sitz im Leben* be transformed into a more Christian and more real locus.

In the same reality, then, there exists the positive that bursts in conjointly with the negative. Not only has evil irrupted, but good as well. Not only has the victims' cry burst in, but their hope and longing for liberation. Therefore, just as we have reformulated theology as *intellectus amoris*, now we wish to reformulate it as *intellectus gratiae*. And the ultimate reason for the latter formulation is in the Christian acceptance of the fact that God is present, patently or concealed, in the victims of this world. Therefore to do theology from amidst, for, and with the victims is to do theology while being borne by reality.

*　　*　　*　　*　　*

We cannot predict what theology will be like in the future, and we have remarked at the outset that others will explore, in this book, new paths for theology. But such as our world is going, and such as God has been manifested in Jesus, we think that substantially the perspective of the victims must continue to be valid — although would that it were to become quickly anachronistic — and in any case giving the primacy to reality in order to transform it. This in no way militates against the equal necessity of "being ever prepared to give reason for our hope," in Gutiérrez's words, "as to tell the poor that God loves them" — the explanatory dimension of theology. But we think that theology must, especially, render that hope productive for the construction in our world of the reign of God: in Ellacuría's words, "taking the crucified people down from the cross" — the transforming dimension of theology. This is what is demanded by reality, and by the God who, at times overtly, at times in a concealed manner, becomes present in that reality.

Whence to extract hope for transforming reality is not something that can be defined beforehand. I have always been encouraged — perhaps because I have happened to live surrounded by martyrs — by the words of Jürgen Moltmann: "Not every life is an occasion of hope, but this life of Jesus, who took upon himself, in love, the cross and death, is." And let us read that carefully, lest we be accused of being dolorists: it is life — although not every life, but the life shot through with mercy and love — that keeps up hope, and that takes on theology.

Theology, Spirituality, and Historical Praxis

Gustavo Gutiérrez

We have always had points of discussion in theology, even disputed questions. The reason for this is that the effort of the "intelligence of the faith," and the terms used to account for the faith, frequently fall short of the wealth of Christian revelation. Furthermore, theology must approach the great Christian truths from changing historical situations — from a variety of concrete challenges. Hence the fact that theological language has so much of the approximate about it, and must be prepared for renewal, precision, and even, if need be, correction. Hence, too, the constant appearance of new perspectives in the discourse on the faith. Let us see some applications and examples.

Theological Language and Its Circumstances

More than twenty-five years ago, something called the *theology of liberation* appeared on the Latin American scene. At that time, for many Christians — despite the impulse of the Council such a short time before — the building of a just society did not seem to be a serious requirement of the faith. In others, however, something no less grave occurred: solidarity with the poor and oppressed in the conditions of Latin America seemed to them an exclusively social or political matter, about which the faith had little or nothing to say. We are speaking of persons for whom, despite all, faith was — or had been — something very important. Both cases expressed a "divorce between faith and life," which the Santo Domingo Bishops' Conference still sees as capable of "producing crying situations of injustice, social inequality, and violence" (n. 24; cf. nos. 96, 161).

And so we had a state of affairs that defied the Christian conscience and challenged theological reflection. Accordingly, the point of departure of that discourse upon the faith was the earnest determination to contribute to the judgment that, in the light of the word of God, ought to be made as to the appropriate commitment: the "commitment that would become more radical, complete, and effective" in the face of the poverty and injustice of our continent. At stake was a Christian commitment inscribed in the process of liberation from everything that prevents the inhabitants of our continent from living as human beings and as daughters and sons of God.[1] The context that throws up obstacles to that worthy life is a complex, conflictive reality, and unprecedented in a number of aspects. Circumstances are in constant evolution, as we might expect, and this dictates that theological reflection be engaged upon a continuous search for the most suitable terms for expressing itself. This theological effort, furthermore, implies an acknowledgment of, precisely, the *mystery* of God's love, the love that swathes human existence and endows it with meaning. No theology, however valid it might be, can be identified with the faith itself.[2] A legitimate theological diversity, within the framework of faith, is an element of wealth in the church.

The theological enterprise is at the service of evangelization. Consequently, it must be very concerned for the communication and comprehension of the Christian message.[3] Theology is a task performed within the church in which there is a deposit of faith. The persons devoted to this commitment, theologians, answer a calling that John Paul II qualifies as "noble and necessary." It arises — the Pope specifies — "within the Church, and is based on the premise that theologians themselves are in the condition of believers, having an attitude of faith to which they themselves must testify in the community." Thus understood — Santo Domingo will say — theological toil "impels an effort in behalf of social justice, human rights, and solidarity with the very poorest" (no. 33). Consequently, theology must employ a language that will speak to our contemporaries. Here it is interesting to observe the place that the evangelizing options open to the church and theology — which latter could have seemed to many to be some kind of esoteric discipline — have acquired, in recent years, in the daily life of numerous Latin Americans: among believers, obviously, but also — although in a different way — among nonbelievers. The result is a new presence of the gospel in Latin American society. From the standpoint of a missionary thrust and inspiration — anxious about the world in which the church lives — we see that we have achieved something very important in these recent years.

From the considerations that we have now set forth, we readily see that

---

1. This is maintained in Gustavo Gutiérrez, *A Theology of Liberation: History, Politics and Salvation*, trans. Caridad Inda and John Eagleson (Maryknoll, N.Y.: Orbis, 1973), from the first page onward.

2. This was solemnly recalled by John XXIII on the occasion of the opening of the Council, in a discourse that was to mark its labors: "The substance of the *depositum fidei*, that is, of the truths that our venerable doctrine contains, is one thing, and the manner in which it is expressed is another" (Address of October 11, 1962).

3. Cf. John Paul II, Inaugural Address at Santo Domingo, no. 7.

theological language is partial, and inevitably indebted to the mentality of its time. History demonstrates this altogether authentically. And so, in all respect for the meaning of the words and terms employed at a given moment, we must approach the theological task by placing it in its context. For simple semantic reasons, terms do not have exactly the same meaning in different mental climates. At stake is not merely the correct meaning of the words, but priorities, balances, and new challenges as well. No one, for example, makes the mistake of thinking that the international and national panorama of two decades ago, whether on the political level or on that of pastoral priorities, is the same today.[4] The social reality in which the faith is lived influences the discourse made upon it.

Accordingly, the effort of a theological grasp of new realities stands in need of constant semantical adjustment. Imperfections of language must be overcome insofar as possible. Accents shift, new questions appear, and an inevitable change in themes and concepts occurs. This state of affairs becomes even more urgent when delicate, disputed questions are under consideration. Then, dialogue is necessary and fruitful. The clarity required for a correct understanding by everyone involved is not always attained. Or else, the delicacy of the point at issue occasions the adoption of formulations that subsequently prove to be open to interpretations going beyond an author's original intent. In order to overcome these obstacles, in order to respond to legitimate misgivings and questions, and in order to render an opinion on the place of these formulations with respect to the common doctrine of the church and their consonance with that doctrine, one must constantly revisit certain topics that, for the reasons we have given, have been and continue to be an object of debate. The political theology of hope constitutes a good example of a series of permanent basic intuitions and at the same time of sensitivity to new questions and of a refinement of theological language.

Theology and Witness

The gift of faith, freely received, leads to following Jesus in deeds and words. This is how the Lord proclaimed the gospel.[5] In the dynamics of faith is the quest for its understanding: "I believe in order to understand," said Saint Anselm, in an expression that has traversed the centuries. This is what we call theology. In turn, theology must contribute to the fidelity and authenticity of our following of Christ.

---

4. It suffices to compare the documents, for example, of Medellín, Puebla, and Santo Domingo, in order to perceive the differences in language. Still, and the Fourth Conference states this on a number of occasions, the fundamental options are the same. See also the diversity of themes addressed by Latin American theology during these years. A number of those points have been present, and brought under consideration anew, at Santo Domingo.

5. Cf. the Constitution *Dei Verbum*, no. 4.

.When Christian faith, lived in the church, experiences new challenges for its communication to others, theology questions itself about the status of the reflection in which it engages on the biblical message. We have numerous historical examples of this. We need not reinvent the task: it is classic in Christianity. We need only plumb its depths, and, often, to renew it by sinking deeper roots into church history and tradition.

This is what happened nearly three decades ago in Latin America. A "reflection, based on the Gospel and the experiences of men and women committed to the process of liberation," arose,[6] and its starting point was the gospel: the Good News brought to us by Jesus Christ. But that News not only reveals the God of our faith. It also unveils the ultimate meaning of human behavior. All theology is a speaking about God. God is in some sense its solitary theme.[7] But by that very fact theology is also, secondarily, a language about those who have been created in the image and likeness of God.

One of our initial questions, consequently, in the early years of the theology of liberation, concerned the nature of the discourse upon the faith. In the first place, we needed to recall that, in a broad and basic sense, every Christian does theology. Indeed, theology "arises spontaneously and inevitably in the believer, in all those who have accepted the gift of the Word of God."[8] This is the floor upon which theology as a systematic discipline is built.

Without faith, which is a grace — faith in the God revealed to us in Christ — there is no theology properly so called. There can only be a consideration of a religious type. After all, theology is seeing things in the light of the word of the Lord (a participation in the science of God, said Thomas Aquinas, in the first Question of his *Summa Theologiae*), which implies receiving that word in faith and making of the latter the ultimate meaning of human existence. Hence the basic, familiar expression of the theology of liberation: theology is a critical reflection upon praxis *in the light of faith* (or of the word of God received in faith). This is the classic *lumen fidei* that constitutes the hinge — or, in the language of the School, the formal object — of theology.

The term *praxis* (or practice) was a relatively new one in the execution of these tasks, and must be understood in a precise manner in order to preclude mistaken interpretations. In this way of understanding the material upon which theology reflects, praxis is intimately and explicitly bound up with the rediscovery of charity "as the center of the Christian life." The establishment of this link is inspired in a celebrated Pauline text that declares that faith works through charity. Hence it is that "love is the nourishment and the fullness of faith, the gift of one's self to the Other, and invariably to others." Charity, accordingly, is "the foundation of the *praxis* of the Christian, of his

6. Gutiérrez, *Theology of Liberation*, p. ix.
7. The point has been developed in Gutiérrez, *Hablar de Dios* (Lima, 1986).
8. Gutiérrez, *Theology of Liberation*, p. 3.

active presence in history."[9] It is to this basing, and this ultimate signification, that we refer when we speak of historical praxis.

The response to God's gratuitous love is love of God and neighbor — two indefectibly united vectors, as Scripture repeats on so many occasions. To separate them is to lie, according to First John (4:20), and we know that, in the Joannine texts, the lie is one of the gravest forms of the rejection of God (cf. John 8:44). We are dealing with the familiar bond between faith and works so heavily emphasized in Matthew's Gospel, for example, and a link that, at one time, was a theme of controversy between Catholic and Protestant theology. But as Karl Barth declares, "the true hearer of the Word of God is the one who puts it to work."

Works are situated on the level of praxis — of acting in concrete history in the service of neighbor. One expression — not the only one — of these works is what the popes call the "struggle for justice": that is, the engagement in favor of an integral liberation. Another expression is the concrete, immediate deed on behalf of the needy. A Christian's ultimate motivation in building a just society is love. In order to be effective, that love must select the necessary means, which can, of course, differ according to circumstance. We must acknowledge that an insistence on these means, which are always provisional, has obfuscated — perhaps because it has not always been suitably presented — the fact that they are only that: means. It is important, then, to avoid all misunderstanding, and restore the profound meaning at stake.

What we have said until now enables the reader to understand texts that otherwise might occasion surprise, and for which we have actually been reproached, such as the following: "In the last instance, the true interpretation of the meaning revealed by theology is given in historical praxis."[10] What is the meaning revealed by the intelligence of the faith? The response can scarcely be in doubt: the love of God, the heart of the revelation that the Father gives us to know by sending the very Son, as John's Gospel says. This is what is meant by the proclamation of the Reign of God, whose coming in our history (and with it, love, peace, justice, freedom) we ask in the Our Father. And it is clear that, unless we love — as a response to God's initiative — unless we seek to contribute siblingship and justice, we do not really believe. "The faith that does nothing in practice," says James — trenchantly — "is thoroughly lifeless" (James 2:17). The love of God in us leads to love of neighbor. This is the meaning at stake. This meaning is equally present in theology as wisdom (the consideration upon Scripture) and in theology as rational and systematic knowledge.

The biblical bases of this focus are clear and manifold. But when it comes

---

9. Gutiérrez, *Theology of Liberation*, pp. 6-7. The historical trajectory of this old notion, which arose with Greek philosophy, is traced in N. Lobkowicz, *Theory and Practice* (Notre Dame, 1967).

10. Gutiérrez, *Teología de la liberación: Perspectivas* (Lima: CEP, 1971), p. 31.

to their application in the present, the contemporary mentality also has a contribution to make. This fact led to our selection of the word *praxis* (with the old, basic precisions that we have here recalled). The use of the word *praxis* enables us to show how our focus on God's love in us, overflowing outward, dovetails with our times, our era — enables us to communicate, with mordancy and wealth, a central point of the Christian message.[11] As Jürgen Moltmann so well says, "Theology exists in order to reflect, in the light of the Gospel, upon all Christian existence and practice."[12]

The truth is that in the deed of love and solidarity the authenticity of our faith in the God of the Reign is verified. It is to that practice that we allude, and not to a practice that would ignore the human condition and the vocation of all to be sons and daughters of God. Rightly does K. Lehmann write: "Christian faith tends inevitably to be verified in works, but it cannot be unreservedly identified with any type of praxis."[13] That perspective has been underscored on various occasions by John Paul II. For example, speaking concretely of the union movement as an element of solidarity among laborers, he says: "The church is intensely committed to this cause, because it considers it as its mission, its service, as a *verification* of its fidelity to Christ, in order to be truly the church of the poor."[14] The "verification" does not create truth as such; it evinces its presence in human acting, and demonstrates its exigencies in a better way.

The entire Bible tells us that in the beginning was God's gratuitous love. All comes from this, that God first loved us, John declares. There is the beginning of all. The author of the book of Job, like Saint Paul, has recalled this with matchless directness. In the history of Christianity, the work of Saint Augustine represents one of the most significant echoes of this fundamental revealed datum. In the Augustinian line, the Second Council of Orange (529), so decisive for our theological training today,[15] emphasized, in memorable terms, the presence and primacy of God's grace in the human being's every good act.[16]

Centuries later the controversy over indulgences led Martin Luther to maintain that nothing, and no one, posits conditions for the salvific activity of God. That activity is something purely gratuitous. Human works never merit it. Faith alone saves (we are saved *sola fide*). This is how Luther understands the Pauline text, "A man is justified by faith apart from observance of the law"

---

11. The Instruction on the theology of liberation likewise refers to Christians' praxis in XI, 4.

12. Jürgen Moltmann, *Diaconía: En el horizonto del Reino* (Santander: Sal Terrae, 1987), p. 14. A few lines earlier he has maintained, "Every believer is a theologian" (p. 13).

13. K. Lehmann, "Problemas metodológicos y hermenéuticos de la teología de la liberación," in his *Teología de la liberación* (Madrid: BAC, 1978), p. 25. Emphasis added.

14. *Laborem Exercens*, no. 82. Emphasis added.

15. Cf. Juan Luis Segundo.

16. Denzinger, no. 200.

(Rom. 3:28). Here is a valuable intuition into the gratuity of God's activity. But it can be misunderstood as a belittling of the human response in the salvific process.

Before all else, salvation is a gift. But it is also a task. It is grace, and it is demand. Human beings respond to God's gift with their freedom, and that freedom is expressed in behavior. God's gratuitous love makes ethical demands. Faith is not reducible to works, but works do express the seriousness — and ultimately the truth, in the biblical sense of loyalty and fidelity — of our acceptance of the gift of faith. Faith — which is life — becomes understood by way of deeds, practice, witness.

Spirituality and Liberation

"Spirituality" is a relatively new word. It made its appearance, in a French context, around the seventeenth century, and denotes what in early times was called the following of Christ *(sequela Christi)*. This following is implemented by persons who live in a determinate historical reality, and in a time marked out by precise coordinates.

"The increasing impoverishment [of] millions of our siblings" to which the Santo Domingo Bishops Conference refers (Final Document, no. 179) — with its causes in injustice, the results of social conflict, and, indeed, terrorism and repressive violence — is a major and inescapable element of the concrete framework in which we are summoned to be disciples of Jesus. Another major and inseparable element of this concrete framework is the effort and generosity of so many persons who defend the right to life and liberty proclaimed in the gospel. These realities challenge Christians, and call them to enter into solidarity with the victims of poverty and violence. A like commitment will take the route of a liberation from everything that keeps these persons in subhuman and unjust conditions — and in a deeper perspective, the route of liberation from the sin, the selfishness, that ignores or even provokes the oppression and suffering of others. At the point of the following of Christ, there is a conversion: the abandonment of one road and the adoption of another that leads us to the divine Parent and the human sibling.

In the 1970s, not a few Christians committed themselves, in their respective countries, to what was called the "Latin American revolutionary process." The essential point here — above and beyond this or that necessary expression of greater distance and an indispensable maturation — rests on the fact that following Christ means making the gospel and its demands of love and justice present amidst the premature death of so many, the mistreatment of the poor, contempt for the Indian and black cultures and races, and the marginalization of women. These are difficult conditions for a Christian life — both for the life of prayer, and for the dimension of solidarity with the suffering. But we must be aware that what is at stake is a challenging, fertile route of fidelity at once to the God of our faith and to the Latin American people.

The gospel does not indicate a precise social or political path to take. But it does present the demands that Christians will have to take into account when they come to select the route they regard as most effective for eliminating unjust inequalities and the marginalization of the most helpless. The question is how to follow a path of holiness — "You must be made perfect as your heavenly Father is perfect" (Matt. 5:48) — in the midst of the demands of solidarity with and commitment to those who suffer poverty, contempt, or injustice. Indeed, these demands not only invite the hearer to give responses of a social or economic kind, but also require an attitude of spirituality.

One of our major challenges is owing to the conflictive nature of the social and the political realm. In this area, *factually,* there are various kinds of confrontations among persons. Social conflict is present — whether we like it or not — in our world. The important thing, in a Christian perspective, is to maintain, amidst oppositions and confrontations, love for every person, even if that person appears in our social reality as an adversary. That is not a simple task. Simple goodwill cannot conjure away a confrontation of opinions. But neither may we for that reason reject — and worse still, fall into hatred of — persons. With respect to these matters, the very Catechism of the Catholic Church says: "Liberation in the spirit of the gospel is incompatible with hatred for the enemy as a person, but not with hatred for the evil he does as enemy."

On the other hand, concrete historical commitment is only a part — a necessary and inevitable part — of Christian life. That life is above all a gladsome experience of the gratuity of God's love, and one of the greatest expressions of this experience is prayer. Prayer is not escapism. In the living experience of prayer are sunk the roots of solidarity with the victims of history, since only God's gratuitous love plunges to the root of ourselves and there arouses an authentic love on our own part. In turn, the latter love translates into deeds of siblingship toward others. Here is the wellspring of the joy that ought to mark the life of the Christian. Love for all, and the gladness that invites others to communication, prevents our commitment (which it is neither human nor Christian to evade) from leading to the rejection of concrete persons, or to a gradual descent into affliction and bitterness.

The following of Jesus (spirituality) embraces the various aspects of the human being.[17] Nothing escapes the acceptance of the gift of life. The historical dimension (engagement) and the contemplative dimension (prayer) are mutually enriching. Although present and appreciated in our theological perspective from the outset, both dimensions have begun to be called, in recent years,

---

17. Among them the ecological aspect, ever more urgent and important. Cf. Jürgen Moltmann, *Gerechtigkeit schafft Zukunft* (Munich: Kaiser, 1989).

"practices," since they correspond to living experience: a praying practice, and the practice of solidarity. At issue is the acceptance of the will of God in our lives. This is the material that, in the light of the Word of the Lord (revelation), constitutes the object of theology's reflection. This is what makes of a lived faith a ruminated one. The ultimate meaning and goal of this effort is that Christians and the whole church be faithful to the message of Jesus, and the means is to make that message more credible, understandable, and effective in the "today" of our history.

Liberation spirituality, which appeared in germ several decades ago, today is a robust reality in Latin America. Emphasis on the contemplative and historical dimensions of the entire Christian life, the study of the books of the Bible that had not been broadly approached in the early stages, the effort to strike bonds with the history of spirituality, and the witness of martyrdom offered by so many persons who have given their lives for the gospel and its preference for the poor, are helping to interpret and nuance initial assertions, as well as to find — in an ongoing quest for the best way to say it — the profound sense of what is at stake.

At bottom, theology is a reflection on the following of Jesus, which postulates the gospel as the path to the Parent who reveals the divine love through God's Child Jesus Christ. That is the point of reference of theology as rational knowledge. It is also, obviously, the point of reference of theology as wisdom (a function of theology that seems to us to be called to a greater development in the Latin American context), which sprang up precisely in the first centuries of the church as a meditation on the Bible for the nourishment of the Christian life. Thus, we continue to believe that any authentic theology is a spiritual theology. Its development is one of the great tasks that lie before us in the future of Latin America.

Martin, Malcolm, and Black Theology

James H. Cone

America, I don't plan to let you rest until that day comes into being when all God's children will be respected, and every [person] will respect the dignity and worth of human personality. America, I don't plan to let you rest until from every city hall in the country, justice will roll down like waters and righteousness like a mighty stream. America, I don't plan to let you rest until from every state house . . . , [persons] will sit in the seat who will do justly, who will love mercy, and who will walk humbly before their God. America, I don't plan to let you rest until you live it out that 'all [persons] are created equal and endowed by their creator with certain inalienable rights.' America, I don't plan to let you rest until you live it out that you believe what you have read in your Bible, that out of one blood God made all [people] to dwell upon the face of the earth.[1]

Martin Luther King, Jr.

All other people have their own religion, which teaches them of a God whom they can associate with themselves, a God who at least looks like one of their own kind. But, we so-called Negroes, after 400 years of masterful brainwashing by the slave master, picture 'our God' with the same blond hair, pale skin, and cold blue eyes of our murderous slave master. His Christian religion teaches us that black is a curse, thus we who accept the slave master's religion find ourselves loving and respecting everything and everyone except black, and can picture God as being anything else EXCEPT BLACK.[2]

Malcolm X

---

1. Martin Luther King, Jr., "Which Ways Its Soul Shall Go?", address given August 2, 1967, at a voter registration rally, Louisville, Kentucky. In Martin Luther King, Jr., Papers, Martin Luther King, Jr., Center for Nonviolent Social Change, Atlanta, Georgia.

2. Malcolm X, "God's Angry Men," *Los Angeles Herald Dispatch*, August 1, 1957.

The prophetic and angry voices of Martin Luther King Jr. and Malcolm X together revolutionized theological thinking in the African American community. Before Martin and Malcolm, black ministers and religious thinkers repeated the doctrines and mimicked the theologies they read and heard in white churches and seminaries, grateful to be allowed to worship God in an integrated sanctuary and to study theology with whites in a seminary classroom.

I remember my excitement when I was accepted as a student at Garrett Theological Seminary more than thirty-five years ago. It was my first educational experience in a predominately white environment. Like most blacks of that time who attended white colleges and graduate schools, I tried hard to be accepted as just another student. But no matter how hard I tried, I was never just another student in the eyes of my white classmates and my professors. I was a *Negro* student — which meant a person of mediocre intelligence (until proven otherwise) and whose history and culture were not worthy of theological reflection.

No longer able to accept black invisibility in theology and getting angrier and angrier at the white brutality meted out against Martin King and other civil rights activists, my southern, Arkansas racial identity began to rise in my theological consciousness. Like a dormant volcano, it soon burst forth in a manner that exceeded my intellectual control.

"You are a racist!" I yelled angrily at my doctoral advisor who was lecturing to a theology class of about 40 students. "You've been talking for weeks now about the wrongdoings of Catholics against Protestants in sixteenth- and seventeenth-century Europe," I continued, raising my voice even higher, "but you've said absolutely nothing about the monstrous acts of violence by *white* Protestants against Negroes in the American South today in 1961!"

Devastated that I — who was a frequent presence in his office and home — would call him a racist, my advisor, a grave and staid English gentleman, had no capacity for understanding black rage. He paced back and forth for nearly a minute before he stopped suddenly and stared directly at me with an aggrieved and perplexed look on his face. Then he shouted, "That's simply not true! Class dismissed."

He stormed out of the classroom to his office. I followed him. "Jim," he turned in protest, "*you* know I'm not a racist!" "I know," I said with an apologetic tone but still laced with anger. "I'm sorry I blurted out my frustrations at you. But I'm angry about racism in America and the rest of the world. I find it very difficult to study theology and never talk about it in class." "I'm concerned about racism too," he retorted with emphasis. We then talked guardedly about racism in Britain and the United States.

The more I thought about the incident, then and later, the more I realized that my angry outburst was not about the personal prejudices of my advisor or any other professor at Garrett. It was about how the discipline of theology had been defined so as to exclude any engagement with the African-American struggle against racism. I did not have the words to say to my advisor what I deeply felt. I just knew intuitively that something was seriously wrong with studying theology during the peak of the civil rights era and never once reading a book about racial justice in America or talking about it in class. It was as if the black struggle for justice had nothing to do with the study of theology — a disturbing assumption that I gradually became convinced was both anti-Christian and racist. But since I could not engage in a disinterested discussion about race as if I were analyzing Karl Barth's Christology, I kept my views about racism in theology to myself and only discussed them with the small group of African-American students who had similar views.

After I completed the Ph.D. in systematic theology in the fall of 1964, I returned to Arkansas to teach at Philander Smith College in Little Rock. No longer cloistered in a white academic environment and thus free of the need of my professors' approval, I turned my attention to the rage I had repressed during six years of graduate education. Martin Luther King, Jr. and the civil rights movement helped me to take another look at the theological meaning of the black struggle for justice. My seminary education was nearly worthless in this regard, except as a negative stimulant. My mostly neoorthodox professors talked incessantly about the "mighty acts of God" in biblical history. But they objected to any effort to link God's righteousness with the political struggles of the poor today, especially among the black poor fighting for justice in the United States. God's righteousness, they repeatedly said, can never be identified with any human project. The secular theologians were not much better. They proclaimed God's death with glee and published God's obituary in *Time* magazine. But they ignored Martin King's proclamation of God's righteous presence in the black freedom struggle.

Although latecomers to the civil rights movement, a few white theologians in the North supported it and participated in marches led by Martin Luther King, Jr. But the African-American fight for justice made little or no impact on their intellectual discourse about God, Jesus, and theology. Mainstream religion scholars viewed King as a civil rights activist who happened to be a preacher rather than as a creative theologian in his own right.

It is one thing to think of Martin King as a civil rights activist who transformed America's race relations, and quite another to regard racial justice as having theological significance. Theology as I studied it in the 1960s was narrowly defined to exclude the practical and intellectual dimensions of race. That was why Albert Camus, Jean-Paul Sartre, and Susan Sontag were read in theology courses, but not Richard Wright, Zora Neale Hurston, W. E. B. DuBois, and James Baldwin. Likewise Harry Emerson Fosdick and Ralph Sockman figured high on the reading lists in homiletics courses, but not Howard Thurman and Martin King. White theologians reflected on the meaning of God's presence in the world from the time of the Exodus to the civil rights revolution and never once made a sustained theological connection between these two liberation events. The black experience was theologically meaningless to them.

Unfortunately black ministers and theologians were strongly influenced by the white way of thinking about God and theology. When Richard Allen and other black Christians separated from white churches in the late eighteenth and early nineteenth centuries, they did not regard their action as having *theological* meaning. They thought of it as a *social* act, totally unrelated to how blacks and whites think about God. That was why they accepted without alterations the confessions of faith of the white denominations from which they separated. But how is it possible to enslave and segregate people and still have correct thinking about God? That was a question that black ministers did not ask.

Even Martin King did not ask that question so as to expose the flawed white liberal thinking about God that he had encountered in graduate school. King thought his theology was derived primarily from his graduate education, and to a large degree it was, especially his ghost-written books and speeches to white audiences. As a result, he was unaware of the profoundly radical interpretation of Christianity expressed in his civil rights activity and proclaimed in his sermons.

But what King *did* in the South and later the North and what he *proclaimed* in sermons and impromptu addresses profoundly influenced our understanding of the Christian faith. King did not do theology in the safe confines of academia — writing books, reading papers to learned societies, and teaching graduate students. He did theology with his life and proclaimed it in his preaching. Through marches, sit-ins, and boycotts and with the thunder of his voice, King hammered out his theology. He aroused the conscience of white America and made the racist a moral pariah in the church and the society. He also inspired passive blacks to take charge of their lives, to believe in themselves, in God's creation of them as a free people, equally deserving of justice as whites.

King was a public theologian. He turned the nation's television networks into his pulpit and classroom, and he forced white Christians to confront their own beliefs. He challenged all Americans in the church, academy, and every segment of the culture to face head-on the great moral crisis of racism in the United States and in the world. It was impossible to ignore King and the claims he made about religion and justice. While he never regarded himself as an academic theologian, he transformed our understanding of the Christian faith by making the practice of justice an essential ingredient of its identity.

It could be argued that Martin King's contribution to the identity of Christianity in America and the world was as far-reaching as Augustine's in the fifth century and Luther's in the sixteenth.[3] Before King, no Christian theologian showed so conclusively in his actions and words the great contradiction between

3. That observation was made to me in a private conversation by theologian Langdon Gilkey of the University of Chicago. It is unfortunate that he never made a disciplined theological argument about King's theological importance in his published writings. If he had done so, perhaps American white theologians would not have ignored the black freedom struggle and would have been less hostile toward the rise of black liberation theology.

racial segregation and the gospel of Jesus. In fact, racial segregation was so widely accepted in the churches and societies throughout the world that few white theologians in America and Europe regarded the practice as unjust. Those who did see the injustice did not regard the issue important enough to write or even talk about. But after King, no theologian or preacher dares to defend racial segregation. He destroyed its moral legitimacy. Even conservative white preachers like Pat Robertson and Jerry Falwell make a point to condemn racial segregation and do not want to be identified with racism. That change is due almost single-handedly to the theological power of King's actions and words.

Martin King was extremely modest about his political achievements and rather naive about the intellectual impact he made on the theological world. Theologians and seminarians have also been slow to recognize the significance of his theological contribution. But I am convinced that Martin Luther King Jr. was the most important and influential Christian theologian in America's history. Some would argue that the honor belongs to Jonathan Edwards or Reinhold Niebuhr or even perhaps Walter Rauschenbusch. (King acknowledged that the latter two, along with other white theologians, had a profound influence on his thinking.) Where we come down on this issue largely depends upon how we understand the discipline of theology. Those who think that the honor belongs to Edwards or Niebuhr or Rauschenbusch cannot possibly regard the achievement of racial justice as a significant theological issue, because none of them made justice for black people a central element of their theological program. Edwards, Rauschenbusch, and Niebuhr were *white* theologians who sought to speak only to their own racial community. They did not use their intellectual power to support people of color in their fight for justice. Blacks and the Third World poor were virtually invisible to them.

I am a black liberation theologian. No theologian in America is going to receive high marks from me who ignores race or pushes it to the margin of his or her theological agenda. But my claim about the importance of race for theology in America does not depend on one being a black liberation theologian. *Any* serious observer of America's history can see that it is impossible to understand the political and religious meaning of this nation without dealing with race. Race has mattered as long as there has been an America. How then can one be regarded as the most important and influential Christian theologian in this land and not deal with racism, its most intractable sin?

Martin King is America's most important Christian theologian because of what he said and did about race from a theological point of view. He was a liberation theologian before the phrase was coined by African-American and Latin-American religious thinkers in the late sixties and early seventies. King's mature reflections on the gospel of Jesus emerged primarily from his struggle for racial justice in America. His political practice preceded his theological reflections. He was an activist-theologian who showed that one could not be a Christian in any authentic sense without fighting for justice among people.

One can observe the priority of practice as a hermeneutical principle in his sermons, essays, and books. *Stride toward Freedom* (1958), *Why We Can't Wait* (1964), and *Where Do We Go from Here?* (1967) were reflections on the political and religious meaning (respectively) of the Montgomery bus boycott (1955-56), the Birmingham movement (1963), and the rise of Black Power (1966). In these texts, King defined the black freedom movement as seeking to redeem the soul of America and to liberate its political and religious institutions from the cancer of racism. I contend that he surpassed the others as a theologian to America because he addressed our most persistent and urgent sickness.

But two other features of King's work elevate him above Edwards, Rauschenbusch, and Niebuhr. The first is his international stature and influence. I do not mean his Nobel Prize, but his contribution beyond the particularity of the black American struggle. He influenced liberation movements in China, Ireland, Germany, India, South Africa, Korea, and the Philippines. Hardly any liberation movements among the poor are untouched by the power of his thought.

Secondly, King was North America's most courageous theologian. He did not seek the protection of a university appointment and a quiet office. One of his most famous theological statements was written in jail. Other ideas were formed in brief breathing spaces after days of exposure to physical danger in the streets of Birmingham, Selma, and Chicago and the dangerous roads of Mississippi. King did theology in solidarity with the "least of these" and in the face of death. "If physical death," he said, "is the price I must pay to free my white brothers and sisters from the permanent death of the spirit, then nothing could be more redemptive." Real theology is risky, as King's courageous life demonstrated.

From King black liberation theology received its Christian identity, which he understood as the practice of justice and love in human relations and the hope that God has not left the "least of these" alone in their suffering. However, that identity was only one factor that contributed to the creation of black liberation theology. The other was Malcolm X, who identified the struggle as a black struggle. As long as black freedom and the Christian way in race relations were identified exclusively with integration and nonviolence, black theology was not possible. Integration and nonviolence required blacks to turn the other cheek to white brutality, join the mainstream of American society, and do theology without anger and without reference to the history and culture of African Americans. It meant seeing Christianity exclusively through the eyes of its white interpreters. Malcolm prevented that from happening.

I remember clearly when Malcolm and black power made a decisive and permanent imprint upon my theological consciousness. I was teaching at Adrian College (a predominately white United Methodist institution) in Adrian, Michigan, trying to make sense out of my vocation as a theologian. The black rage that ignited the Newark and Detroit riots in July 1967, killing nearly eighty people, had revolutionized my theological consciousness. Nothing in seminary had prepared me for this historic moment. It forced me to confront the blackness of my identity and to make theological sense of it.

Martin King helped to define my *Christian* identity but was silent about the meaning of blackness in a world of white supremacy. His public thinking about the faith was designed to persuade white Christians to take seriously the humanity of Negroes. He challenged whites to be true to what they said in their political and religious documents of freedom and democracy. What King did not initially realize was how deeply flawed white Christian thinking is regarding race, and how much psychological damage is done to the self-image of blacks.

To understand white racism and black rage in America, I turned to Malcolm X and Black Power. While King accepted white logic, Malcolm rejected it. "When [people] get angry," Malcolm said, "they aren't interested in logic, they aren't interested in odds, they aren't interested in consequences. When they get angry, they realize that the condition that they're in — that their suffering is unjust, immoral, illegal, and that anything they do to correct it or eliminate it, they're justified. When you develop that type of anger and speak in that voice, then we'll get some kind of respect and recognition, and some changes from these people who have been promising us falsely already for far too long."[4]

Malcolm saw more clearly than King the depth and complexity of racism in America, especially in the North. The North was more clever than the South and thus knew how to camouflage its exploitation of black people. White northern liberals represented themselves as the friends of the Negro and deceived King and many other blacks into believing that they really wanted to achieve racial justice in America. But Malcolm knew better, and he exposed their hypocrisy. He called white liberals "foxes" in contrast to southern "wolves." Malcolm saw no difference between the two, except that one smiles and the other growls when they eat you. Northern white liberals hated Malcolm for his uncompromising, brutal honesty. But blacks, especially the young people, loved him for it. He said publicly what most blacks felt, but were afraid to say except privately among themselves.

I first heard Malcolm speak while I was a student at Garrett, but I did not really listen to him. I was committed to Martin King and hoped that he would accept the invitation offered him to become a professor of theology at Garrett. I regarded Malcolm as a racist and would have nothing to do with him. Malcolm X did not enter my theological consciousness until I left seminary and was challenged by the rise of the black consciousness movement in the middle of the 1960s. Black Power, a child of Malcolm, forced me to take a critical look at Martin King and to discover his limits.

It is one thing to recognize that the gospel of Jesus demands justice in race relations and quite another to recognize that it demands that African

4. *Malcolm X Speaks*, ed. George Breitman (New York: Grove Press, 1965), pp. 107-8.

Americans accept their blackness and reject its white distortions. When I turned to Malcolm, I discovered my blackness and realized that I could never be who I was called to be until I embraced my African heritage — completely and enthusiastically. Malcolm put the word *black* in black theology. He taught black scholars in religion and many preachers that a "colorless Christianity" is a joke. It is only found in the imaginary world of white theology; it is not found in the real world of white seminaries and churches. Nor is it found in black churches. That black people hate themselves is no accident of history. As I listened to Malcolm and meditated on his analysis of racism in America and the world, I became convinced by his rhetorical virtuosity. Speaking to blacks, his primary audience, he said:

> Who taught you to hate the color of your skin? Who taught you to hate the texture of your hair? Who taught you to hate the shape of your nose? Who taught you to hate yourself from the top of your head to the sole of your feet? Who taught you to hate your own kind? Who taught you to hate the race you belong to so much that you don't want to be around each other? You should ask yourself, "Who taught you to hate being what God gave you?"[5]

Malcolm challenged black ministers to take a critical look at Christianity, Martin King, and the civil rights movement. The challenge was so deep that we found ourselves affirming what many persons regarded as theological opposites: Martin and Malcolm, civil rights and black power, Christianity and blackness.

Just as Martin King may be regarded as America's most influential theologian and preacher, Malcolm X may be regarded as America's most trenchant race critic. As Martin's theological achievement may be compared to Augustine's and Luther's, Malcolm's race critique is as far-reaching as Marx's class critique and the current feminist critique of gender. Malcolm was the great master of suspicion in the area of race. No one before or after him analyzed the role of Christianity in promoting racism and its mental and material consequences upon lives of blacks as Malcolm did. He has no peer.

Even today, whites do not feel comfortable listening to or reading Malcolm. They prefer Martin because he can easily be made more palatable to their way of thinking. That is why we celebrate Martin's birthday as a national holiday, and nearly every city has a street named in his honor. Many seminaries have a chair in his name, even though their curricula do not take his theology seriously. When alienated blacks turn to Malcolm, whites turn to Martin, as if they really care about his ideas, which most do not. Whites only care about Martin as a way of undermining the black allegiance to Malcolm.

When Malcolm X was resurrected in Black Power in the second half of the 1960s, whites turned to Martin King. White religious leaders tried to force

---

5. See *Washington Post*, January 23, 1994, p. G6.

militant black ministers to choose between Martin and Malcolm, integration and separation, Christianity and Black Power. But we rejected their demand and insisted on the importance of both. The tension between Martin and Malcolm, integration and separation, Christianity and blackness created black theology. It was analogous to the "double-consciousness," the "two unreconciled strivings," that W. E. B. DuBois wrote about in *The Souls of Black Folk* in 1903.

Martin King taught black ministers that the meaning of Christianity was inextricably linked with the fight for justice in society. That was his great contribution to black theology. He gave it its Christian identity, putting the achievement of social justice at the heart of what it means to be a Christian. He did not write a great treatise on the theme of Christianity and justice. He organized a movement that transformed Christian thinking about race and the struggles for justice in America and throughout the world.

Malcolm X taught black ministers and scholars that the identity of African Americans as a people was inextricably linked with blackness. This was his great contribution to black theology. Malcolm gave black theology its *black* identity, putting blackness at the center of who we were created to be. Like Martin, Malcolm did not write a scholarly treatise on the theme of blackness and self. He revolutionized black self-understanding with the power of his speech.

The distinctiveness of black theology is the bringing together of Martin and Malcolm in creative tension — their ideas about Christianity and justice and blackness and self. Neither Martin nor Malcolm sought to do that. The cultural identity of Christianity was not important to Martin because he understood it in the "universal" categories he was taught in graduate school. His main concern was to link the identity of Christianity with social justice, oriented in love and defined by hope.

The Christian identity of the black self was not important to Malcolm X. For him, Christianity was the white man's religion and thus had to be rejected. Black people, Malcolm contended, needed a black religion, one that would bestow self-respect upon them for being black. Malcolm was not interested in re-making Christianity into a black religion.

The creators of black theology disagreed with both Martin and Malcolm and insisted on the importance of bringing blackness and Christianity together. The beginning of black theology may be dated with the publication of the "Black Power" statement by black religious leaders in the *New York Times,* July 31, 1966, a few weeks after the rise of Black Power during the James Meredith March in Mississippi. Soon afterward the National Committee of Negro Churchmen was organized as the organizational embodiment of their religious concerns. It did not take long for the word *Black* to replace the word *Negro,* as black ministers struggled with the religious meaning of Martin and Malcolm, Christianity and blackness, nonviolence and self-defense, "freedom now" and "by any means necessary."

I sat down to write *Black Theology and Black Power* in the summer of 1968. Martin and Malcolm challenged me to think deep and long about the meaning of Christianity and blackness. Through them, I found my theological voice to articulate the black rage against racism in society, the churches, and in theology. It was a liberating experience. I knew that most of my former professors at Garrett and Northwestern would have trouble with what I was saying about liberation and Christianity, blackness and the gospel. One even told me that all I was doing was seeking justification for blacks on the south side and west side of Chicago to come to Evanston and kill him. But I could not let irrational white fear distract me from the intellectual task of exploring the theological meaning of double consciousness in black people.

Martin and Malcolm symbolize the tension between the African and American heritage of black people. We are still struggling with the tension, and its resolution is nowhere in sight. We can't resolve it because the social, political, and economic conditions that created it are still with us today. In fact, these conditions are worse today for the black poor, the one third of us who reside primarily in urban centers like Chicago and New York.

It is appalling that seminaries and divinity schools continue their business as usual — analyzing so many interesting and irrelevant things — but ignoring the people who could help us to understand the meaning of black exploitation and rage in this society. Why are two of the most prophetic critics of the church and society marginal in seminary curriculums? If we incorporated Martin's and Malcolm's critique of race and religion into our way of thinking, it would revolutionize our way of doing theology, just as class and gender critiques have done.

But taking race seriously is not a comfortable task for either whites or blacks. It is not easy for whites to listen to a radical analysis of race because blackness is truly *Other* to them — creating a horrible, unspeakable fear. When whites think of evil, they think of black. That is why the word *black* is still the most potent symbol of evil. If whites want to direct attention from an evil that they themselves have committed, they say a black person did it. We are the most potent symbols of crime, welfare dependency, sexual harassment, domestic violence, and bad government. Say a black did it, and whites will believe you. Some blacks will too.

With black being such a powerful symbol of evil, white theologians avoid writing and talking about black theology. Even though black theologians were among the earliest exponents of liberation theology, we are often excluded when panels and conferences are held on the subject. One could hardly imagine a progressive divinity school without a significant interpreter of feminist and Latin American liberation theology. But the same is not true for black theology. The absence of a serious and sustained engagement of black theology in seminaries and divinity schools is not an accident. It happens because Black is the Other — strange, evil, and terrifying.

But theology can never be true to itself in America without engaging blackness, encountering its complex, multilayered meaning. Theology, as with

American society as a whole, can never be true to itself unless it comes to terms with Martin and Malcolm together. Both spoke different but complementary truths about blackness that white theologians do not want to hear but must hear if we are to create theologies that are liberating and a society that is humane and just for all of its citizens. Only then can we sing, without hypocrisy, with Martin King, along with Malcolm X, the black spiritual, "Free at last, free at last, thank God almighty, we are free at last."

The Multifaceted Future of Theology

John B. Cobb, Jr.

This chapter describes not what I anticipate, but what I hope for. I abstract from my concern as to whether by the middle of the next century a human society will exist that has the stability and resources to maintain anything like the present university or seminary. I abstract from my concern that the church may lose the ability to attract thoughtful people to its service or have the money that will enable them to have careers in any form of theology. Instead I am, perhaps unrealistically, assuming a context much like our own and describing the roles I hope that theology will play.

By theology I mean intentionally Christian thinking about important matters. It is not the subject matter that makes thought theological. There are quite untheological ways to think about God, the church, salvation, and so forth. Since these are important matters, my point in calling some approaches to them untheological is that they may be motivated by the desire to make a name in academia rather than to be faithfully Christian. Or one may approach them as a historian or a sociologist who makes no pretense to think as a Christian about them.

Equally, any important topic may be thought about from a consciously Christian perspective. One may deal with issues of public policy or of gender or with the frontiers of contemporary physics. If one does so with questions raised by Christian faith and committed to bringing the faith to bear in answering these questions, any subject matter can be treated theologically.

Academic Theology

The definition above intentionally cuts against that which has shaped the academic discipline of theology, which is determined by subject matter. The contrast is not always sharp because most of the treatment of that subject matter has been by persons who are Christian and who intend for their faith to shape their treatment. Also, individual scholars transcend their disciplines and deal with matters outside of them.

But in the United States, the resistance of theology to disciplinization is declining rapidly. Increasingly, those best qualified to deal with the subject matter are favored. Even when these are personally Christian, they are often committed to separating their personal faith from their approach to the subject matter. With the exception of systematic theology itself, which resists disciplinization more than other fields, definition by subject matter sometimes takes priority over the Christian perspective.

Just for this reason, the form of theology whose future is most problematic is the academic discipline. I trust that this form will lose dominance. There are too many urgent tasks for theology to which the academic discipline makes no direct contribution to allow it to continue to absorb most of the human and financial resources for doing theology.

I have been polemicizing against the disciplinization of theology in the United States for some time and have come close to calling for the discontinuance of the discipline. Nevertheless, I do not do so. Although theology is always in danger of a merely incestuous existence, taking its problems from the recent history of the discipline as practiced by other professional theologians and seeking to contribute only to the advance of this isolated community, it is also always more than that. It cultivates the knowledge of a larger and longer tradition, one that in fact shapes the lives and thinking of Christians (as well as others) even when they know nothing about it. It often finds in that tradition facts that throw new light on that process of shaping our present and suggests fresh possibilities open to us today. It recognizes that this larger tradition of Western thought generally undermines, in principle, the way many Christians actually think, exposing their faith to easy dismissal by those who understand that tradition. And at its best, it works to formulate faith in a way that takes account of the real problems posed to it by history.

The lack of interest in this work on the part of the church is partly the church's fault and partly the fault of practitioners of the discipline. The church all too easily gets lost in the weekly routines and forgets that these are all for the sake of a faith whose intellectually responsible continuance in the world is precarious. One shudders to think how Christians would understand themselves today if it had not been for the work of the German theologians of the nineteenth century. How few thoughtful, open-minded people would now be able to call themselves Christian! The church does not sufficiently appreciate the service of its dedicated scholars.

On the other hand, much of the fault lies with the professional theologians. The connection between their research and the real need to maintain a credible theology is often obscure. The more fully theology becomes a discipline in the standard academic sense, or worse, a set of disciplines, the less direct is the concern of most practitioners to provide thoughtful Christians with an intellectually responsible theology. Each practitioner provides a piece. Only a few take responsibility for the encompassing task. Busy churchmen cannot pay much attention. Indeed, even those in different subdisciplines often have neither time nor inclination to deal with these scholarly exercises.

The tendency of the disciplines is to encourage their practitioners to disparage any effort to put the pieces together or establish the relevance of their work to the larger picture. The problem, therefore, is not merely that much of the work is done by specialists who are ill equipped to relate their work to the larger world. The problem is also that an ethos is created that views such tasks with suspicion. The farther the theological disciplines go in this direction, the less reason there will be for their continuance.

Nevertheless, there are always countercurrents within them. And thus far each generation has produced leaders who carry on the task of making contemporary sense of faith. Moltmann himself is a star example from his generation. And he could not have performed the work he has if he had not had a vast array of scholarly research in various theological disciplines on which to draw. The value of the academic disciplines of theology cannot be denied.

I have been speaking thus far of the importance of shaping and reshaping the expression of faith so that it does not ignore or deny valid advances in the history of Western thought. There is another more radical task to which I believe academic theologians are called. That is to take part in shaping the overarching intellectual context in which they do their work. It is not enough to allow the secular mind to define what is real and reliable and then reformulate theology accordingly. Christian faith has a contribution to make to the comprehensive understanding of reality. It is badly truncated when it is merely subservient to other perspectives.

This is a task that runs counter to the self-understanding of academic disciplines, at least in the United States. Each discipline is expected to mind its own business and leave the others alone. Philosophy was once assigned the task of criticizing assumptions and integrating conclusions of the various disciplines. But in the twentieth century it opted instead to become one discipline alongside the rest.

Because the definition of theology that I have proposed still functions, and because few things are more important than our overall vision of reality, the impetus to share in the creation of the vision has not disappeared. In Germany the astonishing work of Wolfhart Pannenberg stands out in this respect as the accomplishment of a single theologian. In the United States we work at this collaboratively under the rubric of "process theology" or "constructive postmodernism." This is not a program that fits any one discipline, including the academic discipline of theology. But it has not yet been excluded altogether by the disciplinary organization of knowledge. I hope to see a revival of this bolder theological effort in the years ahead as the negative consequences of fragmentation of thought and life become ever more apparent. And I am prepared to campaign for university reforms that would be supportive of this kind of work.

There is a another type of theology that occurs around the fringes of the university, almost in spite of the disciplinary organization of knowledge. Thomas Altizer is its most impressive practitioner. While within the academic discipline the tendency is to accept the problems as formulated in the history of the discipline, Altizer focuses on those figures and intellectual movements in which he discerns the greatest spiritual power. He seeks, in a Hegelian sense, to see the history of *Geist*. In the modern world he traces this through Blake and Hegel, Nietzsche and Joyce. Whereas in earlier times *Geist* worked through Christian theologians, this has not been true in the modern world, because their loyalties have been divided between continuing their distinct Christian tradition and taking part in the culture. *Geist* requires totally uninhibited thinking. My point here is not the details of Altizer's position, but to call for theology as discernment of what is shaping and reshaping the Western soul, seeing this also as the work of Christ. In broader terms, it is the theological appraisal of culture.

Altizer is at the farthest extreme from church theology, since in his view the church is not the bearer of *Geist*. But since I find Christ also in the church, and the church as the one place that bears consistent witness to the creative and redemptive work of God in the world, I take a different view.

Church Theology

Church theology is also badly needed. By church theology I do not mean church dogmatics in Barth's sense, but simply Christian thinking that takes its problems, not from the intellectual and scholarly tradition, but from the life of the church. The disciplinization of theology has meant that most members of theological faculties do little of their work in this way. Yet a church struggle is beginning in the United States that threatens to be as disturbing and divisive as the Fundamentalist-Modernist controversy early in this century. It is precipitated by issues of gender, sexuality, liberation, pluralism, and radical critique of the tradition as oppressive and repressive.

Thinking as Christians about these issues is just as intellectually demanding as is the work done in the academic disciplines; and if it is to be done well, it calls for its own kind of scholarship. But the lack of involvement of the great majority of scholars in the academy is striking. In Germany it is once again Moltmann who has shown that the academic theologian need not ignore the struggle for the soul of the church. In the United States, it is chiefly a small band of feminists who take part in the church struggle while maintaining a position within academia. A few conservative white male professors meanwhile give leadership on the other side.

My thesis is that the theological seminary as the church's school should

199

accept a responsibility for theological leadership in the struggles within the church. If professors positioned in academic disciplines cannot, or will not do this, then the church needs to find ways to support others, not so positioned, who will, even if this means a reduction in faculty in the academic disciplines. Although I have defended the value of the disciplines, I cannot see that value as equal to that of bringing the Christian faith to bear upon the actual life of Christian believers, especially when they are in a state of great confusion that threatens to weaken and divide what is left of our mainline churches.

I have described the role of these church theologians in such a way as to show their need for academic theology. They need to know the history of the church and its thought if they are to help the church to bring its tradition responsibly to bear on issues that are new to it. I believe that the church can redirect the energies of many who are now caught up in academic disciplines in this more relevant way if it understands the need to do so. The result would also turn seminaries into far better contexts for the preparation of ministers.

Church theologians, then, are professionals steeped in the tradition. They need to be reflective, as practitioners of the theological disciplines often are not, about *how* the tradition, including the Bible, rightly functions in the life of Christians today. This involves relating traditional Christian wisdom to what we are learning from the social and natural sciences as well, and even from other cultures and religious traditions. Their specialization, therefore, cannot be in a discipline. Their special skill will be in mining the material produced by the disciplines for what is relevant in the ever-changing situation. This means that they must be sensitively involved in the church and its struggle to be faithful.

This complex task demands professional status and freedom from other work. At present there is no other institutional locus for such professionals than the seminaries. But one major role for church theologians must be to work with laypeople. That may require the development of positions separated from the seminary and located in places more accessible to the laity. On the other hand, church theologians are ideal teachers of those preparing for ministry. They are needed in the seminaries as well.

Lay Theology

The work of church theologians cannot be chiefly to inform laypeople what to think. It must also nurture the emergence of lay theology. A certain kind of lay theology existed in the United States in the years after World War II. Church publishers provided books for thoughtful laypeople and there was a magazine called the *Christian Scholar* in which Christian professors in fields other than religion could publish their thoughts. But all of this disappeared. Can lay theology be renewed?

If there is to be a renewal of lay theology, its nature and purpose must be conceived in a different way. In the earlier phase, professionals were asked to write books for laypeople summarizing the findings of their disciplines. In those days this was not pointless, since much of the reflection in the disciplines had not been so far cut off from the concerns of thoughtful lay Christians. Nevertheless, it was primarily a matter of keeping an elite group of laypeople abreast of the work of professionals. As the work of professionals becomes more and more disciplinized, however, it is absurd to suppose that it will interest, or benefit, many laypeople.

There was, however, another dimension to lay theology that is more promising for the future. It was recognized that laypeople were involved in their own professions and that their Christian calling was to live and work as Christians there. Professional theologians made no pretense of offering guidance. Laypeople who knew their professions well were invited to do their own thinking. My impression is that this has gone much further and been much more successful in Germany than in the United States.

There is good reason to revive this kind of lay theology in the United States, and I will turn to something like that below. However, it is far too narrow a role for laypeople to play. They live in churches torn apart by debates about matters they understand just as well as professionals. Professionals provide no guidance in dealing with these matters, and they offer no help to laypeople to think about them as Christians. No wonder the level of the debate is so distressing! It is crucial for the healthy survival of the church that laypeople reclaim their role as theologians. But if this is to happen, we must define a responsible form of theology that does not presuppose years of academic study of the Bible and the history of the church. Is this possible?

I am not proposing that one can think responsibly as a Christian in blank ignorance of the Bible and church history. Part of the problem is that the level of Christian education in our churches is so low that many laypeople are not far from such ignorance. To make introductory survey courses available to laypeople on a wide scale would certainly be desirable. Still, this is not the primary way to empower laypeople to become responsible theologians.

The place to begin is where they are with whatever issues most deeply concern them. Yesterday that might have been the ordination of homosexuals. Today it may be the controversy over identifying deity as Sophia. Tomorrow the exposé of the destructiveness of our economic system to both the poor and the environment may lead to calls for Christians to take a radical stand. We cannot predict which issues will capture the imagination of laypeople. What we can do is encourage them, whatever the issue, to think about it intentionally as Christians.

Some steps in that direction are possible for almost any layperson, however little knowledge she has of the tradition. One does not have to have special historical knowledge in order to become self-critical about the basis on which one's present opinions have been formed. One can ask whether one's opinions are Christian and begin to reflect on how such judgments should be made without extensive study of the tradition.

But once laypeople begin the process of reflecting as Christians about the issues, they will themselves recognize their need to know more. Some of what they need to know they can learn from readily accessible books. Some may require more professional assistance. It is important that that assistance not be directing them as to what to think, but only responding to their recognized need for information and tools.

I do not envision that many laypeople will ever study very extensively in the Christian tradition. But I do envision that many will become aware of the nature of the tradition as ambiguous resource and develop ways of relating to it that are responsible. This will develop in dialogue with other laypeople, so that they will spark one another and assist one another through criticism and suggestion. Laypeople, while remaining lay, can become much better Christian thinkers about the urgent issues now upsetting the church than most professionals are today.

There is no assurance that lay theology will lead to results that are pleasing to all. It may, in fact, intensify debates within the church. But if those debates give expession to genuine efforts to understand what faith calls for at present, rather than to gut level and knee-jerk responses, the debates would take on a Christian character now noticeably lacking. We may hope that one of the most widely recognized features of intentionally Christian thinking would be the effort to hear appreciatively what other Christians are saying. In such a context, the church would have a better chance of being the church.

There is another role for lay theology with or without the collaboration of professional theologians. This can begin with the renewal of thinking about the meaning of faith for work within their own professions and institutions. In the earlier period it not only began there, but also largely ended there. But today there is a good chance that it can go much further.

In the years after World War II there was a fairly complacent sense in the United States that its basic institutions were in good health. When Christian faculty thought about their role in the university, they took the given state of the university largely for granted. Its role in research and teaching, and the methods it employed in both roles, were admired. Christian professors saw their vocation as working faithfully in and for the institution, keeping it true to its own avowed, and largely embodied, purposes.

Today the situation is strikingly different. The universities have grown huge in size at the expense of community and concern for individuals. They have become closely dependent on the military-industrial complex. They have subordinated teaching to research, much of which is trivial. They have encouraged types of specialization that make academic work largely irrelevant to both students and society. They have been corrupted by big time sports. They have abandoned any basis for judging what graduates of their colleges should know. The litany of evils goes on, but these criticisms are now commonplace.

For a Christian to serve responsibly as a Christian in such a context requires serious thinking about what universities should become and how they can move in that direction. Such reflection will raise very fundamental questions about the deepest purposes of the university and what kind of structure would make possible the realization of those purposes.

Similar changes have taken place in the public schools, in law, in medicine, in business, in government, and indeed in virtually every aspect of life in the United States. Serious Christian thinking along vocational lines is unlikely to be as complacent about the institutional context. The question will be more how to bring Christian faith to bear both critically and constructively in reflecting about these institutions and professions.

I have not spoken of the criticism of the church. That is partly because I take that for granted as already far advanced. No major institution has been half so self-critical as the church. It is because we Christians are constantly criticizing the church, sometimes quite well, that we are qualified and justified in critiquing other institutions.

Although I am not writing in terms of realistic projections, but rather of hopes, I do not want to be wholly utopian. I am not supposing that all, or half, or even one tenth of laypeople will become serious theologians in the next century. But perhaps one out of a hundred will. In my own denomination at present that would mean about ninety thousand! That is a goodly number, and it would be supplemented by laypeople from other denominations. If some hundreds of thousands of laypeople were now bringing their faith to bear on the issues confronting our denominations, the discussion would have a dramatically different character. If one tenth of that number, even one hundredth, were engaged in serious theological criticism of the institutions and professions in which they work, the effects would be explosive. There would be little danger that Christianity would appear irrelevant! It might be hated, but it would not be ignored.

One form of theology that I greatly respect is missing from this account of what will be needed in the next century. That is liberation theology. I have assumed that liberation theologians will continue to function in academic disciplines but have a larger scope in church theology and lay theology.

But liberation theology may also need to be a separate locus for theology. In the proposals I have made elsewhere, its contribution to the whole church is given greater space than it now has. But its contribution to ethnic communities within the church may continue to require special and separate location. At present there is enormous power in the achievement by each minority group of its own voice. Long-suppressed energies are expressed and fresh insights emerge. Much of the current church struggle is between those who are committed to making a space in which these voices can be heard and those who resent the barrage of criticism of established leadership and patterns that results. At a certain stage in this claiming of one's heritage and taking pride in the distinct perspective it offers, it is important that there be strong cohesion. At that point, liberation theologies need to be the task of communities of thinkers working together somewhat separate from other such groups and from the mainstream.

As time passes, this becomes less necessary. Already today, I think that feminist theologians could find an adequate context within the several patterns of theology I have outlined. Church theology and lay theology in particular would be places where they could pursue their work, but the academic disciplines also provide a satisfactory context for some of them. For this reason I have not listed feminist theology as a separate category.

On the other hand, it may well be that simply speaking of church theology and lay theology in general is misleading. The image is of a homogeneous church. The needs of blacks will continue to be quite different from those of whites. In addition to facing the same divisive issues as whites, they will continue to need to strengthen their own self-assurance in a context that puts them down, and they will need to continue to critique the dominant church for its persistent racism. This perspective is in danger of being lost if black theologians are simply merged into the general headings I have provided.

As long as U.S. society and its churches are ethnically diverse, as long as each group has a different experience and a different memory from the others, as long as each needs to project its just demands to the larger group, demands that will not otherwise be adequately heard or met, so long it will be important to think of academic theologians, but especially church theologians and lay theologians as including among their number liberation theologians bound to diverse ethnic groups and also speaking for them to the church as a whole.

PART III
THEMES

When Horizons Close: A Reflection on the Utopian *Ratio* of Qoheleth

Elsa Tamez

Professor Jürgen Moltmann has distinguished himself with his contributions on the subject of hope. I wish to dedicate to him, on the occasion of his jubilee, this chapter, which attempts, desperately, to see the light at the end of the tunnel in situations of messianic drought.[1] Qoheleth is a book to read when the chronological times seem to conspire against the human being. Horizons close, the present is frustration, and the glorious past recedes into oblivion.

The Present Time: Total Frustration, *Hebel*

According to theologian and economist Franz Hinkelammert, to have hope in a different future is to threaten the stability of the current capitalistic system, which believes that merely by implementing capitalism we are steaming full speed ahead for the perfect society.[2] The capitalistic system is the hope of everyone. To create other hopes is to be against the only feasible hope. We must have no other expectations, then, but must live the expectation (with readjustments, from time to time) of the promised hope. This being the case, reflection on utopia is a task of primary urgency for those who desire to seek new realities of life for all.

Just as does our present time, the world narrated by Qoheleth declares the nonnovelty of all things under the sun. All is *absurde,* a huge void, a "mess," "a piece of crap." Qoheleth expresses this feeling of frustration through the use

1. Part of this article corresponds to a series of addresses I delivered in Honduras as Strachan Professor of the Latin American Biblical Seminary.
2. Cf. Franz Hinkelammert, "La lógica de la exclusión del mercado capitalista mundial y el proyecto de liberación," in *América Latina: Resistir por la vida* (1994).

of the Hebrew word *hebel*. He relativizes the *theologia communis* of the wisdom tradition that he has received from the past, as well as that of the prophets' messianic promises, and confronts them with daily experience, showing how out of joint they are with that experience. Theoretical theological schemata fail to measure up to the historical challenges of his moment. There are no messianisms in sight, no punishment for the wicked, no reward for the just.

This frustrated, helpless approach permeates the book's discourse. But amidst it all — in fact, on the basis of it — and in an atmosphere of the silence of God, Qoheleth reflects on the concrete opportunities of escape offered in his times of messianic drought. Throughout his book, he will suggest wise counsels in terms of daily life for surviving as well as may be and for resisting the assaults of a society whose motto is: "Every man for himself!"

The book of Qoheleth, or Ecclesiastes, is a book of protest. The Hebrew word *qoheleth* means "member of an assembly," or "one engaged in a dispute or argumentation."[3] Qoheleth's nonnarrated world — that is, the real world in which the text is being produced — asserts just the opposite of Qoheleth's thesis. Everything is new. Scholars of the Hellenistic period point out that an astonishing, unprecedented structural change was transpiring at this time.[4] This was especially the case at the time when the book of Ecclesiastes was written, following the death of Alexander the Great, during the reign of the Ptolemies, with their capital in Egypt (between 280 and 230 B.C.). Novelty reigned in all areas: military technology, the way in which power was administered from Alexandria, the royal administration and its finances, the coining of money, the implementation of fiscal policies in Egypt and the provinces, technology applied to agricultural production, trade on a wider scale, and philosophical discussions — all of these things contributed to the pervading sense of novelty. This was also the period of the creation of mathematical and philosophical concepts that still have currency today. The geographical and economic structure of Egypt under the Ptolemies required a direct and centralized, very organized structure of administration. The Eastern notion of the deification of the ruler was received by the Greeks and put into practice in combination with Greek logic. To the absolute power of the king in his capacity as God, lord of the earth, was added the efficiency of the Greeks.

Why does the author (thought to have been an aristocratic sage) deny the novelty in all of this, without being himself one of the most affected members

---

3. For Ogden, the most appropriate translation is, "one who accuses" (cf. Neh. 5:7): Graham Ogden, *Qoheleth* (Sheffield: JSOT Press, 1987), p. 27.

4. Cf. Michail Rostovtzeff, *Histoire économique et sociale du monde hellénistique* (1989); Martin Hengel, *Judaism and Hellenism: Studies in Their Encounter in Palestine in the Early Hellenistic Period*, trans. John Bowden (Minneapolis: Augsburg Fortress, 1992), pp. 6-57; Michail Rostovtzeff, *Greece*, ed. Elias J. Bickerman, trans. J. D. Duff (Oxford: Oxford University Press, 1963), pp. 258-300; M. Ralf, *La época helenística* (1963); Helmut Koester, *Introduction to the New Testament, Volume 1: History, Culture, and Religion in the Hellenistic Age* (Berlin: Walter de Gruyter, 1982); Stephan de Jong, "¡Quítate de mi sol! Eclesiastés y la tecnocracia helenística," *RIBLA* 13 (1992), n. 11.

of the population? There are a number of possible reasons. It may be that he is endowed with sufficiently incisive and daring powers of analysis to discern the negative consequences (for non-Greeks) of the new Hellenistic economic order, despite all appearances. Or it may be that he is simply a xenophobic conservative, skeptical of anything new. We incline to the former explanation.

This, however, is not the problem with which we are concerned. We are interested in the fact that the author is helpless to shape explicitly a utopia that would organize existence as a structure of possibility in order to go out down the road to something different from enslaving toil *('amal)*, constant self-reproach, lack of solidarity, and the disturbing thought of approaching death, and to struggle for that utopia. Qoheleth does not have the strength of faith in something that would lead him to a transforming praxis. The "hebelian" atmosphere obfuscates all horizons. We shall see below that he will emerge from the dilemma, but only to a limited extent, when, on one hand, he manages to project his incapacity to penetrate the future onto a transcendent God, who acts mysteriously and who organizes times so that there will be a time for everything; and, on the other hand, when he categorically champions an escape into the intense experience of something good about the present (eating and drinking in gladness amidst exhausting labor). This is not his realized utopia. After all, in his logic this, too, will ultimately be *hebel*, since not all can have it. Furthermore, it is fleeting, like adolescence and youth (Eccl. 11:10). All is *hebel*. Nevertheless, this escape will constitute his major perspective, from the viewpoint of feasibility. Let us analyze Qoheleth's particular utopia at greater length.

Qoheleth's Hidden Utopia[5]

In his analysis of neoliberal thought, which claims to be so realistic, and is explicitly anti-utopian, Hinkelammert arrives at the conclusion that neoliberalism, too, has its covert utopia. After all, it repeatedly refers to impossible horizons that transcend the human condition. Thus Hinkelammert is led to assert the positing of utopias as part and parcel of the human condition. Accordingly, he points out:

> No human thought can station itself outside the utopian horizon. One's intention may be to fashion a thinking characterized by a "realism without utopia"; unintentionally, however, one reproduces one's own utopian horizons.[6]

5. We shall employ, in our analysis, Franz Hinkelammert's fundamental categories, basically set forth in his *Crítica de la razón utópica* (1984) and his "El cautiverio de la utopía: Las utopías conservadoras del capitalismo actual, el neoliberalismo y la dialéctica de las alternativas," *Pasos* (1993), n. 50.

6. Hinkelammert, "El cautiverio de la utopía," p. 13.

If this is the case, then our personage, Qoheleth, cannot be anti-utopian or non-utopian, however much he may seem to be, in various of his declarations, such as: "What is crooked cannot be made straight" (1:15; cf. 7:13). And indeed, we find, Qoheleth is not anti-utopian or non-utopian, despite the superabundance of his pessimistic judgments. We shall likewise have to take into account the fact that the text's discourse is in the form of a self-contradicting monologue, so typical of subjectivity. For example, on one side he congratulates the dead, and those who have not been born, since they do not have to see the crimes of violence and injustice that are committed under the sun (4:2-4); and he regards the products of miscarried pregnancies as more blessed than persons who, could they live twice a thousand years, would never enjoy any of the fruits of their toil (6:6). On the other hand, he comes to the conclusion that life is better than death. The dead have no more part in the dynamics of life under the sun since they experience neither love, nor hatred, nor rivalry (9:4-6). Only in this passage does the word *hope* appear: "For any among the living there is hope; a live dog is better off than a dead lion" (9:4). This declaration is not what we would call the most enthusiastic of mottos for keeping hope alive. One must enter into the book of Qoheleth by another route to uncover its utopian horizons. That discovery can be implemented from three angles. First, we may take our point of departure in negativity: if everything is a mess, what can nonmess, non*hebel* be? In other words, what desires are implicit in a rejection of the present? A second level is the utopian horizon of explicit desire, in function of the affirmation of the present life in the ambit of the daily. And a third level is that of explicit faith — trust in an almighty, unfathomable God, who at some time in history will bring about that which is impossible for humans precisely because they are human.

A. The Desires Implicit in a Rejection of the Present

We may posit, as we begin to investigate Qoheleth in this area, four important desires: the desire to know the times, the desire that there may be justice and freedom, the desire for happiness, and the desire to transcend death.

1. The Desire to Know the Times, and the Impossibility of Such Knowledge

One of our personage's major frustrations is the impossibility of knowing the future, and, indeed, of understanding the complexity of what is happening in the present "under the sun." Qoheleth fails to understand the *why* of the "hebelian" present. And tradition's theoretical schemata, which until now had attempted to interpret that *why*, no longer fit.

It seems that, for Qoheleth, salvation is knowing. It is important to know what will happen in order to bear, and to organize oneself in, this "messy" present. But strive as he may, with all of his wisdom and science, he fails to know or understand (6:12; 7:24; 8:7). Knowledge and wisdom cause sorrow and grief (1:17-18). What he finds, to his way of understanding things, is *hebel* alone. And from start to finish, God's projects are inscrutable for him. He says:

> He has made everything appropriate to its time, and has put the timeless (*'olam*) into their hearts, without men's ever discovering, from beginning to end, the work which God has done. (3:11)

The "timeless" (*'olam*) can have various meanings here: unlimited duration; the distant, the occult; or the sum total of all of the concrete — that is, the entire series of the events of history. The human being, then, has the potential to understand beyond the given. Despite that, for Qoheleth it is impossible to understand full reality: the deeds of God take us by surprise and surpass our suppositions. In 8:17 he repeats: despite having observed at length (*rah*), he cannot grasp the deeds of God.

The impotence of not knowing the times or the projects of the divinity causes the writer pain, since now he is unable to organize a consistent practice. This diminishes him as a human being. He gropes his way along, seeking signs that might indicate routes to take (11:1-6), since it is not known what evil may come upon the earth (11:2). Qoheleth takes it as established that wisdom is better than money or strength, and other things besides; but wisdom, too, has its limits. Qoheleth's is a self-critical wisdom.

As the narrator has not been able to master the times objectively and order them in rational fashion, he shifts their dimensions and transfers them beyond his consciousness: he casts them under the dominion of God. The times transcend him; thus, the only thing left for him is to assign them a utopian function. This does humanize him, since it enables him to come to a knowledge of his limits — that is, the limits of the human condition in which he is founded or established. The confident statement that everything has its time and its hour is the utopian phrase that orders life. Only on the basis of faith in that outcome can he return to the rejected present, and bear up under it with some degree of tranquility and security. If there is a time to be born and a time to die, a time to embrace and a time to abstain from embracing, a time to love and a time to hate, there must also be a time of *hebel* and a time of non*hebel.* The new element, denied by Qoheleth himself, would be the proclamation of the time of non*hebel.* The latter is utopian, inasmuch as it occurs independently of human effort. Our writer has faith that it will come someday, but he does not know how. He can identify the signs, as one can see that clouds are filled up with water (11:3), but he cannot master the time of non*hebel*'s coming. In this way, time is converted into a structure of possibility.

2. The Desires of Justice and Freedom in Society

That there be justice for the poor and oppressed is a desire implicit in the rejection of the present. This is obvious. The signifiers of the discourse betray it. Society is topsy-turvy: in place of right there is injustice (3:16); power is in the hands of oppressors; the poor are violently oppressed and there are none to wipe away their tears (4:1). The state fails to discharge its task of administering justice and social welfare (5:7), and the king's tyranny is unbearable. The king cannot even be rebuked because he simply does what he pleases, just as if he were God (8:3-4). And he has his spies everywhere (10:20).

Qoheleth's non*hebel* society is the one where justice, right, and freedom reign. This is his utopia. Since it is not explicit, and he does not believe it feasible, even by way of anticipation, he does not indicate how to approach it, or cause it to approach, on the basis of praxis. Once more, in his faith in a time for everything he finds a possibility, as we understand in 3:17 and 8:4-7.

Let us observe: no structure of possibility affords Qoheleth a knowledge of the times from a temporal perspective, but he does have faith in the existence of ripe or opportune times.

3. The Desire of Happiness

The desire for happiness appears explicitly in the recurring notion that there is nothing better than to eat and drink in gladness. However, a rejection of the present also appears apropos of the toil that enslaves (*'amal*). Let us see how things look from this angle. All of this intensive labor avails nothing for the accumulation of wealth if "riches do not satisfy [one's] greed" — literally, if the soul is cheated of the good (*tob*, 4:8); or if one lives a long life and enjoys none of the fruits of one's labor (6:6). Happiness ought to correspond to exhausting work. Qoheleth rejects not the work process itself, but the enslaving way in which that process is implemented, and the fact that its product is not enjoyed. The enjoyment of that product is the wage that it deserves, its "portion" *(heleq)*: the reward is not the coin that may be given in recompense for work, but happiness in the work process (2:10). For this reason our writer recommends moderation in work: "Better is one handful with tranquility than two with toil and a chase after wind!" (4:6). What, precisely, does happiness mean for Qoheleth? He cannot define it here: he declares only that it ought to be enjoyed, possibly in the measurable time of everyday experience; but neither is he satisfied with the genuine felicity that would extend over long times and short ones alike. Therefore he asks:

> For who knows what is good *(tob)* for a man in life, the limited days of his vain life [the life of his *hebel*] (which God has made like a shadow)? Because — who is there to tell a man what will come after him under the sun? (6:12)

In this last verse we clearly perceive the problem of death that unsettles Qoheleth.

4. The Implicit Desire to Transcend Death

Qoheleth congratulates the dead and the products of miscarried pregnancies who are in Sheol, not because he desires to be among them — we have already seen his preference for being among the living — but because they know not the oppressions and injustices of Qoheleth's world. Our personage does not wish to die. He does not express that in so many words, but it angers him that the just die as do the ungodly, without the slightest distinction between them (9:2-3). Grasping his thought from the standpoint of negativity, we see that for Qoheleth the wicked ought to die, but not the just. Oppressors go through life doing evil, yet they are not condemned, and in the end they simply die. The just do good during their life, their goodness goes unacknowledged, and finally they receive the same wage as the wicked: death. And all of the living forget all of the dead. Qoheleth goes further still: ultimately, death not only equalizes human beings of different conditions, but places the very beasts on the same level as humans (3:20-21). Qoheleth formulates no possibilities of resurrection. In the third century B.C. there was no such discussion in Judaism (unless it had just begun: the case is not clear).

Death is a misfortune against which the human being can avail naught (cf. 8:8). The time of death is characterized as evil: death is a time of darkness (11:8). And it is likewise evil that the human being should be unable to know the time of its arrival:

> Man no more knows his own time than fish taken in the fatal net, or birds trapped in the snare; like these the children of men are caught when the evil time falls suddenly upon them. (9:12)

Insofar as death is an incontestable reality, and no human being knows the beyond or the moment of the coming of death, Qoheleth accepts death, and in accepting it, acknowledges his human condition. On the basis of this acknowledgment, he proposes two feasible alternatives: not to hasten the arrival of death with specific insalubrious practices; and to enjoy the present life intensely, especially before entry into old age, which announces the time of incurable death (cf. 11:7–12:7).

Since one's world is *hebel*, it is of the first importance to know how to cope with life, with an attempt to discern the times. In times of repression, one must be a "pussyfooter." And so in favorable times, says Qoheleth, one ought to make merry and be happy, and in time of adversity, reflect and discern (7:14). Society being set on its ear, since the just do poorly and the wicked do well, one need not be either particularly just or particularly evil: the extremes, in these inverted, repressive situations of ours, may lead to an untimely death (cf. 7:16-19).

Not that this is the ideal solution. Indeed, this solution is sometimes catalogued as *hebel* itself. But it is the best that can be done, at a given moment in daily life, in order to resist the reality of oppression and not to die before one's time. Qoheleth is not being cynical or indifferent. It is only a matter of historical realism at a "countable" or chronological moment. The concept of the fear of God, which we shall analyze below, will afford us a better means of counteracting such frustrating helplessness and thereby of winning the ability to enjoy the sensuous life with freedom and without fault.

The other feasible recommendation for getting a leg up on death is to interrupt, by means of pleasure, the "hebelian" context of the present time, which is much like death — and to do so while it can still be done with all of one's vital energy, and before the coming of death, that world of darkness in which there is no life. The context of future, eternal death, the dwelling place of the human being, is *hebel* too (11:8; cf. 12:5).

These counsels are for the time of youth. Take full advantage of the present. Follow what draws your heart and your eyes; relieve your body of its suffering (11:9-12); enjoy pleasure freely. Qoheleth recommends, for this time of enjoyment, that we be mindful of the Creator, before the world of the present life comes to a close (12:2), before old age saps our strength (12:3-6), and before we enter death, our lasting home (12:5-7). This pleasure must not be destructive of oneself or one's neighbor, so Qoheleth takes care to warn us that in our full enjoyment of it, we must know that God will judge every deed (11:9). God, here, is the sign of the limits that one may not transgress, and is invoked in defense of the subjects of a monarchy.

Qoheleth has no fear of the death to come. He neither loves it nor is summoned by it to suicide. Instead, he conceives of it as an inevitable reality against which one may win an occasional game with many days of material felicity, before it comes. And so he mocks death, although in the end he will have to accept it. Anyone failing to enjoy life amidst so much enslaving toil is permitting death to occur before its time. After all, the opposite of death is not simply life, but life lived in all of its sensuousness. It is faith in a time for everything — a time to be born and another time to die — that enables Qoheleth neither to fear nor to love death, and to take advantage of real life in the interval between birth and demise.

B. An Explicit Viable Alternative: Affirmation of Material and Sensual Life in a Context of Daily Living

After examining his world, and realistically observing that the future bodes only a closed horizon, Qoheleth proposes a solution: reject the present by affirming concrete, sensual life in the present itself. He does not propose a nostalgia for the "good old days," an attempt at happiness through the rumination of memories. Nor does he propose to live now the illusion of a better future, since he knows that everything has its time and happiness will come in its time. And happiness is accepting the present with resignation. Qoheleth's explicit alternative is to live, now, in the midst of *hebel,* that which could seem akin to non*hebel:* a certain unstinting felicity, knowing that everything has its time and hour.

This is a good solution, a feasible one. If the future is opaque, and the past an element of alienation, then our writer must ground his consciousness in the present. Yes, the present can be seen to be a protective breastplate against lack of explicitly shaped utopian horizons or hope of fulfillment of promises made to one's forebears. Of course, various alternatives are available in the present: cynicism, resignation, suicide — or full living governed by a different logic imposed by the "messy" system, that is, by *hebel.*

Let us return to the alternative of a concrete affirmation of life in the present, but let us take account at the same time of Qoheleth's nonnarrated world. The logic of the (Hellenistic) system of production is one of slave labor: the economic and political administration beats a rhythm of labor in a dehumanizing tempo, oblivious of the subject of the labor. The people's religious leaders, for their part, the rulers of the temple, beat a rhythm of persons' acts on the criterion of whether these acts, these persons, fulfill the Mosaic Law and the sacrifices. The subjects of these oppressions, blindly obedient to the law, come to be objectified. It is no longer their consciousness that directs their steps, but the conditioning of the Ptolemaic Hellenistic administration and the requirements of the temple rites. Qoheleth proposes the substitution of a different logic — one governed by the heart (one's own consciousness) and the eyes (what the subject sees). This logic affirms the subject as such. The best way to orientate oneself by logic is not found in terms of a lived experience on the basis of a coherent rationality. This is impossible for the moment. The only thing that this logic indicates to Qoheleth is the negative character of the present: *hebel.* Accordingly, the best logic available to cope with the *hebel* is the affirmation of life in the eating of bread and the drinking of wine with gladness, in the company of the person you love, and amidst enslaving work. This is the central content of the six-times-repeated refrain[7] that spans various sections of Qoheleth's book and becomes the key of his discourse: Qoheleth works, acts, examines, reflects, searches — and comes to the conclusion that there is no better thing than precisely the daily activity just described. With each recurrence of the refrain, new details accompany it. The most complete formula is the last:

---

7. Cf. 2:24-26; 3:12-13; 3:22; 5:18-19; 8:15; and 9:7-16. In 11:9-10 we have the advice to youth to make merry and to take advantage of their youth in order to be happy.

Go, eat your bread with joy and drink your wine with a merry heart, because it is now that God favors your works. At all times let your garments be white, and spare not the perfume for your head. Enjoy life with the wife whom you love, all the days of the fleeting life that is granted you under the sun. This is your lot in life, for the toil of your labors under the sun. Anything you can turn your hand to, do with what power you have; for there will be no work, nor reason, nor knowledge, nor wisdom in the nether world where you are going. (9:7-10)

In this affirmation of concrete life, without being explicit about it, Qoheleth collates the signs of the novelty of the times: the eschatological banquet, Isaiah's familiar utopia (Isa. 62:9).

Let us make no mistake: Qoheleth's proposal is not the utterance of an individualistic, isolated personage who cannot bear the company of any but his beloved. Categorically he argues for oneness with others, since a like relationship of solidarity lends strength and succor for the better living of life (cf. 4:9-12).

This utopia of festival on the basis of daily living is the only possible solution for Qoheleth: reject the present by accepting it in a positive way, that is, by affirming and living that which the present is powerless to offer — rest, gladness, a shared meal — in a rhythm that chronological time cannot mark. In a way, then, one is living eternity within countable time, ignoring time because the minutes do not count. Time here is not gold, as it is for trade, finance, the portfolio of prevailing values, and the production of slave labor. What counts is joy and song, and the shared gladness of festival. What count are living bodies, and the earthly life that precedes everlasting death. If death is our lasting home, as Qoheleth says in 12:5, then life ought to be lived as if it were eternal, and this is done by relishing the life of instants so intense that there is no consciousness of time.

Elsewhere (2:24-26) our refrain is coupled with the assertion that all of this comes from the hand of God. Thus the subject is enabled to enjoy life without guilt feelings. The Mosaic Law, interpreted by the temple leaders, constantly called for rites of purification. Qoheleth follows another logic, and in one place he is even clearer, saying, in 9:7-9, that your works themselves are agreeable to God. In a non*hebel* universe, freedom becomes absolute. This is possible only because liberty is circumscribed by a gladsome world of shared intersubjectivity, a world orientated not by law, but by the logic of acknowledgment of the subject, independently of law.[8]

This is Qoheleth's explicit utopia — even though he does not acknowledge

---

8. It is along these lines that we interpret the Pauline theology of justification by faith and not by the works of the law. The law, absorbed by sin, alienates the subject's conscience, and enslaves. Faith, which is equivalent to taking one's orientation in a different logic, that of the Spirit, transcends the law, and places the human being above it. See Elsa Tamez, *Contra toda condena* (1991).

it as such, as he denies all novelty in the times of history. As a utopia, its full realization is not possible in history for all human beings.[9] Actually, not all time can be that of festival, however Qoheleth may exhort us to that effect. Dressing in white and anointing one's head with perfume means dressing in finery for a banquet. These are poetic, symbolical expressions of the writer's desires.[10] They are based on a reality in which, on the one side, foreign domination determines that in production, trade, the meritocracy, and war, efficiency is the order of the day — leaving human beings, especially farm workers (slave or free), in the lurch; and on the other side, on the local scene, the temple requires sacrifices for purification and compliance with the Law.

But not everyone can rely on having the means to eat and drink, or on a beloved, and thereby be able to enjoy life. Qoheleth's proposal merely represents his desires, manifested not in the subjunctive, but in the imperative mood. The real world is *hebel* for our personage because workers cannot enjoy their product. Others enjoy it, and this is *hebel.* Non*hebel,* for our personage, is the enjoyment of the product of one's own labor. Furthermore, Qoheleth's reflection goes in quest of universality: he refers to all, including the rich (5:19).[11] He proposes to the latter, as well, that they enjoy their goods, for they are unable to do so in their *hebel* world, either because a stranger enjoys them, or because they lose them in unsuccessful business enterprises owing to the fluctuations of the market, or because they strive to accumulate wealth. Their lifestyle does not allow them the joy of daily life or shared bread. They fail to acknowledge their quality as subjects more important than wealth. On Qoheleth's utopian horizon, everyone enjoys material life, and especially, knows how to do so.

On the other hand — and this is important — Qoheleth's alternative of the gladsome experience of a bodily life without anxiety, amidst the rigor of demanding times and the snare of rigorous laws, is not the proposal that his hearers exercise a parallel vital power that would be irresponsible toward the efficient, dehumanizing power of the Ptolemaic machinery. Nor is his proposal the condemnation of the dictates of the Mosaic Law. In question is not an experience of joy that would turn an indifferent back on the dehumanizing havoc wreaked by the power of the times. Nor is it produced by feelings of cynical impotence, or unlove toward the most fragile victims of economic policies. Qoheleth is clear: life is celebrated with gladness in the midst of enslaving labor, in the midst of *hebel.* And this, we think, is the challenge to, and most powerful rebuke of, persons who reject a worthy, full life. Our interpretation is surely plausible. In the glyptic art of ancient Mesopotamia, we have

9. Hinkelammert calls utopia the construction of impossible worlds. Politics would be the art of the possible, orientated by the proposal of the impossible *(Crítica a la razón utópica).*

10. As Rizzante and Gallazzi say *(RIBLA* 14 [1993]: 82), it seems to be a mini-psalm for everyday use.

11. Possibly an allusion to his aristocratic contemporaries, themselves subjected to the rule of the Ptolemaic empire: their goods are at every moment liable to confiscation by the king.

scenes in which, during the course of a funeral, participants are celebrating sacred banquets, with music, dancing, drinking, and lovemaking. What is being represented is the life force in confrontation with death. Death is ridiculed, and life is affirmed and clung to.[12]

In this sense, Qoheleth's proposal, made on the basis of daily living, takes on a larger meaning with respect to the economic, political, and religious macrostructure. There is no question, then, of seeking to advance toward utopia by creating a parallel community, isolated from the *hebel* world[13] and having no effect on it. Ultimately, and perhaps unconsciously, Qoheleth proposes we challenge the logic of the "mess" by living, in the midst of the "mess," a logic of "nonmess," whose synthesis is the eating of bread, the drinking of wine with gladness, and the enjoyment of life with someone we love. Curiously, while until now Qoheleth's ignorance of the times has dehumanized him because it has immobilized him, now, with his proposal, the impenetrability of future horizons humanizes him, inclining him to turn back to himself, to feel his body in gladness, and to share that bodiliness.

C. Impossible Alternative: A Trusting Faith in Almighty God

Qoheleth's frustration is his helplessness before the *hebel* of the world around him. The signifiers in the opening poem (1:4-11) connote the presence of an autonomous machinery that brooks no interference. In that world, daily occurrences are left out of consideration, nor do they affect the all-but-perfect functioning of the monotonous occurrences of the universe. All is *hebel*, and nothing can be done against it (1:14-15). Let us observe the contradictory changes that transpire in Qoheleth's consciousness with regard to meaningless events, and see his theological reading of those events, which helps him read the times. After all, his reading enables him to survive, and survive well.[14]

The task of examining, with wisdom, what happens "under the sun" is an arduous occupation imposed upon human beings by God (1:13). This wise knowledge concerning "madness and folly" is the occasion of "sorrow" and "grief" (1:17-18). The reason is that there is no sure science of the element of absurdity that nests in reality, the enormous void, the *hebel*. The human being's wisdom, inherited from times gone by, is that God has created all things beautifully and well and has made human beings good. Experience in this world contradicts that premise from every angle. Qoheleth fails to understand and

---

12. Cf. Marvin H. Pope, *Song of Songs* (Garden City, N.Y.: Doubleday, 1977), pp. 210ff.

13. Like the utopia of Thomas More that Vasco de Quiroga attempted to create in certain villages of the conquered land of Mexico, where privileges of the utopia were for the inhabitants of the villages. The other natives were brutally exploited, and no one came forward in their defense.

14. In the text they do not appear in order, nor is there any reason why they should, since it was a matter of a struggle of one's own conscience. The order corresponds to our own rereading.

universalizes his failure of comprehension: God made everything beautiful, but the human being fails to understand God's complete work from beginning to end, even though God has placed in our hearts the ability to understand the remotest thing (3:11). However we may strive to comprehend God's designs in history, we do not succeed, even if we are wise (8:17).

Our personage does not understand, and he continues in his theological reasoning: God made human beings just, but they have perverted their situation (7:29). This is a step in the direction of understanding the occurrences of his world. But even so Qoheleth does not manage to understand God's work, since in the divine omniscience God becomes responsible for all events under the sun: then God is responsible for Qoheleth's miserable world. It is God who has made the crooked crooked: "Consider the work of God. Who can make straight what he has made crooked?" (7:13). God is responsible for the fact that some can enjoy the product of their labor and others not. The fact is described as a great and painful evil (6:1-2).

At one point Qoheleth's reasoning reaches its limit: God is God and the human being is a human being. God is stronger: you don't negotiate with divinity. This reality presents itself as a known fact, entailing no mystery: "Whatever is, was long ago given its name, and the nature of man is known, and that he cannot contend in judgment with one who is stronger than he" (6:10).

In taking this step, the narrator projects his impotence upon transcendence, the divinity. Curiously, as he takes this step of acknowledging his help-lessness, the contrary phenomenon is provoked: his soul is dynamized, and the possibility presents itself as concretely viable that a person might enjoy life now, in the midst of *hebel*. This is the indispensable step he must take if he is to reconstruct his consciousness and reorganize his world on the basis of a dimension free from the anxiety, the anguish, and the crushing agony of *hebel*. It is here that the dimension of the fear of God (5:7), which in Proverbs is the "beginning of wisdom" (Prov. 9:10), comes on the scene (Eccl. 5:7). Fear of God is "man's all" (12:13),[15] according to the appendix (12:9-14) of our text, written by a second, later hand.

The meaning of the expression "fear of God" *(yara')* is not "being afraid." In Qoheleth it means rather a recognition of the distance that separates God from the human being.[16] To fear God is to recognize God's numinous, extraordinary aspect, which surpasses human beings because God is inscrutable, unpredictable — an indecipherable enigma. God is mystery. God marks the limits

---

15. The second epilogist, of course, to whom the appendix belongs (12:13-14), does not understand the fear of God in Qoheleth's sense. For Qoheleth, the fear of God has nothing to do with the observance of the commandments.

16. Jenni-Westermann, *Diccionario Teológico Manual del Antiguo Testamento,* 2 vols. (1978), p. 1066.

of human potential. Like a mirror or a clear spring, God shows creatures their condition as humans. In this sense, the acknowledgment of God as God initiates the possibility of human realization. Paradoxically, fear of God means, "Fear not." It invites one to serenity amidst laborious practice. The fear of God bears a relationship to the human being's behavior and attitude toward life. Thus it implies a strong accent on trust.[17] In a recognition of human limits, consciousness unfolds within the margins of possibility. As for the impossible, God will take that in charge, and indeed through creaturely subjects. All is before God. Not that we penetrate the mystery (9:1).

Helplessness, powerlessness casts the human being upon the dimension of faith. In turn, faith bestows on that same being the energy to live. Qoheleth, as we have said, redirects the world toward non*hebel* by assigning propitious times to God. While the time of *hebel* neutralizes or paralyzes us, faith that everything has its time and hour delivers us. God manages times, and things will go well for those who fear God; that is, for those who recognize their limits. This is the power of faith, even though Qoheleth does not experience it in the present "now." Qoheleth has faith that God will act and judge with justice, at the appropriate time (3:17-18; 8:12-13).

Once we have arrived at this point, Qoheleth's explicit alternative becomes feasible: the affirmation of concrete life in the gladness of eating bread and drinking wine and enjoying one's beloved. There is neither irresponsibility nor indifference here, in the face of the events of exploitation under the sun. There is only the wager on life, for we rest in the grace of God in the midst of enslaving toil and against its antihuman logic.

17. Franz Mussner, *Tratado sobre jos judíos* (Salamanca: Sígueme, 1983), p. 98.

The Teaching Office
and the Unity of the Church

Wolfhart Pannenberg

Coming to an understanding concerning ecclesiastical office has frequently been cited as the most difficult task of ecumenical dialogue. This view is certainly justified in the light of the enormous differences between the ways the various organizational structures of the member churches of the World Council of Churches address the tasks of congregational leadership and doctrinal procla-mation. Churches deriving from the Reformation have not only the office of pastor as conferred through ordination, but also various more or less strongly accentuated presbyterial forms of congregational leadership and synodal forms of church leadership at the higher levels. In this context there is little clarity today, apart from the tasks of proclamation and pastoral care, regarding the theological particularity of the pastoral office as compared with other ecclesi-astical service, a particularity characterized by the association of a calling to the ministry on the one hand, and ecclesiastical ordination on the other. This also applies to the relationship between the pastoral office as practiced in Protestant churches today and the ancient church office of the bishop.

The Lutheran Reformation had at its disposal a much clearer and more differentiated understanding in this regard, an understanding also reflected in Lutheran confessional writings. The document resulting from the collective Inter-national Roman Catholic and Protestant-Lutheran Commission on the Spiritual Office in the Church (1981) worked out a detailed understanding on this basis, and also attained a remarkable measure of understanding with the Catholic side. Although the Lutheran churches did indeed respectfully acknowledge the adop-tion of the older church model of a threefold division of the ordination office into episcopate, presbyteriate, and diaconate in the Lima Declaration on Ecclesiastical Office (1982, Nos. 19-21), they did not really appropriate this model. Beginning with the confessional writings of the sixteenth century, Lutheran doctrine has always emphasized the unity of the office commissioned with proclaiming the

Word and administering the sacraments. In 1991, the committee of the Vereinigte Evangelische-Lutheranische Kirche Deutschlands (VELKD) charged with study-ing the doctrinal condemnations of the sixteenth century declared that this one office constituted the office of the pastor, and from it the various supracongre-gational offices were then developed, up to the regional office of the bishop. In this regard, the opinion was to be rejected "that the supracongregational office of the bishop represents the primary, real office of the church," as asserted by the Second Vatican Council. This understanding allegedly fails to realize that "the pastorate's task of public proclamation and administering of the sacraments . . . is the central service of the church," service "for which the office was established" (*Augsburg Confession* [*CA*], V).[1] To be sure, the VELKD-committee did acknowledge that in the ancient church "the office of the bishop was established at the level of the local congregation" *(loc. cit.)*, so that the committee was actually criticizing only the fact that a "supracongregational" office of bishop is placed above the pastoral office as the real office of the church.

The question is whether this correctly portrays the difference from the contemporary Roman Catholic understanding of the office of bishop. That is, the church constitution of the Second Vatican Council refers to bishops not as those standing over the regional church groups, but rather (*Lumen Gentium* [LG], 23) characterizes bishops as the "visible principle and foundation of the unity in their particular churches." The same article (Section 4) also refers to these *ecclesiae particulares* as "local churches," and this concept of *ecclesia localis* appears in Article 26 once more under the designation *congregatio localis* and with reference to the New Testament use of the concept of church. Now, one might certainly object that even though they are referred to as heads of local churches, contemporary Roman Catholic bishops in fact are the holders of regional leadership offices. It is not without significance, however, that the *theology* of the office of bishop associates this office with the concept of the local congregation, though it is admittedly unclear just how this concept is to be understood in its own turn. In any event, LG 26 in particular offers a point of departure for understanding the concept of the local church in the sense of a congregation assembled at a specific place for worship.

In his own commentary to this article, Karl Rahner mentioned the criti-cism expressed at the Council concerning a view of the church oriented too one-sidedly from the perspective of the church as a whole. In his view, LG 26 allegedly tried to do justice to this criticism such that the constitution does after all allow for the "possibility of this view": "One *can* take as one's point of departure the concrete congregation in which the preaching of Christ's word and the proclamation of his salvific death occurs in the Eucharist, in which Christ himself is thus present as eschatological salvation in the Word and

---

1. *Lehrverurteilungen im Gespräch. Die ersten offiziellen Stellungnahmen aus den evan-gelischen Kirchen in Deutschland,* p. 149.

sacrament and in fellowship, and is thus *church* in the true sense of the word. From this perspective, one can then also come to an understanding of the church as a whole, since the church is itself *truly there (vere adest)* in the local congregation."[2] The text of LG 26 does not read *vere adest,* but does say substantively the same thing in its assertion that Christ is present in these local congregations, *cuius virtute consociatur una, sancta catholica et apostolica Ecclesia.*

This entire paragraph is one of the most important points of departure for a *communio*-ecclesiology in the church constitution. Since the statements concerning the office of the bishops as leaders of the particular churches can also be interpreted from this perspective, the explications of the VELKD committee on the Roman Catholic understanding of the office of bishop fail to appreciate its complexity, and in an all too facile fashion contrast this office as a regional office to the Lutheran understanding of office. Instead, they should have pointed out the need for clarification within the Roman Catholic understanding of the concept of the local church with regard to its relationship with the larger church and with regard to the characterization of the office of bishop as a local or as a regional office. By contrast, there should have been no objection to the fact that Catholic doctrine holds fast to the designation "bishop" to refer to "the primary, real office of the church," despite the ambiguity arising from contemporary use, which refers the term almost exclusively to a regional office. We will see that the primitive Christian process through which the bishop's office actually emerged provides good reason for a theology of ecclesiastical office to take as its point of orientation the office of bishop as the classic manifestation of "the primary, real office of the church," though this does not permit the option for any primacy of a regional leadership office over against the office of proclamation and administration of sacraments in the actual worship service at the level of the local congregation. The committee of the VELKD should have insisted on associating the office of bishop with this latter function instead of acknowledging as normal the characterization of the designation "bishop" exclusively as a regional office and instead of tying the Roman Catholic doctrine of office to such characterization.

On the other hand, too little attention is given from an ecclesiological perspective to the substantive reasons for "separating out" supracongregational episcopal offices from the pastoral office as commissioned with proclamation and the administration of the sacraments. Although such separating out is indeed acknowledged as "substantively appropriate in view of the supracongregational identity of the gospel,"[3] it is not associated with the task of maintaining the unity of the church in the unity of apostolic faith, unity that the office of the pastor or bishop already serves in its own way at the level of the local

---

2. *Lexikon für Theologie und Kirche. Ergänzungsband,* I (²1966), 243.
3. See the text cited in note 1 above, p. 149, lines 29-30.

congregation. If this particular context is insufficiently considered, the relationship between the local and supracongregational tasks of ecclesiastical office are not appropriately presented.

In what follows, the primitive Christian roots of the ancient church office of the bishop will serve as a point of departure for clarifying these relationships. Then the relationship between the local and supralocal tasks of ecclesiastical office will be discussed, and in connection with this also the task of a special service directed toward maintaining the unity of the larger church.

1. The Office of Bishop as Service to the Unity of the Local Church in the Teaching of the Gospel

In the beginnings of the gentile-Christian church, the authority of the apostles themselves ensured that the congregations were preserved in their faith in the crucified and resurrected Lord. After the deaths of the apostles, however, the second and third generations of primitive Christianity apparently experienced a period of uncertainty regarding the execution and continuation of this function. Itinerant charismatics and evangelists (Eph. 4:11), who continued to represent that particular type of apostle which journeyed from place to place, could not offer any guarantee for the preservation of the congregations in the faith of their apostolic founders, but rather themselves required testing against just this norm (cf. *Did.* 11-12), as was already the case in Corinth during the lifetime of the apostle Paul (2 Cor. 11). Congregational offices included on the one hand the committee of elders deriving from Judaism, and on the other the offices of local, resident teachers mentioned by Paul (1 Cor. 12:28; Rom. 12:7; cf. Eph. 4:11), as well as the leaders of the house congregations (episcopates), assisted by "deacons" (Phil. 1:1); but these offices had other functions, and initially these functions did not include the authority necessary for continuing the apostolic service of preserving the unity of the congregation in its faith in the gospel as originally received from such authority. Although the Pastoral Epistles do indeed suggest the notion that the apostles themselves installed bishops as their successors, this notion proves to be fictitious if these letters do not come from Paul, but were only written in his name decades after his death, as the majority of exegetes today generally believe. To be sure, just this emergence of pseudonymous Pauline letters can be understood as an expression of the efforts put forth in the decades following the apostle's death for the sake of preserving an orientation toward the doctrine associated with his personal authority, and to assert this orientation in the constitutional problems of the postapostolic age.

The Pastoral Epistles exhibit a tendency to extricate the function of the episcopal office from its restriction to the house congregations and to expand its reference to the overall congregation of a given locale, and to tie its supervisory function to responsibility for doctrine.[4] In the second century, this particular solution asserted itself against other models, above all against a corresponding expansion of the authority of the committee of elders. The deciding factor in this process seems to have been the tying of this responsibility for maintaining the unity of apostolic faith to a single person instead of to a committee. On the other hand, however, congregational leadership by a committee of elders was preserved with an orientation toward the special function of the *episkopos*. Given the special responsibility held by the bishop for the unity of the congregation in the apostolic faith, it is easy to understand that in the congregation's actual worship situation the bishop then also acquired the presiding function at the celebration of the Eucharist, since precisely this celebration of the Eucharist, with the accompanying presence of Christ in the meal, simultaneously portrays the unity of the congregation grounded in him.

This historical evidence has considerable consequences for a theology of ecclesiastical office. Although the notion that the apostles personally installed bishops as their successors and thereby established the ancient church office of the bishop must be considered the product of an idealization of the historically much more complex and apparently much less linear process, in substance these early Christian bishops are indeed the successors of the apostles in their responsibility for preserving the congregations in the unity of the gospel as received from the apostles. This function could be assumed by the recast and expanded office of the episcopate through an association of teaching authority and leadership function, whereby not all the leadership tasks would have to be included in the hand of the bishop, but rather only those immediately connected with the task of preserving the congregations in the unity of the apostolic faith. In the history of the church, the office of the bishop as restructured in this way did indeed prove itself suited for taking on this responsibility for preserving the congregation in the unity of the apostolic gospel. Hence it is not merely an example of a particular "organizational structure" of congregational life whose form was fortuitous and thus might well have been quite different. This association of congregational leadership and teaching, as manifested in the early church office of the bishop, should thus be viewed rather as the solution — one that since then has become classic within the church — to the task of preserving congregations in the unity of apostolic faith.

This task, however, is addressed most decisively through doctrinal proclamation of the Word. Just as the apostolic gospel itself functioned as the given norm in this process through which the office of bishop emerged, so also is the office of the bishop itself now there for the sake of serving God's word by teaching what has been handed down from the apostles (cf. LG 10), whereby the relationship between person and office is no longer the same as with the

---

4. In this connection see J. Roloff, *Der erste Brief an Timotheus. Evangelisch-Katholischer Kommentar zum Neuen Testament*, 15 (Zurich: Benzinger, 1988), pp. 175ff.

apostles themselves. The Pauline gospel is simultaneously vouchsafed by the apostle himself. By contrast, the bishop successors in the apostolic office take the gospel itself, as attested in the New Testament canon, as the standard for their doctrinal proclamation.[5]

Another result is that the commission of the office of bishop is rooted in the faith of the congregation as bound to the gospel, regardless of the extent to which, on the other hand, it does represent the authority of the gospel and of Jesus Christ himself for those congregations. This mutuality is the basis of the demand that the congregations participate in the selection of their bishops and in the exercise of their leadership functions. Because of its ties to the gospel, the community of baptized Christians can also function as a corrective to the activity of the office-holder, since the Christian congregation is, as Luther put it, qualified by virtue of its ties to the gospel and its reception of the spirit "to judge doctrine." The Catholic tradition speaks at this point of *sensus fidelium*. The doctrinal proclamation of the bishops, unlike that of the apostles, does not occupy a position of authority over against the faith of the congregation, but rather is focused and dependent on reception by the congregation's own sensibility for faith.

The Reformation understanding of office, as expressed in an exemplary fashion in *CA* 5, corresponds essentially to this original task and function of the office of bishop. Its designation as an office of preaching contains the Reformation corrective to an understanding of office that had largely neglected the task of proclamation of doctrine. Today, the Roman Catholic understanding both of the office of bishop and of the participation of presbyters in this office also places its main emphasis on the task of proclaiming the gospel (*Presbyterorum Ordinis* 4; cf. LG 21). The task of administering the sacraments corresponds to the presiding function especially during the celebration of the Eucharist, a function ascribed to the ancient church bishop because of his special responsibility for the unity of the congregation in the apostolic faith. The statements of *CA* 5 concerning ecclesiastical office do not especially emphasize this responsibility for unity in faith and the attendant task of leading the congregation. This responsibility is, however, indirectly contained in the statement of *CA* 7 concerning the significance of the gospel teaching and of the administering of the sacraments for the unity of the church; that is, if one considers that according to *CA* 5 the preaching office established by God is responsible for this function. Furthermore, the task of jurisdiction associated with the proclamation of doctrine and the administration of the sacraments is expressly mentioned in *CA* 28:21-22.

More recent ecumenical documents concerning spiritual office emphasize more strongly than did the Augsburg Confession this notion of leading the congregation in the task of doctrinal proclamation. Thus the document of the

---

5. Cf. my discussion of J. Ratzinger's *Das neue Volk Gottes. Entwürfe zur Ekklesiologie* (1969), p. 115, in *Systematische Theologie*, III (Göttingen: Vandenhoeck & Ruprecht, 1993), pp. 415-16.

International Lutheran/Roman Catholic Commission on the Spiritual Office in the Church (1981) asserts that in the postapostolic age a special office "for the sake of leading the congregation became necessary" (no. 17). This office, as pastoral service, is allegedly connected with "serving the unity of the congregation and between congregations" (no. 27). This is also the perspective from which, according to Catholic understanding, the presiding function of the ordained officeholder at the celebration of the Eucharist is to be understood, since it is "the sacrament of unity" (no. 28). According to the Lutheran understanding, too, however, this office stands "in the service of the unity of the church" (no. 29). We might add only that this service is basically put into practice through doctrinal proclamation, through proclamation of the gospel. Here the connection with the Reformation understanding of the office of bishop as a preaching office becomes clear.

The Lima Declaration concerning Ecclesiastical Office (1982) similarly emphasizes the connection between the task of *doctrinal proclamation* and preservation of the *unity* of the church. We read there that the church needs "persons who are publicly and perpetually responsible" for referring the church "to its fundamental dependence on Jesus Christ, and who thereby represent a reference point of unity within its varied gifts" (no. 8). This formulation is also of significance because it makes clear the particularity of the ordained office of the church in relation to the varied charismatic gifts within the life of the congregation. The uniqueness of the ordained office of the church consists in just this responsibility for the unity within the apostolic faith in Jesus Christ, and this responsibility is realized primarily through public doctrinal proclamation.

The Reformation emphasis on the *public nature* of doctrinal proclamation and the administration of the sacraments, which according to *CA* 14 requires appropriate authorization, also contains a reference to the unity of the church. That is, it is a matter of the public as associated with the *church*, of the community of Christians. This is the focal point of the exercise of office in doctrinal proclamation and the administration of the sacraments. The reference to the unity of the larger church inherent in this concept of the church public also establishes the necessity for ordination. If the bishop or pastor in the local church is to address this task of preserving it in the unity of the apostolic faith through doctrinal proclamation, then this involves the faith of the larger church; and this is why appointment to this office is not just a matter concerning the individual local churches involved. The fact that this appointment to office is carried out by the holder of a regional supervisory office of the church, along with the participation of other ordained officeholders, lends expression to the overall relevance of service to the unity of the church, service that is passed on through ordination with the commission to public doctrinal proclamation and administration of the sacraments. Responsibility for the unity of the members of a local congregation in the faith of the apostolic gospel is connected to the unity of all Christendom established in Jesus Christ. The unity of the church as a whole established in Jesus Christ is represented by the ordained office-holder in the local congregation. This is why for the members of the local church this person is also the "point of reference" of their unity, as the Lima document puts it, though only just such a "point of reference," and not the *principium et fundamentum* of their unity, as the Second Vatican Council has said both of the bishops in an unfortunate, because easily misunderstood formulation (LG 23), and similarly also of the office of the pope with reference to the church as a whole (LG 18).

The principle and foundation of the unity of the church is, as 1 Cor. 3:11 puts it, Jesus Christ alone: "For no one can lay any foundation other than the one that has been laid; that foundation is Jesus Christ." The ordained office-holders of the church, regardless at which level of its life, serve the unity of the church grounded in Jesus Christ. That is their commission. To that extent they are, in their various spheres of activity, a "point of reference" of that unity. They are not themselves the "principle" and "foundation" of that unity, but rather *represent* Christ as the principle and foundation of the unity of his church. And that is just what the Lutheran confession also says about church officeholders, namely, that in the execution of their commission for doctrinal proclamation and the administration of the sacraments they represent the person of Christ (*repraesentant Christi personam propter vocationem ecclesiae*, Apol. 7:28); for the officeholder is acting in the place of Christ himself, according to Jesus' own words: "Whoever listens to you listens to me" (Luke 10:16). That is the commission that he (or she) receives through ordination, and it implies that not the bishop or pastor, but rather Jesus Christ himself is the principle and foundation of the unity of his church.

2. The Necessity for Supra-Local Supervision of the Unity of Congregations in the Apostolic Faith

The preceding deliberations have focused on the local character of the ancient ecclesiastical office of the bishop. On the one hand they have presented that office as the church's classic solution to the problem of preserving congregations in the unity of apostolic faith, yet on the other they have identified this same office with the preaching office of the local pastor, an office that according to Reformation doctrine was established by God. In this equation between the local office of pastor and the office of bishop, the Lutheran Reformation consciously took ancient church circumstances as its point of departure, drawing support from explications made by the church father Jerome in his exegesis of Titus 1:5-7, explications also appropriated into the ecclesiastical legal collection *Decretum Gratiani* (I:95, 5), which itself was determinative for the Middle Ages. These explications also profoundly influenced medieval discussion concerning the relationship between the office of presbyter and that of bishop.

In his own writing "Von der Winkelmesse und Pfaffenweihe" (1533), Luther maintained that in the ancient church the bishop and pastor were originally "a single entity."[6] "Every city . . . had a bishop, just as each now has a pastor." This thesis asserting the local character of the ancient church office of bishop is the most important element in this Reformation understanding, and has been confirmed anew by exegetical insights concerning the origin of the office of bishop in the postapostolic age. By contrast, the associated notion — one deriving from Jerome — concerning the original equal status of the office of bishop and that of presbyter is of only secondary significance. Today we realize that in the second century this was only one of the solutions to the question concerning the relationship between what at that time was the relatively new office of bishop and the older institution of congregational leadership through presbyters.

Despite its emphasis on the local office of pastor as the basic form of the preaching office established by God, the Lutheran Reformation did not dispute the necessity of supracongregational, supralocal offices in the church, and even adopted what had become the customary use of the word *bishop* to refer to such regional supervisory office, though it acknowledged the local office of pastor as the original form of the office of bishop. This language is not only the result of a fortuitous semantic shift, but also substantively justified, since the regional office both of the medieval bishops and of contemporary Protestant state bishops are concerned with the same task as was the local office of bishop within the ancient church, namely, with preserving the community of Christians in the unity of apostolic faith, though now with reference to the community of local congregations among themselves and of their pastors. Thus in the case of the regional office of bishop, this involves an office of teaching supervision and of the integration of the various congregations of a given region into the unity of apostolic faith of the church, a unity represented by the bishop.

The necessity for supervising the doctrinal proclamation of pastors had already arisen during the Reformation, in the 1520s in the Electorate of Saxony, and was confirmed by the visitations conducted after 1526. In this sense, the Augsburg Confession also affirmed a regional office of bishop in its final article (*CA* 28). According to *CA* 28:20-21, the task of this office is in principle the same as that of the pastor: "to preach the gospel, forgive sins, judge teaching and discard doctrine that is contrary to the gospel, exclude from Christian congregations the godless whose godless character is apparent, without human force, but rather through God's word alone." The task of doctrinal proclamation is emphatically amplified by the condemnation of erroneous teaching and the task of ecclesiastical discipline. In these things, pastors and congregations are obliged to be obedient to the bishops "according to divine law" (*iure divino; CA*

---

6. *D. Martin Luthers Werke. Kritische Gesamtausgabe* 38 (Weimar: H. Böhlaus Nachfolger, 1912), 237.23.

28:22). Although the Lutheran Reformation expended considerable effort in maintaining and renewing this kind of regional bishop's office, the undertaking was actually not successful in Germany. The reasons for this failure involve the problem of the apostolic succession of office.

Although the historical circumstances cannot be discussed more fully here, it is important to see that the supralocal offices of the church, and thus first the regional bishop's supervisory office, were concerned with the same task that was determinative at the emergence of the office of local congregational leadership in the case of the early Christian *episkopos:* the task of preserving the congregations in the unity of apostolic faith. This task arises not only at the level of local congregations, but also with regard to the community of local congregations. For this purpose, the early church developed on the one hand synods of local bishops, in which each local bishop represented the congregation entrusted to him, and on the other hand the offices of the metropolitan or archbishop, who as the chief administrator within a given church province was responsible for summoning and conducting provincial synods and whose assent was necessary for the election of bishops in his province.

This perspective also makes understandable the extent to which the so-called apostolic succession of office serves the unity of the church in faith, since it is actually the result of the cooperation of the overall church or at least of a given church province in the transferal of office. This in its own turn is an expression of the church community as a whole, which every individual local church is charged with seeking and preserving, since each local church is itself a church only in concert with all other members of the body of Christ, who is present in the center of every local worship service.

In the Christian West, the institution of metropolitan had already deteriorated beginning with the early Middle Ages, or at least its significance was severely restricted — by the claims of kings on the one hand, and of the Roman bishops on the other — to an auxiliary function in the election and appointment of bishops, whereby Rome, as is well known, was able to assert itself in the investiture controversy. From time to time, however, the independence of church provinces has been revived, in the present through the institution of national bishops' conferences.

From the Protestant perspective, the necessity for insuring the unity of the church in its faith in the one apostolic gospel should also not be disputed in connection with the relationship between the various local congregations, or within the context of a given province, nation, and ultimately of all Christendom. To that extent, the point has been emphasized with some justification that the Lutheran Reformation is in principle also open to the necessity of Petrine service to the unity of Christendom as a whole. The only question is just what form such service must assume at the supra-local and ultimately overall church level if it is to take place in accordance with the gospel.

In the first place, one must emphasize that such insurance of the unity of the church on all levels is a task for the teaching of the gospel and of its reception by the community of Christians. Protestant churches suffer from the fact that the task of the teaching office is addressed today almost exclusively at the local level by pastors' proclamation within the worship service. This was not the case during the age of the Reformation. During the entire sixteenth century, an active effort was made to arrive at doctrinal consensus between the various individual territorial churches that had joined the Lutheran Reformation. These efforts manifested themselves in the process leading to the emergence of Lutheran confessional writings and constituted thus also the standard for an effective visitation praxis, and thus for doctrinal supervision of the proclamation actually taking place within the various local congregations.

In later centuries, this doctrinal consensus of the confessional writings was viewed as having been essentially concluded in the sixteenth century, and thus was increasingly historicized. Consciousness of this growing historical distance made it increasingly difficult to implement the doctrinal consensus of the confessional writings within the supervision of doctrine and teaching involving local proclamation. The result is that visitation in the sense of doctrinal or teaching supervision hardly occurs today, since the foundation is lacking, namely, concern with continued development of the doctrinal consensus of the Reformation. In their own turn, Lutheran state bishops only occasionally — here and there — address this responsibility for doctrine in view of current controversies concerning the faith and lifestyle of Christians in the spirit of the apostolic instructions.

In this context, the Lutheran bishops, and even more so the bishops' conference, would be the authorities most likely capable of countering the predominating deteriorization in matters of Christian doctrine, and the authorities that should understand such countering in the sense of the statements of *CA* 28 as the central task of the office entrusted to them. The synods cannot do this on their own, not least because of their composition, since they do not have the authority necessary for judging questions of doctrine in the way the ancient church bishops' synods had such authority. Neither do the synods have the ecclesiastical legal legitimation to carry out the office of teaching, since the didactic foundation of the church is fixed in the confessional status. Only in cooperation with the bishops might contemporary synods take on some of the neglected responsibility for the unity of the present Lutheran churches in the teachings of the apostolic gospel. Here a mere repetition of the confessional status of the sixteenth century is insufficient; what is required are new efforts undertaken on the basis of an understanding of Scripture appropriate for today and in critical discussion with the challenges of modern life.

Hence, the church of the *doctrina evangelii* today lacks at the supralocal levels of church life the necessary concern with the *consensus de doctrina*. This may seem like a harsh judgment, especially if one considers the doctrinal consensus to be adequately secured by the confessional status fixed in church constitutions. Yet the historical foundations of Protestant ecclesiastical self-understanding contained there have proven inadequate for effective teaching supervision if the issue is preserving the unity of the church in the faith of the apostolic gospel amid the current critical problems and discussions of the age. The state churches and their alliances have certainly not without exception neglected these tasks of common teaching and doctrinal responsibility. In addition to declarations of theological committees, whose binding character does, however, remain doubtful, such exceptions include various ecclesiastical missives, though these are actually more interested in current questions of the world than in the central themes of Christian faith. Ecumenical dialogues are another exception, though at least in the case of bilateral deliberations these are largely conducted on the basis of the confessional status of the sixteenth century.

The lament over the extensive disappearance of the teaching office in the Protestant churches above the local level of pastors' proclamation within the context of worship does not *eo ipso* contain an option for the manner in which such an office is exercised in the Roman Catholic Church. Supralocal functions of church teaching need not be concentrated one-sidedly at the single highest point. Their implementation at a mid-level can very well possess a certain ecclesiastically binding character as an expression of the representative formation of judgment of a given particular church within Christendom at a given time, and can do so without claiming finality and without severing critical discussion. To be sure, the faith of such a particular church can only be that particular faith of Christendom as a whole as grounded in the apostolic gospel. This is why the church must again and again put forth an effort at arriving at a worldwide consensus of Christendom concerning its faith. Such efforts find their model in the ecumenical councils of the ancient church. Yet although the doctrinal consensus of a general council can indeed be representative for the whole church and to that extent also binding, it does not have to understand itself as final in the sense of a definitive fixing of doctrinal form.

Perhaps the documents of the Second Vatican Council already provide an example of such openness, and to this extent this council might anticipate the style of future ecumenical councils of Christendom as a whole. In this context, one might also reconsider the relationship between an office that is perpetually responsible for the unity of Christendom as a whole in the faith of the apostolic gospel on the one hand, and the authority of such ecumenical councils on the other. This kind of Petrine service might perhaps be conceived best as a service of mediation between the various constituent churches of Christendom, and specifically also regarding the task of preserving unity in the apostolic faith.

Does Nothing Good Dwell in My Flesh?

Elisabeth Moltmann-Wendel

I

Paul's lament that "nothing good dwells in my flesh" (Rom. 7:18) has generated within both the church and theology a long and tragic history of anxiety, suppression, and hatred toward the body. Like no other theological strand before it, feminist theology has in the meantime disclosed the open or concealed dualism within theology between soul and body, and has uncovered the concrete loci of this division. It is women who through the long history of the church have been rendered invisible and discriminated against, who with their bodies have been objectified and turned into objects of desire and hatred. Violence toward women, as well as sexual exploitation and infringement as evident today everywhere and in every society, has shown once again just how unsuccessful the attempt has been to accept women as equal and to accept their bodies (as well as the bodies of human beings in the larger sense) as part of God's good creation.

Theological women's studies have disclosed the origins of this fatal tradition. Although this tradition did not actually first arise with Christian history itself, it very quickly found fertile soil within Christianity after initial commitments to equality and totality within the Jesus movement and early Christendom. Stages along the way to religious dualism legitimized by Christian thinking included that particular type of conservative ethos already evident in the domestic codes of the New Testament; the influence of the sexual ethics of Stoicism, which viewed the goal of sexuality not in desire, but in reproduction; a turning away from Hebrew conceptual models of totality; and the appropriation of Aristotelian-dualistic thinking. Later critical intrusions — such as that of Hildegard of Bingen — changed little in this regard. Women were identified with nature and with the body, something that made it possible not only to stylize them as mothers and saints, but simultaneously to fear and revile them — because of one's own, unpredictable, feared body — as seductresses, as weak, as whores. In the Western tradition, women's bodies were vessels that men claimed were theirs to fill, control, and possess.

According to Jewish-Christian tradition, the Spirit was poured out upon all flesh and all bodies, and as understood by the Acts of the Apostles and other texts from early Christendom, first seized women and men and gave to them quite different functions within the new congregations. Later, this same Spirit was tied to ecclesiastical office and, in the institutionalized church, thus also to men. The Spirit-filled quality of nascent Christendom was replaced by the hierarchical order of the church that ultimately excluded women from all important offices. Although church history repeatedly witnessed movements in which women came to expression filled with and legitimized by the Spirit, they were always repressed or, ultimately, bound into a hierarchical order. Mistrust of both woman and her corporeality played a role here. Those particular taboos returned that in the Jesus movement and parts of the early church had been suspended. The Levitical purity laws concerning the female body reappeared — laws that along with the other purity laws governing dealings with food and with the dead, had lost their validity. The result was that not only the woman's soul and body, but also spirit and body fell into permanent ecclesiastical discord.

To be sure, for feminist theology, which seeks to aid women in all parts of the world toward self-respect and self-reliance, this conflict between soul and body is merely a secondary contradiction within a larger complex. The primary contradiction resides for them in the unjust structures of racism, sexism, and classism regarding the message of the reign of God. The disclosure and elimination of this contradiction is a societal task. The vision animating feminist theology is a totality in which heaven and earth, immanence and transcendence, soul and body, nature and technology come together once again. This vision, however, is still far from being realized. Totality presupposes that the roots of dualistic theology are overcome. The agenda of feminist theology is to heal the world, and this healing is not an individual, but rather a social task in which women view themselves as midwives seeking to help give birth to a society that allows, encourages, confirms, and even blesses diversity. The liberated body, the body no longer sundered from the soul, the body animated by the spirit — all these are thus merely phenomena on the periphery of a larger healing process.

Consequently, analyses and observations regarding the female body within patriarchal society end up negatively cast. Feminist theology tries to disclose the dependence of this body on men, on male norms, and on a Western value system: the female body serves ideals of beauty determined by others, is supposed to concur with certain norms and standarized proportions, serves as a cult object, and is above all supposed to be tractable and accommodating. The analyses of violence toward the female body presented in the past few years are serious: violence through incest, through marital and public rape, and through coerced impregnation, for example during the war in Bosnia. And even medicine, which actually should be dedicated to the body of human beings as such, still seems caught in the old patterns of domination: the female body has become a public place into which all scientists unabashedly peer without preserving its mystery.[1] Those involved with in-vitro fertilization compare the female body quite simplistically to tubes and ampules, that is, to vessels that are supposed to serve formative male semen as sources of material and as a depository.

Consequently, only a renewal and a healing of the earth, a social alteration of unjust structures will ultimately be able to liberate the bodies of women. The body moves from being an individual to a social category, and for that reason islands of such renewal should be conceived above all collectively: women's collectives such as those envisioned by Frigga Haug, for trying out what it means to walk upright; or the women's church, which fulfills this function in feminist theology. Such collective structures are necessary for eliminating societal wrongs.

II

Within feminism itself, however, and within feminist spirituality, various feminine understandings of the body have emerged that undermine these hardened patriarchal structures and provide new individual points of departure. These have become significant for feminist theology as well.

First: Because the female body is measured against the male standard of accomplishment, against male strength, against a continual capacity for accomplishment and performance, women have begun to discover their own standards. The female body — generally viewed as being weaker than the male body, as being unstable and vulnerable — has now become a flexible, enormously adaptable medical miracle, one whose wounds during birth, for example, heal with surprising swiftness. Its alleged passivity during conception has proven to be a biological error. Today, women can free themselves from false imputations, and can recognize and live according to their own values.

Second: The psychological investigations of Anne Wilson Schaef have shown that healing is a process that takes place within the ill person with the support and assistance of the healer, whereas healing according to the male conceptual pattern comes as an external stimulus.[2] Hence healing needs assistants rather than authorities, assistants who work to free vital energies and support the process of self-healing.

Third: Within the female body, a kind of primal knowledge can be disclosed and vital energies retrieved that hitherto have been held back under false imputations. Instincts can be awakened that have deteriorated in the one-

---

1. Concerning this and the following discussion, see Elisabeth Moltmann-Wendel, *I Am My Body*, trans. John Bowden (New York: Continuum, 1995).

2. Anne Wilson Schaef, *Women's Reality: An Emerging Female System in a White Male Society* (Minneapolis: Winston Press, 1981), pp. 141-42.

dimensional, rational structure of domination. The individuality and originality inherent in every person, formerly concealed under a cloak of fear, passivity, and ignorance, can be released. Self-consciousness and self-determination can shape female lives. Self-determination of the body can then also free a person from all old or new ideologies. Such body-healings are also understood as political processes that dissolve the dualisms on earth. Our survival depends on developing such healing powers. Many of these ideas come from that particular matriarchal spirituality in which the goddess is viewed as the power inhering within us, a power maintaining the cosmos with its vital energy. "The image of the Goddess inspires women to see ourselves as divine, our bodies as sacred, the changing phases of our lives as holy, our aggressions as healthy, our anger as purifying, and our power to nurture and create, but also to limit and destroy when necessary, as the very force that sustains all life."[3]

Traces of such ideas, however, are also evident in feminist theological thinking, for example, in the assertion that "the grace of redemptive life is not beyond nature, but grace or divine gift is the ground of being of nature. Creation is itself the original grace or blessing."[4] Or when slumbering energies in human beings are awakened and mobilized. Or when at the World Conference of Churches in Canberra, the Korean theologian Chung Hyun Kyung draws parallels between the Holy Spirit, whom she usually calls "she," and the East Asian Ki or Chi, the cosmic breath of life. (Ki or Chi can be compared to the original Platonic Eros within Western thinking.) From her constituents she received the message for Canberra: "Tell them that they should not expend too much energy in summoning the spirit, since the spirit is already with us. Do not disturb her by your incessant summoning. She is already intensively at work among us. The only problem is that we do not have the eyes to see her, or the ears to hear her, because we are preoccupied with our own desires. . . . So tell them they should do penance."[5]

Women in feminist theology are generally more reserved with such notions of the body. An impressive foundation for a feminist moral theology, which in 1980 Beverly Wildung Harrison called "embodiment," has hardly been considered and developed. Harrison was keying on ideas presented by James B. Nelson and Tom Fr. Driver, though she also came close to the parallel ideas of Adrienne Rich (*To Think through the Body* [1976]) and Christa Wolf (*Mit dem Körper begreifen* [1978]). Harrison took as her point of departure Ruether's research regarding the unfortunate body-spirit dualisms and attendant negative estimations of women as such. She uncovered a disembodied rationality within

3. Starhawk, "Witchcraft as Goddess Religion," in *The Politics of Women's Spirituality: Essays on the Rise of Spiritual Power within the Feminist Movement*, ed. Charlene Spretnak (Garden City, N.Y.: Doubleday-Anchor, 1982), p. 51.

4. Rosemary Radford Ruether, *Women-Church: Theology and Practice of Feminist Liturgical Communities* (San Francisco: Harper & Row, 1985), p. 86.

5. See Elisabeth Moltmann-Wendel, ed., *Die Weiblichkeit des Heiligen Geistes* (Gütersloh: Chr. Kaiser, Gütersloher Verlagshaus, 1995), pp. 176-77.

male theological thinking, and demanded that feminists begin "with our bodies, ourselves." Ultimately, "all our knowledge, including our moral knowledge, is body-mediated knowledge. All knowledge is rooted in our sensuality. . . . If we are not perceptive in discerning our feelings, or if we do not know what we feel, we cannot be effective moral agents. . . . Failure to live deeply in 'our bodies, ourselves' destroys the possibility of moral relations between us."[6] Why is it that the body has since then so rarely been the central focus in feminist theology? Are women afraid that others will perhaps associate them once again only with these bodies, and that old ideologies regarding women will reemerge?

Rosemary Ruether briefly addresses this question. For her, the theology of the goddess religion contains the proclamation that everything that exists is good, and she finds in this proclamation a lack of understanding for historical sins and a lack of willingness to accept responsibility for the weaknesses and evil of social systems. It is here that the goddess religion allegedly fails to engage in any realistic estimation of the present situation.

Catherine Keller is virtually the only one who has ventured gratifyingly far into the dimensions of the body; although she picks up ideas of Harrison and views personhood as being totally rooted in the flesh, she does also warn against the "simple identification of self and body," against the "celebration of our bodiliness." This kind of materialism allegedly leaves no room for any mutual relationship and transformation of body and soul/spirit.[7]

Hence, in feminist theological thinking the body is both a reminder of the unredeemed and uncomprehending world and a symbol for the possibility of change, for what is possible. Knowledge of our own entanglement in patriarchal structures makes it difficult to view salvation as being already present.

A reflection of the synoptic healing stories involving women might function as a corrective here. The theme here is the presence of salvation, of healing, of making whole, and is presented as such in a fashion hardly equalled in theology. The woman's personality and the healing of the body — that is, self and body — coincide here in a way that gives the lie to all older and newer theological suppressions of the body. "Let it be done for you as you wish" (Matt. 15:28); "go in peace, and be healed of your disease" (Mark 5:34); "you are set free from your ailment" (Luke 13:12) — these three sentences, each of which accompanies the healing of a woman and each of which takes place through touching, show a different view. This unity of body and soul, body and self, body and spirit can already take place here. In the messianic age, salvation or wholeness is always present, and the body, too, is an experienced locus and a sphere of the divine. Feminist theology that remains fixated primarily on the

6. Beverly Wildung Harrison, "The Power of Anger in the Work of Love: Christian Ethics for Women and Other Strangers," in *Making the Connections: Essays in Feminist Social Ethics,* ed. Carol S. Cobb (Boston: Beacon Press, 1985), p. 13.

7. Catherine Keller, *From a Broken Web* (Boston: Beacon, 1986), p. 235.

disclosure of the discredited body is missing its biblical foundation. Salvation, wholeness can already be experienced here, and we already encounter here an inclination to portray the liberated body. The body is not just a social category. Insofar as we are also individuals, the body belongs to us as something that is our own, something individually liberated and something to be renewed.

III

The biblical-Christian traditions rediscovered precisely by women contain various notions that bring together spirit and body into an extremely close connection, and that challenge us to reconsider the relationship between spirit and body.

First: New Testament stories of women, which are always accompanied by healings and for which Jesus becomes a central figure because "he tore down the body-soul dualism by accepting women as they were, including their bodies."[8]

Second: the Holy Spirit as woman and as one who gives birth, of whom the Indian Leelamma Athyal says: "The Holy Spirit is the mistress and giver of life, and woman cooperates with her insofar as she plays an important role in the emergence of life."[9]

Third: the image of the church as body. "Not the soul or the mind or the innermost Self but the body is the image and model for our being church."[10]

The stories of Jesus involving women, the female Spirit that gives birth, and the church as the body of Christ are thus ideas that are hardly sufficiently realized, ideas through which we can overcome our reticence in viewing spirit and body together concretely. Mary Grey's reflections concerning the spirit are helpful: this spirit is conceived as nonhierarchical, as not associated with the beyond, and as something that does not extinguish the person; and it intensifies and transcends the new experiences of the body.[11]

The spirit creates communication in hearing and listening. It solicits the silent, the unheard, the formless, and brings these into being. As early as 1974, one of the early feminist theologians, Nelle Morton, wrote:

> "We experienced God's spirit as a spirit that teaches human beings to listen. The word came and comes as a human word, as a human expression of humanity. The creative act of the spirit does not consist merely in words being spoken, but rather in the word, the breath, and the language of the creature

8. Aruna Gnanadason, *No Longer a Secret: The Church and Violence against Women* (Geneva: WCC Publications, 1993), p. 59.

9. Leelamma Athval, "Frauen und die Lehre vom Heiligen Geist," in *Die Weiblichkeit des Heiligen Geistes*, pp. 143-44.

10. Elisabeth Schüssler Fiorenza, *In Memory of Her* (Eng. trans., New York: Crossroad, 1983), p. 350.

11. Mary Grey, "Wohin fliegt die Wildgans?," in *Die Weiblichkeit des Heiligen Geistes*, pp. 143-44.

being heard. This is experienced wherever the spirit is present in fellowship and where the Pentecostal tongues of fire are at work. It is present in the community, and does not depend on any star, on an expert, or on the specialized knowledge granted to an individual by some hierarchical structure. . . . We learn to hearken with our entire bodies, to listen with our eyes, to see with our ears, and to speak with our hearing, for we know that the spirit is present, and is present dynamically, not statically."[12]

Although the spirit needs the body, it mixes it up: the eyes — which are accustomed to seeing — hear; the ears — which are accustomed to hearing — see; our secured, familiar body falls into fruitful chaos.

The spirit creates totality as well; it binds together corporeal, sexual, and psychological life. In it human beings become whole, and with it one can do justice to human beings in that totality. And finally, the spirit touches us in our innermost being, "on the level of the archaic and the instinctive, and vivifies the playful, joyous, ecstatic element."

Hence the spirit brings to light new dimensions of our being, and binds together human beings in an unaccustomed way. In the process, the spirit profoundly touches the bodies of human beings. In these reflections, spirit and body come together. The body is now no longer despised, rendered invisible, and feared, but rather is viewed again in its most profound experiences and in its capacity as God's creation, a capacity never before seen. It is characteristic of this understanding of spirit that it does not work along some mysterious solo path, but *co*-acts: co-creating, co-forming, co-determining, or it is manifested through movement, processes.

In feminist theology, the locus of such new experiences is the women's church, the counterculture to the patriarchate. Here wounds are healed that result from rape, violence, illness, and incest. Here grief is made possible, hidden currents of energy are motivated, and healing is encouraged by the group. Here liberation from determination by others and from repressive structures is celebrated, so that our true relationship with our physical reality, with the body, the earth, and the divine is reestablished. In such rituals and in such fellowship, the way is opened for the spirit, and the unity of spirit and body comes alive. Church reality is yet far from such reconciliation, and yet needs healing initiatives. Here, however, God and the body are already encountering one another, and spirit and body find their place.

But is there salvation or wholeness beyond such a church? Has not the statement *"extra ecclesia nulla salus est"* not always elicited tension and anxiety?

Feminist theology is a liberation theology that must uncover the unjust structures of society such as sexism, racism, and classism. This requires sociological

---

12. Nelle Morton, "Auf dem Wege zu einer ganzheitlichen Theologie," in E. Moltmann-Wendel, ed., *Frau und Religion. Gotteserfahrungen im Patriarchat* (Frankfurt: Fischer, 1983), pp. 208f.

analyses and theological-historical research. And a sharpened conscience is required for drawing attention to the ever emerging structures of injustice and their victims. Enlightenment and indictment, however, are not the only tasks given to feminist theology. Women today need symbols, images, and ideas with which they can lead their own, self-determined lives. And these images, ideas, and symbols must be characterized by totality; they must encompass body, soul, and spirit. They should not be permitted merely to mediate freedom in a cognitive fashion. They should not be permitted merely to demand a new morality that motivates the will and actions while leaving the unconscious, corporeal dimensions unaddressed.

It is not enough to establish salvation and wholeness and healing in collectives such as the women's church as the only locus of new life. Many women live lonely lives or in out-of-the-way areas where a women's group and women's church are utterly inconceivable. We need images for the presence of salvation and wholeness and healing with which women can live, bear their loneliness, express their hopes, and experience their wholeness. The process of becoming whole, the praxis of experiencing oneself as whole, is a topic hardly addressed by feminist theology. This is not a matter of fleeing reality or of individualizing religious experience. It is ultimately a matter of the body both physically and emotionally, the point of departure of our repression, alienation, and degradation, the body we must once again occupy in a positive fashion.

In my opinion, the following images are helpful:

The notion of God's unconditional, all-encompassing love for us, expressed in the sentences: I am good, I am whole, I am beautiful.[13]

The liberating experience of being able to dissociate oneself from the false imputations that physicians and scientists of all kinds create concerning women and women's bodies, and in the process of being able to arrive at our own standards and values: I am strong, but I can also be weak; I am flexible, I am independent. My body is my male friend/my female friend. I am my body.

The capacity to assure oneself, through the body, of one's own thinking. The capacity to develop and live out one's senses, to enjoy the fullness of aspects, to allow one's own rationality to grow, to say to oneself: I am, therefore I think.

The capacity to open oneself to the experiences of the Holy Spirit, a Spirit that transcends our confining corporeal space and allows us to get past the limits ingrained within us, a Spirit that expands and enriches us in leading us into the cosmic dance.

We need this vision of totality and wholeness; we need the agenda of healing the world and of our cooperation in this healing. We need both lament and indictment. We need the women's church. But we need with equal necessity to take steps toward the personal praxis of becoming whole, for the good is indeed permitted to dwell in my flesh.

13. Elisabeth Moltmann-Wendel, *A Land Flowing with Milk and Honey,* trans. John Bowden (New York: Crossroad, 1986), pp. 154ff.

Christian Anthropology and Gender: A Tribute to Jürgen Moltmann

Rosemary Radford Ruether

Jürgen Moltmann's prolific theological work over more than thirty years has been an inspiration to me in my own theological thought and writing. His concerns have paralleled many of my concerns as well. I read his landmark *Theology of Hope* in 1967 when I was first beginning to think in terms of a connection between Christian hope and social justice. He has been one of the major European theologians in continuous dialogue with the work of Latin-American liberation theologians.

As I turned to an increasing concern for the ecology crisis and its connection with the Christian view of creation, I was greatly aided by his major book, *God in Creation,* a work I regularly assign to students in my class on creation theology. His continuous reflection on Christian anthropology has been helpful in my own thinking on this crucial topic; and feminist theologians and churchwomen have been heartened by the way he has modeled collaboration on this topic with his wife, Elisabeth Moltmann-Wendel, in their joint works *Humanity in God* (1983) and *God His and Hers* (1991).[1] In this chapter I wish to engage in some reflections on Christian anthropology and gender in the spirit of this ongoing dialogue.

Christian anthropology in its classical theological development manifests profound ambiguities toward women. On the one hand, the Pauline credo that in Christ there is neither male nor female (Gal. 3:28) seems to dissolve all differences of gender and to put women on an equal footing with men in the redeemed humanity. If women were defined as inferior and subordinate in the classical societies of the Hebrew and Greco-Roman worlds, Paul's claim seems

---

1. Jürgen Moltmann, *God in Creation: An Ecological Doctrine of Creation,* trans. Margaret Kohl (London: SCM Press, 1985); *Humanity in God,* with Elisabeth Moltmann-Wendel (New York: Pilgrim Press, 1983); and *God, His and Hers,* trans. John Bowden (New York: Crossroad, 1990).

to leave us with two possible interpretations: either this subordination was sinful and contradicts God's intention in creation, or the subjugation of women came about as God's punishment for sin but has now been removed by redemption, restoring and renewing women's original equality with man.

Both of these options have been affirmed in Christian history, the latter in classical tradition and the former in modern liberal theology. A third option, that the patriarchal God of creation and the egalitarian God of redemption are different deities, was ruled out by the Christian rejection of the Marcionite split of the God of creation and the God of redemption. Key to Christian thought is the affirmation that there is one God who is both creator and redeemer. The God of Genesis and the God who is the Father of Jesus Christ is one and the same. Jesus, the Christ, the redeeming Messiah, is the Logos through which the world was created in the beginning; see Hebrews 1:1-5; Colossians 1:15-20.

However, this affirmation of women's equal share in redemption in Christ has been contradicted by an insistence that women cannot exercise representative authority either in society or in the church. This insistence on women's continued subordination in Christian society and church order finds expression in the claim that women by their very nature cannot "image Christ," and that the male is by nature the "head" of the female, mandated by God to exercise domination over her in the family and society.[2]

This insistence on women's continued subordination has been justified by a variety of combinations of two assertions: that women are innately inferior in the very nature of things, and/or that woman has been placed under male subjugation as punishment for (her) sin. We might summarize this view in the following double-bind formula: women are naturally subordinate, but also naturally insubordinate and have been put under male domination both to reaffirm their subordinate nature and to punish them for their sinful rebellion against it.

But how does this claim of original subordination and its reaffirmation in Christian society square with the Pauline claim that in Christ there is "neither male nor female"? The various forms of Christian theological anthropology of gender are more or less conscious efforts to reconcile this contradiction between equality in Christ and continued subordination in Christianity, through various interpretations of the relationship of the status of women in the original creation, in the Fall, and in redemption.

---

2. The first argument is more typical of Roman Catholics; see *The Declaration of the Question of the Admission of Women to the Ministerial Priesthood* (October 15, 1976), §§1-5. The second is more typical of Evangelical Protestants; see Donald Grey Barnhouse, "The Wife with Two Heads," in Letha Scanzoni and Susan Seta, "Woman in Evangelical, Holiness and Pentecostal Tradition," *Women and Religion in America: 1900-1968*, ed. Rosemary Keller and Rosemary Ruether (New York: Harper and Row, 1986), pp. 262-63; also, Letha Scanzoni, "The Great Chain of Being and the Chain of Command," in *Women's Spirit Bonding*, ed. Janet Kalven and Mary I. Buckley (New York: Pilgrim Press, 1984), pp. 41-55.

In this chapter I will explore the various options for combining these relationships systematically, and in their historical development, in classical and modern Christian views. I will then explore a possible reinterpretation of this tradition from a contemporary feminist perspective.

Gender and Creation

Are women created in the image of God? Are women fully and equally *human?* These are the key questions for exploring views of women's status in the original creation. Modern Christian theologies, even conservative ones, affirm that women are equally in the image of God. But they often imply a difference in how women and men image God that justifies subordination. The image of God is seen as reflected in the heterosexual couple, who together make the complete image, but this assumes that neither women nor men are complete in themselves. It also inserts a complementarity into the concept of image of God that makes male leadership over the woman and female auxiliary relationship to the man internal to the "image of God as relationship."

This modern strategy for including women in the image of God by affirming difference in relationship departs from the classical Christian tradition of the Church Fathers. Here there were two options for viewing women's relation to the image of God. In the Eastern tradition, the image of God was identified with the soul, which was seen as spiritual and asexual. Women and men in their spiritual natures have equally redeemable souls. In the original creation there was no subordination but also no gender, sex, or reproduction. Gendered bodies arose as a result of the Fall, which resulted in both sin and death and the necessity of sex and reproduction.[3]

The Latin tradition represented by Augustine, on the other hand, claimed that subordination was intrinsic to the original creation, although sin and death were not. The image of God refers to the soul in both its rational nature and its representation of God's domination over nature. Only men possess this capacity for dominion, while women represent nature or the body that is under dominion. Therefore, for Augustine, women in themselves lack the image of God and are related to God's image only by being included under male headship.[4]

For Augustine, God's image in "man" is androcentric and corporate. Its essence is the quality of rationality as sovereign power to be exercised by the individual male over his own bodily passions and by the male as corporate head

---

3. For example, Gregory of Nyssa, *De Opif. Hom.* 16.

4. Augustine, *De Trinitate* 7.7.10; see Kari Borresen, *Subordination and Equivalence: The Nature and Role of Woman in Augustine and Thomas Aquinas* (Washington, D.C.: Univerity Press of America, 1981), pp. 15-34.

of creation over women and the rest of nature. Augustine's view reflects the patriarchal legal tradition of the male head of the family as corporate individual.

These differences between the Greek, Latin, and modern views raise key questions about the relationship of image of God and gender. How is the soul, spirit, or mind seen as related to sex and the gendered body? Is mind, spirit, or soul sexually neutral, possessed by men and women equally, separate from the sexed body? Or are humans a union of body and soul-mind, and so sexual distinctions also make for differences in women and men's "ways of thinking"? In modern feminist thought, this question is extended by the distinctions of sex and gender, sex being biological differences, while gender is seen as socially constructed.[5]

The differences between the Greek and Latin views of *imago dei* and gender also point to different understandings of the meaning of the image of God as a quality of humanness. Is God's image in humans a shared essence between God and humans or a shared role? The author of Genesis 1:27 intended the latter meaning: that is, humans are like God, not ontologically, but through sharing or representing God in God's dominion over the (rest of) creation. Although this role as God's representative in dominion is given to Adam ("the Human") generically, the priestly author undoubtedly assumed that it was exercised in practice by the patriarchal male.[6]

As Phyllis Bird has shown in her careful exegesis of this passage, the image of God that was given to Adam corporately is not identified with, but distinguished from, gender difference — which humans share with animals, but not with God. Thus image of God cannot be identified literally with male or female biological sex. But since dominion is exercised only by patriarchal males, not by women or slaves, it is patriarchal males who exercise the *role* of image of God as corporate individuals on behalf of the whole community.

With the incorporation of Greek soul-body dualism into Christian thought, Christians also came to think of the image of God as an ontological "likeness" of God and humans, located in the immortal soul, which was seen as participating in the eternal spiritual being of God. The body is seen as the vehicle of both sin and death, while the soul is the part of humans that they share with the divine. The soul is seen as a self-subsistent being, originally without mortal body. The soul is put into a mortal body as a "testing place" or as a fall into sin, but the soul must discard the body in order to return to its pure state.

The soul, although without body originally, was also seen as innately rational, and thus linked with masculinity. The ruling class male is thus the normative human, while women and slaves come about through a failure of

---

5. See Mary Field Belensky et al., *Women's Ways of Knowing* (New York: Basic Books, 1986); also Ann Snitow, Christine Stansell, and Sharon Thompson, *The Powers of Desire: The Politics of Sexualty* (New York: Monthly Review Press, 1975), pp. 157-210.

6. Phyllis Bird, "Male and Female He Created Them: Gen. 1:27b in the Context of the Priestly Account of Creation," *Harvard Theological Review* 74 (1981): 129-59.

the soul to control the body and its reincarnation in so-called lower states.[7] Although Greek Christianity rejected reincarnation, its division of an asexual spiritual soul from gendered body reflects this Platonic anthropology. Augustine synthesizes elements of both the Platonic essentialist and the Hebrew functional views of the image of God. The image of God is normatively male as rational soul exercising dominion over women, body, and nature.

Although Greek Christians identify the image of God with the asexual soul possessed by both men and women, while Augustine assumes a corporate concept of the image as dominion (which women do not possess but are possessed by), both traditions also tend to think of femaleness as a quality of soul as well as body, linked to sense emotions and lack of will power, the psychic qualities of the body. Thus women are also seen as lacking equality of mind, as having a deficient rationality, and hence an inferior soul.[8]

However the ascetic tradition suggested that when women are converted, particularly those who repudiate sex for celibacy, this inferiority of soul is overcome, and they are given "manly and virile" souls.[9] Whether this virility of soul in Christian virgins is a new dispensation of God or a restoration of a quality women originally had but lost in the Fall is unclear. Some radical ascetics claimed that the Christian virgin wins autonomy through her transformation into spiritual "virility." But most Church Fathers, from both East and West, backed away from this implication to suggest that the redeemed woman would express her redemption by redoubled self-abnegation and subjugation to males, particularly her spiritual "heads" in the church.

Gender and Sin

Christian anthropology is unclear about whether or not women were equal in God's original creation and shared equally in the image of God. The Greek ascetic traditions hint of an original equality of soul, and hence a shared image of God, but this is contradicted by views of woman as innately inferior by reason of her bodily and psychic femaleness, and her location in an "order" of creation included under a headship that the patriarchal male exercises as corporate representative of God's dominion.

But all classical traditions agree in stressing women's priority in sin, and its consequences in female subjugation. For the egalitarian tradition, this means that woman lost her original equality and fell into subjugation. For the tradition

---

7. Plato, *Timaeus* 23.

8. Rosemary Ruether, "Misogynism and Virginal Feminism in the Fathers of the Church," in *Religion and Sexism: Images of Women in the Jewish and Christian Traditions,* ed. Rosemary Ruether (New York: Simon and Schuster, 1974), pp. 150-73.

9. Kari Vogt, "Becoming Male: A Gnostic and Early Christian Metaphor," in Borresen, *Image of God*, pp. 172-87.

that saw women as always subordinate, her subordination in the Fall is seen as both redoubled as punishment and as a means of expiation of her primary fault. Women are punished through painful childbearing and subjugation to their husbands, as the Genesis text suggests; but voluntary submission to this punishment is also women's means of salvation.

Thus Christianity reads both gender difference and female scapegoating into its view of sin and the Fall. The silencing of women in church, her marginalization from any public leadership, her repressed and servile status, are both her nature and her punishment for rebellion. Men are thus justified in redoubling this repression to punish any signs of further rebellion in women. Woman's unprotesting acceptance even of unjust repression is her way to salvation through suffering, a suffering that she deserves and yet can use to expiate her sin. This is the theology of the "battered women's syndrome."[10]

Sin is also connected with women in the Christian tradition through the Platonic linking of femaleness, body, sex, mortality, and evil. The body is seen as the source of appetites that draw the immortal soul down into sin and death and cause it to forget its original "pure" nature. Sex is seen as the extreme expression of the sin and death–prone tendencies of the body. The linking of femaleness with this view of sex and body means women are seen as being by nature more sin-prone than men. To shun women is to shun sin. To repress woman is to repress both her sin-proneness and her capacity to tempt men into sin.

A third option lurks in the Genesis 3 narrative; women's subjugation to males is neither a re-ratification of her original subordination or a punishment for the sin of insubordination, but is itself sinful. The original parity of woman and man in Paradise has been lost by the creation of relations of domination and subjugation, and sin reigns in human relations through this unjust form of distorted relationships. But this option will be developed only in modern feminist theologies.[11]

Gender and Redemption

Here we return to the basic Pauline assertion that "In Christ there is neither male nor female." In the Christian tradition, this has meant that women are equally saved by Christ, equally included in the redemption by Christ, to be baptized equally with males. It also has meant that women, although not equal in rationality or power, are nonetheless equally capable of holiness. Since it is

10. Christian women who are trying to break from battering relations often attest to the importance of this theology in their past acceptance of battering; see essays in *Christianity, Patriarch and Abuse: A Feminist Critique*, ed. Joanne C. Brown and Carole R. Bohn (New York: The Pilgrim Press, 1989).

11. Rosemary Ruether, *Sexism and God-Talk: Toward a Feminist Theology* (Boston: Beacon Press, 1983), pp. 159-92.

holiness, not power or learning, that gives rank in heaven, women are as likely to have high rank in heaven as men.[12]

Yet this equality in Christ, in baptism and in capacity for holiness, is related to women's status in the church and society in various ways. For most of the classical tradition, women normatively are to exercise their holiness differently from men. Although humility is appropriate for both holy men and holy women, it is also seen as normative for women as women. Thus voluntary acceptance of subjugation is both her place in "nature" and her path to holiness as expiation of sin.

Radical ascetics suggested that the redeemed woman overcame her sub- jugation to man, particularly as a celibate, and hence attained a new "virility" and independence; but this idea was read differently by male and female ascetics. When female ascetics asserted it as independent control of their own religious communities, it was generally opposed by male church leaders.[13]

Only in modern feminist theologies has there begun to be developed another option for reading gender relations in terms of creation-sin-redemption. If original equality is our true natures, and domination-subjugation the expres- sion of sin, then restoration-development of egalitarian relations is both the means and the expression of redemption.

However, this affirmation of equality as original-redeemed gender rela- tions raises the underlying question of how gender is related to humanness. Do we assume a gender-neutral or gender-inclusive (androgynous) definition of humanness shared equally by men and women? Can we then speak of redemp- tion as both men and women becoming "fully human" and affirming a parity in which the full humanness of each affirms that of the other? Or is it impossible to extricate the concept of generic humanness from its androcentric history in which the male is the norm of humanness and the female deficient in relation to this norm?[14]

Do women need to claim a new definition of "good femaleness" that will be different from androcentric normative humanness? Is there a sufficiently greater difference in gender than a similarity of species between human males and human females that we cannot construct a concept of a common species ideal to which men and women can/should aspire equally? Do we need different

12. See Eleanor McLaughlin, "Women, Power and Holiness in Medieval Christianity," in *Women of Spirit: Female Leadership in the Jewish and Christian Traditions*, ed. Rosemary Ruether and Eleanor McLaughlin (New York: Simon and Schuster, 1979), pp. 99-130.

13. The history of Catholic nuns as a struggle for self-government against the clerical hierarchy, based on the implied theology of celibacy as giving women independent personhood, is yet to be written, but it is implied in many accounts. See, for example, Mary Ewens, "Women in the Convent," in Karen Kennelly, *American Catholic Women* (New York: Macmillan, 1989), p. 1747; and Madonna Kolbenschlag, *Authority, Community and Conflict* (Kansas City: Sheed and Ward, 1986).

14. Lynda M. Glennon, *Women and Dualism: A Sociology of Knowledge* (New York: Longman and Green, 1979).

ideals for male and female humanness? And, if so, can we avoid a hierarchical valuation of these different norms, whether the male norm is valued as superior or the female norm as superior? These questions plague modern Western anthropology and prevent feminist thought from having a consensus about what is meant by the equality of women and men.

From Classical to Modern Christian Anthropologies

Classical Christian anthropology in the Western tradition, shaped by Augustine, is characterized by a dominant patriarchal view that asserts some combination of woman's subjugation in original nature, deepened through the Fall, which women expiate through continued subjugation in the church and in Christian society. This continued subjugation in the order of redemption expresses both woman's nature and her punishment for sin, while affirming her ultimate redeemability and equality in heaven through voluntary acceptance of humility.

Augustinian anthropology was reworked by Thomas Aquinas in the thirteenth century through the incorporation of Aristotelian philosophy. Aquinas appropriated Aristotle's view of the female as innately inferior in mind, will, and body and hence lacking complete humanness. Her subjugation is thus the expression of her inferiority and incapacity for self-rule. In Aquinas the idea that women are subordinate in the original order of creation is read through the assumption of female inferiority in nature in a way that was absent in Augustine.[15] This leads to the further assertions that Christ had to be male to possess full or perfect humanness and that only the male can represent Christ as priest (the anthropology that lies behind the contemporary papal assertions that women cannot "image" Christ).

In the Reformation Luther and Calvin express variants on the classical anthropological tradition. Luther leans to the ascetic tradition that woman was originally man's equal in Paradise, but her primacy in sin caused her to lose this original equality. Now woman's subordination stands as the expression of her punishment for sin.[16] Calvin, by contrast, comes closer to Augustine's view. Woman's subordination to man is an expression of a divinely given order of creation, but implies no innate inferiority of nature. As sinners elected by God's grace, women and men stand on equal footing, but woman is to express her election through voluntary submission to her rightful place as man's subordinate and "helpmeet."

---

15. Thomas Aquinas, *Summa Theologica*, pt. 1, q. 92; see also Borresen, *Subordination and Equivalence*, pp. 141-78.

16. Martin Luther, *Lectures on Genesis:* Gen. 2:18, 3:16, in *Luther's Works*, vol. 1, ed. Jaroslav Pelikan (St. Louis: Concordia Publishing House, 1958), pp. 115, 202-3.

Side by side with this dominant patriarchal anthropology runs a minority tradition found in the mystical and millennialist lines of Christian thought. This minority tradition suggests that women and men were spiritually equal as androgynous beings in the original creation. The Fall created sex, death, and separation of genders. In redemption both sex and mortality are overcome, and humanity regains its original androgynous nature. Redemption is linked to celibacy and restoration of spiritual wholeness overcoming gender division.

In redemption women are freed from the "curse of Eve" — painful child-bearing and subjugation to their husbands. They become whole, regain their "virile and manly" natures, and are able to co-lead as teachers and prophets in church.[17] Elements of this theology of original and redeemed spiritual equality were found in early Christian gnosticism and have been rediscovered in ascetic mystical and millennialist movements in the medieval and Reformation periods, as well as modern movements, exemplified by the Anglo-American Shakers.[18]

Nineteenth-century American thought saw a shifting in the ideology of gender. The classical division between patriarchal and millennial traditions was transmuted into a new division between liberal monism and romantic binary anthropologies.

Liberal monism asserts that there is one universal generic human nature shared by all humans equally. This human nature is characterized by rationality and moral conscience. Human rights and equality before the law are identified with the possession of these generic human qualities. Since all humans have these qualities, all have the same human rights and are to be equal before the law. Liberalism identified this equality with an original nature that all humans have by virtue of "creation." Inequality of legal rights or social hierarchy is not based on a divinely created "order of nature," but on a human disordering of nature that caused unjust differences of rights. The liberal revolution is thus both a restoration of original nature and a redemptive new era in which governments are created based on "natural equality."[19]

Liberal feminists sought to claim this same equality before the law for women. But they were frustrated by the unstated androcentrism of the liberal definition of human nature. Normative humanness was identified with male

17. For Gnostic anthropology see Vogt, "Becoming Male"; also, Rosemary Ruether, "Women in Utopian Movements," in *Women and Religion in America: The Nineteenth Century*, ed. Rosemary Ruether (New York: Harper and Row, 1981), pp. 47-48.

18. For Shaker theology, see Marjorie Procter-Smith, "In the Line of the Female: Shakerism and Feminism," in *Women's Leadership in Marginal Religions*, ed. Catherine Wessinger (Chicago: University of Illinois Press, 1993), pp. 23-40. For Shaker church order and its historical development, see Karen Nickless and Pamela Nickless, "Sexual Equality and Economic Authority: The Shaker Experience, 1784-1900," in *Women in Spiritual and Communitarian Societies*, ed. Wendy Chmielewski et al. (Syracuse: Syracuse University Press, 1993), pp. 119-32.

19. For a classical statement of liberal egalitarianism, see "Condorcet's Pleas for the Citizenship of Women," *Journal de la Societé de 1789* (3 July 1790). English trans.: *Fortnightly Review* 13:42 (June 1870): 719-20; see Rosemary Ruether, *Sexism and God-talk*, pp. 102-4.

public roles from which women had been historically excluded. In the liberal constitutions of the eighteenth and nineteenth centuries, women and other subordinate people continue to be excluded from the "rights of man" because the rights that belong to all men "by nature" continued to be assumed to be rights that are to be exercised by the white propertied male. The patriarchal male continued to be assumed to be a corporate self, acting for both himself and those "under him," that is, dependent women, children, and servants.

Through a series of social revolutions and reforms such as abolition, universal manhood suffrage, and women's suffrage, the rights of "man" became extended to all adults (who are not either imprisoned or mentally incompetent) in a more throughgoing individualism that partly breaks the idea of a family head as corporate personality. But women continue to be disadvantaged in a scheme of equality based on public roles and jobs that ignore the private sphere and women's role and work in it. Thus women in liberal systems are both overworked and defeated in their quest for equality by having to be simultaneously the "same" as men in public employment, while also doing the lion's share of the work in the family.

Romantic binary anthropologies affirm the distinct roles of women in the family, and the distinct "feminine" psychic qualities associated with it that were ignored by androcentric liberal monism. Men and women are defined as complementary; that is, a supplementary relation of distinct and opposite psychic qualities. Men are masculine; that is, rational, aggressive, and autonomous. Women are feminine; that is, intuitive, passive, and auxiliary. Only together are these distinct halves brought together in an ideal whole. Romantic anthropology often saw the feminine qualities as morally superior, linked to love and altruism. Male aggression and egoism need to be refined and "uplifted" by female altruism.

This binary understanding of male and female as masculine and feminine lent itself to several distinct social ideals. In conservative romanticism, male and female differences are linked with public and private spheres. Women are to stay out of the public sphere and uplift the male by their devoted mothering at home. Victorian women reformers shifted this view by insisting that women must crusade into the male public sphere and uplift it through social reform that made the public sphere more "homelike." Separatist feminists exaggerated the implied moral superiority of women by suggesting that women should shun men altogether, creating an autonomous female world based on superior female qualities.[20]

Feminist anthropology today is divided between the dual heritage of liberal monism and romantic dualism. It is still seeking some satisfactory synthesis that can affirm that women are simultaneously equal and yet different in ways that are often tacitly assumed to be morally superior to masculine tendencies.

20. Ruether, *Sexism and Godtalk*, pp. 104-9.

Beyond Androgyny: Toward a Feminist Anthropology

A feminist anthropology must transcend both androcentric monism, which identifies generic humanness with what have been male qualities of public life, and the romantic binary split of masculine men and feminine women. We need to start by asserting that the qualities labeled masculine and feminine in patriarchal culture — rationality and autonomy, intuition and altruism — are capacities of both men and women. Only when we bring together all the qualities split into these binary opposites do we get a glimpse of what a whole human being might be.

However, it is not enough to paste these qualities together in their traditional forms as an androgynous union of masculine and feminine, for their binary splitting also expresses a distorted relation of men as dominant and women as subordinate, and hence a distortion of the appropriate relation of these qualities. We need a transformed synthesis in which rationality and intuition, autonomy and relationality, are mutually transformed.

We also need to recognize that men and women, through a combination of biological development and socialization, make this journey into wholeness from different sides, and thus gradually come to wholeness and mutuality by helping each other to develop those aspects of the self that gender stereotypes have tended to repress. Women need to help men develop more relationality, and men need to help women develop more independence. While women have traditionally been assumed to do something of the first task for men, men have seldom called themselves to the second task on behalf of women.

What does this understanding of humanness as a journey into wholeness beyond gender stereotypes mean for our understanding of the theological concepts of image of God, sin, fallenness, and redemption? I believe it means that our understanding of the image of God cannot be based on gender stereotypes, including an androgynous complementarity of both masculine and feminine. Further, it cannot be based on concepts of either domination over subjugated people and the natural world or on the splitting of mind and body. The whole creation must be seen as the bodying forth of the Word and Wisdom of God and as sacramentally present in all beings.

If God is thought of as present in creation by bringing forth all things in life-giving interrelations and by a constant process of renewing life-giving relations, then humans are most expressive of God's presence by manifesting this creative and healing process. Sin breaks this creating and healing process and creates distorted relationships of domination and exploitation that aggrandize one side of a relationship by inferiorizing and impoverishing the other side. Sexism and all forms of exploitative domination are thus not parts of the image of God, but forms of sin. Salvation is the process of conversion from distorted relationships and the regrounding of selves in healing relationality.

How then can we think about human gender at all as related to the image of God? First, we must affirm that God, not being a mammal of any kind, does not literally have gender. God is neither male nor female and yet is in and through all relations, including those of gender. Insofar as we use gender images metaphorically for God, we must do so in a way that clearly reveals them as metaphorical, not literal. Our metaphors must include both male and female, and in a complex transformative synthesis that points us beyond stereotypes toward our journey to wholeness. This wholeness, furthermore, is not a known ideal, but goes ahead of us into an uncompleted future, as redemption itself is still incomplete.

The image of God cannot be identified with dominion. Moreover, dominion can be reinterpreted as "stewardship" only with the cautionary proviso that we recognize that our call to care for *all* of creation is a corrective to the very recent emergence of humans as the dominant species and the destructive use of such dominance. We do not possess, but instead are called to be converted to a caring for the earth that is sustaining, not destructive.

Finally, we need to ask how individuation and family or community are connected in our anthropology of gender. Patriarchal anthropology was based on the assumption that the (free, ruling class) male was not just an individual, but a corporate person who exercises "headship" over a "body" of persons: women, children, servants. Women were credited with legal autonomy only through dissolving this concept of the family as the base of rights for an individualism in which each adult is autonomous. Liberal individualism abstracts men and women from their social context as isolated atoms, each motivated by self-interest.

A feminist anthropology needs to restore an understanding of men and women as embedded in and responsible to the corporate life of the family, but not in such a way as to cause the personhood of women to disappear in the corporate representation of the male "head of family." Rather, we need to think of men and women as both relational and individuated as an interactive process. The marriage relation of men and women thus becomes a mutual covenant for interdependence and individuation of both partners. Childrearing is a cooperative process of both parents to raise children, male and female, capable of this same mutuality in interdependence and individuation as persons in their own right.

Feminist anthropology must reject both the patriarchal family, where only the patriarch is fully a person, and liberal individualism, where all are assumed to be autonomous persons but only as isolated from relationship, in order to envision new families in a new society where individuation and community can be interrelated.

The Future of Theology
in a Commodity Society

M. Douglas Meeks

Christian theology in the twenty-first century will be faced with the threat of having no place. Theology belongs where the triune God is redeeming the creation — that is, among the poor and the threatened places of the creation. But theology cannot exist without something like the university as the place in which the spirit can reflect, and the church as the place in which the Spirit can form the people of God. Both the university and the church are radically threatened by the market society. Theology will no longer be able to presuppose these institutions as they have existed for several centuries. The work of theology has to entail its engendering of its own *oikos* within the massive oikic crises of ec-onomy, ec-ology, and ec-umene. In this chapter I will concentrate on theology as a function of the church and on the shape of theology's growing struggle to find space and time in a market society.

Jürgen Moltmann, more than any other contemporary theologian, has provided a wealth of resources for reconceptualizing the church. His contributions will become all the more crucial toward the end of the twentieth century as theology turns its attention in a more concentrated way to the question of the church's faithful existence and even survival in the market society. In this chapter I will expand Moltmann's notion of the immanence of God's triune love as it creates space and time for the church within the social conditions of the market society that increasingly truncate the church's possibilites of appearing publicly.[1] I will do this by pointing to the concretization of God's being as love in terms of gifting relationships as opposed to commodity exchange relationships. The viability of the church and thus of theology in the market society

---

1. See especially Jürgen Moltmann, *God in Creation: A New Theology of Creation and the Spirit,* trans. Margaret Kohl (Minneapolis: Fortress Press, 1992), pp. 104-214, and *The Spirit of Life: A Universal Affirmation,* trans. Margaret Kohl (Minneapolis: Fortress Press, 1992), pp. 217-67 and passim.

will depend on whether it can become a gifting community in a commodity society where gift becomes increasingly problematic.

The Church in the Market Society

No contemporary historical reality is so pervasive as the expansion of the market into every region, town, and village of the world. The market is working wonders. It is changing the world, in many ways for the better. But the market will not redeem the world. The market has no power against sin, evil, and death, despite our pretensions about its universal spread and effectiveness. And in many respects it is a juggernaut that is devouring the lives of people and communities; dissolving civic, national, and state identities; and threatening the life of nature.

The forces of the market, combined with accelerating technological innovations in the flows of information and capital, undermine capitalist society. The "end of organized capitalism" does not mean the end of the market, but rather the disintegration of many of the social, civil, and cultural structures that have accompanied the rise and predominance of the capitalist societies of the nineteenth and twentieth centuries.[2] A core assumption remains — namely, that our individual material futures, pursued according to the rules of the market and directed by the invisible hand of technology, will result in a beneficent common future for all. It is in this sense that we may still speak of a market society in the midst of disorganized capitalism.

The church in the North Atlantic rim has largely come to understand itself as one of the institutions comprising the civil sector of capitalist society. As this sector disintegrates, the church loses its institutional embeddedness and its various rationales as a necessary constituent of this sector. At the same time, the church's self-understanding and organization are increasingly ruled by market logic. According to Robert Heilbroner, the nature of our society is *accumulation of wealth as power* and the logic of our society is *exchange of commodities*.[3] Everything dances around these realities. We believe them so implicitly that we are willing to serve them and shape our lives according to their logic. It is the language with which all people are fascinated. It is increasingly the logic through which people expect life, security, and future.

The market logic is in and of itself a human good. It is perhaps the most successful human social device ever conceived. No one can deny its awesome effect in modernity. But many of the so-called neoclassical assumptions of the modern market destroy the possibility of Christian discipleship within economy and are

2. Scott Lash and John Urry, *The End of Organized Capitalism* (Cambridge: Polity, 1987).

3. Robert Heilbroner, *The Nature and Logic of Capitalism* (New York: W. W. Norton, 1985), pp. 31-32, 141-48, and passim.

increasingly narrowing the public space of appearance in which the church can exist.[4] These assumptions also destroy the possibility of democracy shaping property, work, and consumption in ways that preserve equality, participation, and access to livelihood and community. The market can flourish without these assumptions and many of the institutions to which they have given rise. It is not the market per se, but rather what Karl Polanyi calls "the market society" that should be criticized; that is, a society in which all the spheres in which social goods have to be distributed are controlled by the market logic itself.[5] All social goods are produced and distributed as if they were commodities.

What cannot appear under the rules of the market is the reality of God's self-giving love, which is expressed in the logic/logos of *grace*. The logic of the market, exchange of commodities and the accumulation of wealth as power, gives no space for those biblically narrated relationships and practices that are governed by the excess of gifting, such as mutual self-giving, diakonia, and stewardship. Since gifting is the primary biblical way of concretely describing God's being as love, as well as the peculiar modality of *ecclesia,* the problematic of speaking of God's presence in the market society is comparable to the problematic of speaking of the presence of *ecclesia* in the market society.

If we speak biblically of the church as the "household of God" or the *oikonomia tou theou,* then we have to ask whether the church is actually appearing or can appear in the market society. Where concretely is the space and time of the church when the church itself has been absorbed into the market society and is itself largely organized according to the market logic? How concretely does the presence of God the Spirit make room and make time for the embodiment of the church so that it can actually appear publicly and make a historical difference? How can the church block the spread of the totalitarian market so that, dwelling in God, it can be an alternative *oikonomia?*

What has become clear since the *Wende* of 1989 is that Marxist, Keynesian, and neoclassical economics do not hold the key to the future. The assumptions of neoclassical economics about the human being, history, nature, and the state are still governing our perceptions of the market, while the market itself, combined with new technology, seems to function out of control of neoclassical expectations and laws. The ethical tasks facing humanity and perforce the Christian church are: (1) How to humanize the market so that it can serve a human future, and (2) How to create economy beyond the market so that the full meaning of *economy* can be realized for human beings and nature.[6] There can be no question of overcoming the market. For the foreseeable future all public economy will be market oriented.

---

4. M. Douglas Meeks, *God the Economist: The Doctrine of God and Political Economy* (Minneapolis: Fortress Press, 1989), pp. 47-73.

5. Karl Polanyi, *The Livelihood of Man* (New York: Academic Press, 1977), pp. 9 and passim. Cf. also Charles E. Lindblom, *Politics and Markets: The World's Political-Economic Systems* (New York: Basic Books, 1977).

6. For older meanings of *economy* see Meeks, *God the Economist,* esp. pp. 75-97.

But the rules of the market are human constructions and can be reshaped in order to make the market more humane.[7] Furthermore, neither the market as presently conceived and practiced nor any future theory and practice of the market will be able to bring about on its own accord the global household in which the conflicts among peoples and with nature can be made less than exterminating.

What are the economies of life that must be added to the market for a humane *oikonomia?* If it is possible for human beings to direct the market in more humane ways, what instruments other than the state are available for this task? Is it possible for us to get beyond the neoclassical ways in which we have defined ourselves, our possessions, our work, our consumption? What could replace these definitions in our public life? Our problem, then, runs something like this: The market cannot be modified in a humanizing way without communities, since no civil or political means exist for humanizing the economy without communities to bear them. But the market society tends to destroy community. The ancient construal of *economy* included questions of how to form and sustain community, questions of how the members of the household are related to each other. The impoverishment of modern economics is its exclusion of these questions. Recently it has become commonplace to ask whether there *are* any communities that can nourish democratic values or that can bear politics.[8] Our question is to what extent there can be any genuine communities of transformation in the church.[9] The church must be engaged in these questions because they touch on both its own survival and its mission as defined by the triune God.

Globalization and the Disorganization of Capitalism

Few contemporary economists doubt that we are undergoing a worldwide structural transformation of the economy. The *industrial age* is giving way to the *information age.* Massive reorganization of business and government combined with the unprecedented influence of high technology, global financial systems, and the power of electronic media have led to the destructuring of organized capitalism. Organized capitalism once consisted of approximately a dozen complexly organized capitalist societies, all located in the North Atlantic rim.[10] Beyond

7. See Jürgen Moltmann, "Ist der Markt das Ende aller Dinge?" in *Die Flügel nicht stutzen. Warum wir Utopien brauchen,* ed. W. Teichert (Düsseldorf: Patmos Verlag, 1994), pp. 84-108.

8. See, for example, Robert Bellah et al., *Habits of the Heart: Individualism and Commitment in American Life* (New York: Harper & Row, 1985) and idem, *The Good Society* (New York: Alfred A. Knopf, 1991); John Kenneth Galbraith, *The Culture of Contentment* (New York: Houghton Mifflin, 1992); Christopher Lasch, *The True and Only Heaven: Progress and Its Critics* (New York: W. W. Norton, 1991).

9. See Steve Tipton's chapter, "The Public Church," in Bellah et al., *The Good Society,* pp. 179-219.

10. For the following see Scott Lash and John Urry, *Economies of Signs and Space* (London: Sage Publications, 1994), pp. 1-10, 314-26, and passim.

were many societies in more or less colonial or semi-colonial relations with this organized core. Disorganized capitalism is the epoch in which various processes and flows have restructured this pattern. For example, capital and technologies have flown to 170 or so sovereign countries with market economies, each determined to defend its territory. The mobility of business agents, tourists, migrants, and refugees has increased enormously. There has been a time-space compression in financial markets that makes market transactions almost instantaneous. This has produced a generalization of risks that knows no national boundaries and the fear of such risks.[11] Major parts of the world economy are now international producer and consumer *services*. The "market" has discovered that it can function without producing work for people. Those who master knowledge, the "symbolic analysts," as Robert Reich calls them, segregate themselves from those who are producers and service givers.[12] As they secede from the commonwealth, they create separate living spaces, schools, and cultural sites and no longer contribute their work and wealth to the common good of society. Globalized culture and communication structures become increasingly free of particular regions and locate in global cities more closely connected to each other than to their provinces. In these cities, a service and information class develops with cosmopolitan taste, especially for fashionable consumer services, usually provided by one or another category of immigrant. Social classes, conventionally organized around symbolic place and hierarchy, give way to a new kind of cosmopolitan, postmodern individual in re-engineered cultural spaces (for example, art world, financial world, drug world, advertising world, academic world). And, perhaps most importantly, the disorganization of capitalist society is marked by the declining effectiveness and legitimacy of nation states, which are unable to control such disorganized capitalist flows. The state can no longer regulate the economy.[13]

The process of globalization is accompanied by utopian and dystopian predictions. The end of the Cold War brought the lifting of enormous financial,

---

11. John Maynard Keynes already referred to the world's financial markets as *casinos*. Because of information technology innovations, today's integrated, 24-hour casino is transforming itself from a classic free-market place of win-lose competition to a "new form of electronic commons, where each 'rational actor's' self-interested behaviour can endanger the entire system — unless rapid cooperative, collective action is taken." Hazel Henderson, "New Markets and New Commons," *Futures* 27/2 (March 1995): 113. As much a $1 trillion in virtual securities (derivatives of stocks, commodities, and bonds) can be traded in one day. The global securities and financial industry is increasingly unable to address the multiplying risks to all players in currency speculation, as we witnessed in the Savings and Loan fiasco in the United States and the Barings Bank collapse in the United Kingdom. Mammoth losses in derivatives and hedging strategies can cause untold suffering for millions of people and destabilize institutions all over the world. Risks cannot be reduced without new global rules. What is the social innovation that can match the global casino's computer and satellite-based technological innovation?

12. Robert B. Reich, *The Work of Nations: Preparing Ourselves for 21st-Century Capitalism* (New York: Alfred A. Knopf, 1991).

13. Richard Barnet and John Cavanagh, *Global Dreams: Imperial Corporations and the New World Order* (New York: Random House, 1994).

social, and psychological burdens and the expectation of unprecedented opportunity symbolized by the computer chip and fiber optics. But the dystopic perspective sees the possibility of cataclysmic collapse due to the debt crisis, the poverty crisis, and the ecological/energy crisis and the increase of wild, ungovernable zones in the world and its cities.

Community

Much of contemporary sociology deals with the decline of community in this new global economy. In the information-based economy, the self comes up against an ever faster circulation of goods, images, money, ideas, and other human beings.[14] The shared meanings and background practices of community are emptied out as a deracinated "I" is set adrift from community in a process of individuation and atomization. More sanguine theorists believe that the development of multiple forms of reflexivity can counter the dystopic view of the collapse of community in the global information economy. Economies of "signs and space" are the networks, the flows of a "we" of global community that can give rise to a reflexivity in which the "I" is empowered to shape the rules and resources of social structure as well as to direct his or her own life.

Scott Lash and John Urry treat two models of the embodiment of "global" community: (1) the universalistic represented by the Marxist world system[15] and Parsonian functionalism, and (2) the particular and immediate represented by the nonrule regulated customs *(Sitten)* of Hegel's *Sittlichkeit*.[16]

The *universalistic* approach emphasizes the development of ever more abstract social relations, an evolutionist understanding of history, and a liberal or proletarian vision of emancipation. It imagines communities in abstract time and space which social events and relations happen *in*. This view of community still works with Enlightenment abstract forms of individualism.[17]

---

14. Lash and Urry, *Economies of Signs and Spaces,* pp. 314ff.

15. Immanuel Wallerstein, *The Modern World-System* (New York: Academic Press, 1974, 1980).

16. Lash and Urry, *Economies of Signs and Space,* pp. 315ff.

17. According to Michael Welker, such abstract individualism generates the false appearance of realized equality and of "an endless capacity for dialogue and for change. The clouds of indeterminacy swallow up tall promises about full equality and the change of individuals and 'structures' at will by means of dialogue, trust, and a willingness to learn. The pluralism of the Spirit makes it possible to see through this illusion. Men do not become women and women do not become men. The young do of course become old, but the old do not become young. The oppressed who have been liberated must also live with their history of suffering. These factors, as well as racial and national background and location in a specific phase of historical development, impose considerable limits on the capacity for dialogue. . . . It is necessary to pay heed to limits that are creaturely and enriching as well as to those that are unrighteous and oppressive. It is necessary to pay heed to limitations that are good and bad, salutary and isolating, liberating and demonic." *God the Spirit,* trans. John F. Hoffmeyer (Minneapolis: Fortress Press, 1994), p. 26.

It fails to render a genuinely historical sense of community that can acknowledge the limits of human embodiment and of tragedy. Furthermore, those in the liberal theological tradition have a predilection for large claims for the possible transformations toward wholeness in individuals and justice in society, without paying attention to what could be the actual historical bearers of such transformation. The result is ecclesiastical institutions that have less and less public influence. Much theological discourse, therefore, tends to succumb to the pervasive fatalism about changing massive institutions that has a stranglehold on our society given the unaccountability of the market to democratic process and the seeming impossibility of democratically structured change.

The *particularistic* approach to community stresses immediate engagement in the nexus of shared meanings and background practices. The Cartesian understanding of time, space, and society is castigated as metaphysical obfuscation of being. The community is constituted by the nonrule regulated (though learned) *habits* of Bourdieu's *habitus* or MacIntyre's networks of immediately available *tools and practices* in which goods and other meanings are routinely produced or by the *prejudgments* of Gadamer's theory of hermeneutics.[18] According to Lash and Urry this "worldedness" in aesthetic or hermeneutical reflexivity points to the possibility of local versions of the "we" and seems to open up political space for new communities and new social movements. Such aesthetic or hermeneutic reflexivity in its interpretive relation to social conditions and the self is active in production and consumption, in critique, and as a foundation for community.

But the antidiscursive world of shared meanings and background practices can also be the world of racist, sexist, and classist hate. Thus Lash and Urry look for a "cosmopolitan" mode of such rooted being in "invented" communities. But, though Lash and Urry are able to demonstrate that through aesthetic reflexivity many new communities are invented and selves reinvented in order to enter new communities, they do not show any way by which the prejudgments and habits and shared meanings of a community can be invented or transformed in such a way as to include the radically other, the stranger. This leads us to a consideration of the peculiar character of the "economy" of the household of Jesus Christ in which God's love as gift is embodied in relation to the stranger, thereby breaking through the fixations and sediments of society and creating new time and space for community.

18. Pierre Bourdieu, *Distinctions: A Social Critique of the Judgment of Taste*, trans. Richard Nice (London: Routledge, 1984). According to Bourdieu, prejudgments of taste do not involve the subject-object mode. They are already background practices, the shared assumptions of taste communities. We already dwell in them, and therefore they are not rules about which we can be objective. They are the predispositions and unreflected background practices of the judgments of taste. See also Alasdair MacIntyre, *After Virtue,* 2nd ed. (Notre Dame, Ind.: University of Notre Dame Press, 1984).

God's *Oikonomia* in the Community of Face

We have seen that the church has been to a large extent absorbed into the market society and is itself in significant ways organized according to market logic. Can we speak concretely of the presence of God in the Spirit making room and time for the embodiment of the church so that it can actually appear publicly and make a historical difference? How does the church block the spread of the totalitarian tendencies of the market so that, dwelling in God, it can be an alternative *oikonomia?*

Unless we are focused on ecclesial community, we have little actual means to address in any significant public way the transformation of the economic and political subjugating realities that are causing massive human misery in the global community. We have been too much caught up in the Enlightenment sciences of the individual subject and of the social to the virtual exclusion of the interhuman community, which is the primary mode of *ecclesia*. Without what Immanuel Levinas calls "the community of face," the radical criticism and alternative community necessary to freedom from subjugation will not take place.[19] Here Edward Farley's distinction of three spheres of human reality is helpful: (1) the sphere of subjectivity or the agent, (2) the social sphere, and (3) the sphere of reciprocal human relations.[20] In their increasing dependence on the psychological and sociological sciences, theology and ethics have lost sight of the fact that both evil and redemption have a primary locus in the community of face.

In the sphere of individual selves, evil thrives in alienation, resentment, guilt, and violation stemming from idolatry. In the social sphere, evil occurs when a group's self-absolutizing of its particularity violently utilizes other groups.[21] The peculiar power of evil is that it separates the spheres of the self and of the social from the interhuman, thus rendering redemption in any sphere impossible. Market relations, once they determine all relations, separate communities of face from selves and social entities, agencies and strategies, and become seemingly benign masks of subjugation. Because idolatry and self-absolutizing can be overcome only in the interhuman, redemption takes place in the sphere of the mutual coinherence of human beings with each other and with nature. If culturally mediated norms for regulating human action as sedimented in the market culture can be criticized and changed only with reference to the interhuman, then we should search for new social forms and new space and time for what we may call *oikic perichoretic relationships*, in the depth of the community of face.

---

19. Immanuel Levinas, *Totality and Infinity: An Essay on Exteriority,* trans. A. Lingis (Pittsburgh: Duquesne University Press, 1969).

20. Edward Farley, *Good and Evil: Interpreting a Human Condition* (Minneapolis: Fortress Press, 1990).

21. Farley, *Good and Evil,* pp. 260ff.

Communities of face express themselves in relatively constant modalities or relationships; and they call forth strategies and practices, agential and political disciplines. Many distinctive disciplines of the church's practice under its own criteria of face must be remembered, retrieved, reimagined, and practiced. Here I will refer to the ecclesial community of face formed at the Lord's Table as a primary locus of the alternative economy of the household of Jesus Christ.

Economy in Eucharistic Practice

Ecclesia is a community of face in which the sin and fear of human beings and the power of evil and death are taken into the life of God's love, and the power of God's love is given the community for the sake of God's redemption of the world and God's reign of glory. This love creates an *oikonomia* whose habitus and background practices are epitomized in the Lord's Meal. The self-giving love of the community in the Lord's Table is the shaping power of the household of Jesus Christ. It is the site of God's creation of time and space for God's alternative economy. The eucharistic economy of God expresses itself in patent, objective table manners that structure the ethos, the time, and the space of the economy of the triune God, under the conditions of history, within the community of face.

Table manners are as old as human society itself, the reason being that no human society exists without them. Every society obeys eating rules that epitomize and symbolize the widest social agreements.[22] The primary rules of eating are simple: If you don't eat, you die; and no matter how large your meal, you soon will be hungry again. If you want to get invited to dinner, you have to know and keep the table manners of the someone who is in the position of inviting. Thus all parents and communities sense that table manners are life-and-death concerns, and every meal is ritualized to some extent in light of these concerns. The peculiarity of the eucharistic meal is that it aims at the comprehensive inclusion of God's creatures in livelihood, in what it takes to live and live abundantly.

Anthropologically, table manners assure *sharing* and prevent *violence*.[23] Human beings developed the kind of hips they have, allowing them to stand up erect with free use of hands and arms, because they reached out to give food to other human beings. We human beings decided to eat together, to share our meals, and that is what made us human. With the occasional exception of a few

22. Margaret Visser, *The Rituals of Dinner: The Origins, Evolution, Eccentricities, and Meaning of Table Manners* (New York: Grove Weidenfeld, 1991).

23. For the following see Visser, pp. 2-78. Every community, of course, also distorts itself through table manners, for they can be used not only to make sure one is included at the table, but also to exclude others from the table through snobbery and class systems.

species like chimpanzees, human beings are the only creatures who bring food home to share with adults as well as children. It is this sharing that is at the heart of table manners. Table manners also exist because of the fundamental threat of violence. As soon as human society existed, there were manners that assured that at meal times we eat rather than are eaten. Eating is aggressive by nature and the implements required for it could easily become killing instruments around the table. Table manners are social agreements devised precisely because violence could so easily erupt at dinner.

The strange table manners at the Lord's Table are practices of the *oikonomia tou theou* and thus intend more than prevention of violence and sharing of what is necessary for sustenance.[24] They embody the oikic perichoretic relationships that actually constitute life against death, evil, and sin. They are expressions of the interdivine, interhuman relations created by the Word (logos/logic) of the gospel in the power of the Holy Spirit.

The oikic perichoretic relationships of a world open church depend on the real presence of the Host, Jesus Christ, to create the community of face in which idolatry and subjugation can be overcome. The real presence of Jesus Christ means the mediation of the past of Jesus (including Israel and creation) and the future of Jesus (including the reign of the Triune Community's righteousness over death, evil, and sin).

The Stranger's Face. The economy of grace depends on who is invited to dinner. If we do not eat with the stranger, we will never be able to establish oikic relationships with the poor in any conceivable way that approximates the intention of the Triune Community's righteousness/justice. Conventional moral norms sedimented in North Atlantic culture are thoroughly egoistic. The theology and life forms of the church also often reflect these criteria functioning in market society: self-possession, the individual as one's own hermeneutic and arbiter of truth, and humanity judged as most human insofar as one distinguishes oneself from the other. In such a privatistic culture, all public responsibility has to be defended in terms of self-interest in some kind of social contract.[25] The church is merely a voluntary association of like-minded people who help each other with individual choices.[26] World-openness in this context can

---

24. At the Lord's Supper we have the same questions of manners and rituals that any meal has: Who is the host? Who is invited? How are hosts and guests greeted? What should be served? How should we serve it? What is the seating arrangement or how should the weakest be assured of their portion? When should we start eating? What should we talk about? How should we thank the host? How should we depart? What provision for the next meal should be made? These of course are the primary questions of economy, notwithstanding their eclipse in modern economics, that is, the primary questions of relations of the household toward life against death. The ways in which these questions are answered in practice in the community of face determine the possibility and shape of the church's witness in economy.

25. John Rawls, *A Theory of Justice* (Cambridge: Harvard University Press, 1971).

26. M. Douglas Meeks, "Hope and the Ministry of Planning and Management," *Anglican Theological Review* 64 (April 1982): 147-62.

also be conceived in terms of egoism: the other completes me, helps me to come to my own self-understanding, makes me more human. The market culture retrieves with ardor every ethical argument for egoism; we are profoundly predisposed to understand rights in terms of prudence. There is no wonder, then, that the discourse of justice is so strife-torn.[27]

Only the encounter of the stranger can break self-absolutism. The encounter of the stranger at the Lord's Table is the beginning of life, the possibility of justification before God, the stuff of redemption.[28] There are two ways to encounter a stranger, someone who is radically different. The philosopher of individual freedom, Jean-Paul Sartre, claims that when we encounter a stranger we come upon a *look,* a look that threatens us, because the other might define us and take away our identity and freedom. Thus, for Sartre, "Hell is other people." On the other hand, the Jewish philosopher Levinas asserts that when we encounter a stranger, we come upon a *face.* A face is the expression of the way another person is in the world, of his or her way of experiencing the world. Levinas says that the face of a stranger shocks us, but it is our one chance of becoming truly human. Our salvation is wrapped up in the face of the stranger. We don't discover ourselves and our salvation by self-discovery, by looking deeper into ourselves, but in encountering the face of the stranger. The other's call or appeal is the beginning of life; it is the other's appeal that gives us the opportunity to be free and just. The face of the other provides the means to break our absorption in agency or institutional forms and policy.

Scarcity, Satiation, and Gift

Like the rest of culture in the North Atlantic rim, the church is impacted by the numbing effect of the experience of artificial scarcity and satiation. The deepest and most necessary assumption for the practice of market logic is scarcity.[29] The effect of the practice of market logic is satiation. Both scarcity and satiation deaden the spirit and impede life with the other. Artificial scarcity spawns the lottery culture: The others may not make it, but I may. Satiation slakes the thirst for righteousness. Scarcity and satiation leave only one possibility for the distribution of what is necessary for life and life abundant: the logic of exchange. The genuinely other cannot appear in this logic. The Eucharist undermines or

---

27. Alasdair MacIntyre, *Whose Justice? Which Rationality?* (Notre Dame, Ind.: University of Notre Dame Press, 1988).

28. See Meeks, *God the Economist,* pp. 82-89; Michael Ignatieff, *The Needs of Strangers* (New York: Viking Press, 1985); Thomas W. Ogletree, *Hospitality to the Stranger: Dimensions of Moral Understanding* (Philadelphia: Fortress Press, 1985), pp. 35-59; Walter Brueggemann, *Interpretation and Obedience: From Faithful Reading to Faithful Living* (Minneapolis: Fortress Press, 1992), pp. 290-310.

29. Meeks, *God the Economist,* pp. 17-19, 170-77.

blocks the logic of exchange and creates a new reciprocity or mutuality of giving. Eucharistic oikic relationships create the space and time in which we may be gifted and give ourselves. It is an economy in which God's gifting of Godself gives us room to give.

Moltmann's treatment of the internal life of the triune God is also a picture of the coherence, structure, and substance of Christian generosity. Moltmann has returned the doctrine of the Trinity to its practical roots in the economy of God, that is, to the ways in which God organizes the household of God's creation. This view of the Trinity opens up the possibility of thinking about God's being through the hyperbolic logic of giving. The gratuity of God's giving is the mystery of God's being. God creates out of the diffusion of goodness, not an act of free will. This fecundity is at once God's withdrawal to give space to God's creatures and God's indwelling in God's creation. The Trinity is the community of extravagant, overflowing, self-diffusive goodness. The gift is nothing other than Godself. God's being as love is essentially other-related, ecstatic, and passionate. Primordial giving follows the passion that inheres in the act of giving. God's being as love seeks affiliation, a society of individual persons who are both free and connected through acts of excessive and mutual giving.

What kind of economy does God embody and encourage? The biblical narratives point to God's overwhelming generosity to human beings and the creation. God's giving is hyperbolic, excessive, and intrusive giving and as such initiates all our giving. The gift always precedes the act of passing it along. But God's love should not be made so transcendent and idealized that God's gratuity excludes human giving in return. Response to God's giving should not be the logic of exchange, but God's giving does create more than gratitude. It creates human mutuality and further giving. Giving is the way in which God must be received. God aims at a community that responds to giving with further giving, creating relationships of obligation and responsibility. God's excess creates space and time for human reciprocity. Being a Christian means being involved in a structure of demands and benefits.

Forgiveness is the beginning of a new economy and a new logic of distribution called grace. What is served at the eucharistic meal is the gift of God's own life, the body and blood of Jesus Christ, which is the gift of God's forgiveness as the sole power that can break the bonds of sin, evil, and death.[30] Those who are forgiven are capable of extraordinary love (Luke 7:36-50). Those who are forgiven little, love little. They hoard, for they have constantly to justify themselves and construct their own immortality. If we are forgiven and loved so much that God gives God's own life for us, then much is expected of us. And so we leave this meal, not just having shared with each other and having prevented violence, but as new creatures empowered to live with the other.

---

30. See Farley's helpful reflections on forgiveness in *Good and Evil*, pp. 247ff.

A commodity is truly consumed when it is sold, because nothing about the exchange assures its return. The peculiar reality of gifting, however, is that when the gift is used, it is not used up. The gift that is passed along remains abundant. Gifts that remain gifts can support an affluence of satisfaction, even without numerical abundance.[31] Gifting replaces the bloated satiety that results from narcissistic consumption and competition for scarce goods with the liberating fulfillment that stems from sharing.

The eucharistic modality is joy so great that it judges and transforms, a judgment that is so absolute that we cannot help but be thankful that it is gift. Joy and judgment make us outraged by poverty because of the endless generosity of God and shock us with the recognition that not being in the mode of being gifted and gifting is blasphemous. The *oikonomia tou theou* depends upon the retaught and relearned generosity of God, upon gifts that give in being given and that create dignity in being received. Only the gratuitous language of praise can break the suspicion and hatred of being gifted and gifting in our public household. No one in our public household wants to be "much obliged," for it would mean by definition the loss of freedom for exchange. But unless we will mean by oikic relationships only what the market intends, the miracle by which we come to understand ourselves and our community as gift would have to take place.[32]

The table manners at the Lord's Table become our manners for the whole of our lives. Our manners at this Table are meant to be our manners at all tables. If the question of the Lord's Table is the question whether all of God's creatures will have daily bread, then the church must become a trustee of political responsibility. It must practice responsible life together, the life of common decisions that include the face of the radical other, the life of conference, the life of conciliar and synodical existence with the stranger.

For the church as God's household to participate in the public household in ways that lead to life is a project so awesome, complicated, and next to impossible that we should not even think about it far removed from the Stranger who invites us to a meal in which the earth and all its creatures are promised a home and in which we have a realistic because crucified place from which to be so bold as to speak of an economy of life against death.

---

31. Meeks, *God the Economist,* p. 179.

32. "And God is able to provide you with every blessing in abundance, so that you may always have enough of everything and may provide in abundance for every good work. As it is written, 'He scatters abroad, he gives to the poor; his righteousness endures forever' " (2 Cor. 9:8, RSV). "He who supplies seed to the sower and bread for food will supply and multiply your resources and increase the harvest of your righteousness. You will be enriched in every way for great generosity, which through us will produce thanksgiving to God; for the rendering of this service not only supplies the wants of the saints but also overflows in many thanksgivings to God" (2 Cor. 9:10-12).

The *oikos* of Theology

I have argued that not only the shape but the viability of theology in the twenty-first century will depend on the public space in which the church exists. Theology's work will literally depend on the creation of an alternative *oikonomia* in which oikic perichoretic relationships embody self-gifting and life-gifting relationships in the presence of the stranger. Since this *oikonomia* is primarily the work of God the Spirit, theology's agenda will be a trinitarian pneumatology in the face of utopian and dystopian social systems.

Twenty-first-century theology will have to search for its own peculiar *oikos* or place. It is extraordinarily difficult to say where a theology shaped by eucharistic *oikonomia* will find its locus. Almost no institution in the market society embodies communion of stranger in gifting. It is clear, however, that as the conditions of the market society deconstruct the traditional places of theology, it will be those theologies serving the *oikonomia tou theou* that actually discover a new place and time for theology's life and work.

Global Ethics and Education

Hans Küng

The cry for orientation, perspectives, and ethical foundations in an increasingly differentiated industrial society is being sounded today precisely from within the pedagogical sphere. Educators who deal every day with children and young people confirm the often horrifying degree to which many of their pupils have lost those particular foundations that for earlier generations were a given: commandments, rules, standards, and ideals. The need for a binding ethos applicable within this very pedagogical sphere is thus greater than ever. For the sake of entering into a discussion of these problems, I would like to throw some light on what has been called the present "orientation crisis," or even the "orientation jungle." The question concerning a global ethic does not represent a problem merely among religions. Society as a whole is challenged to reflect self-critically upon its ethical foundations.

Violence in the Media

The portrayal of violence in the media has reached disturbing proportions since the 1970s and 1980s, though especially in the most recent years; this has come about through the mass distribution of what earlier generations — including young people — would have considered inconceivably realistic portrayals of the most brutal violence and cruelty, both in films shown on (primarily "private") television and in easily dubbed videos, though also in what are in part voyeuristic television reports. These portrayals of violence, which are utterly void of any sympathy, love for one's fellow, or humanity, are now added to all the other threats to youth, both old and new (for example, drugs).

Of course, these threats should not be exaggerated, as if the more or less fortuitous or occasional viewing of such films or videos of necessity results in enduring harm. On the other hand, however, neither should one present these threats as being less harmful than they actually are, as if — as one particular 'catharsis theory," which has since been discredited, asserted — a person's inclination to violence might be ameliorated through the addictive consumption of such videos, as if the process of becoming inured to violence could be reversed, or as if the viewing of torture, rape, sadomasochism, and killing would ever make a person more peaceful. According to new studies,[1] quite the contrary is the case: images of violence excite, stimulate, and de-inhibit the inclination to commit acts of violence and to engage in aggressive behavior, even to the point of prompting criminal acts.

Four considerations make it easy to understand that a causal connection exists between portrayals of violence in videos or television programs on the one hand and the inclination to violence on the other, especially on the part of young people, in the sense of a strengthening of that inclination to violence. Excessive viewing of portrayals of horror and violence can lead to compensation, identification, imitation, and projection.

(1) *Compensation.* Young people who from childhood on have suffered from disturbed notions of self-worth, who have constantly feared that they appear weak and powerless, who have been helplessly subjected to the strict discipline and harsh punishments of authority figures — such young people are able to compensate their own weakness with the aid of (forbidden!) violent videos via fantasies of their own strength and the strength of their clique.

(2) *Identification.* Especially those with impaired self-worth wish to identify with the characters in the films, though not (as is normally the case with adults) with the victims, but rather with the perpetrators. Like these main characters, they want to be strong, cool, hard men, Rambos who will dispose of all their adversaries and challenges and ultimately emerge victorious. Young people are especially apt to incorporate into their own behavioral repertoire those particular patterns of behavior portrayed on television (cf. the "Monday syndrome" on school playgrounds).

(3) *Imitation.* A person becomes accustomed to violent images, appropriates the strategies of justification (the self-defense and self-help argument broadly portrayed in film), and neutralizes his or her own deed. This facilitates imitation. Examinations of incarcerated persons have revealed particular susceptibility to these trends; these persons assimilate such patterns differently than do nondelinquents. Incarcerated persons observed more closely, recognized the potential for realizing a given act, and in some cases imitated an individual crime in every detail.

1. Cf. the field studies of R. H. Weiss concerning the behavior of pupils in Baden Württemberg and Saxony, published under the title "Gewaltmedienkonsum Video-Gewalt 1992," as well as "Sächsische Jugendstudie 1992," available from the Oberschulamt Stuttgart. Cf. similarly M. Scheungrab, *Filmkonsum und Delinquenz* (Regensburg, 1994).

(4) *Projection.* A person whose feelings of self-worth have already been disrupted is extremely gratified at being able to project his or her own dark side onto others — into minorities, weak persons, and those despised by society. In this way, such persons are able to exalt themselves, since they do, after all, belong to an elite group — as whites, Germans, natives, and so on. This is why sympathy for the political right and for skinheads is found not only among certain underprivileged strata but also in so-called normal families in bourgeois settings (more so in smaller towns than in large cities); subconsciously burdened by a plethora of problems, such groups fear competition and their own social decline.

The destructive potential of inhuman, sadistic videos, of videos inimical to both women and foreigners, videos glorifying violence and dangling it before us as the only solution to conflict — the destructive potential of such videos is enormous. This is why broadly based citizen movements today[2] demand with good reason television programming that is at least more humane if not completely violence-free, and seek an end to advertising in the context of violence and human suffering; that is, they seek responsible programming regarding the portrayal of violence, and the effective enforcement of existing legal regulations.

And yet one particular finding of previous research should be kept in mind: the individual who is actually consuming these portrayals of violence is the real factor determining whether such visual consumption of violence does indeed result in any enduring damage and personality change. This does not refer merely to the individual psychological point of departure, that is, whether this consumption takes place in a solitary setting or in a clique, whether merely for the sake of diversion or in order to transport oneself into a certain world. Rather, it refers above all to an individual's familial, educational, and social milieu, that is, whether the child experienced rejection and insecurity in the family sphere or feelings of safety, security, and openness that enabled him or her to develop a stable feeling of self-worth; whether the school fostered a strong sense of self in the child that made him or her capable of dealing successfully with the internal and external problems of puberty; and finally, whether the child's social milieu is open or hostile toward what is foreign, unaccustomed, and new. But how are children to develop a stable sense of self-worth, a strong sense of self, and an open mind if children — who until they are eleven or twelve years old are in any event able to distinguish only with difficulty between fictional violence in movies on the one hand and actual violence in news broadcasts on the other — are living today in an "orientation jungle"?

2. For example, the "Initiative for the Elimination of Violence in Television" of Detmold psychologist K. A. Richter with its quarter-million signatures; cf. *Focus* 26 (1994).

HANS KÜNG

The Orientation Jungle

Am I exaggerating the problem? Probably not much. For we are living in an age in which a two-year-old in Liverpool was slowly and deliberately murdered by two ten-year-olds, an age in which young people set fire to houses, desecrate tombstones, band together in gangs, and carry out excesses of violence against foreigners. Even the magazine *Der Spiegel* could not avoid lamenting the "orientation crisis" — indeed, the "orientation jungle" — in a 1993 title article,[3] alleging that a "detabooization has come about today that is without precedence in the history of culture": "The most recent generation must come to terms with a confusion of values whose dimensions can hardly be estimated. They hardly recognize any clear standards for right and wrong or good and evil of the sort still provided in the 1950s and 1960s by parents and schools, churches, and sometimes politicians."

Thus while it is true that the media and the profit-mongering of their shareholders do indeed share the blame along with their reality-, brutality-, and porno-television, one must look deeper for the real causes of the increasing physical brutalization; degeneration of language; unbridled self-realization; the sunken threshold of shame; and the spiral of cynicism, violence, and obscenity. After numerous scandals in politics, economics, and labor unions, Theo Sommer, editor of the largest German weekly, *Die Zeit,* addressed the conscience of the intellectuals:

> Certainly, the intellectuals of this country must also take a look at themselves. Many of them have preached self-realization to the point of excess; they have derided virtue, propriety, and style; and for a time they have taken postmodern *laissez faire* so far that for the sake of "anything goes" absolutely nothing more was condemned. In this way, community was sacrificed on the altar of society. Standards dissolved in the corrosive acid bath of criticism.[4]

All of this means that, in addition to other factors (politics, legislation, courts), countermeasures will be primarily an educational matter, that is, a matter of prudent pedagogical thinking that is neither authoritarian nor anti-authoritarian, and that respects the freedom of young people while not dispensing with authority. For it is precisely the young child who must be both told and shown what ethical duty is, what is humane and inhumane, what is just and unjust, fair and unfair, honest and dishonest. And in the family, school, and church the child must learn how to get along humanely with others and how to solve conflicts without the use of violence. Basic behavioral models in the family do, after all, bear much of the responsibility if a young person cannot get along in life, experiences anxiety regarding the future, does not really find the right

3. *Der Spiegel* 9 (1993).
4. *Die Zeit,* 21 May 1993.

vocation, becomes violent, and so on. And if children do not learn anything either in the family or in school about the central commandments of the great religious traditions — "you shall not kill," "you shall not steal," "you shall not lie" — it should come as no surprise when many of them adhere to no values at all, conducting their lives rather according to whatever is "fun." Educators quite correctly point out that prevention of violent behavior must begin early and focus on long-term results.

I am not arguing here as some sour moral apostle, who with a raised finger preaches ethics as the enslavement of human beings. The question of ethics is in any event not merely addressed to the "young" (this is not intended as a cultural-critical *lamento*), but rather to contemporary society at large, a society that in view of the democratically legitimized plurality of lifestyles and life concepts must continually question itself anew concerning that which is ethically binding, unless it is to end one day in either chaos or dictatorship. To this we may add that, as is well known, this crisis in orientation is a problem not merely for Europe but also for America and especially for the regions of the former Soviet Union and for China; that is, it is a worldwide problem. For this reason, the question of ethics literally becomes a question of a global ethic.

Religions: Incapable of Peace?

Where, however, are credible authorities, traditions, or persons capable of mediating such an ethos to today's youth? Can one here simply invoke, in a general fashion, the great religious traditions? Can one simply refer to these religions and their representatives in order to get a handle on the global problem of ethical deficit and orientation crisis? Hardly. For have not precisely these religions, because of their backward orientation and their focus on power, forfeited so much credibility today that they are of hardly any pedagogical use as authorities and models? Has the abundant aggressiveness precisely of religions not again and again proven their own incapacity for peace? Are religions, like nations, not from the very beginning incapable of peace and by their very nature aggressive? And now precisely they are to be the ones implementing or even guaranteeing a global ethic in a credible fashion?

This is no doubt a serious question. Precisely because religions deal with the absolute and with absolutely valid truths, is not aggressiveness, so to speak, in their blood? Does not an arrogant consciousness of being chosen foster a division of the world into the chosen and the damned, the redeemed and the pagans, the good and the evil?[5] Is the inclination for hostility not inbred in

---

5. This is the point of departure taken by the research project of Professor R. Friedli, *Religionen und Friede. Der Einfluss spirituell-religiöser Erfahrungen in Konfliktsituationen. Eine*

them, so to speak, so that the result again and again has been aggression and hostility, either as impulsive and spontaneous defense or as deliberate action with the conscious intention of harming or wounding whoever happened to believe differently?

Is such aggressiveness not found especially among the prophetic religions of Semitic origin (Judaism, Christianity, and Islam), which do after all take as their point of departure a juxtaposition of God and human beings, that is, a model of religious confrontation?

But is aggressiveness also not entirely unfamiliar to the religions originating on the Indian subcontinent, despite the considerable extent to which they are carried by a basic proclivity toward mysticism and unity, standing as they do under the sign of religious inwardness (early Indian religion of the Upanishad, Buddhism, and Hinduism)?

Indeed, do we not find aggressiveness even among those religions shaped by wisdom teaching, religions that in and of themselves stand under the sign of harmony, the religions of the Chinese tradition (Confucianism, Taoism)?

Is this aggressiveness then a posture of threat, attack, and battle against non-Christians, non-Muslims, non-Hindus, non-Hän-Chinese? Everywhere we look, is it not religions that have generated strife both internally and externally, bloody conflicts, "religious wars"; is it not religions that, while not always directly causing wars, nonetheless often legitimized and inspired them, or at least silently approved and did not prevent them? Nonreligious persons are not the only ones asking whether religions are not more of a hindrance than a help in educating a person for peace. Indeed, are religions not virtually a textbook example of the basic contemporary pedagogical thesis that aggressiveness is, as a matter of fact, a given of human nature, and thus also of religion — itself a basic feature of human beings?

Aggressiveness and Educating toward Peace

Biologists, psychologists, and anthropologists today agree to a greater degree than ever before that a certain measure of aggressiveness is simply necessary if an animal or human being — and thus also a small child — is to survive in its given society. So one might ask whether aggressiveness is not simply our fate, already genetically inherent in us, so that we should be not at all surprised that religions, too, contribute their share to the *homo homini lupus*, that is, that they, too, have received that particular measure of aggressiveness which happens to characterize the beast in human beings.

---

empirische Untersuchung zur Friedenserziehung, funded by Schweizer Nationalfonds (1989-92) and published in two volumes under the title *Religionen und Friedfertigkeit. Untersuchungen zur Friedenserziehung*, with contributions by G. Gebhardt, C. J. Jäggi, and R. Friedli.

To be sure, today we may view as outdated that great controversy between biologically oriented scholars, orthodox psychoanalysis, and German behavioral research or ethology from the school of Konrad Lorenz on the one hand and American psychologists and natural scientists such as the American behaviorists à la B. F. Skinner on the other. This controversy involved, on the one hand, those who view human beings primarily as genetically preprogrammed, that is, as beings whose behavioral forms, modes of action, and reactions are motivated and guided by inherited programs,[6] and on the other hand those who view human beings primarily as guided by their surroundings, shaped and influenced by their environment, dependent on social conditions, variously conditioned by society itself, and thus largely predictable as far as behavior is concerned.[7]

General consensus today holds that basically both views apply: human beings are both genetically preprogrammed and shaped by their environment, though not totally determined by either. For a person totally preprogrammed by inherited factors or totally conditioned by the environment would not really be a human being at all, but rather an animal or a robot. Expressed positively, and in a way that is fundamental to any pedagogical considerations, within the parameters of inherited features on the one hand and conditioning by the environment on the other, a person is free, free in contrast to dependence on instinct, coercion, and power, free in the sense of choice, of self-determination, of autonomy, and thus also quite free to follow or to resist any one particular instinctive impulse.

As far as aggressiveness is concerned, it, too, is inherited, anchored in the genome as assumed by the theories of impulse (Freud) or instinct (Lorenz). This means that it cannot simply be religiously satanized, morally combatted, and as it were eliminated through legislation. To that extent, aggressiveness is indeed, as Konrad Lorenz admittedly formulates somewhat one-sidedly, "so-called evil," merely apparent evil, evil that in any case also contains its element of good. But to what extent exactly? Without aggressive energy, a human being — like any animal — would be unable to maintain its own terrain over against other creatures or to insure its necessary distance from other creatures. There is no such thing as coexistence without tension. Without aggressive energy, even children could not assert themselves against their parents' restraints or over-zealous sheltering; they could not develop and enhance themselves in what is, as a matter of fact, a kind of competition with others that begins with childhood itself; they would not learn to act and to react, to assert themselves and to struggle. In short, without some aggressiveness, the child would be utterly

6. Cf. Konrad Lorenz, *On Aggression,* trans. Marjorie K. Wilson (New York: Harcourt, Brace, & World, 1966); and Lorenz, *Studies in Animal and Human Behavior* (Cambridge, Mass.: Harvard University Press, 1970-71). A good overview can be found in I. Eibl-Eibesfeldt, *Ethology: The Biology of Behavior* (New York: Holt, Rinehart, and Winston, 1970).

7. Cf. B. F. Skinner, *Beyond Freedom and Dignity* (New York: Knopf, 1971).

unable to develop any self-confidence and to become independent and an adult. To that extent, the aggressive social exploration that takes place in the defiant stages of childhood and in adolescence, for example, is simply necessary for sounding out and expanding the child's realm of activity and for developing those reason-guided skills the young person needs for asserting himself or herself against the resistance of both the human and the objective world. Only in this way does the development, self-assertion, and self-realization of a person come about.

These considerations already make it quite clear that any education toward peace that tries from the very beginning, by means of prohibitions, sanctions, and restrictions on personal activities, to prevent a child's natural impulses of aggressiveness, aggravation, rage, anger, and irritation from coming to expression even in games, contests, and tussling, as well as in serious arguments, can only lead to frustration that sooner or later will surface as genuine aggression (or, if such frustration has been internalized, in neuroses). In other words, such authoritarian education toward peace, one that represses all aggressiveness and demands essentially a cowardly posture, will miss its mark. Aggressiveness can indeed be valuable, and it need not include harm to others as long as it manages to demonstrate personal strength with crushing arguments instead of crushing blows.[8]

But this is only one side of the problem. Aggressiveness is, after all, not entirely inherited; it is also learned, conditioned. It is not only guided by the genome but also tested and shaped by one's surroundings. Aggressiveness is thus also the result of a learning process involving observation and reinforcement, as understood by the aggression theory of social learning (Bandura, Walters). In the course of her socialization, a child learns how to act and react both in play and in serious situations. Although a child naturally always learns on the basis of inborn learning mechanisms, this does not mean that the child cannot also relearn based on new experiences. In view of biologically conditioned impulses or motives, too, human beings are by no means instinctively predetermined for specific behavior, as are animals, since a person is, after all, capable even of participating in a hunger strike to the point of exhaustion for the sake of spiritual or political goals.[9] And so, too, a child is by no means

8. Hence, coercion or harm directed toward others need not be included in a definition of aggressiveness from the very beginning. E. von Gebsattel correctly observes: "Studies of animals that are after prey, in heat, pursued, or are defending self or young demonstrate that living creatures have no natural inclination focused primarily on harming and destroying spheres of life alien to their own; all the aggressive acts demonstrated by animals — including those clearly intent on destruction — are to be interpreted merely as modes of self-preservation or of the sexual drive." See E. von Gebsattel, "Aggression," *Lexikon der Pädagogik*, vol. 1 (Freiburg, 1952), p. 40.

9. In the following discussion I am following the illuminating explications of the Freiburg *Privatdozentin* Dr. Gabriele Haug-Schnabel, *Das neue Verhältnis biologischer Grundlagen von aggressiven Verhaltensweisen* (manuscript, 1994).

simply at the mercy of those particular stimuli that might precipitate aggressiveness. Rather, the child is able to check them voluntarily and in this way is able to learn to bridle her aggression. The community and models normally help the child to distinguish between those situations in which aggression is appropriate and those in which it is not, between those in which an impulse can be satisfied and those in which it cannot.

In the meantime, more recent discussion has found that by no means every aggression is based on frustration, as the frustration-aggression theory of the American team of Yale psychologists (J. Dollard, N. Miller) still assumed in the 1930s, as if every aggression were prompted by nongratification of some impulse and might be prevented by wish gratification, so that the prevention of aggression might be attained through a prevention of frustration on the one hand and a gratification of impulses on the other.[10] For contemporary behavioral biology, too, all monocausal aggression theories are outdated, and frustration is viewed as merely one cause among others.

This second aspect of aggressiveness has no less significant pedagogical consequences than the first: education toward peace that takes the approach that one must simply "allow the child to grow" and must gratify all his wishes as far as possible in order to allow an aggression-free, peaceful person to emerge will not result in the envisioned dismantling of aggressiveness but rather in what in the long run is a fateful release of this allegedly pent-up aggressive energy. What might seem somewhat amusing in a little house-tyrant can prove to be quite dangerous in an egomaniacal or violent pubescent or adolescent. But this is simply the way it is: if one wish after another is gratified for a child, and if that child's closest contact persons avoid all confrontation in a posture of extreme indulgence, the result is not at all freedom from aggression but rather the aggressive appearance of ever-new needs and wishes. So quite the opposite is the case here: only if at an early stage and in a consistent fashion a child encounters insightful and fair boundaries will the result be a clarification — one ultimately also desired by the child himself — and ebbing of that particular aggressive social exploration which is socially so important. As a result of such guidance, the child learns to react constructively instead of aggressively to threats. The young person then understands in principle how far he or she may go, and that a person cannot simply be an individualist and egoist. In other words, antiauthoritarian education toward peace that believes it must tolerate all aggressiveness also misses the mark. It merely takes a blind posture toward the dangerous dynamics of aggressiveness, dynamics that in the long run can have extraordinarily destructive social consequences; every aggression begets further aggression.

---

10. Cf. L. Berkowitz, ed., *Roots of Aggression: A Re-examination of the Frustration-Aggression Hypothesis* (New York: Atherton, 1969).

Elements of Aggression and Peace in Religion

Hence one by no means must assume, with Sigmund Freud or Konrad Lorenz, the presence of a biologically based, unified impulse source, a "universal death impulse" opposed to the "life impulse," a violent, lethally destructive instinct serving as the basis of all aggressive behavior; nor should one assume, with Alfred Adler, the will to power as the unified motivating source. And especially if one assumes, as most scholars do today, a multiplicity of causes of aggressiveness, one can hardly avoid acknowledging that a religious person, too, or religions as such, possess a certain element of aggression, one that is, of course, similarly ambivalent. Religions, too, if they wish to survive, exhibit a certain inclination toward aggression, with the goal of acquiring power or possessions, of defending territory, of acquiring adherents; this is especially the case, for example,

- when they feel that the substance of their faith is threatened and that they must defend themselves (genuinely so in the case of religious persecution, allegedly so in the case of fundamentalism);
- when they feel threatened in their own territory by the "mission" activities of another religion (or confession) (e.g., Eastern Orthodoxy in the face of the Roman reevangelization offensive);
- when they feel frustrated because of historical failures that they can no longer deny (as in the case of conservative Islam in the face of accommodating and yet threatening modernization or secularization);
- when in the hard reality of competition among religions one particular religion (or confession) seems to come up short.

Hence, in such cases, both religious persons and religions as such also exhibit aggressive behavior that is then associated with the questions of salvation and truth. In and of itself, this aggressive tendency need not be necessarily bad, but rather can be understood as self-assertion — as long as it is not directed toward harming others, and as long as it does not aim at what is principally unpeaceful coexistence, or at cold war or even actual war, as unfortunately has repeatedly been the case. Indeed, it is precisely in the great crisis areas of our time that we see just how ruinous religiously colored aggressiveness can become if it is not consciously checked; nothing should be glossed over in this regard.

On the other hand, it is precisely in recent decades that religions have demonstrated in different ways than ever before that they are capable of dismantling among themselves and among others these dangerous elements of aggression, and of developing the dynamics of peace inherent in their fundamental documents and guiding figures. It is well known that the relationship especially among the formerly hostile Christian churches has changed in a fundamental way since Vatican II.

A number of facts from the political sphere are also well known:

- peace between Germany and France has come about not through Euro-technocrats, but through morally and religiously motivated people;
- the understanding between Germany and Poland was essentially prepared by religious-ecclesiastical circles;
- the revolutions in the former German Democratic Republic and in Eastern Europe were guided in a decisive fashion by religiously motivated people, people who also prevented the use of violence and the spilling of blood;
- the peaceful end to several dictatorships — for example, in the Philippines and in South Africa, though also in Central and South America — would hardly have been possible without the mediation of religious persons, in this case Christian churches.

A Global Ethic as the Contribution of Religions to Peace

One further important area is that of ecumenical understanding between world religions. Here, too, noteworthy progress has been made that is capable of strengthening the credibility of religions with regard to the legitimization of a shared global ethic. For the first time in the history of religions, representatives of all the religions were able, at the Parliament of the World's Religions in Chicago in September 1993, to agree on a common basic ethical text, a declaration entitled "Toward a Global Ethic," formulating a minimal basic consensus with regard to binding values, fixed standards, and basic moral attitudes.[11] With this "global ethic," the representatives of all the great world religions did not intend to establish a new world ideology or any unified world religion beyond all existing religions, and they certainly did not intend to establish the predominance of any one religion over the others. Instead, with this "global ethic" they wanted to bring to expression an already existing general consensus regarding binding values, fixed standards, and basic personal attitudes. For they were borne by the conviction that there will be no new world order without a global ethic. And without a global ethic, there will be no world peace.

The "Toward a Global Ethic" declaration is also of great significance in the field of education today, since it combines the principle of focusing on elemental factors with the principle of concretization. "Toward a Global Ethic" considers all religions to be in agreement concerning the basic demand that "every human being (whether man or woman, white or of color, rich or poor) must be treated humanely," and furthermore concerning that particular "Golden Rule" that for millennia has been a part of and has been preserved in many religious and ethical traditions of humankind. This Golden Rule is expressed

11. Cf. Hans Küng and K.-J. Kuschel, eds., *A Global Ethic: The Declaration of the Parliament of the World's Religions* (New York: Continuum, 1993).

positively in the words "that which you would have others do to you, do also to others." It is precisely from the perspective of this basic humane orientation that one can avoid that sterile, exclusively aggressive counterposition that combines self-love with xenophobia, one's own success with the defeat of others, one's own power with the powerlessness of others — and that does so in a fashion void of any human fellowship and mutual caring.

This Golden Rule should become the immovable, unconditional norm for all spheres of life — for family and community, for races, nations, and religions. This principle can be actualized concretely through four comprehensive, ancient imperatives of humane behavior found in most of the world's religions:

(1) "You shall not kill": the commitment to a culture of nonviolence and reverence for all life;
(2) "You shall not steal": the commitment to a culture of solidarity and to a just economic order;
(3) "You shall not lie": the commitment to a culture of tolerance and a life of truthfulness;
(4) "You shall not engage in fornication": the commitment to a culture of equality and to the partnership of man and woman.

All of this is directed not only to adults but to children as well and to the young in general. Well-considered pedagogical thinking aims at effective prophylaxis already during childhood.

Childhood as the Time to Begin Learning Ethics

There is no doubt that the present situation is often enough to make us despair. On the basis of a "detabooization without precedence in the history of culture," the imperatives of humane behavior preserved for millennia in most religious and ethical traditions are in many cases no longer being persuasively passed on. The element of hope in the present situation, however, is that on the basis of what in religious history is an unprecedented ecumenical movement, it is precisely these ancient rules of humanity that are being revived, and ever larger numbers of people are being seized by the need for a change of consciousness, not only in the sphere of economics and ecology, with regard to war and peace, and in the partnership of man and woman, but also in the sphere of morality in the larger sense.

Hence it is precisely the field of education that finds itself here facing an enormous task, and the declaration of the Parliament of the World Religions brings to abundantly clear expression just this pedagogical component of a global ethic regarding those four imperatives of humane behavior.

(1) Concerning the first imperative, from the ancient, great religious and ethical traditions of humankind we receive the instruction: You shall not kill. Or, phrased positively: Revere life. So let us reflect anew on the consequences of this ancient maxim. Every person has a right to life, to physical inviolability, and to a free development of his or her own personality insofar as this does not violate the rights of others. No person has the right to torment another person physically or mentally, to wound another person, and certainly not to kill another person. And no people, no state, no race, and no religion has the right to discriminate against a minority that is different or of a different faith, nor to "cleanse," exile, and certainly not to liquidate such a minority.

Without doubt, where there are people, there will be conflicts. Such conflicts, however, should be resolved basically without the use of force and within the framework of a system of justice. This applies both to individuals and to states. Indeed, those with political power especially are called to adhere to the system of justice and to support peaceful resolutions that are as free as possible from violence. They should become involved in an international order of peace that in its own turn will need protection and defense against those who would employ violence. The arms race is a dead-end street; disarmament is the order of the day. Let no one be deceived: Humankind will not survive without world peace.

This is why young people should already be learning both at home and at school that violence is not acceptable as a means of settling conflicts with others. Only in this way can a culture of nonviolence come about.

(2) Concerning the second imperative, from the ancient, great religious and ethical traditions of humankind we receive the instruction: You shall not steal. Or phrased positively: Act justly and fairly. So let us reflect anew on the consequences of this ancient maxim. No person has the right to rob from another, in whatever form, or to violate that person's possessions or those of the community. At the same time, however, no person has the right to use his or her possessions without considering the needs of society and of the earth itself.

Wherever extreme poverty abounds, helplessness and despair become widespread, and people will always steal for the sake of survival. Wherever power and wealth are ruthlessly accumulated, the disadvantaged and marginal will unavoidably develop feelings of envy, of resentment, and even of mortal hatred and of rebellion. This, however, leads to a devil's circle of violence and counterviolence. Let no one be deceived: There will be no world peace without world justice.

This is why young people should already be learning both at home and at school that possessions — be they ever so few — come with obligations. Their use should at the same time also serve the welfare of the community. Only in this way can a just economic order be developed.

(3) Concerning the third imperative, from the ancient, great religious and ethical traditions of humankind we receive the instruction: You shall not lie. Or phrased positively: Speak and act truthfully. So let us reflect anew on the consequences of this ancient maxim. No person, no institution, no state, and no church or religious community has the right to speak untruth to others.

This applies especially to the mass media; to art, literature, and science; to politicians and political parties; and finally to representatives of religions: whenever religious leaders stir up prejudices, hatred, and hostility toward those of different beliefs, whenever they preach fanaticism or even initiate or sanction religious wars, they deserve the condemnation of their fellow human beings and the loss of their followers. Let no one be deceived: There will be no world justice without truth and humane behavior.

This is why young people should already be learning both at home and at school that they should practice truthfulness in thought, speech, and action. Every person has a right to truth and truthfulness. Every person has a right to the information and education necessary for making the fundamental decisions affecting his or her life. Without a basic ethical orientation, however, a person can hardly differentiate between what is important and what is unimportant. In the daily flood of information in our world, ethical standards serve as an aid to discernment whenever facts are skewed, interests concealed, inclinations flattered, and opinions absolutized.

(4) Concerning the fourth imperative, from the ancient, great religious and ethical traditions of humankind we receive the instruction: You shall not engage in fornication. Or phrased positively: Respect and love one another. So let us reflect anew on the consequences of this ancient maxim. No person has the right to debase another person into a mere object of sexuality, or to make or keep that person sexually dependent.

We condemn sexual exploitation and gender discrimination as among the worst forms of human degradation. Wherever — especially in the name of religious conviction — the dominion of one gender over the other is preached and sexual exploitation is tolerated, wherever prostitution is supported or children mistreated, we must resist. Let no one be deceived: There will be no true humanity without coexistence in partnership.

This is why young people should already be learning both at home and at school that sexuality is not basically a negative-destructive or exploitative power, but rather a creative-formative one. It functions as a life-affirming formative element of fellowship and can flourish only if it is lived with consideration for the happiness of one's partner as well as oneself.[12]

---

12. Cf. *A Global Ethic*, III.1-4 (abbreviated).

The Challenge for Education Today

Experience has long showed us that processes of change in consciousness must be implemented in both a short- and long-term fashion. This is why it is of the utmost significance that at every level we begin to discuss the declaration "Toward a Global Ethic," and to disclose it especially to students and young people through special didactic measures. For me there is no question that this kind of text should be discussed in classes on ethics and religion today, and that it should become an integral part of overall instruction. I believe this for three reasons:

(1) A special credibility attaches to this document. It does not come out of an ecclesiastical institution whose interests it represents, which would engender mistrust among many young people today. Instead, it is supported by people from all the world's religions and regions, people who have brought to expression here their own convictions.

(2) This document is an expression of actualized plurality. Not only people from different religious traditions but also nonreligious people will be able to accept this document. This is important especially for young people who have grown up in environments ranging from agnostic to fully atheistic. The declaration "Toward a Global Ethic" also expressly demands the cooperation of believers and nonbelievers: "The principles expressed in this declaration can be supported by all human beings with ethical convictions, whether religiously based or not."

(3) At the same time, this document demonstrates a close connection between religion and ethics, and in this way can help keep religion and ethics from drifting ever more widely apart. This document can also help build bridges between the different convictions present among students of today, bridges that can bring ethically and religiously oriented students closer together again.

In this way, a kind of social discourse can be put into motion that must extend far beyond the pedagogical sphere, since not only teachers and students but also other societal groups are being addressed here: physicians as well as business people, lawyers as well as journalists. I have already tried to make this clear in my *Projekt Welthethos,* but I will restate these considerations here.[13]

We need people on all continents who can better inform and orient us regarding people of other lands and cultures, who can pick up on the impulses of other religions and in the process simultaneously deepen the understanding and praxis of their own religion.

13. Cf. Hans Küng, *Projekt Weltethos* (Munich: Piper, 1990), pp. 168-71. The English translation is *Global Responsibility: In Search of a New World Ethic* (New York: Continuum, 1991).

We especially need men and women in politics who do not just view the newly arisen problems of world politics from the perspective of strategic commanders or of the world market, but who seek to actualize an international concept of peace in which the religiously nourished yearnings of people in Europe and the rest of the world for reconciliation and peace are addressed.

Beyond this, we need men and women in economic life who view people of other lands and cultures — both at home and abroad — not only in their role as those who render a certain service or in a purely economic sense as trade partners, but rather who are able to transcend their own narrow economic thinking and view these people as a whole, becoming acquainted in a sympathetic fashion with their variously different histories, cultures, and religions.

We need scholarly thinkers not only with predominantly quantitative-statistical background knowledge but also with fundamental historical, ethical, and religious insight. The mediation of knowledge without standards of value can only lead us astray.

Finally, we also need churches that are able to counter all of today's inclinations toward restoration, and instead of reacting hierarchically-bureaucratically to new spiritual and religious challenges act both internally and externally in a fashion that is close to their constituents and fully conscious of the problems at hand. Such churches should be organized pluralistically rather than centralistically. They should be focused on dialogue rather than on dogma. Instead of circling with self-satisfaction around themselves, they should address self-critically and innovatively the questions of the future, and should do so despite all the doubts of faith.

In a practical sense we need theology and theological writing that advances in a spiritual-intellectual fashion interreligious dialogue in the interest of peace; we also need instruction in religion, teachers of religion, and books of religion that stand in the service of interreligious intellectual exchange and that pursue this work of enlightenment as practical education toward peace.

Hence it might be helpful here to consider how the following learning goals of ecumenical pedagogy for peace might be attained for children and young people.[14] We must

- learn to follow a value system in which respect for human dignity occupies the first position;
- learn to become acquainted in a sympathetic fashion with others;

---

14. Cf. Verein für Friedenspädagogik e. V., ed., *Gewaltfrei leben. Informationen für Eltern, Erzieherinnen und Lehrerinnen* (Tübingen, 1993), p. 9. Valuable insights can be found in G. Gebhardt, *Zum Frieden bewegen. Friedenserziehung in religiösen Friedensbewegungen* (Hamburg, 1994). This involves a presentation of the work for peace undertaken by Pax Christi Suisse Romande, the World Conference of Religions for Peace, and the Japanese-Buddhist movement Rissho Kosei-kai.

- learn to express feelings and to discuss feelings in dialogue with others;
- learn to address conflicts constructively and to deal with aggression non-violently;
- create space for personally responsible action;
- create credible models and orient oneself toward their achievement.

Human life is never without strife. But the rules of humane conflict, rules that despite all personal engagement and loss can nonetheless lead to mutual understanding and mutual respect, must be learned already during childhood.[15] Only thus can the kind of religiosity our age needs emerge in today's religions for a new generation: religiosity with a foundation, but without fundamentalism; religiosity with religious identity, but without exclusivity; religiosity with certainty of truth, but without fanaticism.

---

15. The work mentioned in n. 14 from the Verein für Friedenspädagogik (Tübingen) develops "several rules for successful conflict resolution" (p. 11):

(1) Discuss the problem immediately. Do not wait until hostile feelings become pent up. If at all possible, discuss the problem in the situation itself or shortly thereafter, when the occasion arises.

(2) Speak in the first person. During conflicts, the more I speak about my own feelings and my own emotions, the better will my partner get to know and understand me. Saying "I" instead of "you" in a conflict situation has an additional advantage: I must reveal my colors and clarify for myself what I really am after. My own openness also encourages the other person to be open.

(3) Don't interrupt one another. I let my counterpart say what she/he wants, and I listen attentively without interrupting her/him. Here I pay attention especially to the feelings, needs, interests she/he expresses. I try to listen closely to these expressions of the other person and to address them.

(4) Address the other person directly, looking at that person in the process. If I want to say something or get it out, I speak directly to the person concerned. That is, I do not speak to the entire group if I am actually addressing only a particular person.

(5) Find a common perspective on the problem. What is the issue? Where do I see the causes, and where does my conflict partner see them? Is it possible to find a common perspective on the problem?

(6) Stay on the topic. I keep to the problem to which I am seeking a solution. Neither do I allow my conflict partner to jump from one topic to another.

(7) Avoid accusations and insults. Mutual reproaches clarify nothing and do not solve the problem, but rather merely harden the positions.

Theonomy and/or Autonomy

Paul Ricoeur

I have selected as a critical point of the idea of revelation, the revelation of the Mosaic law, concentrated in the so-called "ten words." Two things have directed my choice. On the one hand, the moral axis can be regarded as the backbone of the Hebrew Bible — although there surely are other modalities of revelation, which we shall not pause to consider. On the other hand, the idea of a law of divine origin, transmitted by an inspired legislator, gives occasion for a radical confrontation with one of the claims of modernity — that of moral autonomy, which we receive in the canonical formulation bestowed on it by Kantianism. At least at first blush, the idea of a legislation of divine origin must appear as a form of heteronomy, diametrically opposed to the presumed autonomy of moral conscience.

I shall develop my discussion in two steps. In part one of this essay, I shall ask whether it is possible to endow the idea of theonomy with such a form as will thereupon prevent its confusion, in the further course of the discussion, with heteronomy understood as contrary to autonomy. In part two, I shall sketch a dialectic of theonomy and autonomy in which, I shall suggest, autonomy itself ought to be conceived in new terms — rendering it, if not positively compatible with heteronomy (likewise conceived in new terms), at any rate not antagonistic to it.

I. Conceiving Theonomy

Under the heading "Conceiving Theonomy," I should like to discuss two points. The first bears on the situation of the ethical moment of revelation vis-à-vis all of the relational modalities that combine in the "naming of God," to employ the most flexible expression available. This first undertaking will consist to a large extent in determining what one might call the "scriptural site" of the divine legislation, keeping in mind the variety of literary genres present in the Hebrew

Bible — the narrative, legislative, prophetical, hymnic, sapiential, and other genres.

1. The first intersection that must surely be emphasized consists in the entangling of the bestowal of the law with the story of the liberation, the deliverance (the departure from Egypt, crossing of the desert, trek to the promised land, etc.). This interconnection will appear all the more remarkable if it is true that the *stories* and the *laws* belong to two different traditions, bound together after the fact by a skillful redactor. This is the hermeneutical situation that we shall have to take as our point of departure. It is important for us to see that, on one side, the bestowal of the law is linked to an act of deliverance that founds the "narrative" identity of the people of Israel: "I, the Lord, am your God, who brought you out of the land of Egypt, that place of slavery" (Exod. 20:2; Deut. 5:6). The law, then, will be that of a free people, or at least of a people called to freedom. But the counterpart is also important. Thus restored to its narrative framework, the law is seen to be inseparable from a gift consisting in a memorable event, an event worth the recounting. Thus, the bestowal of the law becomes a foundational event in its own right. The effect of this intersection is twofold: the story of the deliverance receives a prescriptive coloration, and the prescriptive element, part and parcel, becomes narrative.

A second remarkable intersection is to be found apart from the narrative framework of Exodus but not apart from that of the Pentateuch. It concerns the relationship between the memory of the foundational events and the *creation* stories reported in Genesis. Actually, the latter are not limited in their number to the two familiar stories of Genesis 2–3 and Genesis 1 but include the entire chain of foundational events of all kinds that in some fashion prolong throughout history the energy of a commencement belonging to a mythic time that cannot be spliced into the time of history. The call of the Prophets, from Abraham to Moses, belongs to this chain of foundational events. What is the importance of the proximity between the law and the stories of the foundation of a world for an understanding of the notion of theonomy? The essential contribution of the creation stories is the idea of an origin older than all history, the idea of an anteriority antecedent to all memory. In a sense, the law participates in this antecedence of a creation always "already there." But there is more. The creation stories present a paradox that consists in the reporting of an event that has had no witness. As a result, the event cannot be "re-presented" in the quasi-presence of a past recalled to memory. This paradoxical situation elucidates a surprising trait of our creation stories: they constitute not only scriptures but re-scriptures of other stories, themselves ever antecedent. It is as if it were only by correcting, by rectifying, ever earlier stories that the idea of an absolute beginning could be signified — precisely by the fact of its escape to the rear of all story. If we relate this surprising trait of the creation stories to those bearing on the bestowal of the law, we are led to think of the latter perhaps not as event without witness, but at least as event all testimony to which is withdrawn from

285

narrative appropriation. This observation may shed light on certain anomalies in concurrent stories of the meeting between Moses and God and the engraving and receiving, breaking, and rewriting of the tablets. To boot, we have the data provided by historical criticism when it comes to the work of rewriting ever older writings, and these data evince a parallel between the status of writings that may be called legislative and those that are creational. Thus, it is by way of a series of layers of ever anterior legislation that we have the radical antecedence that withdraws the origin of the law from any appropriation.

It is against this background that we can note as well the relationship between the Pentateuch en bloc and the *prophetical* writings, which the ancient rabbis placed in two different categories and the New Testament designated in tandem, at once unified and distinct, as "the Law and the Prophets." The important thing here is not the forecast of particular events, but the rhythm of death and resurrection stamped on these writings by the succession of prophecies of catastrophe and restoration. While the identity of the people was rooted in the traditional stories bearing on past deliverances, confrontation with the imminence of destruction introduces the note of fundamental threat into the perception of history, a threat to which no response is available but the hope, without guarantee, of a messianic salvation. Inescapably, the ensemble of the legislation of a liberated people must be resituated under the sign of the dialectic of menace and hope. One of the most remarkable effects of placing things in this perspective is a qualitative change in the injunction as such, which appears less and less as imposed from without and more and more as carved on hearts instead. We have the prophets Jeremiah and Ezekiel as witnesses to this interiorization of injunction. In the prophetical future, it is said that the law will be no longer carved on tablets of stone but will be written on hearts of flesh. The word will remain a word of the Other, but of the Other in us.

We must not leave this section of the essay without noting the retroactive effect of the sapiential writings on the stories, the laws, and the prophecies. The meditation of the sages, in all of its extreme variety (Proverbs, Qoheleth, Job), establishes a communion between the narrative identity of Israel and the wisdom of the nations — a wisdom thousands of years old that, all through the ancient Near East, dealt with what we might call speculative problems concerning the origin of evil, justice and retribution, and above all the enigma of unjust suffering. But this wisdom is not all concentrated in the sapiential writings. It pierces to the heart of the other literary genres. A good example would be that of the stories of catastrophe, which can be considered "narrativized" forms of wisdom. It is by way of wisdom that all of the beginnings, all of the foundational events — of the world and of the law — are set in their proper problematic perspective and, we might say, conceptualized. It is in terms of wisdom that we may speak of the bestowal of the law as theonomy.

2. Having entertained these general background considerations bearing on, shall we say, the biblical framing of the imperative, we must now focus on

the law itself, with a view to elucidating what we may call its *consistency*. By "consistency," we mean not only what the law consists in but the *solidity* of both the seemingly monolithic bloc of the "Ten Commandments" and the whole legislation gravitating around these commandments in a textual space of a legislative tenor.

I should like to emphasize three traits, which I shall present in an ascending order.

The first trait concerns the *relational* character of the law, both in its horizontal dimension, as a link among human beings, and in its vertical dimension, as a relation between God and the human being. Here we touch on a familiar problem — that of the relationship between the idea of law and the category of *covenant*. Covenant brings a relational God into confrontation with an equally relational human being. To be sure, the divine-human relation is a relationship of inequality, and this is of crucial importance for the very notion of theonomy. Exegetes have cited, in this regard, the Hittite model of the unequal traits of suzerain and vassal. But however unequal this covenant relation, it also comports a remarkable reciprocity, in its quality as an exchange of *promises*. To the *sought* promise of obedience there corresponds the *proffered* promise of succor. Thus is instituted a bond of "fidelity to fidelity": two "words given" are welded together. This doubly "promissory" character of the covenant is essential for an understanding of the notion of theonomy. On one hand, the Other is not the Utterly Other, for he accompanies human beings' history and establishes for them their position of standing "before God." On the other hand — and here we begin to anticipate our further discussion — we may say that the promise from on high imposes a responsibility for a promise from below. Here is the other side of the coin of the "before God" category: free consent is sought within a nonetheless unequal relation. In Deuteronomy, especially, we find a powerful accent on human initiative, an initiative enclosed in the divine injunction thus: "I have set before you life and death, the blessing and the curse. Choose life, then, that you and your descendants may live" (Deut. 30:19).

The second trait that I should like to emphasize now regards the *hierarchy* of the norms at issue. The problem is a familiar one to modern jurists: not all laws rest on the same level, especially in the constitutional domain. True, one can speak of "a" constitution as a single legal entity; nevertheless, there is a distinction to be drawn between general principles of law and determinate constitutional "rules." (Here philosopher Dworkin insists on a distinction between *principles*, which arise in an ethico-political perspective and are open to interpretation, and *rules*, which are at once more determinate and more nearly approaching univocity.) The case is no different with the "legislation" of the Pentateuch, taken in its ensemble. Historical criticism has taught us to recognize a distinction between the "covenant code" of Exodus 20–22ff. and the Decalogue proper, and, more importantly, between apodictic laws ("Do this," "Do that") and casuistic laws ("When someone does this or that," then "such and such a sanction").

More important than this diversity, reflecting traditions and redactions that are, to be sure, different, is the more precisely hierarchical structure emerging from the juxtaposition and composition of the codes. We might say that the codes are subject to a twofold pulsation: on one side toward the fundamental or principal, and on the other side toward the concrete and everyday. The thrust toward the fundamental tends to gather, to simplify, to unify, "from above." This impulse is expressed in the commandment "You shall love the Lord, your God, with all your heart, and with all your soul, and with all your strength" (Deut. 6:4). The other impulse effects a ramifying, complexifying, almost infinite multiplication of ever finer layers of the legislation. This hierarchical structure is essential to an adequate understanding of the notion of theonomy. Before we come to the precisions of the third trait, we are enabled to distinguish — that is, set in opposition — the law and the laws.

But it is the third trait that puts the final touch on this important dialectic.

It is apropos of the third trait that I have spoken above of an "ascending order." While we have crowned the laws with the law that enjoins loving God with all one's heart, with all one's soul, and with all one's mind, we have not yet underscored the essential — namely, that the commandment in question is the commandment to *love*. But here is the surprise. Can loving be a commandment? Can love be the object of an order, an injunction? Kant solved the problem by removing love from the affective sphere and relocating it as practice, under the heading of "practical love." Freud, for his part, saw in this injunction the impossible commandment that, in his eyes, utterly subverted the Judeo-Christian pretension to a divine foundation of love.

For my own part, I have found the beginnings of a response to this huge enigma in Franz Rosenzweig's *Star of Redemption*. The Jewish philosopher, contemporary of the disaster of the First World War, comes right out and distinguishes between commandment *(Befehl)* and law *(Gesetz)*. It is in its quality as a commandment, according to Rosenzweig, that love can be ordained, ordered. Are we dealing with a rhetorical device? Not at all. This commandment is simply the one addressed by the lover to the beloved: "Love me, thou!" But then is it still a commandment? Yes it is, if behind the commandment we understand the conjuration, the supplication, of love insistently appealing for reciprocity. "The commandment of love can only come from the mouth of the lover. Only one who loves, but that one indeed, can say, and indeed says, 'Love me'" (French trans., p. 210). And, unexpectedly, the Sinai imperative rings like the Song of Songs. This was not evident when we were situating the massive structure of the Sinai material in its scriptural place. The Jewish Sabbath liturgy implements this kinship — incongruous as it is, prima facie — right in its ritual framework. I have not the space here to explain how Rosenzweig arrives at this radical declaration. Let us only recall the *Star of Redemption*'s tripartite structure, in which a meditation on the commandment occupies the median position, the one to which the philosopher gives the title of "Revelation," placing it between "Creation" and "Redemption." "Creation," in Rosenzweig's altogether special vocabulary, denotes the "perpetual foundation of things"; "Revelation" is the "ceaselessly renewed birth of the soul"; and "Redemption" refers to the "eternal coming of the Reign." The commandment of love, then, is situated at the hinge between what one might call "creation behind us" and "messianism before us." Three profound temporalities are thus intermingled, three figures of eternity are sketched, under a distinction dividing an immemorial past, a ceaselessly renewed present, and a perpetually imminent future (or, better, futurity or futuration). We note the exclusive character of the relation of love governing the one-to-one of God and the soul: it is only in the future, messianic dimension that this relationship is exteriorized in works: then it is that the commandment is multiplied and dispersed in the laws, and the human being receives the face-to-face of a neighbor.

The first and second traits of theonomy are at once complete, and re-capitulated in the third. By "recapitulated," I mean that the commandment is settled in the perpetual foundation of the immemorial past of creation, it arises in the incessant present of the injunction to love, and it spreads out to the future in the ever-more-crowded network of the laws of life in common. But it is only with this third trait that the description of theonomy is complete. A formula is in order here, one that will govern our whole discussion of the ideas of heter-onomy and autonomy. And the formula is: "Love obliges." Only sundered from its source — the commandment to love — is there any scandal in an inter-human love (a "horizontal" love, so to speak); that a lover's love obliges is a surprise, but not a scandal. We may have some antecedent understanding of this great enigma in life's most ordinary situations, beginning with the birth of a child. Simply by virtue of the fact that it is "there," the newborn's frailty obliges. Here two Jewish thinkers come together who may never have met. They are Franz Rosenzweig, author of *Star of Redemption,* and Hans Jonas, who wrote *The Responsibility Principle.* That to which love obliges is precisely what Jonas calls responsibility for the frail, the *fragile.* We can view the commandment to love in terms of this responsibility, a responsibility very precisely orientated toward that which is fragile and placed in our care. The implications are vast, even in the political order: Hans Jonas unhesitatingly compares the fragility of the state, which has been entrusted to us, to that of the newborn, whose fragility obliges us.

Now we need the formula: "Love obliges its appropriated counterpart." I propose speaking here of a *loving obedience.* The correlation between the two formulas respects at once the asymmetry of obligation and obedience *and* the reciprocity between two loves.

With this correlation between two loves, I bring the first part of this essay to its conclusion, observing that a new set of problems arises at this point. In the context of these problems, theonomy can confront autonomy without mutual exclusion, and occupy a place different from that of heteronomy.

II. From Theonomy to Autonomy

I should like to submit the following thesis for discussion: far from being opposed to a morality of autonomy, theonomy (understood in the sense of a loving obedience) assists autonomy to *go to its limit;* but, conversely, in order to be adapted to a loving obedience, autonomy must dissociate its lot from *self-sufficiency;* and this self-criticism on the part of the idea of autonomy has a positive counterpart in the equation between autonomy and responsibility for the other, in a sense akin to that given this expression by Emmanuel Levinas.

In this second part, as well, I should like to proceed by stages.

1. I shall begin at the point reached above: love obliges. Thus we have underscored the *origin* of the moral obligation residing in the commandment to love. Now we must blaze the *trail* the obligation is to follow. In order to do that, I propose to take my point of departure in the dialectic between love and justice. I know very well that this opposition is not presented in these terms in the Hebrew Bible or, in the last analysis, in the New Testament. In both Testaments, love is justice and justice is love. But one may legitimately maintain that later history has rendered explicit a tension that may well have been present from the outset; for that matter, I appeal to this tension precisely in order to resist a disjunction between the two terms and in order to enrich each by the other, my intent being to show that love demands not less than justice but more than justice. At this point, we must speak of this *more-than-justice* among human beings that is required by a loving obedience.

(a) It is to Kierkegaard that we owe a reflection on the supraethical dimension of love. He sees, in the story of the "binding of Isaac" (Gen. 22), mistakenly called the "sacrifice of Isaac," the model of the destabilizing exception to the routine of duty. Abraham, the knight of faith, is justified because, for love of God, he has dared to brave the commandment that forbids murder. The exception of Abraham can be held as revelatory of the *fundamentally excessive* character of love as over against justice. It was along these lines that a number of times in my earlier works I set the logic of superabundance, characteristic of what I call an economy of gift, in opposition to the logic of equivalency that governs the various spheres of justice.

The "excess" of the logic of superabundance vis-à-vis the logic of equivalency is expressed first of all in a disproportion that opens, between the two terms, a space for the practical mediations that can bolster justice in its most basic moral project.

The disproportion in question appears first of all in language. Love speaks, but in a different sort of language from that of justice. Love's discourse is primarily a discourse of praise. In praise, persons rejoice in the sight of a particular object, which reigns over all of the other objects of their concern. The play of language appropriate to praise, then, is hymn, acclamation: "Happy the one who. . . ." Bringing this observation on the language of love into line with what we have said above concerning the curious character of the commandment to love, I shall speak of a poetical use of the imperative, ranging from loving invitation, to supplication, to the wrath of love betrayed. Indeed, it is under the aegis of the poetry of hymn, extended to that of commandment, that the power of metaphorization attaching to expressions of love may be situated. It is thus that love generates a rising and falling spiral among the affects distinguished by the terms *erōs, philia,* and *agapē.* Thus, an analogy is "invented" — that is, at once discovered and created — among the affects that we should be mistaken to set in opposition after the fashion of Nygren in his celebrated *Eros and Agape.* In contrast to love, which is not argued but declared (as we see in 1 Cor. 13), justice is recognized first of all within an activity of communication characterized by a confrontation between claims and arguments in type-situations of conflict and process and then subsequently with a decision that cuts off debate and terminates the conflict. The rationality of this *processus* is ensured by the procedural dispositions controlling all of its phases. The procedure, in turn, is controlled by a formalism that, far from betraying any defect, is the mark of the strength of justice, joining the sword that sunders to the balance that weighs. It is this formalism that, in the dialectic of love and justice, boasts of the logic of equivalency, the very first expression of which is the equality of all before the law. To treat similar cases similarly: behold the rule of justice in its judicial application. Distributive and commutative justice are likewise subject to procedural rules, and these rules are just as formal as those presiding over the judiciary order.

It is on this level of formalism that love may well have a role to play — at the very heart of the institutions that invest love with the observable shape of positive law, to which citizens are directly subject and which they are summoned to obey. My suggestion here is that the *sense of justice* underlying these formalisms does not have the univocal character so dear to the laws of positive law. The sense of justice, which we may call a reasonable sentiment, oscillates between two different levels. Thus we see its equivocity. On the lower level, the level basing the contractualist conceptions of the origin of law from Hobbes to Rousseau to Kant to Rawls, the basic attitude of the contractants, placed in the hypothetical situation of an antecedence to the contract, is that of *mutual disinterest,* in the strong sense of an interest unsullied by envy, which interest each of the contractants seeks to promote. On the higher level, the ideal aimed at by the sense of justice and revealed by our indignation at the crying injustices of the world as it is, is expressed by a desire for mutual dependence — *mutual indebtedness.* Social cooperation, which Rawls's justice principles, for example, aim to reinforce, illustrates this oscillation between competition and solidarity: the calculations culminating in the contract install a loftier sentiment than a mutual disinterest but a shallower sentiment than mutual indebtedness. Would it not be the function of love, then, to *assist* the sense of justice to rise to the level of an authentic acknowledgment such that each person has a sense of being the debtor of each? A bridge must be thrown, then, between a love simply praised for itself, for its eminence and moral beauty, and a sense of justice that rightly holds in suspicion any recourse to a charity that would seek to substitute itself for justice — that would pretend to dispense men and women of goodwill from their obligations in justice. The dialectic must ensue, after a separate examination of the titles of love and of justice. It is a delicate thing to maintain the tension between love and justice and thereby learn where that tension would become the occasion of responsible behaviors. What I have already said with regard to the obligation engendered by love dispatches the moral subject in quest of such behaviors. For if love obliges, it is first and foremost to justice that it obliges — but to a justice reared in the economy of gift. It is as if the economy of gift sought to infiltrate the economy of equivalency.

It is mainly in the exercise of the moral judgment in the concrete situation, when one must choose sides in conflicts of duties, or in conflicts between respect for the rule and solicitude for individual persons, or in the difficult cases where the choice is not between good and bad but between bad and worse that love undertakes its plea, in the name of compassion and generosity, for a justice that would frankly place the sense of a mutual indebtedness above the confrontation between disinterested interests. But it is also at the level of institutions that this compassion and this generosity come to expression. Penal law knows attenuating circumstances, exemption from penalty, amnesty. In the face of social exclusion, corrective justice somewhat represents the voice of love on the plane of distributive justice. International politics itself is not out of the reach of love under the form of unwonted acts of repentance, as when Chancellor Willy Brandt went to Warsaw and knelt there, or Václav Havel asked forgiveness of the Sudatenlanders, or the president of the Republic of Portugal, then King Juan Carlos of Spain, begged forgiveness of the Jews for their expulsion from the Iberian peninsula at the close of the fifteenth century. And there are other instances.

(b) A second way in which love might convert justice to its highest ideals would be to contribute to the *actual universalization* of the moral rule by way of the exemplary power of the exception. This suggestion is a prolongation of the Kierkegaardian interpretation of the binding of Israel in Genesis 22. The "suspension" of ethics, Kierkegaard averred, marks the limit of law. My proposition is a bit different, and complementary. Might it not be that the exception serves to reveal a different sort of limit than that to which the categorical, as such, would be subject? I am thinking of *limits of fact* imposed upon the categorical by *historical experience*.

The suggestion that I here make directly concerns the discussion dividing contemporary moralists, who are split between a formal universalism, as professed by Karl Otto Apel and Jürgen Habermas, and a concrete contextualism, represented by M. Sandel, M. Walzer, C. Taylor, and A. MacIntyre. The former camp effectively espouses the procedural conception of law that I have evoked above. The latter places the accent on the cultural limitations affecting the juridical and political practices of communities whose internal consensus rests on a necessarily limited apprehension of the good and the obligatory. Confronted with this seemingly insurmountable antinomy, may we not hold that the universalism expressed by Kant in the idea of obligation *without exception,* and in Apel and Habermas by that of an ideal community of communication without limits and unfettered, is realized, in the crucible of actual practice, only under the form of an "inchoative" universalism — that is, a universalism merely adduced, a universalism awaiting acknowledgment by the other cultures? The advocates of this universalism must be prepared to listen to the other cultures, who will also have authentic universalisms to turn to account — but universalisms embedded, like our own, in concrete practices wearing the mark of cultural limitations symmetrical with ours.

Would it not be the role of love, then, to contribute to the reduction of the gap between this universalism ideally without restriction and the contextualism in which cultural differences prevail? The biblical world — first the Jewish, then the Christian — offers examples, since become paradigmatic, of this extension of culturally limited spheres outward toward an actually universal acknowledgment. The Old Testament's repeated call to the people to include in their hospitality "the alien, the orphan, and the widow among you" (Deut. 16:11, etc.) — in other words, the "other" beneficiary of hospitality — presents us with a first example of the pressure exerted by love upon justice, leading the latter to a frontal attack on practices of exclusion that may well be the counterpart of every strong social bond. The commandment to love one's enemies as we have it in the Sermon on the Mount constitutes the strongest example. The imperative form in which the "new commandment" is couched inscribes it in the ethical sphere. But its kinship with the commandment "Love me," which Rosenzweig distinguishes from law, qualifies it as supra-ethical: it proceeds from an economy of gift, renouncing from the start all reciprocity. For that matter, Jesus associates the commandment to love one's enemies with other exceptional behaviors that fly in the face of the logic of equivalency of ordinary justice. But the commandment to love one's enemies occupies an eminent place among all of these challenges to good moral sense, inasmuch as it directly concerns the sixth commandment of the Decalogue. The commandment to love one's enemies is "new" only by the extension it bestows on the concept of the neighbor, which does not escape the cultural restrictions emphasized by the contextualist theories. The gravity of the injunction results from the fact that the restrictions in question seem constitutive, to our very day, of the political bond. Does Carl Schmitt not set up the category friends/enemies into a criterion of politics? The current state of international law confirms this analysis. And has not war, as so shatteringly illustrated by the terrible twentieth century, always been the moving force of the history of nations and states? The fact is that international law is incapable, today, of furnishing the universality-without-restrictions of the rule of justice with the appropriate institutional form. A "project of perpetual peace," to borrow the title of Kant's celebrated opusculum, will long be utopian. At least Kant argues in favor of the elimination of war from the field of relations among states precisely in terms of justice due and right required. Thereby he demonstrates that peace is an exigency of law and right itself.

Does it not fall to the part of love, then, to *motivate* the concrete approaches of international policy in the direction of perpetual peace? The end of the sufferings inflicted by peoples on one another does not seem to constitute sufficient reason or motivation for "making peace." It is altogether as if a desire for murder, stronger than the fear of death, roused peoples from time to time and thrust them to disaster. Without this collective push toward death, how can one explain the hatred that seems consubstantial with so many peoples' claim to identity? On the contrary, people ought to begin by recalling the memory of the sufferings they have inflicted on others before harping on their own past of such glory and trial. But this *metanoia* of the memory seems accessible only through love — through that *Eros* of which Freud asked, on the eve of his own death, overshadowed by the events we know, whether it would ever tire of *Thanatos!*

2. A seemingly different effect from this pressure exerted by love on justice concerns the singularity and irreplaceability of persons. It is not only in extension, as we have just seen, but in intensity as well that love acts. Perhaps we must return here to the "God alone" of the monotheistic proclamation of the Hebrew Bible. I have attempted to show above that the Johannine formula "God is love" did not abolish the "God alone" but developed it metaphorically. Thus, a kind of "mirror" relationship would obtain between the first and the sixth commandment. Indeed, Rosenzweig understands the commandment "Love me" to be addressed to the individual, thereby reserving for what he calls "redemption" the transition to a plurality of neighbors. Might we not say, then, that the Hebrew and Johannine professions of faith buttress the recognition of persons as being each of them *unique?*

Why is this *aid* on the part of love in behalf of justice desirable? A first reason is that there seems to be no absolutely constraining moral reason why the difference in persons should be in itself an object of obligation. Surely, the practice of an exchange of roles in conversation, the difference in position of social actors in all transactions, the irreducible difference among memories individual and collective, and finally the search for individual responsibility in cases in which damages are to be recovered or punishment meted out — all of these social situations seem to make of the difference between persons an irreducible component of the *humana conditio*. But all of these considerations seem to be of the order of fact, not of law. We see this clearly in terms of the possibility on the horizon of genetic engineering — a horizon reserved to our imaginations for the time being — of manufacturing an indefinite number of clones, copies of human beings. Why would this be forbidden? Is it because, in the common morality, difference is bound up with otherness and otherness is a condition of mutual acknowledgment? To be sure. But what could forbid us from making an exception to this ordinary conviction? And whence does this conviction draw its force?

The need for a "buttress" is sensible in another way as well. Justice differs from friendship, and from interpersonal relations generally, in that it does not rest on the one-on-one of personal confrontation — that is, on the power of the injunction emanating from the face, from each face, saying to me, in Emmanuel Levinas's mighty expression, "Do not kill me!" Justice finds the object of its confrontation in the "faceless" other — in all others to whom I am bound by bonds of right and law through a multitude of institutions. The object is no longer "thou," but *each*. Now, how to keep the *each* from sliding down the slippery slope of the "they," the "someone," the "anybody"? The *each* is still distributive: "To each his own," to each his or her just portion, with a validity extending even to unequal distribution. "One," in the sense of "someone," is anonymous: he or she congeals into an indistinct mass. Does it not fall to love's *imagination*, then, and to its *singularizing* glance, to extend the privilege of the one-on-one, the face-to-face, to all relationships, even to those with the faceless other or others? The case is like that of a love for enemies, which denies the validity of the political difference between friends and enemies. In the problematic of the *each*, love would seek to deny the gap between the "thou" and the "someone else." This is how love would contribute to the preservation of the irreplaceability of persons in all exchanges of roles.

3. Another reason to look to love to protect justice against its own wanderings emerges from the contemporary discussion concerning the foundations of justice. I have referred to the debate between universalism and contextualism. Another debate is broached by the objection addressed to Kant by his rebellious disciples, Apel and Habermas among others, in the name of an ethics of communication. According to these writers, the test of the rule of universalization to which a subject ought to submit the maxim of his or her action would unfold in a monologue conducted within the moral subject alone. The objection is probably ill-founded to the extent that it is conceived as an attack on Kant. Kant's *Doctrine of Law* presupposes various type-situations in which the co-existence of spheres of free action is threatened by enmity, and by all of the adversities to which the social bond is exposed. Whatever be the case with Kant, the question is whether an ethics of communication entirely succeeds in safeguarding its dialogical vocation from slipping back into the solitude of monologue. If subjects called to argumentation must lay aside everything that our moralists hold for simple conventions, then what remains of the singularity and otherness of the partners in the discussion? If their convictions are only conventions, then what distinguishes the partners from each other, apart from their interests? Only a vivid sense of the *otherness* of persons can safeguard the dialogical dimension against any reduction to a monologue conducted by an

undifferentiated subject. Singularity, otherness, and mutuality are the ultimate presuppositions of the dialogical structure of argumentation. Now, what better guarantee of this trilogy than love?

4. In the preceding sections, the accent has fallen on the various ways in which love can come to the assistance of justice by helping it to rise to and maintain itself on its highest level of demand. In this section, I should like to put forward the idea that love can also place justice on its guard against excessive ambitions. Here the excess is no longer from the side of love, under the form of the exception, but from that of justice, under the form of *hubris*. In this fashion, the dialectic of love and justice takes on a decidedly more polemical form.

I should like to return to the sense of dependency with which I characterized the religious sentiment at the outset. Left to itself, this sense of dependency implies a theonomic regime that would seem diametrically opposed to a moral autonomy. But our subsequent observations concerning the metaphorical identity between the "God alone" of Exodus/Deuteronomy and the "God is love" of the apostle, and then concerning the priority of the commandment of love to all of the laws, enable us to complement the sense of *dependency* with that of *antecedence* — which latter necessarily comports what I propose to call a certain *foundational passivity:* "Because you have been loved, love in turn." We need not hesitate to extend this sense of antecedence to the laws that have been called apodictic: one can call them God's comings — not, to be sure, under the mythic form of the Sinai accounts and the bestowal of the tablets of the law upon Moses, but in virtue of their proximity to the commandment of love, which proceeds from the love that is God. This, in my opinion, is the only acceptable sense of the notion of theonomy: love obliges, we have said; that to which it obliges is a loving obedience.

This last must not be set in confrontation with the autonomy of the Kantian imperative and its communicational version.

On the one hand, I would emphasize that a loving obedience arouses us to responsibility with regard to the other, in the sense in which Emmanuel Levinas says it of the face, whose injunction compellingly invites me to care for the other to the point of bending me to the posture of hostage and the act of substitution. In this sense, theonomy, understood as the call to a loving obedience, generates autonomy, understood as call to responsibility. Here we touch on a delicate point, where a certain foundational passivity joins with an active acceptance of responsibility. But the acceptance of responsibility has no other space of exercise than communication, the quest for acknowledgment, and, in the last instance, the vow of consent. This juncture between an antecedence of law and a responsible spontaneity finds an echo in the common moral consciousness itself: it is under the figure of the "voice of conscience," and not merely oppressive and repressive consciousness, that the law attests its structuring. Of course, there is no finding a particular law that has not been instituted by human beings in the course of history. The theory of positive law is not without its argument. But the legality of law is not only instituted but also instituting. In a sense, it is always "already there," along with any symbolic order on which, in the last analysis, all education, and perhaps all psychotherapy, rely.

On the other hand, I would warn against any "superelevation" of moral autonomy. Grasped in its rational core, moral autonomy entails a number of propositions that take on a meaning only in an ethics of responsible spontaneity. What are these propositions? First, on the level of a semantics of obligation, we have the assertion that law is the *ratio cognoscendi* of freedom, and freedom the *ratio existendi* of law. In other words, there is no law but for free beings, and there is no freedom without subjection/submission to an obligation. If, on the human level, obligation takes the form of the imperative, the reason for this is the recalcitrance of the sensible inclinations; and if the imperative is categorical, it is so in the sense of the absence of any restriction attaching to obligation. Now, how does one recognize the categorical character of an imperative? By the capacity of certain maxims of our action to pass the test of universalization. This being said, we can precisely locate the points at which moral autonomy apparently turns out to be incompatible with theonomy, even understanding theonomy as loving obedience. The confrontation takes place at two precise points: first on the level of the *bond between freedom and law* and then on the level of the *rule of universalization.*

In my view, the rule of universalization should give no occasion for conflict, since it constitutes only a criterion, a test, a touchstone for recognizing the morality of an intention and distinguishing it from a disguised interest. The responsibility to which a loving obedience issues its call is not only not incompatible with this criterion but actually requires it if that responsibility is to be reasonable and not emotional.

There remains the critical point of the definition of autonomy in terms of *self-sufficiency.* It may be doubted whether Kant managed to found this principle on itself. Does he not characterize the consciousness we have of this synthetic a priori judgment, which places law and freedom in solidarity with each other, as a "fact of reason," which is equivalent to holding morality as a given? Granted, this given is practical reason itself — in other words, the practical *capacity* of reason. Now, apart from the obscurity of the notion of a "fact of reason," we may well wonder whether human freedom does not open out upon something other than itself when we put this capacity itself to the question on the level of individual consciences. True, the human being can be defined as the *able* subject — able to speak, able to act, able to recount, able to accept responsibility for his or her acts. But is this ability actually available? Does not evil consist in a radical incapacitation? This is Kant's own thesis in *Religion within the Limits of Reason Alone.* In that work, reflection on religion actually starts out with a meditation on radical evil, and continues with an examination of the conditions for the regeneration of a moral subject: Is it on his or her own strength that that subject is regenerated, or is it with help from without? Expelled from moral philosophy, autonomy reappears in the philosophy of religion. The little that Kant concedes here to the idea of a gracious assistance suffices to prevent practical philosophy from being forbidden to open itself to the very particular dialectic between autonomy and what is called, on the strict plane of morality, heteronomy. To be sure, the philosophy of religion is not moral philosophy. But how can the dividing wall between, on the one hand, a morality that separates the *principle* of obligation from any taking account of the human *ability* to obey the law, and on the other, religion, which has no other object, according to Kant, than the regeneration of the moral subject — in other words, the restoration, or, better, the inauguration of an *able* moral subject — be kept watertight?

The next question would be whether the communicational ethics better succeeds in founding upon itself the obligation of discussion and argumentation, which is presumed to eliminate the difficulties involved in the "fact of reason," and to bestow on the criteria of the universalization of the maxim a form that is dialogical from the outset. The self-founding character of the ethics of communication seems to me to proceed from a *hubris,* to which I have referred above, of the practical reason, a *hubris* to which Kant had taken care not to fall victim. But let us suppose that Apel succeeds in convincing skeptics of the solidity of his transcendental pragmatics. (Apel is more radical than Habermas, who is more concerned with the mutual attraction between the theory of morality and the social sciences of interaction.) Even under this supposition, Apel, like Kant, will still have to take into account the *ability* and the *goodwill* of the protagonists of the public discussion. It is at this level, that of motivation, of disposition (which the Germans call *Gesinnung*), rather than at the level of argumentation properly so called, that I should seek to strike an articulation between loving obedience and what one might call entry into discussion, access to the ability to dialogue. Why, after all, to cite the celebrated opposition posited by Eric Weil at the beginning of his *Logic of Philosophy* — why discourse rather than violence? The problem is deemed resolved the moment the protagonists decide to have no recourse in their conflicts but to the argument of the better argument. They succumb to the objection of the "performative contradiction" only once they have abandoned argumentation.

These last observations merge with those we have sought to develop in the preceding sections: should the ethics of communication not accept the supra-ethical assistance of a love that obliges, in order to be in a position to hold firm to the distinction that ultimately is most dear to it, that between communicational reason and instrumental or strategic reason? In truth, when it comes to safeguarding the gap between the two levels of practical reason, what could be mightier than love of neighbor?

Printed in the United States
43517LVS00005B/65